Language Arts

Sandra B. Cohen
Stephen P. Plaskon

University of Virginia

Charles E. Merrill Publishing Company
A Bell & Howell Company
Columbus   Toronto   London   Sydney

for the Mildly Handicapped

Published by
Charles E. Merrill Publishing Company
A Bell & Howell Company
Columbus, Ohio 43216

This book was set in Optima and Americana.
Cover Design Coordination: Will Chenoweth.
Production Coordination: Cynthia Norfleet Donaldson.

Photo Credits: Myron Cunningham, p. 82 (right), p. 83 (bottom);
Celia Drake, p. 9 (top), p. 82 (bottom), p. 83 (top left; center),
p. 170 (left), p. 171 (left; top right); Larry Hamill, p. 8 (right);
University of Southern California, p. 82 (left); Dan Unkefer, p. 170
(bottom right); Cynda Williams, p. 8 (left); all other photographs
property of Charles E. Merrill Publishing Company.

Library of Congress Catalog Card Number: 79–92793
International Standard Book Number: 0–675–08131–9

Printed in the United States of America
1 2 3 4 5 6 7 8 9 10—85 84 83 82 81 80

Contents

iii

Contents

Contents

DEDICATION

To Patrick . . .

SBC

To SueAndrea Plaskon, for her encouragement and patience throughout the duration of this project.

To Keegan Paul Plaskon, for the stimulation his arrival provided to see it completed.

SPP

Acknowledgments

In developing this book, we have drawn on numerous sources. The writings of special educators, regular educators, speech and language specialists, and countless other professionals have, in essence, made this work possible.

In particular, S. P. P. would like to thank Donald W. Protheroe, Betty Liles, and Jacqueline Sachs, all of the University of Connecticut, whose perspectives concerning the teaching of the language arts and the language acquisition and development process influenced a portion of this text.

The blending of different viewpoints has helped to make this text more than the sum of its parts. The compromises struck between the teaching strategies of the special and regular educator stem from our contacts with students in our respective areas. We owe them a special thanks for the insights they gave us in developing practical procedures for teaching language skills.

Also, the suggestions of our colleagues and students significantly changed the contents of this text. The objective reviews of our manuscript in its formative stages verified our perceptions and the value of the course that we chose. We therefore wish to acknowledge our colleagues who served as the reviewers for this text: Virginia Lucas, Wittenberg University; Patricia Gillespie-Silver, Boston State College; John Vokurka, Eastern Kentucky University; Johanna DeStefano, Ohio State University; John Carney, University of New Hampshire; Eldonna Evertts, University of Illinois; Andrew Johnston, Miami University; and William Palmer, University of North Carolina-Chapel Hill.

ACKNOWLEDGEMENTS

Without the contributions of our editors and their assistants, this text would never have been a reality. Their enthusiasm for our ideas, their assistance in the concept development, and their tolerance for our sliding deadlines deserve this special note. We would like to thank Thomas Hutchinson, Executive Editor, Gil Imholz, Regular Education Editor, Cindy Donaldson, Production Editor, and in particular, Marianne Taflinger, Special Education Editor, all of Charles E. Merrill Publishing Company.

Given a text of this size, there is an array of typists and proofreaders we must thank for the countless hours that they spent deciphering our handwriting and incorporating all those last minute changes into the manuscript. Thanks to Patricia Dunn, Diane Farrish, Suzanne Haggard, Sharon Hall, and Martha Lundin for their assistance in typing the manuscript. Thanks to Diane Browder, Shelly Glick, and Joan Safran for their help in securing all the necessary permissions. And thanks to Karen Huff, Jennifer Kenaga, and Kathy McQuail for the time they spent in proofreading the manuscript. We owe a special thank you to Patricia Crook, Laurie DeBettencourt, and Michael Gerber for their contributions of children's work samples.

While this text has been influenced by these particular individuals, the responsibility for the organization and the interpretation of the information that it contains rests with us.

SBC
SPP

Introduction

Children entering school are expected to acquire specific patterns of behavior and learning. If a child deviates from the established norms we, as teachers, attempt to bring him as close as possible to a recognized criterion.

Ever since compulsory education laws required that "all children" receive a public education, the American school system has dealt with diversity. However, as history bears out, the recognition of individual differences has not always been successfully achieved, and handicapped children were either segregated or left out of the educational mainstream.

During the 1960s and 1970s education entered a judicial and legislative era which resulted in the right to education being recognized for every handicapped child (Mills vs. Board of Education, 1972; Pennsylvania Association for Retarded Children vs. Commonwealth of Pennsylvania, 1972). One by one, states incorporated legislation which elevated the educational rights of the handicapped child to those of his normal peer. The parents of educationally deprived chilren were a major force behind this movement.

These same parents continued to bring their concerns forward until attention was given at a national level. The result of their efforts in conjunction with educators and legislators was PL 94-142, The Education for All Handicapped Children Act, a comprehensive legislation which attempts to remedy educational inequities. Three major components of PL 94-142 have direct implications for teachers of the language arts.

First, the public law provides that a child should receive instruction in the "least restrictive environment." Although "least restrictive" is an individually defined term based on the abilities and needs of the child, it often implies integration with nonhandicapped peers. This is especially true with

1

the population of mildly handicapped children. As a result, many previously segregated children are returning to the regular classroom for instruction at some point during the day. The goal of integration is to allow the child to learn to function within the larger society. A society made up of people from many backgrounds, of many different abilities, and with many different outward appearances. Within this diverse structure children, including the mildly handicapped, must learn to communicate with one another. The language arts curriculum is the appropriate place for developing this potential. The teacher of the language arts must bring each child to mastery of the essential communication skills through an orderly step-by-step progression.

Second, the federal legislation dictates that evaluation procedures be regulated in order that they be nondiscriminatory, be valid measures for placement decisions, and provide an accurate means of program planning and progress. Assessment has become a focal point in the instructional process. The educational strategies we use in the language arts program for the mildly handicapped must relate directly to the assessment process and continuous evaluation is of great importance.

The third implication of PL 94-142 mandates that each handicapped child have an Individualized Educational Plan (IEP). The IEP includes the evaluation of the child's present level of functioning, goals, objectives, and activities written as a management and instructional tool to benefit the child under consideration. The IEP is written as a team effort, combining the knowledge of the parents, the child's teachers, and the school administrator. The intent of the IEP is to design an instructional guide for the teacher to follow when working with the problem learner. Structuring the environment, sequencing skills, and modifying materials are important aspects of this guide.

Looked upon in a more unified way, PL 94-142 forces the language arts teacher of the mildly handicapped to:

1. Establish realistic objectives—both long- and short-term for the child to achieve during a one-year period.
2. Assess specific skills as well as the child's ability to integrate and apply skills in the communication process.
3. Promote the interaction of the mildly handicapped child with other children and adults in as many diverse situations as possible.

The Individualization of Instruction

Throughout this text, we emphasize the need to individualize instruction to the maximum extent possible. The placement of the mildly handicapped child in the classroom necessitates the modification and adaptation of materials and methods in all the areas of the language arts curriculum. The teacher of the language arts can respond to the ever increasing demand to meet the needs of the individual student and, in particular, those of the mildly handicapped.

The phrase "individualization of instruction" is one that has been decidedly overworked in recent years. The phrase now has numerous definitions, connotations, and implications for teachers. Just what do administrators, legislators, and teacher educators mean when they state that emphasis must be placed on providing for individual differences? What are parents looking for in a school environment when they ask how does the curriculum meet the needs of individual students? Where does the definition of "individualization" begin and end?

No one single approach to individualization should be advocated over any other particular model for instruction. However, in this text we do appropriately refer to various, accepted procedures for instructional programming. *To us, individualization means the development of an instructional program that is based on a diagnosis of the performance capabilities of individual children in each of the areas of the language arts.* This process of individualization may require the modification of existing materials or skill sequences or even the creation of completely new techniques that are only appropriate and suitable for use with a particular child. In either case, the program that is devised is based on a thorough knowledge of the child and an understanding of the techniques and procedures for facilitating language acquisition and development. By working from information that is obtained through assessment and evaluation of behaviors in speaking, listening, reading, and writing skills, the individualization of instruction in the language arts can be achieved.

All attempts at individualization require an evaluation of program effectiveness. We have attempted to include recommendations for determining the degree to which an instructional program has met with success. We have not ignored this fact in our discussion of each of the areas of the language arts. Evaluation, it is pointed out, is a key ingredient in determining the "next step" in an instructional sequence. To individualize means to evaluate *both* the performance of the student and the degree to which the methods, materials, and procedures employed by the teacher contribute to the child's success in mastering a skill.

The ability to effectively communicate in spoken and written language is a fundamental condition for survival, and facility in the language arts is important enough to warrant considerable attention in the school curriculum. Emphasis on communication effectiveness can be achieved *only* when instruction is individualized to the maximum extent possible.

The Integration of the Language Arts

In many school systems, the language arts curriculum is divided into time blocks or segments, with each skill area being allocated a set number of

3

minutes each day or week. Generally the curriculum coordinator responsible for this scheduling wishes to have each teacher spend a specified amount of time on each language arts skill in order to ensure that all the language arts are taught each and every day. While such a rationale seems at first glance to be quite logical, experience has shown that whenever such division of instructional time occurs, there is generally *less,* not more, emphasis placed on language arts instruction! This occurs simply because the language arts skills can not be factored out and isolated into time blocks that require independent treatment. The skills of listening, speaking, reading, and writing require integration.

In this text, we have by necessity presented and discussed each of the language arts skills in separate chapters. What may not be readily apparent, however, is that we believe strongly in the integration of all the language arts skills into a single, combined curriculum and instructional procedure. We maintain that each of the language arts:

1. Is interdependent and that none of them can be taught in isolation as they each depend on the other.
2. Exists symbiotically in that instruction in one area actually benefits the other.
3. Is mutually reinforcing and to instructionally distinguish among them will have a negative effect on the child's ability to experience success in any of them. Activities that are used to teach reading skills, for example, actually reinforce spelling, composition, and aural language.

There are numerous benefits that can be derived from an integrated approach to language arts instruction. The teacher of the language arts has the flexibility to determine the extent to which a child or class of children will explore one area over another rather than being locked into a rigid time or block schedule. The integration of the language arts permits the utilization of materials produced in one situation (e.g., composition or handwriting) to be used in another (e.g., reading or spelling instruction). Considerable overlap exists in the teaching of the language arts, and, to ignore this conveys the message that skills in communication are not in any way related to each other. We do not believe this to be the case. An effective user of language employs numerous skills on a daily basis that integrate speaking, spelling, reading, writing, and listening. The language arts curriculum in our opinion should reinforce, not negate, this fact.

In terms of evaluation of performance, the best estimate of skill achievement is the degree to which those skills are incorporated into settings other than those in which they initially occurred. Does the child who consistently performs well on spelling assignments show the same level of proficiency when it comes to composition assignments? Are talents in listening or oral speaking seen also in reading? Is the child who attends carefully to directions also a significant contributor to class discussions and conversations? It is not possible to determine just how effective an instructional program has been *unless* performance is sampled across skill areas. An integration of the language arts provides the teacher with numerous opportunities to observe and to record a child's performance in more than one area. Any statements that are made about the rate at which a child is improving his communication effectiveness should be based on observations of that child in several related situations.

The integration of the language arts, in terms of instruction and evaluation of performance, is, in our opinion, clearly the more desirable of the approaches to curriculum design that can be taken. Through this text, we advocate just such an approach.

A major premise of this text is that sound teaching principles be applied to the teaching of all language arts. Consideration of each child's learning needs is the predominant force behind the development of the language arts program. This concentration on the individual child is not peculiar to the instruction of the mildly handicapped. It is a reasonable expectation for instruction of all children.

Most of the materials and methods advocated in this text are suitable for use with any child involved in a language arts curriculum. All children, normal and mildly handicapped, will benefit from instruction which is based on an assessment of their present level of functioning, learning style, and specific educational needs as stated in instructional objectives. A deemphasis on age and grade level achievement norms is strongly recommended in order to allow all children to develop at their own rate and to the highest level of their potential.

As teachers of the language arts, our job is to develop communication skills for each child. The adjustments we make to the "general" language arts curriculum are designed with this goal in mind. Good communication begins with the creation of a warm, receptive, and stimulating environment, the basis of which is the relationship between the teacher and student. The teacher's attitude is paramount as it influences communication throughout the instructional sequence.

The teacher who recognizes the unique differences expressed by *all* children is able to accept each child as an individual. By understanding how each student learns, the teacher can make reasonable decisions regarding what he learns. The educational sequence becomes a practical reality when it is conceived, not according to labels, but according to the individual concerns of the child. The aim is to posture the reader toward a noncategorical approach for educational intervention of learning problems.

At this point it is understandable to ask why this book is specifically designed for teaching language arts to the mildly handicapped. Why can't the reader use any language arts text? What difference will this one make?

The answer to these questions is not as simple as one would expect. Instructional strategies for the exceptional child are based on the following assumptions:

1. Behavior is observable and develops in orderly patterns (*theoretical base*).
2. Patterns of behavior can be changed using consistent and planned strategies.
3. The language arts, (i.e., communication) are essential patterns of behavior which each child must achieve to an adequate level for ultimate self-sufficiency (*reality base*).
4. Mildly handicapped children experience combinations of learning problems which require modifications to the general langauge arts curriculum (*practical base*).
5. Modifications include:
    a. Programming for a slower *rate* of achievement
    b. Extended readiness periods
    c. Alternative instructional procedures
    d. Increased stimulation and reinforcement (*instructional base*)
6. Using appropriate modifications for the mildly handicapped child's learning needs will result in successful communication (*achievement base*).

Much of the theory, procedures, and instructional activities presented in any specific chapter could be adapted for teaching any language arts skill. Perhaps to stress their application, each theory and strategy should have been restated from chapter to chapter, but limited space and a desire to avoid redundancy dictated that we trust the reader to carry over an understanding of instructional principles from one chapter to another.

Facility in the language arts will enable the mildly handicapped child to learn and to achieve throughout life. The ability to communicate with one's peers, to read for information or pleasure, and to express oneself in writing are daily necessities. The teacher who helps the mildly handicapped child acquire skills in listening, speaking, reading, and writing is giving the child those tools he needs to function independently and to be self-sufficient.

PART
I

Fundamentals

1

The Mildly Handicapped

All children experience school-related problems at one time or another. During the course of a *typical* school day, the regular classroom teacher may deal with problems ranging from aggression to disinterest. The causes of these difficulties may vary from an unknown family conflict to a simple stomachache, and their impact may be directly related to the immediacy of the solution. Although these situations may result temporarily in poor academic performance and abnormal behavior, they tend to be short lived and to resolve themselves. The competent teacher is alert to these instances and adjusts the learning program only when necessary.

There are other children whose presence in school is associated with problems that require attention and planned remediation. Children who display characteristics related to prolonged learning difficulties, unsatisfactory interpersonal relationships, and/or inappropriate behavior deserve closer observation by the teacher and school personnel (Bower, 1969). These children are often referred for special education services and require additional support in order to achieve their potential. The majority of these children are mildly handicapped and can function within the regular class program when support services are provided.

This chapter focuses on understanding classification and labeling in special education and on the characteristics and learning potential of mildly handicapped children. The evidence strongly suggests that a noncategorical

11

approach is appropriate for the education of the majority of exceptional children and that regular classroom teachers, as well as special educators, need to focus on a child's learning deficits rather than on educational labels.

Labeling and Mislabeling

The American education system has become rooted in labeling children, segregating according to classification and then assumably applying specific teaching techniques to each group. The limitations of this system are numerous and have presented serious problems for both the development of educational curriculum and the training of teachers. In general, classification for special education has been based on a model of labeling children according to etiology and behavior characteristics. Such a system is derived from the medical treatment of physical illness and reflects the belief that systematic learning and behavioral problems can be cured once the individual's medical history is determined. The heavy emphasis placed on the etiology of the difficulty has been a major consideration in the practice of classification and segregation of children in the educational system. Educators are now realizing that such a focus is irrelevant to educational achievement and that classification and subsequent labeling of children is largely detrimental to all concerned.

The intent of educational classification is to group children according to orderly relationships, such as homogenous learning arrangements. Labeling is the practice by which such groups are identified. Initially labels were developed for communication among members of the many disciplines concerned with exceptional children. The fields of education, medicine, psychology, sociology, and law have all influenced the nomenclature used to identify children who differ from the norm. The input of these various disciplines is evident in classifications which still predominate: brain damage, neurological impairment (biomedical); mental retardation, emotional disturbance (psychometric); socially maladjusted (sociological-legal) and slow learners (educational). Any child within a classification presumably displays a set of problems common to the other children with the same label.

The enhancement of instruction has been given as a major rationale for classifying and thereby labeling exceptional children. By grouping similarly labeled children it is believed that a specified educational program can be more easily provided and remediation would be more likely to occur. The fallacy is in the failure of professionals to provide educationally functional definitions that can produce specified programs. It is also believed that labels provide a diagnostic service and therefore are advantageous. Basically, to identify children who manifest certain characteristics we have developed a linear system of classification, labeling, diagnosis, and program prescription.

12

(See Figure 1.1.) The logic of the cycle breaks down, however, since the classification system does not establish homogenous groupings; and, for the mildly handicapped, labels do not provide diagnosis nor can they prescribe treatment.

Lovitt (1975) makes a strong case against categorical grouping/labeling and uniform treatment for learning disabled (LD) students. His arguments can also be applied to educable mentally retarded and emotionally disturbed children as well as to most other categorically labeled children. Simply stated, Lovitt believes that deviant behaviors must be dealt with on an individual basis. Single behaviors which have contributed to the deviant label should be remediated one at a time, rather than dealing with all possible behaviors associated with the categorical label.

Contrary to what many educators and psychologists claim, we still are not able to make diagnostic decisions that are completely accurate in distinguishing among mental retardation, emotional disturbance, learning disabilities, and slow learners. Agreement among the professionals in defining group labels has never been a reality and as a result multiple labels have been applied to any one specific problem. Table 1.1, a classification chart with an associated list of characteristic labels for children having learning or behavior problems, illustrates the confusion.

After reviewing this partial list of labels, it is possible to understand the difficulty in ascribing any predetermined set of characteristics to a given group. The successful use of labels to describe the less visible deficiencies, such as mild mental retardation, emotional disturbance, and learning disabilities, is debatable. The characteristics so often associated with each label show a great deal of overlap or similarity. The task of differentiating among each of these special education categories and assigning the appropriate label to a child is an enormous one. Although professionals seek to identify

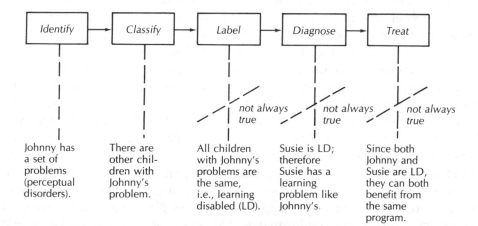

FIGURE 1.1   Identification-Treatment System

13

Table 1.1

Mental Retardation	Emotional Disturbance	Learning Disabilities
slow learner	underachiever	underachiever
hyperactive	impulsive	sensory dysfunction
emotional problems	hyperactive	hyperactive
poor self-concept	socially maladjusted	brain damaged
brain damage	aggressive	minimal brain dysfunction
dyslexia	withdrawn	perceptual disorders
perceptual difficulties	autistic	neurologically impaired
poor attention	brain damaged	dyslexic
language disability	distractible	dysgraphic
socially maladaptive	language disorders	aphasic
memory disorders	poor self-concept	distractible
poor coordination	short attention span	inattentive
poor socialization		poor motivation
culturally disadvantaged		emotional difficulty
distractible		memory disorders
short attention span		low self-concept
		poor coordination
		short attention span

the child's primary disability area, it is not always possible to accurately do so; and mislabeling, followed by inappropriate placement, is the result.

Another problem associated with the practice of labeling children is the negative effect the label itself has on the child. Research tends to support the belief that labels influence the way people view others. When a special education label is applied to children, their teachers, both in regular and special education, often lower their expectations. For example, a child who is labeled mentally retarded may act in a particular way, not because of actual intellectual retardation, but because of the significant effect the label has on the teacher's expectation of his academic abilities. (Gillung & Rucker, 1977; Salvia, Clark, & Ysseldyke, 1973; Forness, 1974).

It is also commonly assumed that labeling a child as deviant in any way produces a decrease in self-concept and weakens interactions among the peer group (Meyerwitz, 1962; Jones, 1972; Haywood, 1971). Yet, a thorough review of the research literature in mental retardation by MacMillan, Jones, and Aloia (1974) found "no evidence of a direct relationship between self-concept and labeling" (p. 246) and ". . . the evidence on the effect of labeling . . . on peer acceptance is open to several conflicting interpretations," (p. 247). The issue of labeling is a complex one since it can not be separated completely from the effects of class placement, personal interaction, and actual performance. However, few would disagree that labels do alter the child's environment in some manner. MacMillan et al. (1974) summarize the issue of labeling effects as follows:

> In fact, the issue of the impact of the ... label on a child entails two subissues. What is the consequence of mislabeling when the label is appropriate for some children but not for others? The assumption here is that labels only damage when they identify a child as less able than he really is. A slightly different concern relates to the impact of the label on any child, regardless of the appropriateness of that label. The assumption here is that a label, if denigrating, suppresses performance measures of a labeled child below the level at which he would score despite the behavioral limitations that led to his being labeled. ... (p. 242)

With all this mounting concern and evidence against the use of labels, why do we continue the practice? Hallahan and Kauffman (1978) cite four reasons for the use of labels.

1. It is often noted that *federal and local funding of special education programs* is based upon labeling and therefore labeling is necessary in order to secure funds.
2. It is maintained by some that *labeling a population helps professionals communicate* to one another about what kinds of children are being referred to.
3. We can make a relatively strong case for the opinion that with the *abolishment of the present labels a new set of labels and/or descriptive phrases would evolve to take their place.*
4. Whether it is right or wrong, *labeling helps to spotlight the problem for the general public.* (pp. 38–39)

Hallahan and Kauffman qualify each of the four reasons for labeling children and pointedly remind the reader that there are two sides to the labeling issue. In an in-depth examination of the problem of labeling children, Hobbs (1975) looked at the advantages and disadvantages provided by our present classification system. Although classification (labels) provides beneficial services, the negative effects outweigh the positive. Labels act as powerful instruments of control dictating instructional arrangements and programs and creating expectations for children without a careful assessment of their individual abilities and potential.

Finally, the use of categorical labels is often justified as a means of describing children who need support strategies in order to learn. The practice of labeling is intended to help differentiate among groups of children. Unfortunately, a side-effect of such differentiation is the use of labels (seldom admitted to) as an excuse for poor teaching. "Of course we didn't teach that child because she had a disability. Our teaching was just fine. It was her learning that was faulty" (Bateman, 1975, p. 319). It is important for teachers to carefully examine the use and effect of labels upon the students they represent and upon their own teaching style.

Categorical Versus Noncategorical Special Education

Educable mental retardation (EMR), learning disabilities (LD), and behavioral disorders (BD) are the most common special education labels applied to children. Traditionally these groups are considered distinct categories that are homogenously arranged and require unique instructional strategies. The application of group definitions hallmarks the differences among the classifications. The categorical approach to special education resulted from the belief that children within each group manifested similar characteristics, as stated in the categorical definition, and had common learning needs, evidenced by the fact that teachers were prepared exclusively to teach one speciality. It is now becoming clear that the distinction among these groups—EMR, BD, and LD—is an artificial one which has confused educators and parents alike. Hallahan and Kauffman (1976, 1977) discuss the overlap in definition, etiology, behavioral characteristics, and instructional methods among the areas of mildly handicapping conditions and suggest that the present classification system does not distinguish among unique groups of children. A detailed examination of these four areas should clarify the lack of distinction among the major special education classifications.

Definitions

A careful examination of the definitions used in categorical classification provides evidence of group interaction.

Mental retardation
... refers to significantly sub-average general intellectual functioning existing concurrently with deficits in adaptive behavior, and manifested during the developmental period. (Grossman, 1973)

Behavior disorders
Children ... who chronically and markedly respond to their environment in socially unacceptable and/or personally unsatisfying ways but who can be taught more socially acceptable and personally gratifying behavior. (Kauffman, 1977, p. 23)

Learning disabilities
... those children who have a disorder in one or more of the basic psychological processes involved in understanding or in using language, spoken or written, which disorders include such conditions as perceptual handicaps, brain injury, minimal brain dysfunction, dyslexia, and developmental aphasia. Such terms do not include children who have learning problems which are primarily the result of visual, hearing, or motor handicaps, of mental retardation, of emotional disturbance, or environmental,

16

cultural, or economic disadvantage. [Public Law 94-142, Section 5(b) (4), 1975]

The definition of mental retardation uses a dual criteria for classification: reduced intelligence and a deficit in adaptive behavior, measured by IQ and social adjustment, respectively (Figure 1.2). Adaptive behavior is also a primary criterion for behavior disorders.

To further complicate matters, the definition of learning disabilities states what the learning difficulty cannot result from more succintly than what the disability actually is. The purpose of establishing Learning Disabilities, a relatively new category of exceptional children, was to assist in further defining problem children, or rather children who presented problems to the educational system. While the intent was to create a homogenous classification of children, the actual result was to set apart a group of children who manifested a wide range of abilities and difficulties. The educational divisions among categories became more complex and difficult to distinguish. "Whenever it is necessary to say what something is *not* in order to say what it *is,* suspicion must be aroused regarding whether the 'definers' are sure what the problem is" (Hallahan & Kauffman, 1977, p. 140). The definitions of EMR, BD, and LD are not succinct; and, when analyzed, tend to confuse the classification issue even further, leading one to conclude that a noncategorical approach would be more appropriate.

Etiology

Although separate bodies of literature and research have evolved concerning the causes of retardation, behavior disorders, and learning disabilities, there appears to be a commonality of etiological factors. Regardless

INTELLECTUAL FUNCTIONING

		Retarded	Not Retarded
ADAPTIVE BEHAVIOR	Retarded	mentally retarded	not mentally retarded
	Not Retarded	not mentally retarded	not mentally retarded

Source: From H. J. Grossman, *Manual on terminology and classification in mental retardation.* American Association on Mental Deficiency. Special Publication Series, No. 2, 1973.

FIGURE 1.2   Dual Criteria of Retarded Functioning According to AAMD Definition

of classification, the majority of handicapping conditions result from un-known causes. In fact, an estimated 80 percent of the educable mentally retarded have no known etiology (Hallahan & Kauffman, 1976). It should not be assumed, however, that because there are so many cases of unknown causation that no causes exist. The truth is, that our present means of measurement most likely lack the sophistication necessary to detect many specific etiologies.

In those cases where etiology is known, it is generally accepted that handicapping conditions result from biological factors, environmental factors, or a combination of the two. Examples of biological factors are: genetic dysfunction, neurological disorders, glandular defects, and physiological factors and malfunctions. In each classification—mildly retarded, behavior disordered, or learning disabled—there are children who show evidence of neurological dysfunction, commonly referred to as brain injury or minimal brain dysfunction. All such disorders result from injury or trauma to the central nervous system; but, since there is no criterion by which a certain extent of damage is associated with any one classification (EMR, BD, or LD), the diagnosis is somewhat arbitrary.

Etiology in other cases has been linked to genetic factors. The association of genetic factors and lowered intelligence is commonly accepted in many instances. The reader is most likely aware of genetically transmitted cases of moderate and severe retardation, such as Downs' Syndrome and PKU (phenylketonuria), as well as the genetic link, hypothesized by Jensen (1975) as an explanation of the lower IQ scores and academic achievement of black children. Professional interest has also increased in possible genetic causes of behavior disorders and learning disabilities. Although direct association is somewhat obscure, it is believed that genetic factors may predispose children to specific character disorders (Bakwin & Bakwin, 1972). Instances of learning disabilities, such as dyslexia, have shown possible transmission from father to son (Stephens, 1977). As early as 1937, Orton, an authority in reading disabilities, believed that heredity was responsible for mixed dominance (right-eyed and left-handed preference) which is often associated with reading difficulties. Orton's theory has not received much recent support; however, the idea of a heredity factor in reading disorders has prompted continued research (Hallahan & Kauffman, 1976), and distinctions between EMR, BD, and LD can not be assumed on the basis of genetic linkage.

Probably the most frequently stated etiology for the various handicapping conditions is environmental factors. The child's innate potential for learning is largely influenced by such elements as poor instruction, lack of stimulation, inadequate learning environment, and low reinforcement for achievement. When the environment is not conducive to learning, even a child with an average or higher IQ will fall short in actual achievement. The position that the child's performance is largely caused by environment is also assumed to be the cause of children's behavioral/emotional difficulties. Few professionals would doubt the influence of situational factors, such as inadequate social models, inconsistent rewards and punishment for appropriate and inappropriate behaviors, and conflicting value systems of the home, school, and peer group.

Closely tied to the environmental point of view is a combination of biological and environmental factors. Proponents of this approach believe that the child's predisposition for behavior is strongly affected by environmental conditions. Therefore, the child's ultimate achievement will be within a predetermined range of performance. If the environment offers the best conditions in which to learn and grow, the child's greatest potential eventually will be attained. However, the reverse is also true, given less ideal conditions the child's potential for performance is lowered (Jensen, 1969; Dobzhansky, 1955).

It is a mistake to think that labels, such as retardation, behavior disorders, and learning disabilities, can be applied on the basis of etiology alone. Since children in each of these categories share common etiologies, this factor can not be used as a differential attribute of any one classification.

Behavioral Characteristics

Children who exhibit any problems in personality/social adjustment, intellectual development, and academic achievement can be found in all the areas of special education that have been discussed—EMR, BD, LD. Separately, each of these characteristics is commonly cited as the primary disability in a particular classification. Research, however, does not support the claim that one disability is primary in each category; and, in fact, provides evidence that it is extremely difficult to separate children into a special education area by assessing their behavioral characteristics (Stephens, 1977; Kauffman, 1977; Stott, 1976).

As early as 1852 the historic American educator, Samuel Howe, noted the similarities between the mildly retarded and behaviorally disordered, and he applied the term *simulative idiocy*. Today this term has been replaced by the expression *pseudoretardation* which is defined as, ". . . the problem of knowing the difference between children who are *truly* retarded and those who only appear to be retarded" (Kauffman, 1977, p. 47). Pseudoretardation is the result of confusion between the assumed characteristics of the different areas of special education. For example, a child whose current functioning is within the mentally retarded range will be so labeled, according to definition (AAMD, Grossman, 1973), even though the child may not be retarded in a cognitive sense. The presumed retardation may actually be the result of motivational factors, poor teaching, inadequate adjustment, and/or other personality deficiencies. As educators become aware of the interation among intellectual abilities, emotional characteristics, and situational variables, the insistence on labeling a child either mentally retarded or behavior disordered will decrease and so will the probability of mislabeling, (e.g., pseudoretardation).

Although problems in personal-social adjustment are the primary characteristics associated with the behavior disordered child, they are also prevalent in the mentally retarded and learning disabled. It is often assumed that, due to their lowered intellectual ability, the mentally retarded experience greater personal adjustment problems than their normal peers. MacMillan (1977) cites "rejection, overprotection, failure and ridicule, which result in frustrations and strong feelings of guilt, shame and inadequacy" (p. 412) as the most common reasons for the maladjustment of the retarded. As mildly retarded children grow, their self-concept is often affected by comparing themselves with children of normal intelligence. The predominance of failure experiences, both in reality and in the child's view, can result in abnormal social behaviors which further support the deviant label. Similar effects have been noted for children with learning disabilities. These LD children have been described as social isolates who manifest hyperactive, distractible, and aggressive behaviors (Bryan, Wheeler, Felcan, & Henek, 1976; Keogh, Tchir, & Windeguth-Behn, 1974; and Wallace & McLoughlin, 1975). Many EMR and some LD children are victims of unstable home situations and grow up unable to cope with the psychological demands placed on them in the school environment. These children are often described by their teachers as manifesting inadequate adaptive skills, such as interpersonal skills and self-management. Therefore, it is relatively safe to assume that EMR and LD children share the maladaptive label with BD children.

Intelligence has been isolated as a major factor differentiating the mentally retarded from other classifications. By definition the retarded are considered to have a lower IQ than either the behaviorally disordered or the learning disabled. Although this may be true, the distinction is not as great as previously believed. Intellectual abilities, stated in terms of IQ, for both the disturbed and the learning disabled have been shown to be at the lower end of the continuum than would normally be anticipated (Kauffman, 1977). Current research on the IQ of learning disabled children has provided evidence that the mean IQ for this group is below the population mean of 100. In fact, specific studies have estimated that between 25 and 37 percent of sampled LD children are functioning at a level below normal intelligence (Ames, 1968; Kirk & Elkins, 1975; Smith, Coleman, Dokecki, & Davis, 1977). But, can these statistics be interpreted to mean that so large a percentage of LD children are actually below normal in measured intelligence? Instead, it is possible that the majority of these identified children with low IQs are actually mislabeled and therefore misplaced in an LD situation.

The final behavior characteristic that we must examine to understand categorical overlap is underachievement. Learning disabled children, in particular, are identified by this criterion, which is often defined in terms of a discrepancy between a child's potential learning ability and present level of functioning. Using a discrepancy criterion to measure underachievement is not always a successful technique. The many inherent problems associated with assessing learning potential, such as test selection and bias and the questionable accuracy of the IQ score itself, further complicate discussion of the issues. Why some children do not work up to their greatest potential is a question that has not been sufficiently answered. However, we do know that environmental, personal, biological, and behavioral factors all exert an influence. Such things as motivation, the quality of teaching, self-concept, learning strategies, and specific learning disabilities are related to the child's achievement level. If any one or a combination of these elements presents a serious problem, the child will function as an underachiever. A strong argument can be made that the underachievement factor is applicable to the characteristics of many educable retarded and behavior disordered children, as well as the learning disabled. Underachievement for EMR and BD children is relative to the expectations established for the child's mental age. Children in any classification who are not performing at the level of their potential ability should be considered underachievers (Hallahan & Cohen, 1977).

This brief discussion of the overlap in behavior characteristics, specifically adjustment, IQ, and underachievement, should convince the reader that these are unlikely avenues for successful application of categorical labels. Even a historical perspective reveals elements of confusion and mislabeling. Analysis of behavior characteristics, for the purpose of classification, shows the three criteria are common to each area—EMR, BD, and LD—with little, if any, elements of distinction.

Instructional Methods

One of the major reasons for classification and labeling within the educational system is to provide instruction designed to meet specific learning needs. The intent has been to develop an educational program uniquely formulated for each categorical group. Past attempts at program development, based on classification and labels instead of student needs, have generally failed. Teachers of the retarded realized that they could benefit from strategies developed by LD and BD teachers. In addition, the field of learning disabilities seems to have *borrowed* much of its instructional strategies from mental retardation and all three areas have shared in the development of behavior modification programs in the classroom. The technology of one group soon became the technology of all.

Recently the traditional view of program development based on group needs has given way to a goal of individualization. This contemporary approach establishes educational procedures based on individual student performance. Education begins with assessment of student needs; followed

21

by instruction, which relates directly to the needs assessment, and reassessment to determine if objectives actually have been achieved. In line with the current approach, assess-teach-reassess, children of varying disabilities can be taught within one program. When teachers are prepared to instruct a wide variety of learning and behavior programs, it is realistic to successfully group EMR, BD, and LD students (Taylor et al., 1972).

> A child with the symptoms of dyslexia, under this system, may work in a classroom side by side with retarded children or children with psychiatric problems. He may be taught with materials and techniques devised previously exclusively for these children. In terms of instruction, traditional distinctions between himself and other exceptional children are being increasingly diminished. (Forness, 1974, p. 57)

Once again, the expected division among the major classifications is not apparent. Instructional methods are similarly applied on an individual basis for EMR, BD, and LD children; and a trend toward noncategorical teacher preparation is increasing.

The Venn diagrams in Figure 1.3 illustrate the extensive overlap among the classifications of educable mentally retarded, behavioral disorders, and learning disabilities. Diagrams a-b-c represent the commonalities of etiology, teaching methods, and behavior characteristics and show that differentiation among the groups is almost impossible and meaningless. The actual difference must ultimately rest with a distinction of behavioral frequency (diagram d). That is, certain behaviors occur more often in BD (d-1), EMR (d-3), or LD (d-5). The extent to which a behavioral characteristic exists, its rate of occurrence and duration, is the factor which in some way distinguishes the EMR, BD, and LD classifications. The analysis, however, reveals that the greatest percentage of behavioral characteristics occur with an equal frequency in all three areas (d-7) and that even a distinction based on frequency is a relatively weak one.

The following statement summarizes the classification dilemma that presently involves the field of special education:

> In particular, there is no research to support the claim that the mildly retarded and the disturbed . . . differ much from the learning disabled in the behaviors they do and do not exhibit. In light of this, it is not surprising that teaching methods for the mildly retarded and disturbed and the environmentally disadvantaged do not differ widely from those for the learning disabled. These realizations are what have convinced many that non-categorical special education for the mildly handicapped is a more sensible alternative to the present practice of spending large amounts of time and money attempting to diagnose whether a child is retarded, disturbed, or learning disabled. (Hallahan & Cohen, 1977, p. 133)

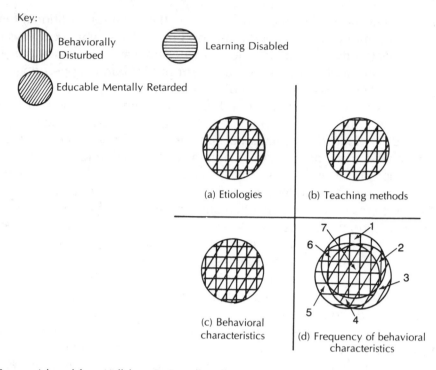

Key:

Behaviorally Disturbed

Learning Disabled

Educable Mentally Retarded

(a) Etiologies

(b) Teaching methods

(c) Behavioral characteristics

(d) Frequency of behavioral characteristics

Source: Adapted from Hallahan, D. P. and Kauffman, J. M. *Introduction to learning disabilities.* Englewood Cliffs, N.J.: Prentice-Hall, Inc., 1976, p. 37.

FIGURE 1.3 Venn diagrams illustrating the similarities and differences among the conditions of emotional disturbance, learning disabilities, and educable mental retardation.

In light of the large amount of overlap in definition, etiology, behavioral characteristics, and instructional methods, it is inappropriate to pursue a categorical approach for educating the majority of children with learning and behavior problems. Continued controversies and a general lack of consensus among professionals over special education classification and labeling practices have led to irresolvable problems and confusion. It is therefore important that educational efforts, in both regular and special education, be redirected toward a noncategorical focus.

Definition of the Mildly Handicapped

An alternative to our present classification system is to focus on a broadly defined and conceived label which assumes the positive objectives of labeling, such as grouping for special instruction, differentiation of *problem* students from their *normal* peers, and a focus on the need for additional funding. The term *mildly handicapped* is an appropriate label which conveys the positive aspects without implying the many negative associations of our present categorical labels. In addition, the term mildly handicapped does not imply an etiology or specify a remediation.

Mildly handicapped children differ in learning, behavioral, or physical traits from the average child, to such an extent that they require specialized or supportive educational programming. The degree to which a child must differ from the norm in order to be considered mildly handicapped is determined in several ways. Such disabilities as sight loss and hearing loss are determined by federal guidelines; State Departments of Education and local systems may establish IQ cutoffs for mental disabilities; and professional organizations often define specific disability populations. However, in almost all cases the significant question is whether or not the children can profit to the limit of their ability from the learning experiences provided in the regular classroom (Neff & Pilch, 1976). Children who cannot meet this criterion do not need to be segregated from the existing classroom, rather they may need adjustments in the regular education program and/or additional support in a resource, consultative, or tutorial experience. The mildly handicapped differ from the severely handicapped in that the latter are not considered for regular class placement and are generally more easily distinguishable from their normal peers.

For the purpose of this text the special education categories to be included under the general rubric of the mildly handicapped are: the mildly retarded (educable retarded), the mildly disturbed (behaviorally disordered), and the learning disabled (specific learning disabilities). Children in each of these classifications have similar basic needs as normal children in addition to specific needs associated with their learning and behavioral problems. Also included in this group of exceptional children are the slow learners, sometimes referred to as being dull normal, borderline, culturally disadvantaged, or dull average intelligence.

Until 1973 the most commonly accepted definition of mental retardation included all individuals with an IQ of one or more standard deviations below the mean (IQ = 100). (See Figure 1.4.) In essence, this meant that all children with an IQ of 85 or less were considered mentally retarded and were eligible for a special education program. Using this cutoff a disproportionate number of minority and low socioeconomic children were represented in self-contained special education classes. In an attempt to rectify this situation the definition was revised to a cutoff of IQ 69 (AAMD, Grossman, 1973). Those children previously considered mentally retarded and who still exhibited the same learning and behavioral difficulties were no longer classified within the special education structure. However, a change in definition did not mask the children's educational problems or increase their achievement. The children who were no longer identified as retarded still required atten-

24

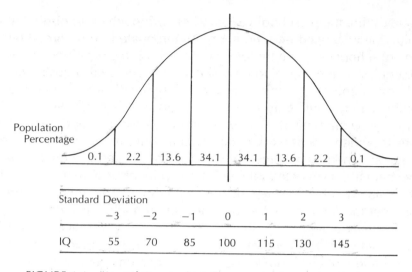

Population
Percentage

| 0.1 | 2.2 | 13.6 | 34.1 | 34.1 | 13.6 | 2.2 | 0.1 |

Standard Deviation

| | −3 | −2 | −1 | 0 | 1 | 2 | 3 |

| IQ | 55 | 70 | 85 | 100 | 115 | 130 | 145 |

FIGURE 1.4 Normal Curve of Intelligence and Population Percentage

tion to their specific learning needs and became known as slow learners. Special educators often debate whether this group should be considered as exceptional children, and specifically as mildly handicapped. Slow learners qualify, if the mildly handicapped are thought of as children who are unable to meet the standardized criteria established by the schools and who cannot reach their potential achievement without specially designed assistance. Slow learners, like other mildly handicapped children, require curriculum modifications, additional teacher attention, and specialized methodology in order to learn adequately. Inclusion in individualized programs devised for mildly handicapped children increases the slow learner's achievement level.

Regrouping or relabeling children from a categorical label to identification as mildly handicapped does not guarantee that they will be *declassified* or that appropriate instruction will be given. There is still a tendency to seek specific labels and to associate stereotypic patterns of behavior. The mildly handicapped should be considered a heterogenous group of individuals who exhibit a broad range of problems. Children are unique in that their present problems are the result of the interacting effects of cognitive ability, personality traits, perceptual-motor performance, and the surrounding environment. In as much as we focus on the child, and not the disability label, the term mildly handicapped is a noncategorical designation.

Prevalence Estimates of the Mildly Handicapped

The majority of mildly handicapped children are not recognized as having problems prior to school entrance. Social and physical growth are generally

25

adequate during the preschool years and only through close observation can the mildly handicapped preschooler be differentiated from normal peers. At the time of school entrance the general focus is on the development of social competencies, achieving readiness skills, and personal adjustment to the school environment. In many cases the mildly handicapped child meets the minimum requirements that are expected up to this point. With increased academic programming the child is asked to assume additional responsibilities for independent work habits, social conformity, and increased cognitive development. The pressures applied by the educational system for achievement at an expected rate and the continuous comparison of all children to a standard tends to segregate those who are different. Children who do not meet the norm are labeled as deviant and classification is sought.

Figure 1.5 represents the number of mildly handicapped children identified between the ages of 0 and 21. Since few mildly handicapped children are identified before school age, the percentages are extremely low. It is during the elementary grades that the majority are brought to the attention of their teachers and parents. As academic demands increase, problems become more evident until finally a referral is made for evaluation and individualized programming. During late adolescence many of these children become involved in vocational training programs and begin to blend into the mainstream of their peer group. Beyond school age a very limited number of mildly handicapped children can be identified.

Another way to predict the prevalence of the mildly handicapped is to examine the percentage of problem learners within the schools. Once again, estimates vary widely according to diagnosis, definition, and program resources. Many mildly handicapped children are not brought to the attention of the educational system, and they remain without assistance in the regular classroom. Therefore, it is almost impossible to state the number of educationally handicapped children presently enrolled in our public schools. Even if we were to examine the number of identified mildly handicapped children, the task would be enormous.

The prevalence rate of this population can best be estimated by combining percentages given for individual categories of special children (Figure

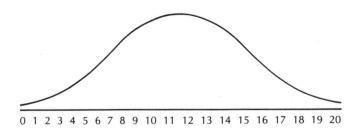

FIGURE 1.5 Estimate of Incidence of Mildly Handicapped Children by Age Group

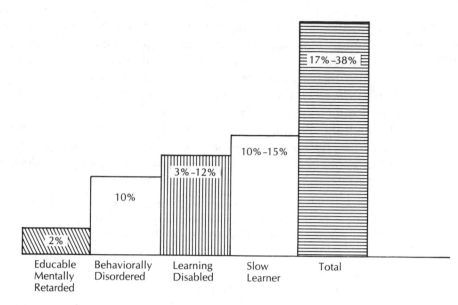

FIGURE 1.6   Estimates of Mildly Handicapped Children in the School Population

1.6). Caution, however, is advised in assuming the accuracy of any population statistics. Because prevalence rates vary according to the definition employed, community variables which affect identification, financial factors, and available resources (children are often labeled EMR, LD, or BD based on which placement is available, not on unique behavioral traits), estimated ranges are included on the graph. To illustrate this point, Samuel Kirk, a noted special educator, once responded to an HEW directive concerning a high percentage figure of learning disability by saying, "Tell us how many you want and can afford, and we will find them by definition and degree of severity" (Kirk, 1972, in Neff & Pilch, 1976, p. 19).

Whether you examine the percentage of handicapped children who are mildly handicapped or the number of school-age children within this identification, the conclusion is the same. The majority of handicapped children are mildly handicapped and are experiencing learning and behavior problems which significantly affect their ability to function within the school environment.

Common Learning and Behavioral Difficulties

Learning problems are often cumulative. Children who go unidentified for a long period of time tend to fall farther behind and increase their learning difficulties until someone notices them. By then, unfortunately, the complexity of the problem, the lack of appropriate instructional resources, or the child's own discouragement may make it almost impossible to remediate the handicap. Early recognition of a child's learning difficulties can lead to remediation and ultimately the prevention of more serious problems.

Children *perform* continuously throughout the school day and their behavior, when closely observed, often provides clues for potential learning handicaps. Although the child generates a great deal of behavioral information, the teacher must decide what elements constitute a learning problem. Pasanella and Volkmor (1977) have determined two basic criteria to identify a learning problem:

   a. The extent to which the child's behavior deviates from what may be considered *normal* or typical for children of his/her age or grade level; and
   b. the teacher's tolerance for and ability to deal with behavioral and academic differences. (p. 38)

Identification of a learning problem is not synonymous with classification—a point that many educators seem to confuse. Identification is the process of isolating specific characteristics which provide stumbling blocks to learning. Both informal and formal assessment are necessary to analyze those classroom behaviors which are indicative of the learning handicap. Identification does not imply either a label or a group placement but rather provides a description of the child's actual performance.

The teacher should be *alert* to both the general behavioral characteristic and the associated classroom behavior of the learning difficulty. For instance, the child who has a slow rate of learning needs more learning trials to acquire a skill than a normal peer. Not all children who present one or more of these problem characteristics need special assistance. It is the combination of the behaviors and the environment which may determine the actual handicap. The following list provides common characteristics associated with the types of learning problems presented by mildly handicapped children. The reader is cautioned to interpret the list with a clear understanding that, "it is the frequency, intensity, and clustering of discrete behaviors that provide evidence of a problem" (Pasanella & Volkmor, 1977, p. 41).

   I. *Characteristics of Cognitive Learning Problems*
      1. Learns at a slower rate
      2. Relies on concrete learning rather than abstract learning
      3. Finds it hard to retain information
      4. Lacks judgment and *common sense*
      5. Highly distractible
      6. Learning sets are difficult to form
      7. Has trouble establishing concepts
      8. Learning is rigid; cannot transfer learning

9.   Learns from direct teaching; cannot acquire skills inciden-
tally
10.   Is an underachiever
11.   Cannot attend to the relevant stimulus dimension
12.   Has a short attention span

II.   *Characteristics of Language and Language-Related Problems*
1.   Verbal expression is difficult
2.   Verbal reception appears inadequate for learning
3.   Articulation problems are evident (omissions and substitutions)
4.   Oral reading is more difficult than silent reading
5.   Inappropriate speech quality (e.g., pitch, tone)
6.   Stuttering
7.   Finds it difficult to carry on a conversation
8.   Does not respond in complete thoughts

III.   *Characteristics of Auditory-Perceptual Problems*
1.   Cannot attend to verbal directions
2.   Gives inappropriate responses to verbal questions
3.   Prefers visual tasks that require very little listening
4.   Cannot determine the main idea from orally presented material
5.   Finds it difficult to discriminate between similar sounding
words (e.g., tap-top; pen-pin)
6.   Cannot retell a story that was read out loud
7.   Has difficulty identifying sounds (e.g., train whistle, dinner
bell, ambulance siren)
8.   Has trouble identifying rhyming words
9.   Leaves off common prefixes and suffixes
10.   Cannot repeat a series of words or digits that were orally
presented
11.   Has difficulty learning to count by memory
12.   Has trouble writing from dictation
13.   Strains to hear what is said

IV.   *Characteristics of Visual-Motor Problems*
1.   Easily distracted by visual stimuli
2.   Awkward movements
3.   Cannot comprehend something seen
4.   Unable to discriminate shapes, colors, size relationships
5.   Poor handwriting
6.   Reversals in handwriting
7.   Cannot remember something seen

8. Fine motor tasks are difficult
9. Prefers oral learning tasks
10. Reacts to parts, rather than the whole (e.g., letters rather than words)
11. Complains of physical problems
12. Must point at each word while reading
13. Evident body tension
14. Cannot recognize common objects
15. Confuses similar letters (m-n; d-b; p-g; f-t) and numbers (1-7; 3-8; 6-9).

V. *Characteristics of Social-Emotional Problems*
1. Cannot sit still for an appropriate amount of time
2. Achieves below expectancy
3. Unable to make friends
4. Aggressive toward peers
5. Withdrawn, hypoactive
6. Anxious to try new things
7. Inconsistent behaviors
8. Frequent mood changes
9. Extremely fearful
10. Constant fantasizing or lying
11. Excessive daydreaming
12. Excessive body movement or twitching
13. Extremely self-conscious
14. Antischool attitude
15. Does not work well in a group
16. Nail-biting
17. Inappropriate or excessive verbalization

Source: Adapted from Dexter, 1977; Pasanella & Volkmor, 1977; Neff & Pilch, 1976.

When a child exhibits any one or a combination of the above learning characteristics it is easy to begin *identifying the child in terms of learning problems alone.* The tendency at such times is to lose sight of these children as individuals who are *more like their normal peers than they are different.* Mildly handicapped children, like their normal age-mate, need affection, attention, and understanding. They want to, and will, learn when something is presented in a manner that they can grasp and that is relevant to their needs. In addition, the mildly handicapped child is generally not *handicapped* equally in all areas. Identification of a learning problem should not cloud the recognition of the child's strengths.

Teachers need to closely examine the child's present problem as well as areas of strength in order to develop an accurate picture of the child's abilities. The following incident between a teacher and a supervisor illustrates this point.

> Ms. Lewis, a first-grade teacher had revealed to her supervisor that she was unable to deal with Alexandra and was frustrated in each new attempt. When the supervisor asked Ms. Lewis to describe the problems, she received this brief statement.

> > "Alexandra just can't seem to do what's asked of her. She doesn't follow directions and constantly repeats the other children's answers."

> The supervisor decided to observe the class focusing on Alexandra for most of the visit. She noticed that most of the interactions between Alexandra and the rest of the class were positive and that during certain activities the child was an eager participant. The supervisor then asked Ms. Lewis to complete a Problem Analysis Form (Figure 1.7). The form was used to structure Ms. Lewis's observation of Alexandra's behavior beyond a general statement of the learning problem. Ms. Lewis realized several positive aspects of Alexandra's behavior and became more willing to continue working on the problem. Together the teacher and supervisor were able to develop a remediation plan.

Learning Styles

To fully understand a child's learning and behavioral characteristics it is important to examine learning style. Learning style is simply the way the child *attacks* learning. More specifically, it is the process by which the child learns best. Learning styles vary from child to child in a manner similar to the variance among teaching styles. Some teachers are best at lecturing, others use written work more effectively, some like a small group arrangement, while others find working one-to-one is best for them. To some teachers the chalkboard is essential, while to others it is a forgotten part of the room. No two teachers structure their classroom in exactly the same manner. Each teacher develops a teaching style that personally is most effective and comfortable. The way mildly handicapped children approach learning varies in much the same way.

Learning styles are multifaceted and include, among other things, modalities of learning (i.e., auditory, visual, kinesthetic, and tactile), task approaches (i.e., impulsive, reflective, and trial and error), environmental factors (i.e., works well when it's quiet or noisy), psychological factors (i.e., expects to succeed or fail) and social conditions (i.e., works best in a group or alone). Elements of a child's learning styles may vary depending on the specific skill being worked on and the child's particular learning and behavior problems.

31

Child Alexandra	Date 4/5	Teacher Ms. Lewis
Age 6		

General Description of Problem	Specific Behaviors	Consequences of Behavior
Evidence of language problems	— Can't follow verbal directions. — Has trouble answering verbal questions. She never volunteers an answer, but when called upon repeats answers heard previously or gives nonsensical responses. — She scored at the preschool level of the *Santa Clara Inventory* in auditory memory and perception and language development.	Because Alexandra doesn't follow directions, she is out of step with the group and needs to be redirected. She is often embarrassed by giving the wrong answer and seems not to want to be included in group discussions. Works harder when working alone.

Areas of Strength	Things (s)he likes to do	Things I like about this child
She is very well liked by her peers and is sought after as a playmate. Alexandra is able to do concrete tasks very well. She recognizes her letters and numerals and some beginning sight words, and can do simple arithmetic.	— Music (rhythm instruments) — Listening to records — Writing	I enjoy watching Alexandra's social interaction. She is always well behaved and usually tries to do the work.

Remediation:
1. Break directions down into simple steps
2. Have child repeat directions
3. Appropriate questioning sequence: ask the question, model response, question again (prompt if necessary), and reinforce
4. Practice exercises to increase auditory memory

FIGURE 1.7   Problem Analysis Form

For example, Dillion has an auditory memory problem and seems to learn best by observing a demonstration and then trying the task himself. The teacher understands that this learning style includes visualization and participation and thus structures spelling so that Dillion sees the word, writes the word with a model, and then writes the word from memory. Adam, on the other hand, is a disabled reader who learns best through the auditory-vocal channel and is most motivated by novelty. His teacher arranges for him to use the Language Master (a recorder-player teaching machine) to learn spelling words. Adam first hears the word being spelled, then orally spells the word, and finally plays back his own recording of the word he has just dictated. The overlapping elements of a child's style helps him approach learning without anxiety and with some sense of conformity. A teacher should note the logical progression of the child's learning styles and how the application of these factors leads to achieving the desired goal.

It is not necessary to use formal scales and measures to assess children's learning styles. Observation by the teacher and, when appropriate, by the children themselves is an effective means of evaluation. The Learning Style Checklist is a simple form to help structure the assessment of a child's learning style. The form takes a few minutes to complete and provides summary statements to keep in mind when designing the learning experience.

Directions: Check each factor that applies to the way the child learns best.

Learning Style Checklist

Name _____   Date _____

Appropriate
Statement

I.   *Environmental Conditions*
——————   **1.** Studies best when it is quiet
——————   **2.** Works with a little noise
——————   **3.** Can block out noise and confusion
——————   **4.** Needs background sound
——————   **5.** Can sit up in a chair and work well
——————   **6.** Works well on the floor
——————   **7.** Relaxes in a chair to work
——————   **8.** Falls asleep if too relaxed

II.   *Affective Conditions*
——————   **1.** Feels good when he does well
——————   **2.** Achievement stimulates more achievement
——————   **3.** Feels like work is too difficult
——————   **4.** Feels inadequate for the work
——————   **5.** Thinks work load is too great
——————   **6.** Takes pride in work
——————   **7.** Displays an interest in achieving
——————   **8.** School is no burden
——————   **9.** Sees no benefit in learning

III.   *Social Conditions*
——————   **1.** Likes to work alone
——————   **2.** Works well with one other child
——————   **3.** Likes to work in small groups
——————   **4.** Likes to work in a large group
——————   **5.** Will volunteer for a task
——————   **6.** Needs teacher direction to complete a task
——————   **7.** Can work independently on familiar tasks
——————   **8.** Likes working with the teacher
——————   **9.** Feels teachers are the "bad guys"

IV.   *Behavioral Conditions*
——————   **1.** Works well from a model
——————   **2.** Responds to reinforcement (increases behavior)
——————   **3.** Reacts to punishment (decreases behavior)
——————   **4.** Easily frustrated
——————   **5.** Needs to be stimulated to work

*Appropriate
Statement*

_____	**6.** Seeks attention from peers
_____	**7.** Seeks attention from teachers
_____	**8.** Has a failure set

V. *Task Conditions*
  1. Approaches a task:
  _____ **a.** Impulsively
  _____ **b.** Reflectively
  _____ **c.** Learns by trial and error
  2. When learning something new, learns best by:
  _____ **a.** Reading about it
  _____ **b.** Hearing it
  _____ **c.** Seeing it
  _____ **d.** Doing it
  _____ **e.** Reading and hearing
  _____ **f.** Seeing and hearing
  _____ **g.** Hearing and doing
  _____ **h.** Use of media
  3. The amount and organization which lead to the best results:
  _____ **a.** Small units of work
  _____ **b.** Alternating reading and doing or hearing
  _____ **c.** Directions given for each part
  _____ **d.** Working in a group, then alone
  _____ **e.** See a demonstration, then respond
  4. Responds best:
  _____ **a.** In written form
  _____ **b.** Orally
  _____ **c.** Through demonstration
  5. Approaches a task with expectancy to:
  _____ **a.** Complete the assignment
  _____ **b.** Succeed at the task
  _____ **c.** Fail at the task
  _____ **d.** Require assistance
  _____ **e.** Work at a slower rate than the rest of the class

Summary Statements

Complete the following statements based on the responses that were marked.

1. The best environment for learning is _____
   _____ .

2. The child's attitude toward learning is _____
   _____ .

3. The child approaches a task _____
   and expects to _____ .

4. The child likes to work _____
   _____ .

Educational Programming

By now the reader should be convinced that categorical labels are of little use beyond the broadest set of circumstances. It is what the child does, or does not do, that is educationally relevant. For example, it does not matter that Patrick is EMR, what is important is that he cannot recognize sight words; and the LD label is not nearly as significant as the fact that Robin is not able to repeat a series of sounds.

The trend toward analysis and careful description of actual learning performance developed parallel with the increased application of behavioral technology in educational settings. This mutual growth probably could have been predicted, since a behavioral approach focuses on actual performance and gives no credence to implied characteristics or labels (Forness, 1974). The present orientation is to treat performance problems by using information attained in a systematic manner. The Instructional Programming Model (Figure 1.8) illustrates the direct relationship between educational assessment and instructional programming. The teacher who closely observes this procedural model will be aligned with a diagnostic-prescriptive instructional approach. Ysseldyke and Salvia (1974) contend that there are four critical assumptions to effective diagnostic-prescriptive teaching;

1. Children enter a teaching situation with strengths and weaknesses.
2. These strengths and weaknesses are causally related to the acquisition of academic skills.
3. These strengths and weaknesses can be reliably and validly assessed.
4. There are well identified links between children's strengths and weaknesses and the relative effectiveness of instruction. (p. 181)

This systematic approach to teaching the mildly handicapped provides the teacher with a functional structure for planning and implementing an educational program. Although the emphasis is on individual handicapped children and their specific needs, criteria for satisfactory performance are often based on the standards set for children of normal ability. The attainment of established performance levels in the regular classroom provides instruc-

Frank and Ernest

I FOUND OUT THE TROUBLE, SIR; WE'RE INSIDE A BOTTLE.

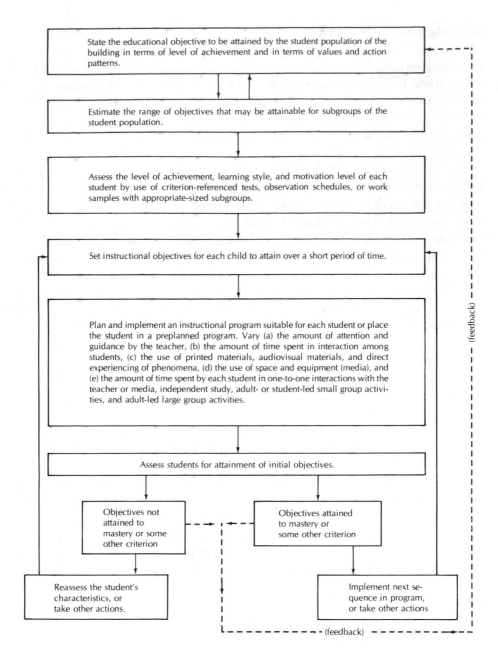

State the educational objective to be attained by the student population of the building in terms of level of achievement and in terms of values and action patterns.

Estimate the range of objectives that may be attainable for subgroups of the student population.

Assess the level of achievement, learning style, and motivation level of each student by use of criterion-referenced tests, observation schedules, or work samples with appropriate-sized subgroups.

Set instructional objectives for each child to attain over a short period of time.

Plan and implement an instructional program suitable for each student or place the student in a preplanned program. Vary (a) the amount of attention and guidance by the teacher, (b) the amount of time spent in interaction among students, (c) the use of printed materials, audiovisual materials, and direct experiencing of phenomena, (d) the use of space and equipment (media), and (e) the amount of time spent by each student in one-to-one interactions with the teacher or media, independent study, adult- or student-led small group activities, and adult-led large group activities.

Assess students for attainment of initial objectives.

Objectives not attained to mastery or some other criterion

Objectives attained to mastery or some other criterion

Reassess the student's characteristics, or take other actions.

Implement next sequence in program, or take other actions

(feedback)

(feedback)

Source: Klausmeier, H., Quilling, M., Sorenson, J., Way, R., and Glasrud, G. *Individually guided education in the multi-unit elementary school: Guidelines for implementation.* Madison, Wisconsin: Wisconsin Research and Development Center for Cognitive Learning, 1971, p. 19.

FIGURE 1.8   *Instructional Programming Model*

tional goals for the mildly handicapped. The reader should not interpret this to mean that group goals are the focus. It is simply that children are considered mildly handicapped when they deviate from the norm. All attempts at intervention should, therefore, be aimed at narrowing the gap between the mildly handicapped and the standards set for the education of the average child.

Achievement Goals

Mildly handicapped children are capable of learning along with their normal counterparts in the regular classroom, since the educational objectives developed for them are identical to those of the general school population.

> The goals of regular education are directed towards insuring economic, vocational, and social independence: active participation as a citizen in the affairs of the community, state, and nation; and educational competence. (Lowenbraun & Affleck, 1976, p. 3)

When identified early and given proper instructional programming, mildly handicapped children ultimately reach these general goals. Specifically, the mildly handicapped have potential in three areas of development:

1. Academic programming
2. Social adjustment
3. Occupational achievement

An estimate of potential in each of these domains must be based on the individual child's abilities, the child's specific set of learning problems, and the interaction of the child with the environment. A closer examination of academic, social, and occupational achievement for the mildly handicapped reveals that the major differences in instructional planning between the mildly handicapped and their normal peers are the curricular adaptions necessary for mildly handicapped children to reach the general education objectives and the somewhat lower level of achievement ultimately attained by these children.

Mildly handicapped children generally function at the lower end of the continuum in academic achievement. They tend to have a slower rate of learning than their regular classmates, but the heterogeneity of this group makes it impossible to describe academic characteristics and potential in any manner other than on an individual basis. Keep in mind that, in most instances, mildly handicapped children do not exhibit equally slow or abnormal characteristics in all areas of learning. As a result, learning profiles vary from child to child.

An estimate of a child's learning capacity is most accurately determined by using the mental age as a reference point. Mental age (MA) is defined as:

$$MA = \frac{CA\ (chronological\ age) \times IQ}{100}$$

Although the MA as an estimate of potential seems clear, it must be interpreted with caution since MA and CA are highly related, and the MA relies on IQ. As such, there is some error of measurement and imperfect reliability. However, even if the reader does not accept the mental age as an absolute predictor, this estimate can be used to arrive at some measure of achievement potential relevant to a child's educational grade level. Achievement potential can be derived by subtracting 5 from a child's mental age:

Achievement Potential (grade level) = MA − 5

Accordingly, a child with a mental age of 12 would be functioning at approximately a seventh grade academic level (Otto, McMenemy, & Smith, 1973). Using the achievement potential formula a teacher can estimate a starting point for assessment and instruction and then appropriately select materials and activities.

For children whose learning problems are primarily related to a slower learning rate, yearly academic growth can be estimated. Figure 1.9 represents a learning expectancy chart which correlates academic growth with intellectual ability. The expectancy chart allows the teacher to estimate long-term objectives for achievement on the basis of the child's growth expectancy.

For example, a child with an IQ of 70 will probably complete ¾ of a grade level per year and may ultimately attain a sixth grade level. The long-term objectives for this child should be based on assessed learning needs and expected year's growth relative to normal peers.

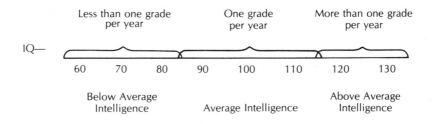

FIGURE 1.9   Learning Expectancy Chart

Social development throughout the school years is as important to the child's individual growth as academic achievement. Mildly handicapped children tend to display a variety of minor adjustment problems. Whether these problems are the cause or the result of the child's learning difficulties is uncertain. We do know, however, that in most cases a child who is experiencing learning problems also needs assistance in the area of social development. For the child, adjustment is tied to his sense of self-worth, his potential for achievement, coping with his environment, and his acceptance of responsibility. Mildly handicapped children eventually achieve social independence to the point that they can live within the community as self-sufficient adults.

The final objective pertains to occupational achievement. As adults, most mildly handicapped persons find work in unskilled, semiskilled, and some skilled trade jobs. How successful these adults are at their occupations depends partly on past training and social adjustment, making it impossible to separate out any of these three goals. In the vast majority of cases mildly handicapped children will no longer be so identified when they reach adulthood. School departure signals an increased rate of assimilation within the society.

Language Arts for the Mildly Handicapped

The communication skills commonly associated with the language arts program are perhaps the most important skills to the mildly handicapped child's future. The ability to receive and provide information, social acknowledgment, and vocational knowledge influence the child's eventual acceptance in the adult community. It is commonly believed that communication is the essential element in the development and maintenance of interpersonal relationships. This point is illustrated by the phrase "communication breakdown," often used to refer to faltering personal interactions.

The mildly handicapped demonstrate a wide range of communication related difficulties which influence their school achievement. The interactive effect of language and cognition has been posited by both language and educational authorities (Vygotsky, 1962; Bruner, Oliver, & Greenfield, 1966; and Nelson, 1973). The characteristics of the child's language problem may be very broad. For example, an expressive language difficulty limits a wide range of the child's social and academic interactions. These children may have a limited vocabulary due to lack of experiences, poor motivation, inadequate comprehension, and/or faulty instruction. Unless intervention is initiated, these children will fall further behind their peers until the language problem has permeated all aspects of the learning environment. Early remediation of language-related problems is essential for continued growth.

39

For some children, difficulties in the language arts may be much more specific. Even a very narrow language-related problem, such as a spelling disability, will interfere with effective communication and personal growth. A very clear example of the impact such a language-related handicap can present is conveyed in the following letter written to a Dr. Fonerden who published it in the American Journal of Insanity (1850) in the hope of illustrating psychological principles. The article was entitled "Mental Embarrassments in Orthography, as Experienced by the Relator, from His Childhood to the Twenty-fifth Year of His Age." The misspellings represent those of the original manuscript.

> Dr. Fonerden: I wish to explain to you a strange mental weakness, to which I have been all my life a victim. At the age of seven or eight, I could read quite well, but shut the book and I could not spell the smallest words. My aunt who instructed me, beleeving that it was obstinancy on my part, turned me over to my grandfather, and he punished me severely gave me a collum of words to commit by a certain time; but ala, when the time had expired, I could not spell the first word, which was *urn*. Hour after hour and day after day was I compeled to study over this word; but let me shut the book for ten minutes and I could not spell it right, except by chance, and to my utter mortification a little collored boy was called up to spell it for me, he having lurned it from hearing it repeated to me so often. After I could see that I was looked upon as little better than a simpleton, and years afterwards grandfather kept me at home, whilest he expended hundreds on the education of my eldest sister . . . Now this peculiarity of my youth sticks by me still. When I went to see, I took a dictionary, with the determination never to return home until I had lurned to spell, but it was of no use. If I had kept my resolve I should never have returned. The hours of study I have wasted in endeavoring to become a good speller would have given me a profession. For that which I read, if it excite any interest, becomes stamped upon my memory indelibly, with this single exception, that which I wonce lurn I never forget. When I left school I wrote a very good hand, but spoilt it in indeavoring so to disguise the letters, that they might pass for what they should be, instead of what they were. I had occasion very recently, to direct letter to my sister, but could no do so untill I had loocked over many books to find the name Rachal, which I could not spell. I have been puzled to distinguish between the agative too the preposition to, and between the article the and the pronoun thee. Were I to write this over from memory a great majority of the works would be spelled differently.
>
> It were a painfull task for me to attempt to innumerate the many occasions on which I have been made to suffer the most bitter mortification on account of this misfortune. But your insight into character will enable you to form some estimate of what I must have endured. It was this that induced me to give up the business to which I was raised, and to go to sea, and has turned me aside from many things that I would have attempted, otherside. The chief difficulty that I have to contend with is

this; that when I write the most firmiliar words, and then ask myself are they spelt right, some jugling friend whispers in my ear many ways of spelling them, and I become lost in a maze of doubt and conjecture. To no other than yourself would I make this humiliating confession; and only to you in the faint hope that you may suggest a remedy. If you can, all that you have done to develope my mind, and to strengthen my character, will be as noting in comparison. Yours, truly, ―――――

Had the letter writer been in school today it is likely that he would have received special education services and his spelling disability could have been remediated. However, the point is made that any language-related difficulty will have an impact on the child's total educational program.

The objectives of the language arts program for the mildly handicapped child are the same as for the normal child. Specifically, the goal for all children is to achieve proficiency in communication skills and critical thinking. Adjustments in methods and materials may be required for the mildly handicapped child to acquire these skills, however, these variations are not significant enough to require separation of the mildly handicapped for language arts instruction. The teacher should be knowledgeable in assessing language-related skills, describing child behavior and developing appropriate intervention strategies.

Most academic tasks are based on language facility. To progress through school and to meet the demands of complex tasks, the child must master the skills of listening, speaking, reading, and writing. The interaction of various language skills can affect the child's learning and achievement. It is important to develop an understanding of the relation of one language skill to another.

Unique categories of the language arts are artificial in that they can not be separated naturally into exclusive bodies of knowledge and performance. It is not possible to talk of a child's receptive language problem as affecting only oral conversational skills, or a child's deficits in decoding as peculiar only to reading ability. The interaction of the language arts skills is such that it is not feasible to totally separate the different stages of cognitive development which lead directly to listening, speaking, reading, and writing. These abilities occur as the result of internal processes, but the need to communicate about language and language functions forces us to label the skills as separate external entities.

The mildly handicapped child may need much more systematic instruction in order to master the rudiments of the language arts curriculum. Many of the related skills of the language arts are acquired or enhanced by participation in reading and writing, or social interaction by speaking and listening. Children with reading problems, expressive problems, or even motor dysfunctions which inhibit their involvement have less chance to learn and practice communication skills.

SPEAKING AND PREREADING

Labeling

names common objects
names body parts
gives own name
names real objects, e.g., apple
names parts of objects, e.g., seeds
names aspects of objects, e.g., flavor
names objects from pictures and
  models
identifies words
identifies letters and names
names coins

Speaking

responds to questions
initiates conversations
relates experiences
tells stories from pictures
uses appropriate greetings
uses courtesy words

Writing

uses pencil or crayon for drawing
prints some letters and numbers
prints own name
prints some words

DECODING SKILLS AND CONCEPTS

Listening

follows verbal directions and
  instructions
relates listening experiences
repeats verbal directions

Reading

reads from left to right
names all letters of alphabet
matches lowercase letters with uppercase letters
reads basic sight words
uses word-attack skills to decode
  unfamiliar words
reads sentences
reads stories

reads for information
reads for pleasure
follows written directions
reads orally
reads with inflection
demonstrates meanings of punctuation symbols

Numbers and Math Symbols

reads number symbols
reads math symbols
associates amounts with number
  symbols
does simple addition
does simple subtraction
carries in addition
borrows in subtraction
does one-step problems
does two-step problems

Writing from Dictation

uses capitalizations correctly
uses punctuation correctly
uses correct tense
spells common words correctly
forms letters and words legibly

ADVANCED SKILLS AND CONCEPTS

Reading

uses reference skills
reads maps, graphs, tables, and other
  illustrative devices
uses study skills when reading
reads newspapers, magazines, and
  other recreational matter
scans and skims for selective reading
draws inferences and conclusions
  from printed matter

Mathematics

uses mathematical symbols
adds, subtracts, multiplies, divides
  whole numbers
adds, subtracts, multiplies, divides
  common fractions

FIGURE 1.10   Language-Related Academic Skills and Concepts

Figure 1.10 (*continued*)

adds, subtracts, multiplies, divides
   decimal fractions
changes decimals to percents
changes common fractions to percents
changes percents to decimals
changes percents to common fractions
determines interest
reads and uses roman numerals
describes and lists elements of
   number sets
uses common measures, e.g., feet,
   yards, miles, pounds, tons
reads time
reads temperatures
uses constant symbols
uses variable symbols
uses equations and inequations
uses distributive property and its
   inverse
factors polynomial expressions
derives sets of quadratic equations by
   factoring
transforms algebraic fractions
performs fundamental operations
   with algebraic fractions
uses ratios to compare quantities
develops and uses proportions
formulates direct and inverse
   variations
uses tables of powers and roots
extracts square roots of numbers
derives solution sets for quadratic
   formulas
derives and uses quadratic formulas
uses trigonometric ratios to measure
   distances
uses tables of trigonometric ratios
solves problems using trigonometric
   ratios

Spoken Expressions

participates in group discussions
shares time in group discussions
speaks to audiences
modulates voice

pronounces combinations of letters
   and words correctly
differentiates between colloquial
   expressions and formal expressions
uses terms and phrases correctly
uses plural nouns correctly
uses possessive case of nouns when
   modifying verbal nouns
uses pronouns for definite antecedents
uses verbs in agreement with subjects
   in number and person
uses nouns and pronouns in proper
   case

Written Expressions

uses period, question, and exclamation marks
uses commas
uses pair of commas to enclose
   phrases
uses semicolon
uses colon
uses parentheses
uses single dash
uses pair of dashes
uses quotation marks
uses brackets
uses three dots
uses capital letters in spelling proper
   names and for beginning sentences
uses abbreviation point
uses decimal point
uses comma in numbers
uses hyphen for compound words
uses apostrophe for writing contractions and plurals
divides words into syllables
pronounces words correctly
identifies roots of words
identifies prefixes
identifies suffixes
uses words with different meanings
   in various contexts
forms plurals of nouns
adds suffixes to words

(*continued*)

Figure 1.10 (*continued*)

uses a dictionary as a tool in writing	combines supporting thoughts with main thoughts
writes personal letters	uses prepositions and conjunctions correctly
writes business letters	
addresses envelopes	
writes bank checks	uses adverbs in reference to verbs
combines equal thoughts with conjunctions	uses adjectives in reference to nouns and pronouns
combines equal sentences to form compound sentences	engages in creative writing

Source: Adapted from Stephens, T. M., *Teaching skills to children with learning and behavior disorders.* Columbus, Ohio: Charles E. Merrill Publishing Co., 1978, pp. 108–109.

Being concerned for any noted deficit, teachers often develop intensified learning activities directed at remediation of an isolated learning problem. Instead, the teacher should be aware of the multiple relationships of language skills and plan an instructional sequence to help the children make sense of the language they use.

The language arts program for the mildly handicapped child is not always remedial in nature. The child's inability to use language may result from developmental problems. In either case, a remedial or developmental dysfunction, the instructional program should emphasize: extended readiness, gradual introduction of sequential skills, modeling, multiple practice, planned generalization activities, and reinforcement.

Within the language arts the mildly handicapped child is expected to formulate and apply concepts. Concepts help us learn about and simplify our environment by classifying elements and ideas that are related in some manner. Concepts are essential to language and academic achievement. Most mildly handicapped children, like their normal peers, learn concepts through daily interaction. Unfortunately, children with learning problems may be limited in their experiences, such as reading, and therefore, may be less able to acquire concepts independently. In these instances, systematic instruction is necessary.

Thousands of concepts exist. Many of these are presented during the school years and are interrelated with the skills the child acquires. Examples of language-related concepts and skills that the child is expected to acquire during schooling are presented in Figure 1.10. The majority of these language concepts are referenced at different points in this text. Again, it must be pointed out that, although these concepts and skills are enumerated as separate entities, in reality they interact and overlap a great deal.

The language arts program for the mildly handicapped child should be structured to provide a wide variety of concrete language experiences. *Experience is the key to language development*; and, in the case of the mildly handicapped child, many experiences are necessary for adequate growth.

The teacher must provide opportunities for the child to generalize language skills from one experience to another and to transfer old learning to new concepts. Primarily, the mildly handicapped child should be encouraged to communicate with the teacher and other students throughout the day and in a variety of situations. The remainder of this text is devoted to the language arts and specific teaching strategies.

SUMMARY

Reviewing the concepts and literature of labeling children with learning and behavioral problems reveals the difficulty in assigning appropriate labels and classifications. There is no clear-cut differentiation among the major special education classifications to justify a categorical approach. Instead, it is advocated that a noncategorical approach, which focuses on the individual child's abilities and deficits, be instituted and that a general designation of *mildly handicapped* be applied to children needing support services to effectively remain in the regular education program.

Mildly handicapped children are more similar to their *normal* peers than they are different. The characteristics they display are not uncommon among normal school-aged children. However, the extent and duration of the child's learning and behavior problems are such that they require special education services for remediation. Teachers need to be aware of persistent problems which affect the child's learning potential. A list of common learning and behavioral problems and a learning style checklist are provided to assist the reader's observation and understanding of the mildly handicapped child.

The basic educational objectives established for all children are appropriate for the mildly handicapped including those for the language arts. The ultimate goal is for the child to become economically and socially independent. To do this, the child must achieve proficiency in communication skills known as the language arts.

POINTS FOR DISCUSSION

1. List all the adjectives you associate with the label "culturally disadvantaged." Which terms are educationally relevant? Compare your list with one written by someone else. Do you have the same associations? Could you have communicated clearly? What implications does a label have for teachers? parents? the labeled child?

2. Divide the class into five small groups. On a large piece of newsprint, have each group list with a marking pen all the stereotyped problem behaviors associated

with one of the following categories of children: educable mentally retarded, learning disabled, behavior disorders, slow learners, and normal youngsters (in the case of normals, stress that the list should reflect problems occurring in the regular classroom). Compare the lists. How are the groups alike? How are they different? Which group appears to have the most problems?

3. In this chapter we established the diagnostic-prescriptive model as the framework for language arts instruction. Why is this particular model pertinent to the education of the mildly handicapped child in the regular classroom? What difference would it make if, rather than a diagnostic-prescriptive approach, the mildly handicapped child received a completely grade-oriented language arts program?

4. Once labels have been established, it is extremely difficult to do away with them. Why do you think educational labels continue to exist while evidence mounts contrary to their benefit?

5. Try to brainstorm what would happen if all labels were done away with and teachers, parents, administrators, and children were forced to communicate without them. What effect would it have on the educational environment and programs? Think of as many alternative methods for communication as you can that could be used instead of labels.

6. Have each member of the class develop a case study on a mildly handicapped child. Include family history, academic profiles, and a description of the child's social-peer relationships. Discuss your findings in class, making comparisons and contrasts among different children. What, if any, generalizations can you make about mildly handicapped children as a group?

REFERENCES

Ames, L. B. A low intelligence quotient often not recognized as the chief cause of many learning difficulties. *Journal of Learning Disabilities*, 1968, *1*, 45–48.

Bakwin, H., and Bakwin, R. M. *Behavior disorders in children* (4th ed.). Philadelphia: Saunders, 1972.

Bateman, B. L. D. leaders strike back at distorted reporting. *Journal of Learning Disabilities*, 1975, *8*, 316–325.

Bower, E. M. *Early identification of emotionally handicapped children in school* (2nd ed.). Springfield, Ill.: Charles C. Thomas, 1969.

Bruner, J. S., Oliver, R. R., and Greenfield, P. M. *Studies in cognitive growth*. New York: Wiley, 1966.

Bryan, T., Wheeler, R., Felcan, J., and Henek, T. "Come on dummy": An observational study of children's communications. *Journal of Learning Disabilities*, 1976, *9*, 661–669.

Dexter, B. L. *Special education and the classroom teacher: Concepts, perspectives and strategies*. Springfield, Ill.: Charles C. Thomas, 1977.

Dobzhansky, T. *Evolution, genetics and man*. New York: Wiley, 1955.

Fonerden, (Dr.) Mental embarrassments in orthography, as experienced by the relator, from his childhood to the twenty-fifth year of his age. *American Journal of Insanity*, 1850, *7*, 61–63.

Forness, S. R. Implications of recent trends in educational labeling. *Journal of Learning Disabilities*, 1974, *7*, 445–449.

Gillung, T., and Rucker, C. Labels and teacher expectations. *Exceptional Children*, 1977, *43*, 464–465.

Grossman, H. J. *Manual on terminology and classification in mental retardation*. American Association on Mental Deficiency. Special Publication Series, No. 2, 1973.

Hallahan, D. P., and Cohen, S. B. Learning disabilities: Problems in definition. *Behavioral Disorders*, 1977, *2*, 132–135.

Hallahan, D. P., and Kauffman, J. M. *Introduction to learning disabilities*. Englewood Cliffs, N.J.: Prentice-Hall, Inc. 1976.

Hallahan, D. P., and Kauffman, J. M. Labels, categories, behaviors: ED, LD, and EMR reconsidered. *Journal of Special Education*, 1977, *11*, 139–149.

Hallahan, D. P., and Kauffman, J. M. *Exceptional children: Introduction to special education*. Englewood Cliffs, N.J.: Prentice-Hall, Inc., 1978.

Haywood, H. C. *Labeling: Efficacy, evils and caveats*. Paper presented at the Joseph P. Kennedy, Jr. Foundation International Symposium on Human Rights, Retardation and Research, Washington, D.C., October, 1971.

Hobbs, N. *The futures of children*. San Francisco: Jossey-Bass, Inc., 1975.

Howe, S. G. Third and final report of the Experimental School for Teaching and Training Idiotic Children: Also the first report of the trustees of the Massachusetts School for Idiotic and Feebleminded Youth. *American Journal of Insanity*, 1852, *9*, 20–36.

Jensen, A. How much can we boost IQ and scholastic achievement? *Harvard Educational Review*, 1969, *39*, 1–123.

Jones, R. L. Labels and stigma in special education. *Exceptional Children*, 1972, *38*, 553–564.

Kauffman, J. M. *Characteristics of children's behavior disorders*. Columbus, Ohio: Charles E. Merrill Publishing Company, 1977.

Keogh, B., Tchir, C., and Windeguth-Behn, A. Teachers' perception of educationally high risk children. *Journal of Learning Disabilities*, 1974, *6*, 367–374.

Kirk, S. A. *Educating exceptional children* (2nd ed.). Boston: Houghton Mifflin Company, 1972.

Kirk, S. A., and Elkins, J. Characteristics of children enrolled in the Child Service Demonstration Centers. *Journal of Learning Disabilities*, 1975, *8*, 406–420.

Klausmeier, H., Quilling, M., Sorenson, J., Way, R., and Glasrud, G. *Individually guided education in the multiunit elementary school: Guidelines for implementation*. Madison, Wisconsin: Wisconsin Research and Development Center for Cognitive Learning, 1971.

Lovitt, Thomas. Applied behavior analysis and learning disabilities. Part II: Specific research recommendations and suggestions for practitioners. *Journal of Learning Disabilities*, 1975, *8*, 504–518.

Lowenbraun, S., and Affleck, J. O. *Teaching mildly handicapped children in regular classes*. Columbus, Ohio: Charles E. Merrill Publishing Company, 1976.

MacMillan, D. L. *Mental retardation in school and society*. Boston: Little,

Brown and Company, 1977.

MacMillan, D. L., Jones, R. L., and Aloia, G. F. The mentally retarded label: A theoretical analysis and review of research. *American Journal of Mental Deficiency*, 1974, *79*, 241–261.

Meyerwitz, T. H. Self-derogation in young retardates and special class placement. *Child Development*, 1962, *33*, 443–451.

Neff, H., and Pilch, J. *Teaching handicapped children easily*. Springfield, Ill.: Charles C. Thomas, 1976.

Nelson, K. Structure and strategy in learning to talk. *Monographs of the Society for Research in Child Development*, 1973, *38* (1 and 2 Serial No. 149).

Otto, W., McMenemy, R. A., and Smith, R. J. *Corrective and remedial teaching* (2nd ed.). Boston: Houghton Mifflin Company, 1973.

Pasanella, A. L., and Volkmor, C. B. *Coming back . . . or never leaving: Instructional programming for handicapped students in the mainstream*. Columbus, Ohio: Charles E. Merrill Publishing Company, 1977.

Salvia, J., Clark, G. M., and Ysseldyke, J. E. Teacher retention of stereotypes of exceptionality. *Exceptional Children*, 1973, *39*, 651–652.

Smith, M., Coleman, J. M., Dokecki, P., and Davis, E. Intellectual characteristics of school labeled learning disabled children. *Exceptional Children*, 1977, *43*, 352–357.

Stephens, T. M. *Teaching skills to children with learning and behavior disorders*. Columbus, Ohio: Charles E. Merrill Publishing Company, 1977.

Stott, D. H. Pseudo-retardation as a form of learning disability: The case of Jean. *Journal of Learning Disabilities*, 1976, *9*, 354–364.

Taylor F. D., Artuso, A. A., Soloway, M. M., Hewett, F. M., Quay, H. C., and Stillwell, R. J. A learning center plan for special education. *Focus on Exceptional Children*, 1972, *4*, 1–7.

Vygotsky, L. *Thought and language*. Cambridge, Mass.: MIT Press, 1962.

Wallace, G., and McLoughlin, J. A. *Learning disabilities: Concepts and characteristics*. Columbus, Ohio: Charles E. Merrill Publishing Company, 1975.

Ysseldyke, J., and Salvia, J. Diagnostic-prescriptive teaching: Two models. *Exceptional Children*, 1974, *41*, 181–183.

2

The Course of Language Acquisition and Development

The course of language acquisition and development is one of the most fascinating areas of study for a teacher. Regardless of one's area of specialization, exposure to the strategies children employ to develop language skills can be a rewarding experience. Few other professionals have as high a degree of contact with children's language as do educators. For most, the study of children's language is a study of children themselves.

Whether working in a regular classroom or serving as a resource teacher, there is a need to be aware of the child's communication skills. Each day's activities consist of countless verbal encounters. Some are with children in one's direct care. Others are casual interactions with children in different grades. There might even be contact with children in different schools. Whether working in an instructional, supervisory, or consultant role, a teacher's sensitivity to children's language can improve relationships. A teacher who is aware of the major characteristics of children's language will undoubtedly feel just a bit more comfortable in the presence of children.

To effectively develop children's skills in speaking, listening, reading, and writing, the teacher must have a working knowledge of language acquisition and development. So often educators look at language arts instruction in terms of units, lessons, or themes. Very seldom does a discussion of instructional strategies focus on language acquisition as a developmental and sequential process. To help children acquire functional language skills, the teacher must be aware of the process by which the child acquires the basic features of the language system. Quite likely, teachers who become familiar with the language learning process will adapt their methods of language arts instruction to reflect aspects of the developmental sequence.

What Do We Know About Language?

What is language? How is it defined? How often do we stop to think about it? We know that it is essential to our existence. We know that without it we would not be able to function as efficiently and as effectively as we do. Yet, how often do we seriously consider the dimensions of this particular aspect of our nature? When asked to define language, most people describe the basic characteristics commonly associated with language—there tends to be a general set of beliefs about what language is. Thus, if several individuals were asked to define language, the resulting definitions would be quite similar.

Assume you are given the task of writing a general definition of language. You are asked to simply put down your thoughts; to respond to the question: "What is language?" What would you do? What descriptors would you make use of? Would you find yourself referring back to previous experiences? Would you think about relationships with people? Would you think how language affects you and your daily life? What strategies would you use to come up with a definition of language?

Regardless of your technique, whether you refer back to childhood experiences or think of present situations, you would probably find yourself making statements such as these:

> *Language is a form of communication.*
> *Language is a symbol system that is understood by a large number of people.*
> *Language is vocal, visual, verbal, and rhythmic.*
> *Language can be physical and written.*
> *Language is interpreted through the senses.*
> *Language is instinctive.*
> *Language is knowledge and understanding.*

Each of these is a partial definition, in some cases satisfactory and in others quite limiting. But, there is a commonality among these hypothetical definitions. While they may differ slightly in their form, each statement tends to focus on language as a form of communication that is essential to our being, that shapes our view of the world, and helps in the interpretation of new experiences.

A Dictionary Definition

According to Webster (1966), language is defined as: "the expression or communication of thoughts and feelings by means of vocal sounds, and combinations of such sounds, to which meaning is attributed . . . or the written symbols for them" (p. 821). The significant overlap is apparent between the informal definitions that could have been generated by a group of individuals and the formalized or classic dictionary definition of language.

Language Redefined

While the definitions of language, both formal and informal, appear to be adequate, they by no means constitute a complete and thorough definition of language. The dictionary definition is simply a description of what language *does*. It tells us basically what we already know to be true about language. It re-emphasized that language is a form of communication that makes use of both verbal and nonverbal forms of interaction to express thoughts and feelings. Though the current dictionary definition does not tell us what language *is*, how it is learned, or how it comes to be understood; it is useful as a summation of common beliefs. Yet, from the point of view of an educator, it provides few instructional guidelines.

In addition, the dictionary definition of language is to an extent simplistic and misleading. For example, the definition states that language involves the use of vocal sounds in meaningful patterns, and, when they exist, corresponding written symbols. Does this mean that language and language ability are contingent on the ability to speak and to see? Is language really this limited? Are these particular physical processes necessary in order to use language? The answer is clearly no. A normal, functioning adult suddenly paralyzed in a serious accident does not lose facility with language, despite the loss of mobility and the power of speech. Language survives these disabilities. Once acquired and refined, language survives the inability to produce sound and the inability to see. Language plays an extremely significant role in our existence and is not so easily destroyed.

According to Cazden (1972), language might be defined as a rule-governed but creative behavior that possesses levels of structure, is hierarchical in nature, and consists of transformations. This definition of language as compared to the definition contained in Webster's dictionary is by far more comprehensive and specific. This definition tells us specifically what lan-

51

guage is, not just what language does. It builds on understandings inherent in the dictionary definition. Let us look at each component of this definition in greater detail.

The Rule-Governed but Creative Process of Language

Language is a rule-governed but creative process. This characteristic of language is very seldom included when people are asked to describe language. Perhaps it is so obvious that a set of rules governs the use of language, people do not incorporate this fact specifically into their definitions. Also, few people will describe language as a creative process. For some reason, this aspect does not appear to be consistent with most people's beliefs about language.

Language is certainly a rule-governed activity. While not specifically called forth in every communication situation, the rules are used unconsciously to construct and to generate sentences. Early studies (Davis, 1938; Piaget, 1932; Smith, 1935), based on the transcribed utterances of children's speech in various settings, suggested that there was a system at work that influenced the speech samples obtained. Very obviously the utterances generated by young children were clearly and distinctly nonadultlike in nature. The children's speech samples were unique and specific to a particular age group.

Certainly adults have a sophisticated rule system which they use to construct and generate sentences. The fact that language is rule-governed as far as adults are concerned is fairly obvious. We might describe our rule system in terms of traditional grammar. Although we do not rely on it to speak and to communicate, we do use the rule-governed nature of our language to describe what it is that we do when we are speaking or writing. The rule-governed nature of young children's language was not described until recently. The fact that the child's grammar is unique and is quite different from that of an adult has contributed significantly to what is known about the language acquisition and development process.

The creative aspect of language can be dealt with at both the adult and the child level as well. Language is indeed a creative process. Each sentence generated by an adult or child is constructed fresh, with the obvious exception of idiomatic expressions. We certainly do not have a storehouse of sentences available to draw from each time we are in a communication situation. It would be quite a cumbersome and difficult process to speak if we had to call forth from a memory bank previously constructed sentences that were suitable for each communication situation. Speaking would become a very tedious, stilted, and awkward means to express thoughts and feelings.

In the case of young children, the creativity of language is certainly obvious. Young children have been known to produce unique combinations, interpretations, and descriptions that are far from commonplace. Perhaps the best way to discuss the creative aspect of language as far as children are concerned is to cite a few references from Chukovsky's book *From Two to Five* (1963). Consider the three-year old who says half asleep:

> *Mom, cover my hind leg! (p. 2).*

Or, another speaking to her father over the telephone for the very first time who says:

> *Daddy, why do you have such a dusky-dusky voice today? (p. 2).*

Think, too, of the child who tells us so seriously that:

> *A bald man has a barefoot head, (p. 2).*
> *A mint candy makes a draft in your mouth, (p. 2).*
> *A husband of a grasshopper is a daddyhopper, (p. 2).*

One observer of children's creativity with language is Art Linkletter, who has recorded in his book *Kids Say the Darndest Things* (1957) a number of children's statements that can be described as extremely creative. Whether one is talking about the use of vocabulary, new concepts, or the generation of definitions, children below the age of seven tend to be quite unique in their responses.

For instance, the child who was asked by Mr. Linkletter on his CBS-TV program, "House Party," to describe himself:

> *"Well," he faltered, "I'm mostly dependable."*

> *"What do you mean by that?" Mr. Linkletter encouraged him.*

> *"Well," the child replied. "Nobody can ever depend on where I'll be or what I'm going to do!" (p. 16).*

Then there were the children who described for Mr. Linkletter what they thought an inferiority complex was. The children replied:

> *"It's interference on a radar screen."*
> *"It's a sort of disease you can catch if you're not careful" (p. 116).*

Another child was requested by Mr. Linkletter to define for him the phrase "a good sport." The child replied:

> *"A good sport is a guy who is no good at any kind of sport like tennis or football or swimming so the only thing left for him is to be a good sport," (p. 118).*

"What is alimony?" Mr. Linkletter asked.

> "It is something that Davie Crockett fought for and finally lost!" (p. 120).

The creativity of children's language is not hard to document. Most of us have had experiences with children quite similar to these. The fascinating part is that all children experience creative thrusts while they are learning language. While interpretations may vary, definitions be unique, and statements range from the entirely possible to the absolutely absurd, children are indeed extraordinarily creative in their use of language forms and expressions.

The Levels of Structure in Language

Having established that language is indeed a rule-governed but creative process, let us take a look at the second characteristic of the definition of language—levels of structure. While much of the work done on creative aspects of child language was based on descriptive studies, the research related to levels of structure is considerably more formal. Levels of structure include the four areas of:

1. Syntax
2. Semantics
3. Pragmatics
4. Phonology

These four levels of structure exist within language, and each level contains specific developmental hallmarks that are significant. Syntax means the development of grammar; Semantics, the acquisition of meaning; Pragmatics, the assignment of function to utterances; and Phonology, the acquisition of sound. These are the four levels of structure referenced in this component of our definition of language.

Development of Syntax

By the development of syntax we mean the acquisition of grammar. Recent studies of child language indicate that the process by which children acquire a knowledge of grammar is a fairly consistent and standard procedure across cultures and languages (Slobin, 1970). The comprehensive study that was done by Brown (1973) on the speech of Adam, Eve, and Sarah revealed that children do proceed through a series of stages in the process of

54

learning to use grammar. To understand this aspect of language, let us look at some of the basic stages in the development of grammar.

Age Ranges

It should be mentioned here that while there are approximate chronological ages at which various skills are achieved, no set requirement can be applied universally to all children. It does appear that the average age at which the single word utterances begin to be produced is twelve months. This is followed by a transition period of about six months before the appearance of two-word utterances, or the beginning of what is called the duophrastic stage. These ages are used simply to approximate the points at which most youngsters tend to develop particular vocalizations. There is no reason to believe that if a child has not begun to produce single-word utterances by twelve months that there is a serious disability or language delay. By the same token, some children begin to generate these utterances quite a bit earlier than twelve months. These dates, while useful in terms of describing stages, must be dealt with rather cautiously. It is perhaps best to understand that when a specific age is given, there can be a variation of four to six months on either side of the given age. It would be entirely correct to report that the holophrastic stage can occur between ten and fourteen months. Similarly, the duophrastic stage can begin from around fourteen months to approximately twenty months. Remember the flexibility of these particular ages.

The studies reported in Figure 2.1 clearly show the general agreement among researchers that specific skills do occur at a particular age level. There is, however, quite a bit of evidence that a wide range of abilities is possible for any of these skills.

The Holophrastic Stage

On or about the child's first birthday, the first words appear. These are generally single-word utterances. The child will say such things as "Milk," "Daddy," "Cookie," "Wet," and "Go." These first words or single-word utterances have often been referred to as self-imperatives. In listening to a twelve-month-old child speak, you could almost believe that the child was indeed issuing a command to respond to those very same utterances. It is as if the child were saying "Walk!" or "Go!" or "Wet!" Certainly this interpretation does not apply to all the child's utterances, but there appears to be some relationship between these single-word utterances and the development of the related psychomotor skills.

Up until the appearance of the first words, much of the child's speech has been mere babbling and playful vocalizations. Assuming that we are not dealing with a language-delayed or language-deviant youngster, we would expect that, prior to twelve months, the child has become engaged in a number of activities that are related directly to the eventual production of recognizable speech sounds. Many parents readily admit that their child,

Language Skill	Age In Months	Authority
Attends readily to speaking	1.3	Bayley
Understands gestures	9.0	Cattell
Responds to "bye-bye"	10.0	Gesell, Thompson
Adjusts to commands	10.0	Gesell, Thompson
Comprehends simple verbal statements	12.0	Gesell, Thompson
Says "hello, thank you"	18.0	Gesell, Thompson
Names one single object	18.0	Bayley
Names pictures in a book	18.7	Bayley
Comprehends simple questions	18.0	Gesell
Understands a command with gestures	21.0	Buhler
Names three objects	21.0	Gesell
Identifies objects by name	24.0	Terman & Merrill
Refers to self by name	24.0	Ilg & Ames
Points to body parts	24.0	Terman & Merrill
Follows simple directions	24.0	Terman & Merrill
Understands number concepts	30.0	Gettell
Can be taught basic colors	48.0	J. Tracy Clinic
Comprehends semantic relations	30.0	Stutsman
Comparison of objects	42.0	Terman & Merrill

Source: Adopted from Butt, D., and Chreist, F. A speechreading test for young children. *The Volta Review*, 1968, *70*, 228–229.

FIGURE 2.1   Language Skill Development

prior to the appearance of first words, engaged in a number of "conversations" that were quite unintelligible. This type of "baby talk" is certainly a prerequisite to the appearance of the single-word utterances. From the point of view of the acquisition of syntax, however, these preliminary vocalizations are not of real significance. Only when recognizable speech begins and actual words are produced can we begin to talk about the acquisition of syntax.

The holophrastic stage continues for a short period of time. Usually a short transition phase occurs between the single-word utterances ("Walk," "Play," and "Go") and utterances that appear in closer proximity to each other such as "Door, Open." "Daddy, Slippers." "Walk, Play." As the child makes use of these initial words, the rate at which they occur tends to increase dramatically. It is natural to find that once the first words appear, they are quickly joined by other words. The child moves from what is considered the holophrastic stage to the duophrastic stage—two-word utterances.

Duophrastic Stage

The duophrastic stage is the actual beginning of syntax and occurs at about eighteen months. The two-word utterances produced during the duophrastic stage have been analyzed rather extensively by Brown (1973), who generated what is referred to as the Pivot Open Class grammar system. The term Pivot Open Class grammar seems to aptly describe the syntactic system utilized by the child at this age.

The Pivot Open Class grammar system consists of two-word utterances in which one word is a pivot word and the other serves as an open class word. The pivot words expand very slowly—they are extremely important for the child and therefore are held onto. Other words are introduced around a pivot word. The open class, by contrast, is quite large and contains all the words that are in the child's vocabulary. Such examples would be: "Allgone cookie." "Allgone milk." "Allgone wet." "Allgone soap." "Allgone Daddy." "More cookie." "More ice cream." "Big train." "Big rug." "Big hat." "Big ball." These are quite typical of the utterances produced by a child of 18–20 months. In describing the utterances obtained from the children in his study (Adam, Eve, and Sarah), Brown (1973) generated a series of categories that can describe the Pivot Open Class grammar system. The categories that Brown discovered existing in children's speech are as follows:

Nomination	Locative
Notice	Movement
Recurrence	Agent-Action
Nonexistence	Agent-Object
Attributive	Action-Object
Possessive	Conjunction

Each of these categories can be described by specific vocalizations. Figure 2.2 shows those utterances most common to each of the categories listed.

These categories are good descriptors of a child's speech at approximately eighteen months. These two-word utterances are certainly the basis of the beginning of syntax. Once they occur, they tend to be elaborated upon extensively by the child. The number of items that appear in each of the categories grows quite rapidly. Through the processes of differentiation and elaboration, the child's vocabulary and utterances tend to become considerably more complex. By differentiation, or the splitting of classes, the child begins to group together several of the categories. For example, the nomination and attributive categories are grouped together so that the child begins to form utterances, such as "That Big Train." The child is expanding on the knowledge that has been gained in the use of these particular categories. The differentiation and the splitting of classes tends to produce utterances that are

Structural Meaning	Characterization	Example
Nomination	Is the child's attempt to identify a particular object in the environment.	That book
Notice	Refers to recognition.	Hi belt
Recurrence	Occurs frequently in young children's speech; is identified by the word "more."	More . . .
Nonexistence	Is identified by the frequent occurrence of the word "allgone."	Allgone . . .
Attributive	Refers to the assignment of a particular attribute to an object in the child's environment.	Big train
Possessive	Is the child's attempt to assign ownership	Mommy . . .
Locative	Is the child's attempt to identify the particular placement of an object.	Sweater chair
Movement	Is identified by the child's use of a verb and a noun; movement in a particular setting or place is often depicted.	Walk street
Agent-Action	Is the child's specific attempt to assign activity to a particular individual.	Eve read
Agent-Object	Refers to assignment of association but not ownership.	Daddy sock
Action-Object	Refers to movement related to a particular object in the immediate environment.	Put book
Conjunction	Is the grouping together of like items.	Umbrella boot

Source: Adapted from Brown, R. Psycholinguistics. New York: Free Press, a division of Macmillan Company, 1970, p. 220. Reprinted with permission.

FIGURE 2.2   Pivot-Open Class Grammar

much more complex than the two-word vocalizations that have been produced prior to this time. Elaboration refers to the simple addition of modifiers and articles to the child's statements. "Big train" easily becomes "That big green train." Or "A big green train." Or perhaps "The big green train." The categories as described by Brown are accurate descriptions of what takes place with respect to the child's use of syntax between eighteen and twenty-four months.

The Addition of Stress

The development of syntax has been discussed thus far in a rather structured fashion. As the child makes use of the categories described by Pivot Open Class grammar, there is a growing awareness of the utility of what is referred to as suprasegmental phonemes—stress, intonation, rate, jesture, facial expression, and pitch. Of these suprasegmental phonemes, a child uses stress in a unique way. It has been shown that the child uses stress to clarify whether a particular item in an open class category is being referred to in terms of ownership or in terms of location. An example from Dale (1972, p. 42) will clarify this use of stress.

When uttering the phrase "Christy room," the child could mean that Christy is in her room or that this is Christy's room. It was discovered that the statement "Christy *room*" (stress on room) meant that Christy was *in* her room. The statement "*Christy* room" (stress on Christy) meant that the child was assigning ownership to the room, implying that it was Christy's room.

According to Wieman (1974) the child apparently uses stress in an increasingly more obvious fashion as reference proceeds from agent to a pronoun object to action to noun object to locative and finally to new or contrasting information, at which point stress is most obvious. Wieman's observations indicate that the child is quite conscious of the need to request additional information or to distinguish between items through some variation in the speech signal. At this point, the only tool available to the child is that of stress and stress production. Figure 2.3 shows the shifting stress patterns children use as the basis of reference changes.

At the age of approximately thirty-six to forty months a shift begins to take place with respect to the types of sentences the child constructs and uses. Perhaps the next most significant phase in the development of syntax is that of the child's use of questions and questioning techniques. It is usually said at this point that the child is entering a new stage in the development of syntax. Dale (1972) demonstrates three specific stages that children seem to pass through in the development of questions.

Figure 2.4 delineates the types of speech produced by children at various stages. We can see a distinct difference between the type of questions children ask early in their awareness and use of questions and those produced several months later. Bellugi's (1965) description of the development

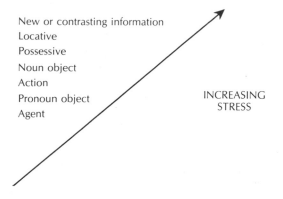

FIGURE 2.3   *The Usefulness of Stress*

Stage	Mean length of utterance	Ages (months)		Examples	Structures
I	1.8–2.0 morphemes	Adam Eve Sarah	28 18 27	a. No ear? See hole? Mommy eggnog? b. What's that? Where Daddy going?	S^a + Q What NP (doing)[b] Where NP (going)[b]
II	2.3–2.9 morphemes	Adam Eve Sarah	32 22 32	a. You can't fix it? See my doggie? Mom pinch finger? b. Who is it? What book name? Why not he eat? Why you smiling? Why not cracker can't talk?	S + Q Wh + S
III	3.4–3.6 morphemes	Adam Eve Sarah	38 25 38	a. Do I look like a little baby? Can't you get it? Can't it be a bigger truck? Am I silly? Does turtles crawl? Did you broke that part? Does the kitty stands up?	Aux + (n't) + NP + VP (result of question and do transformations)
				b. Why you caught it? What we saw? What did you doed? What he can ride in? What you have in you mouth? Why the kitty can't stand up?	Wh + NP + VP (result of wh-transformation; question and do transformations usually omitted)
				c. Who took this off? What lives in that house?	Wh + VP (wh subject question)

Source: From Language Development: Structure and Function by Philip S. Dale, p. 86. Copyright © 1972 by the Dryden Press. Reprinted by permission of Holt, Rinehart and Winston.

FIGURE 2.4   Stages in the Development of Questions

of questions as contained in Dale (1972, p. 86) tends to be rather straightforward. There are four basic types of questions: the yes-no question, the *wh*-question, the tag question, and indirect questions.

Yes-no questions are obviously the easiest to produce and require the least amount of linguistic effort on the part of the child. Yes-no questions can be generated by a change in prosaic features. Asking a yes-no question does not require a sophisticated knowledge of the English language. A simple shift in tone and emphasis alerts a listener that a question is being asked. Examining in Figure 2.4 the speech Adam and Sarah obtained when the mean length of their utterances was between 1.8 and 2.0 demonstrates rather clearly the use of simple intonation and prosaic shifts. The examples cited such as "No ear," "See hole," "Mommy eggnog," are not questions in a strict sense. However, when spoken using a variation in stress and intonation, it is apparent that a question is being asked.

The *wh*-questions are considerably more complex. What does it take to produce a *wh*-question? Consider a conversation that you might have recently overheard. In all likelihood, you heard sentences being generated such as:

> "Why wasn't he there?"
> "Why didn't you go?"
> "Where could he have put your number?"
> "What didn't he do, that is the question!"

These *wh*-questions and most questions used in informal conversations make use of a subject verb inversion as well as a contraction. Because these two linguistic forms are generally incorporated into *wh*-questions, these questions are a bit more complex and require quite a bit more skill to produce on the part of the speaker. Here, simple shifts in prosaic features are not sufficient to convey the message and question appropriately. The child must rely on a particular syntactic construction as well as changes in stress, pitch, and intonation to properly utilize this questioning form.

The third kind of question, the tag question, is quite common as the following examples show:

> "She is going to the party, isn't she?"
> "You have made up your mind to complete this assignment, haven't you?"
> "You will take this letter to the post office for me, won't you?"

Tag questions are considerably more sophisticated—a basic declarative sentence can convey information as well as ask a question. It is certainly a much more aggressive linguistic form. It invites comment on the part of the speaker. Not only do tag questions alter the impact of a declarative sentence,

61

they make use of, almost exclusively, contractions—a form that is difficult for children to acquire.

The fourth kind of question, the indirect question, occurs quite a bit later in the child's development. Examples of indirect questions are as follows:

"He asked me if I had a ticket to the movies."
"He wondered out loud if Martha had enough money."

Indirect questions incorporate, in many cases, most of the complexities associated with question asking. There can be, and generally is, a description of a past event taking place. As can be seen from the examples, emphasis is placed on *both* the situation and the question. Indirect questions do require a bit of mental manipulation on the part of both the speaker and the listener. They can be difficult to comprehend and answer. In many instances, the indirect question is asked in more of a rhetorical sense. The speaker is not necessarily looking for a reply. In the example, "He asked if he had a ticket to the theatre," the answer is probably not as significant as the situation in which the statement occurred. Indirect questions are often used in story telling situations. More than likely a third person is involved who is describing the situation. The story might go something like: "*And then*, he asked him if he had a ticket to the theatre." This implies that an entire sequence of events was at work here and the question comprised only a minor part of the exchange being described.

Once the child becomes fairly comfortable with these particular techniques and has learned how productive questioning can be, they become an integral part of the child's speech.

Refinement of Relationships
At this point it is important to remember that while the child has become a rather sophisticated language user, a number of skills still require further development. Although the child has made use of a number of forms before the age of five, there is a need to explore and to manipulate language for years to come. The child continues to:

1. Refine the use of affirmative versus negative.
2. Develop a better understanding of singular versus plural pronouns.
3. Refine subject-object relationships.
4. Increase awareness of present versus future tenses.
5. Experiment with collective nouns (e.g., audience, committee, family, or jury).
6. Exhibit signs of confusion over passive versus active voice.
7. Lack a fully developed awareness of indirect versus direct objects.

These particular skills are refined after the age of five. However, the speech of the five year old is, syntactically speaking, sophisticated and highly developed.

The Development of Semantics

The development of semantics is the second of the four levels of structure. Having become aware of the acquisition of syntax, you might suspect that the development of semantics would follow a similar pattern. This is not the case. The development of semantics is not well understood. There is no specific pattern or sequence of events to describe the acquisition of meaning.

Difficulties Involved in the Study of Semantics

Perhaps the most difficult obstacle to overcome in studying children's acquisition of meaning is the lack of knowledge about how adults acquire meaning. In the development of syntax, we could work backwards from adult syntactic structures. The knowledge of the adult syntactic system provided a baseline of information that could be compared to the speech of the young child. With this data available, statements and hypotheses could be generated with respect to the syntax or syntactic awareness of the child. In the case of semantics, however, no such structure currently exists. Of the various theories concerning adult semantic structures, none appears to be completely adequate. If a specific set of characteristics were available that could describe the adult semantic system, then it would be possible to work backwards, in this case as well, to the semantic system used by children. Until the adult semantic system is more fully understood, the processes children use in acquiring meaning will remain somewhat of a mystery.

In addition, the acquisition of meaning is very closely allied with the cognitive development process. A high degree of relationship seems to exist between cognitive strategies and the development of semantics. The ability to acquire meaning is directly contingent upon the ability to function in our society and to rapidly acquire those skills and insights necessary for survival. Simply recognizing the high degree of correlation between these two similar elements of human behavior does little to help us describe the acquisition of meaning. In fact, it contributes to the problems associated with study in this area.

As a result of these particular considerations, the study of the acquisition of meaning is extremely difficult. The lack of information about the adults' structure, the involvement with cognitive development and the real failure of vocabulary studies to contribute significantly to our understanding of the acquisition of meaning have all created numerous problems with respect to attempting to define the course of semantic development.

Theories of the Acquisition of Meaning

Three distinct theories that deal with this particular topic are, according to Dale (1972): the referential, the behavioral, and the conceptual approaches.

Referential Theory. The referential theory of the acquisition of meaning holds that most words have a referent that exists in the universe. A specific item in the universe or the environment that is being referred to can be identified by a given speech segment. For example, one might say that the meaning of the word chair is that particular thing that consists of four legs, a seat, and a back. Certainly the word "chair" has a particular referent in our environment. Those proponents of the referential theory believe quite strongly that the meaning of the word "chair" is acquired by children, and adults as well, through specific experiences. Contact with chairs and with individuals who have referred to such particular constructions as chairs leads us to use that word only in those specified contexts. Numerous examples are easily generated. "Lamp," "bird," "automobile," "pavement," "building," "window," "shelf," "flower," and "book" all have specific referents in our environment. In fact, a specific grammatic class of words, commonly referred to as nouns, is an essential element of language. A noun by definition is "a class of word that names or classifies people, animals, things, and ideas" (Guth, 1965, p. 368). Nouns occur typically as subjects of clauses or as objects of verbs and prepositions. They are indeed a substantial part of our vocabulary.

Certainly, citing noun classes as examples of what is meant by the referential theory is extremely simplistic. It is important, however, to be aware that this ability to recognize specific objects as referents may be an essential aspect of the acquisition of meaning. Proponents of the referential theory believe strongly that many words not classed as nouns also have a particular referent in the environment. Most of us will agree that, given the word "beauty," we can point to something in the environment that represents "beauty." This might be a slightly fluctuating type of designation and the referent might take on subtle characteristics, yet in all likelihood the particular object that represents beauty for one person will correspond to some extent to another individual's referent for the word "beauty." It also might be difficult to assign a referent to the word "honesty." However, we all could point to a historical figure, to a particular incident, to a particular situation, or to a set of circumstances that represent the meaning of the word "honesty." "Honesty" might be represented by Abraham Lincoln for some; for others, George Washington.

Perhaps it is through these common experiences that the acquisition of meaning is developed. Our continued growth as adults and exposure to varied interpretations contribute to our on-going understanding of particular concepts and words. The referential theory, while not a completely adequate explanation of the acquisition of meaning, does provide some insight into how meaning is learned and assigned.

However, there are distinct difficulties with the referential theory. For example, particular phrases may have exactly the same referent; particular words may have constant meaning but different referents, depending upon the situation; cultural concepts may be different and therefore influence the meaning of a particular word; and there are many words in our vocabulary to which it is utterly impossible to assign meaning. Each of these examples points out the specific limitations of this theory and demonstrates clearly that it is not a totally adequate explanation of the acquisition of meaning (Dale, 1972, pp. 133–134).

Behavioral Theory.   The second of the three theories, the behavioral theory, is a bit more complex than the referential theory. The behavioral theory maintains that the meaning of an utterance is the response it produces in the listener. This attempt to explain meaning is built on the relationship that exists between prior experience and current behaviors. Behaviorists maintain that our conditioned response to a statement *is* the actual meaning of the statement. There can be no one specific meaning for any statement or phrase, since there can be so many subtle variations in responses to a single vocalization. The behavioral theory of the acquisition of meaning rests heavily on the classical conditioned response paradigm. We are, in essence, conditioned by previous experiences to act and to feel in a particular way when confronted with a particular statement.

For example, imperative sentences are those commands so frequently used in day-to-day conversation that generate specific responses. The intent of the utterance is by no means questionable. The phrases or commands, "Open the window!" or "Shut the door!" or "Be quiet!" are not often subject to widespread interpretation. Each utterance produces a particular response.

The behavioral theory would be rather simplistic if it stopped at this point. Yet, it does take into account the fact that circumstances may contribute significantly to the type of response an utterance generates. "Bring me an apple" might be a simple command that produces no anxiety in the listener, if apples are plentiful or readily available. "Bring me an apple" when nothing but oranges are at hand might produce a series of responses that involve questioning, anxiety, negation, or confusion.

Note from these examples that the behavioral theory of the acquisition of meaning focuses on the responses that a particular statement produces in the listener. This response act might also be described as a tendency to respond, since it does not necessarily imply that overt activity must occur.

A number of difficulties are associated with the behavioral theory of the acquisition of meaning. A heavy reliance on the classical conditioning model is certainly one difficulty. Some would maintain that such a parallel is completely artificial and holds no value. The opponents of the behavioral approach claim that almost any human activity can be described in terms of a conditioned response. Therefore, applying this model to the acquisition of meaning is hardly novel or appropriate.

Another difficulty is that complex sentences and statements initiate numerous response tendencies in the course of a single conversation! When taken at face value, the behavioral theory seems to attribute unique capabilities to the human mind. The example "John is a liar" shows perhaps two particular tendencies to respond inherent in it. The same phrase can become much more complex. "John is a liar only in the company of Joe" creates additional considerations that must be met. "John was a liar but is reformed now" is still another set of circumstances that needs responses. According to the behavioral theory, several different responses must be made in order to understand the meaning of the last statement. In each case, then, one would have to respond, correct, shift gears, and respond again. The process could occur several times over in any one utterance. This aspect may in some sense detract from the theory, since most of us will agree that some manipulation of responses and feelings does not consciously happen in our conversations and communications. People would state that they are left only with an overall reaction or tendency to respond as a result of a communication encounter. Few would summarize a conversation by listing a series of responses. It would be quite difficult to communicate and to ask for reactions if we knew that the respondent was going to say: "Well, at first I felt like this, and then like this, and then what he said made me feel this way, and then. . . ." Response in the behavioral theory, if adhered to strictly, would almost necessitate that kind of reaction. Everyday experiences obviously do not support that particular notion.

The referential theory and the behavioral theory cover two of the most significant attempts to describe the acquisition of meaning. Each theory provides some information on the development of semantics. However, one theory often gives rise to a second or a third, and such is the case with theories related to the acquisition of meaning. The inadequacies of the referential and the behavioral theories prompted Bolinger (1968) to advance an entirely new approach to the acquisition of meaning—the conceptual theory.

Conceptual Theory. The conceptual theory of the acquisition of meaning states that our ability with words, our ability to acquire meaning, and our ability to use language effectively are all contingent upon the development of concepts. Take, for example, the concept of time. Most educators are quite aware of the difficulties associated with the teaching of the days of the week, the months of the year, and seasons. Most teachers explain that before young children can use such words as "yesterday," "today," and "tomorrow" appropriately, they must develop an understanding of the concept of time. It is only after that particular ability—to distinguish between the past, present, and the future—has been acquired that children can use the appropriate word forms. Only when the concept of time is acquired does the term "Monday" or "Tuesday" take on added meaning for the child. Another example and one also frequently referred to by classroom teachers is that of space relations. Teaching the young child the meaning of the words "above," "below," "besides," "under," and "upon" requires an understanding of space relations. Dealing with that concept in the classroom contributes significantly to the children's ability with those particular vocabulary words.

The list of concepts and related vocabulary can become quite extensive. The point, however, is to be aware that our vocabulary appears to be related to particular concepts that we understand and use. Meaning is acquired in conjunction with the development of ideas and the understanding of particular relationships. Concepts may be the key to the acquisition of meaning.

It is interesting to note that Bolinger's theory builds on both the referential and behavioral theories. Both are recognized and virtually incorporated into what we have called the conceptual theory. The development of concepts for one person requires a certain amount of experimentation and contact with items in the environment. A number of referents are necessary before a particular idea can be understood. For another person physical responses, physical manipulation of objects, or total immersion in the concept is a fundamental aspect of the process of acquiring it; and some people require a combination of referents and immersion in the topic before it is learned or understood.

The Importance of Concept Development
in the Acquisition of Meaning

Although the development of semantics is not well understood, there are several aspects of this component of the definition of language that are not indefinite. It has been found that concept development, an understanding of word relationships, the ability to classify information, the ability to identify distinguishing characteristics, and an awareness that semantics and syntax are highly related, are all particularly important to the development of meaning.

Perhaps the most significant contribution to the knowledge about the acquisition of meaning rests in the notion that meaning is acquired as concepts are developed. Piaget's 1932 experimentation with children's awareness of perspective, sometimes referred to as egocentrism, and conservation (Piaget & Szeminska, 1952) has shown that the meaning of a particular term for a child is directly related to the concept involved.

A child under the age of five has difficulty with the terms right and left. We all have observed young children correctly identify their own right and left hands yet fail consistently to identify the right and left hands of a person seated directly in front of and facing them.

This particular demonstration raises the question: do these children understand the meaning of the terms "right" and left." It is a perplexing situation because they have just demonstrated that, yes, they do know their own right and left hands. However, when asked to show another person's right and left hands, they fail in both situations. In this situation, the children do not understand the meaning of the words right and left. Until the concept of perspective acquired, they will continue to make such errors.

The Importance of Word Relationships

Besides Piaget's work in concept formation, studies of a limited nature have been conducted with respect to word relationships. It has been found that children do acquire particular word relationships as they learn vocabulary. The relationships of synonymy, antonymy, reciprocity, and inclusion are but four word relationships that contribute to the acquisition of meaning. As these particular concepts are acquired and developed, there may very well be additional vocabulary growth. The full meaning of many words seems to be based on one's ability to relate those words to similar and dissimilar situations.

Very little is known about children's acquisition of word relationships. Very young children appear to make use of syntagmatic classes, such as "hot-bath," prior to making use of paradigmatic classes, such as "hot-cold." Observations on the use of synonyms and antonyms show that young children use synonyms much more frequently than antonyms. When confronted with particular one-word stimuli, older children tend to respond in opposites. Younger children tend to respond with similar classes or words that have similar characteristics. These concepts are important in the acquisition of meaning.

The Importance of Classification

From an adult point of view, a similar type of relationship is at work with respect to the acquisition of meaning. Osgood, Suci, and Tannebaum (1957) in the development of the "semantic differential" have generated what is referred to as a "three-dimensional semantic space" in which all individuals operate. When asked to rate individuals, objects, places, or situations, three particular concepts were found to permeate the adult's rating scale. It appeared that the concepts of evaluation, potency, and activity were all significant in terms of defining the meaning of a particular event, place, person, or situation in our lives. Specifically, adults tend to evaluate situations in terms of correctness or incorrectness, to define things in terms of their heaviness versus their lightness, and to look at events in terms of the degree of activity that the particular situation will generate or require.

Children, however, when asked to respond to a particular situation using the semantic differential technique, tend to confuse the categories.

Adults will be much more discriminating whereas a child will describe something that is good as also being clean and pretty. A child who finds a particular object quite heavy also associates slowness with it. As children become older, the meaning of a particular situation in terms of this three-dimensional semantic space tends to become more refined. After the age of eight the categories of evaluation, potency, and activity stand independent of each other.

The Importance of Distinguishing Characteristics

With respect to the acquisition of meaning, the concept of classification of events, objects, places, and situations as outlined by Osgood's semantic differential suggests that there may be a set of distinguishing characteristics that describes each word we use. These distinguishing characteristics or feature bundles probably play a very important role in determining meaning. Every word apparently has a set of feature bundles or distinguishing characteristics inherent in it. The awareness of these particular characteristics permits us to determine the appropriate meaning of the words that are encountered or utilized.

Figure 2.5 is a diagrammatic representation of the word "bachelor." As can be seen in this diagram, the word "bachelor" has the characteristic of being a noun as a grammatic classification, of being male, of being human, and of being animal. These particular aspects of the word "bachelor" determine appropriate meanings. The categories human and male generate different definitions of the word than do the characteristics of male and animal.

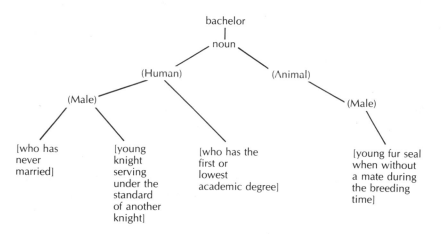

Source: From *Child language and education* by C. Cazden, Copyright © 1972 by Holt, Rinehart and Winston, Inc. Reprinted and adapted by permission of Holt, Rinehart and Winston. Originally found in Katz, J., and Fordor, J. *The structure of language: Readings in the philosophy of language.* Englewood Cliffs, N.J.: Prentice-Hall, Inc., 1964, 523. Adapted by permission of Prentice-Hall, Inc.

FIGURE 2.5 *Diagrammatic Representation of "Bachelor."*

From this example, it is evident that we must be aware of the characteristics or feature bundles of the word "bachelor" in order to successfully determine its meaning.

Perhaps the best example of our use of semantic feature bundles rests in pronoun selection. Applying the concept of semantic feature bundles to the acquisition of meaning with respect to pronouns, we can see that such strategies are equally as prevalent with this grammatic class. According to Waryas (1973), awareness of the following semantic features are necessary in order to make appropriate pronoun selections:

+/−	Pronoun
+/−	Speaker
+/−	Listener
+/−	Other
+/−	Singular
+/−	Male

Source: Waryas, C. Psycholinguistic research in language integration programs: The pronoun system. *Journal of Psycholinguistical Research,* 1973, 2(3), 221-237.

These particular semantic features determine our selection from the pronoun lexicon. In almost any situation, our ability to select a pronoun as a noun substitute is contingent upon the identification of the necessary features and the appropriate association with a given vocabulary word. For example, if a situation were to call for the pronoun "her," we would have to identify "her" in the following manner:

+	Pronoun
−	Speaker
−	Listener
+	Other
+	Singular
−	Male

Such an application of these categories can be made with any pronoun. It is quite apparent that the use of semantic features is not all that unusual, especially since such an approach can be applied so readily to such a significant aspect of our language.

As in the case of pronouns, the concepts of speaker, listener, other, singularity, and sexuality are necessary before appropriate pronoun selection can be made. The use of these concepts in pronoun selection parallels the concepts suggested by Osgood of evaluation, potency, and activity. Certainly the pronoun semantic feature bundles are much more specific than Osgood's categories. Yet, specific concept awareness seems necessary to making particular vocabulary selections.

Importance of Syntax

Another aspect of what is known about the acquisition of meaning was already mentioned in the discussion of the development of syntax. The relationship that exists between syntax and semantics is quite strong. The meaning of many unfamiliar statements, phrases, or words can often be derived by an understanding of the syntactic considerations. Consider the following:

GLOOPY & BLIT EXERCISE

Gloopy is a borp.
Blit is a lof.
Gloopy klums like Blit.
Gloopy and Blit are floms.
　　Ril had poved Blit to a jonfy.
But lo had not poved Gloopy.
　　"The jonfy is for lofs,"
Blit bofd to Gloopy.
　　"Rom are a borp."
　　Gloopy was not klorpy.
Then Blit was not klorpy.

Questions: Answer in complete sentences.

1. What are Gloopy and Blit?
2. Who does Gloopy klum like?
3. What did Blit bof to Gloopy?
4. Was Blit klorpy?
5. Why wasn't Gloopy poved to the jonfy?

Source: From *Language and Thinking in School,* 2nd ed., by E. Brooke Smith, Kenneth S. Goodman and Robert Meredith. Copyright © 1970 by Holt, Rinehart and Winston, Inc., © 1976 by Holt, Rinehart and Winston. Reprinted by permission of Holt, Rinehart and Winston.

To read this nonsense passage and to answer the questions correctly, knowledge of the English syntactical system must be used to an extent. By defining classes of words, and by examining the relationships that exist syntactically, one should be able to respond appropriately. Without a knowledge of syntax, the answers to those questions could be quite difficult to obtain. The nonsense paragraph Gloopy and Blit is indicative of the relationship that exists between syntax and semantics.

Summary of Semantic Development

Regardless of the theory subscribed to, children seem to begin exhibiting signs of an awareness of semantic relationships by age eight. Around age eight, children develop a greater sensitivity to word meaning and to a variety of forms. While the development of semantics is an on-going process, it appears to stabilize at this point in the child's development.

The Development of Pragmatics

The definition of language used in this text has a third level of structure—pragmatics. The development of pragmatics is also a little-understood area. It is quite similar to the development of semantics. Information regarding children's ability to use language in subtle ways is still quite sketchy. By pragmatics, we mean the assignment of function to particular utterances. Speier (1969) demonstrated that the function of a single-word question in a conversational setting can vary significantly. The example provided by Speier as contained in Cazden (1972, p. 13) is as follows:

Child (C) is talking with his father (A):

  (C): Dad
  (A): What?
  (C): At the end of all the counting there is an eight on its side.
  (A): What?
  (C): At the end of all the counting there is an eight on its side.
  (A): Where did you learn that?

As can be seen from this particular exchange, the use of the word "what" served two different functions. Initially, the word called for attention on the part of the listener. Once that was achieved, the child was able to proceed with the statement. The next "what" that the listener used was a question, signifying to the speaker that there was a problem in communication and that further elaboration would be necessary. In this case, the child elected to repeat the same sentence over again. The fact that a word such as "what" can serve such a function places it in the class of a paradigmatic expression. While the form of the word stays the same, its function is subject to variation. The ability to interpret the meaning of words such as "what" is one that is acquired. Certainly the awareness of word function is a subtle skill.

A significant relationship exists between semantics and pragmatics, but the overlap is not quite clear. What has been said about the development of semantics might also apply to the development of pragmatics. That is, a particular cognitive strategy is necessary to understanding the relationship between form and function. It does appear that children, at an early age, are sensitive to the various phrases and statements used by adults that are not meant to be taken literally. This skill is one that is indeed a refinement of semantic understandings.

The Development of Phonology

The fourth level of structure in our definition of language is the acquisition of phonemes. Because a relationship exists between phonology and reading, a good deal of research has been conducted in this area. It is important to realize that the acquisition of phonemes is a logical and sequential procedure. This section deals with only the major aspects of the acquisition of phonemes and discusses only those elements necessary to complete our definition of language.

There is no doubt that the ability to produce and to discriminate sounds is quite commonplace. Knowledge of the rules for combining sounds into words and larger units appears to be acquired quite readily. The exposure to vocal stimuli contributes significantly to the development of phonemes. From a developmental point of view, one needs only to be aware that there is a skill progression. Cazden (1972) points out several myths that have been perpetuated with respect the acquisition of phonemes.

The first myth has been that the development of phonemes is a slow and gradual process. Much of the research that has been done with respect to the acquisition of phonemes indicates quite clearly that the rate at which particular phonemes are introduced and made use of is rapid. Forms do appear quite quickly and new sounds are learned by the child readily. Young children can discriminate between phonemes at an early age.

The second myth discussed by Cazden is that the learning of the production of sounds is developed by a process of gradual shaping of infant babbling into acceptable sounds. Cazden reports that this is simply not true. In fact, a period of silence occurs between vocalic play or babbling and actual speech production. From these observations it seems there is not a direct progression from babbling to speech sounds, but rather a period of time when little speech is produced.

With respect to the acquisition of phonemes, Figure 2.6 shows that, at a very early age, particular sounds are acquired and correctly used by children. The progression of sounds generally found in children's speech between the ages of three and seven years, five months is delineated. The reader can see that a progression does exist and that there is an apparent order to phoneme acquisition.

Comparison of the Ages at which Subjects Correctly Produced Specific Consonant Sounds in the Templin, the Wellman, and the Poole Studies*

		Age Correctly Produced	
Sound	Templin (1957)	Wellman and others (1931)	Poole (1934)
m	3	3	3.5
n	3	3	4.5
ŋ	3	—[a]	4.5
p	3	4	3.5
f	3	3	5.5
h	3	3	3.5
w	3	3	3.5
j	3.5	4	4.5
k	4	4	4.5
b	4	3	3.5
d	4	5	4.5
g	4	4	4.5
r	4	5	7.5
s	4.5	5	7.5[b]
ʃ	4.5	—[c]	6.5
tʃ	4.5	5	—[c]
t	6	5	4.5
θ	6	—[a]	7.5[b]
v	6	5	6.5[b]
l	6	4	6.5
ð	7	—[c]	6.5
z	7	5	7.5[b]
ʒ	7	—[c]	6.5
dʒ	7	6	—[c]
hw	—[a]	—[a]	7.5

*In the Wellman and others and Templin studies a sound was considered mastered if it was articulated correctly by 75 percent of the subjects. The criterion of correct production was 100 percent in the Poole study.

[a] Sound was tested but was not produced correctly by 75 percent of the subjects at the oldest age tested. In the Wellman data the "hw" reached the percentage criterion at 5 but not at 6 years, the medial "ŋ" reached it at 3, and the initial and medial "θ" and "ð" at 5 years.
[b] Poole (Davis, 1938), in a study of 20,000 preschool and school-age children reports the following shifts: "s" and "z" appear at 5.5 years, then disappear and return later at 7.5 years or above: "θ" appears at 6.5 years and "v" at 5.5 years.
[c] Sound not tested or not reported.

Source: Templin, M. C. Certain language skills in children, their development and interrelationships. Minneapolis: University of Minnesota Press, 1957, 54(26), 53 (Monograph of the Institute of Child Welfare).

FIGURE 2.6   The Acquisition of Phonemes

The Hierarchical Nature of Language

This particular aspect of our definition is easy to deal with—there is no question that language is hierarchical in nature. Acquired forms are made use of in the acquisition of new forms. The work of Brown (1973) has served as the basis for this fact. It was observed in the study of three children (Adam, Eve, and Sarah) that the language forms being used were direct outgrowths of previously acquired forms. Basically, one need only to refer to our discussion of syntax or semantics to confirm this fact. Naturally, the acquisition of syntax is clearly more organized than that of semantics, but the notion of an order is implied in both. With respect to the development of syntax, we saw that the holophrastic stage gave way to the duophrastic stage—a move from one-word statements to two-word statements. Our discussion of the duophrastic stage and the Pivot Open Class grammar system pointed out quite clearly that the categories used initially by children begin to be combined to produce longer statements. Adult sentences can also be shown to be hierarchical in nature. Each can be diagrammed to demonstrate the combination of elements comprising a given sentence. The hierarchical nature of our language is indeed a given.

Language Transformations

The final component of our definition involves the use of transformations. Chomsky (1957) advanced the theory that there was a high degree of correspondence between surface structure and deep structure within language. He provided the notion that we make use of surface structure in order to convey deeper meaning. All our utterances can be looked at in terms of surface structure and deep structure. To arrive at an appropriate type of surface structure for the meaning that we have in mind, a number of transformations may be required. Three of the most basic transformations according to Cazden (1972, pp. 19–21) are:

1. Separation transformation
2. Passive transformation
3. Indirect object transformation

Each transformation is basically a set of rules that must be learned and acquired in order to convey information correctly. The rules that are represented by the term transformation refer only to changes in form, not necessarily in meaning.

The separation transformation deals with the ability to transpose certain verbs and their participles. An example of a separation transformation would be the following:

> *"Please take out the garbage."*
> *"Please take the garbage out."*

The verb form "take out" can be used in this case in both situations correctly. We must be aware that, if the pronoun "it" is substituted for the word "garbage," a separation is required. We then have a separation transformation at work in the example. Pronouns are an exception to the rule, because there must be a separation around pronouns. We would then say:

> *"Please take it out."*

not

> *"Please take out it."*

The separation transformation is an example of a change in form that can occur without altering meaning.

The passive transformation is frequently used by adults and children alike. It is also one of the later-occurring skills. The passive transformation requires an understanding of the elements of our language. A sentence such as: "He shoveled the snow" can be readily converted into a passive voice sentence: "The snow was shoveled by him." Many studies have been done regarding children's understanding of the passive transformation. It is apparent that children at an early age rely heavily on word order. If the examples provided were: "The cat chased the dog" or "The dog was chased by the cat," young children asked to draw a picture of the particular situations would submit different responses. Children would insist that in one case the cat did the chasing—which, of course, would be correct; while in the other the dog did the chasing—even though that is completely incorrect. The passive transformation is one that is not learned until much later in the child's development.

The indirect object transformation is quite easy to understand. The statement: "The clerk gave the bag to the girl," can be easily rephrased to read "The clerk gave her the bag." The indirect object transformation is a streamlining process, although the same amount of information is being conveyed. The prepositional phrase is simply removed. While this transformation is simple to use, it also has been shown to be a later-occurring developmental skill. Children after age five continue to experiment with both passive and indirect object transformations.

Language Acquisition and the Mildly Handicapped

Having discussed the general aspects of the course of language acquisition and development in normal children, we might wonder to what extent the

Area of Language	Typical Construction	Possible Variation
Development of Syntax	"Is the boy going home?"	"The boy going home?"
	"Mary has a small ball she is playing with."	"She playing with ball."
	"What else can you make?"	"What else you make?"
	"You can touch these dots."	"You touch dot."
	"You can't reach the top of this table."	"No reach table."
	"Draw a line up to the corner of the top of the paper."	"Draw line top paper."

	Typical Construction	Possible Interpretation
Development of Semantics and Pragmatics (Wiig & (Semel, 1976, pp. 186–188).	"He hit the roof."	The man reached out and actually hit the roof with his hand.
	"I'm all tied up at the office."	The person speaking is actually bound to a chair.
	"Bill caught a cold."	Bill actually was able to catch a cold with his hands and hold onto it.
	"The advertising business is a real jungle."	This business is one that has trees and wild animals in it.
	"When Bill received the award, he was as pleased as punch."	Bill, when he got the award, looked like a bowl of punch.

	Typical Construction	Possible Pronunciation
Development of Phonology	"The boy caught two fish yesterday."	"The boy caught two pish yesterday."
	"Martha had three sheep in the barn."	"Martha had thrwee theep in the barn."
	"Jeri ran after the round ball."	"Jeri wran after the wround ball."
	"Stephen slipped on the step."	"Thephen thlipped on the thep."

FIGURE 2.7 Examples of Possible Deviations from Normal Speech Patterns

mildly handicapped child deviates from this particular pattern. How different is the syntax of the mildly handicapped child? What difficulties in understanding word or sentence meanings do mildly handicapped children frequently experience? Are pronunciations radically different? Is speech unintelligible? Do the mildly handicapped understand how language forms may differ from their intended functions? Are transformations utilized appropriately?

Figure 2.7 provides a few examples of how the speech and language of the mildly handicapped child *might* differ from that of the normal youngster. This listing is to serve only as an example of the kinds of variations that may occur. The following chapters in this text specify how the mildly handicapped child typically writes, speaks, reads, and spells.

Language Acquisition and the Teaching of the Language Arts

Besides serving as a basis for decision-making regarding the quality of the speech of the mildly handicapped child, the information concerning the course of language acquisition and development should assist the teacher in the design, implementation, and evaluation of each of the language arts skill areas. It is our contention that the information contained in this chapter concerning the definition of language and the sequence of events surrounding its development is of value to the teacher of the language arts. Throughout the text, references will be made to the information that has been presented here.

In the chapters that follow, the suggested skills and activities are based on the knowledge that the normal child acquires language in an ordered, sequential fashion and that skill in each of the areas translates to a facility in the various aspects of the language arts. The relationship between the two might be seen as follows:

Area of Language Acquisition	Related Area of the Language Arts
Acquisition of Syntax	Oral Language Development ·Question asking Functional Writing Skills ·Sentence completion
Development of Semantics and Pragmatics	Listening Skills Multiple Meaning Vocabulary Sensitivity to Nonverbal Cues and Clues
Development of Phonology	Spelling Improvement Reading

FIGURE 2.8   Relationship between Acquisition of Language and Facility in Language Arts

Within each language arts area, there are numerous points of overlap between curriculum components and the knowledge presently available concerning the manner in which language is acquired. This chapter serves as one part of the base upon which the ideas, activities, and techniques that follow are built. Reference should be made frequently back to this chapter as this text is utilized.

SUMMARY

This chapter has attempted to expand upon commonly held notions concerning the language acquisition and development process. It was stated that the popular definitions of language are somewhat inadequate. They tend to deal only with myths and generalizations about language. A popular definition of language taken from *Webster's New World Dictionary* was compared to a definition advanced by Cazden in her text *Child Language and Education* (1972). Using the latter definition, the aspects of language could be explored from a developmental point of view. This chapter then focused on language as:

1. A rule-governed but creative activity.
2. A structure consisting of syntax, semantics, pragmatics, and phonology levels.
3. Hierarchical in nature.
4. Made of transformations.

This chapter attempted to provide an overview of the child language acquisition and development process. The information that has been presented here should serve as a basis for understanding the activities, the ideas, the concepts, and the recommendations to be made in subsequent chapters. It is hoped that the definition discussed will serve as a basis for language arts instruction. By dispelling some of the popular notions with respect to the child language acquisition and development process, the reader should be better able to structure the child's language environment. It is indeed possible to facilitate the acquisition of language by providing an environment that contributes significantly to the child's ability to experience new forms. Stimulation and varied linguistic encounters are indeed keys to growth in language ability.

POINTS FOR DISCUSSION

1. Write a definition of language. Try to be as concise yet as complete as possible in your description. Share your definition with a classmate. Discuss those features

of language that are common to both, different, or in conflict. See if you can generate a common definition of language. Present your definition to the entire class for discussion.

2.   Trace the course of syntactic development describing those stages that the child apparently passes through in the development of syntax. Include in your discussion examples of the child's language one could anticipate encountering at each stage.

3.   What should teachers know about the acquisition of phonemes? Pretend you are given the assignment of sharing information with your peers regarding the development of phonemes. What would you say? What would you include in your presentation?

4.   Share with a peer your understanding of the development of semantics. In your conversations, try to review the major theories related to the acquisition of meaning and discuss some of the beliefs that currently exist with respect to the child's acquiring of meaning.

5.   Describe, if you can, a recent experience with a young child. Discuss your encounter with this youngster from a language standpoint. What impressed you the most about the child's speech? What types of creative behaviors did you experience? What was most unusual about this child's ability to communicate?

REFERENCES

Bellugi, U. The development of interrogative structures in children's speech. In K. Riegel (Ed.), *The development of language functions*. University of Michigan Language Development Program, Report No. 8, 1965, pp. 103–138.

Bolinger, D. *Aspects of language*. New York: Harcourt Brace Jovanovich, 1968.

Brown, R. *Psycholinguistics*. New York: Free Press, 1970.

Brown, R. *A first language*. Cambridge, Mass.: Harvard University Press, 1973.

Butt, D., and Chreist, F. A speechreading test for young children. *The Volta Review*, 1968, *70*, 228–229.

Cazden, C. *Child language and education*. New York: Holt, Rinehart and Winston, 1972.

Chomsky, N. *Syntactic structures*. The Hague: Mouton, 1957.

Chukovsky, K. *From two to five*. Translated and edited by M. Morton. Berkeley, Calif.: University of California Press, 1963.

Dale, P. *Language development: Structure and function*. Hinsdale, Il: Dryden Press, Inc., 1972, 2nd ed., 1976.

Davis, E. Developmental changes in the distribution of parts of speech. *Child Development*, 1938, *9* (3), 309–317.

Ervin-Tripp, S. Language development. In L. W. Hoffman and M. L. Hoffman (Eds.), *Review of child development research*. Vol. 2. New York: Russell Sage Foundation, 1966.

Guth, H. *The concise English handbook* (2nd ed.). Belmont, Calif.: Wadsworth Publishing Company, 1965.

Jakobson, R. *Child language, aphasia, and phonological universals.* Translated by A. Keiler. The Hague: Mouton, 1968.

Katz, J., and Fordor, J. The structure of a semantic theory. In J. Katz and J. Fordor (Eds.), *The structure of language.* Englewood Cliffs, N.J.: Prentice-Hall, 1964.

Linkletter, A. *Kids say the darndest things.* New York: Pocket Books, 1957.

Osgood, C., Suci, G., and Tannebaum, P. *The measurement of meaning.* Urbana: University of Illinois Press, 1957.

Piaget, J. *The language and thought of the child* (2nd ed.). London: Routledge and Kegan Paul, 1932.

Piaget, J., and Szeminska, A. *The child's conception of number.* Translated by G. Gattegno and F. M. Hodgson. London: Routledge, 1952.

Slobin, D. L. Universals of grammatical development in children. In G. B. Flores d'Arcais and W. J. M. Levelt (Eds.), *Advances in psycholinguistics.* Amsterdam: North Holland Publishing Co., 1970.

Smith, E., Goodman, K., and Meredith, R. *Language and thinking in the elementary school* (2nd ed.). New York: Holt, Rinehart & Winston, 1976.

Smith, M. A study of some factors influencing the development of the sentence in preschool children. *Journal of Genetic Psychology,* 1935, 46, 182–212.

Speier, M. *The organization of talk and socialization in family household interaction.* Unpublished doctoral dissertation, University of California at Berkeley, 1969.

Templin, M. *Certain language skills in children, their development and interrelationships.* Minneapolis: University of Minnesota Press, 1957, 54(26), 53. (Monograph of the Institute of Child Welfare).

Waryas, C. Psycholinguistic research in language integration programs: The pronoun system. *Journal of Psycholinguistical Research,* 1973, 2 (3), 221–237.

Webster's New World Dictionary, College Edition. New York: The World Publishing Co., 1966, p. 821.

Wieman, L. A. *The stress pattern of early child language.* Unpublished doctoral dissertation, University of Washington, 1974.

Wiig, E., and Semel, E. *Language disabilities in children and adolescents.* Columbus, Ohio: Charles E. Merrill Publishing Company, 1976.

PART II

Assessment

3

The Language Arts and Communication

"When *I* use a word," Humpty Dumpty said in rather a scornful tone, "it means just what I choose it to mean—neither more nor less."

"The question is," said Alice, "whether you *can* make words mean so many different things."

"The question is," said Humpty Dumpty, "which is to be master—that's all."*

The language arts represent to teachers that aspect of the curriculum that stresses communication. For most, the teaching of reading, writing, penmanship, oral language, listening, and spelling represents the extent to which instructional emphasis is placed on communication skill development. While this focus on reading, writing, listening, and speaking as communication is appropriate, it often does not stress the interrelationship that exists between these skills. Teachers of the language arts need to identify commonalities between these skills to construct an instructional program that is oriented toward *total* communication skill development.

*From Lewis Carroll as found in Miller, G. *Language and Communication*. New York: McGraw-Hill, 1963, p. 1.

Many teachers have found themselves in "Humpty Dumpty-Alice" situations with children whose communication skills were simply not all that they should be. Usually the children's behavior in such situations is viewed as immature or even "cute," and the fact that little, if any, communication at all was taking place probably was not of concern. At some point, every teacher begins to help children understand that they cannot "make words mean so many different things," and that, in order to successfully communicate with others, certain skills simply must be developed.

The Process of Communication

Teaching mildly handicapped children basic communication skills requires that the teacher have some understanding of the communication process and knowledge of communications theory. The teaching of communication skills, as with the teaching of writing, penmanship, oral language, listening skills, and spelling, cannot be successful without an understanding of the underlying principles at work. In this case, the successful teaching of communication skills rests on the teacher's view of the communication process.

What then is communication? What does it involve? Who participates? How many people are necessary? At what levels can communication occur? How much of our interaction with others can be considered "communication?" Numerous other questions can be raised with respect to the communication process. These are only a few, but they do represent the most basic concerns that must be addressed in the teaching of communication skills.

Let us begin with a definition of communication. Byker and Anderson (1975) suggest that "human communication is a sharing of information between two or more people" (p. 4). Nothing more, nothing less. This is indeed a simple definition. It appears to be logical and accurate, but what is the rationale behind it?

Byker and Anderson based their definition on Burke's (1969) concepts of "autonomy and consubstantiality."

> In Burke's scheme there is no autonomy, hence, no need for communication (Figure 1). If each is completely separate, absolute autonomy prevails; hence, no communication is possible (Figure 2). If each is separate yet also joined to others, consubstantiality reigns and communication can occur (Figure 3).

Burke's definition is unique because the notion of consubstantiality can account for the sum total of all the elements of an interaction. The process of communication enables one individual, with all the ensuing

86

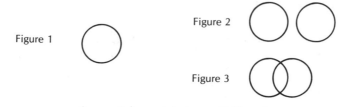

Figure 1

Figure 2

Figure 3

Source: Byker and Anderson, 1975, p. 3.

characteristics of personality, intelligence, emotion, and language capacity to share common experiences with another. The situation, the environment, the time of day, month, and year, and the variables of vocal action (e.g., articulation and voice quality), bodily action (e.g., stance, poise, and gesture), language utilized (e.g., vocabulary and grammar), the feedback provided (e.g., amount and nature), and listener traits (e.g., sex, social status, age, intelligence, experience, and knowledge of the topic) can all influence the outcome of the exchange.

This process of "sharing of information" from a "consubstantially" based viewpoint results in a process that can be depicted as in Figure 3.1. The visual display incorporates all the elements that have been discussed thus far with respect to the communication process.

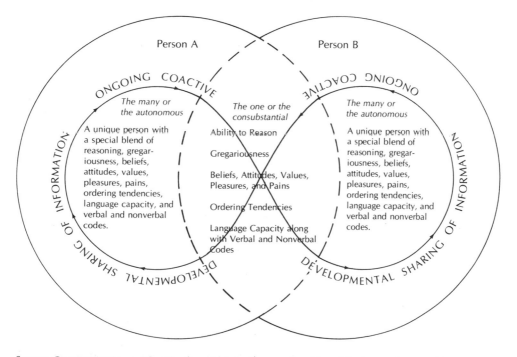

Source: Communication as identification: An introductory view. Copyright © 1975 by Donald Byker and Loren J. Anderson. Used by permission of Harper & Row, Publishers, Inc.

FIGURE 3.1   The Byker-Anderson Model of Communication

Communication Models

The process of communicating an idea, feeling, or concept involves at least two people with some sort of *transmission device* that produces or *encodes* a *signal,* that travels along some *channel* to a *receiver,* who *decodes* the signal and *reacts* to it. A graphic representation of this process *and* the numerous factors that constitute both independent and dependent variables is a communication model. Since the process of communication is of concern to business, industry, government, and the professions, it is not surprising to find numerous communication models available.

Historically, public speaking has always received an unusual amount of attention. Prior to the invention of the printing press, oral communication was the primary vehicle for conveying ideas and shaping behaviors. It is no secret that ancient Greece contributed significantly to modern-day communication theory. In fact, Aristotle's view of the communication process (Figure 3.2) outlined the three key elements found in all models.

Aristotle's model, however, appears to treat communication in a very linear fashion. A noticeable omission in Figure 3.2 is any indication of interaction between the speaker and the listener. It is almost as though the speaker in Aristotle's view is isolated from the listener in much the same sense that a lecturer is separated from the audience by the podium and the formality of the situation.

Those communication models that have followed from Aristotle's work have elaborated on these dimensions of the communication act. In fact,

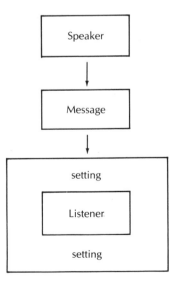

Source: From Howard H. Martin and Kenneth E. Andersen, SPEECH COMMUNICATION: ANALYSIS AND READINGS. Copyright © 1968 by Allyn and Bacon, Inc., Boston. Reprinted with permission.

FIGURE 3.2   *Aristotle's View of the Communication Process*

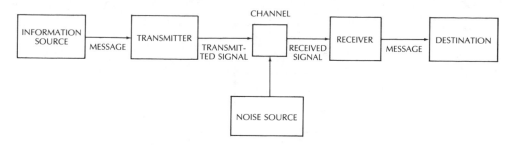

FIGURE 3.3   Shannon's Communication Theory Model

the tremendous surge of information processing that occurred in the early part of this century did much to stimulate the generation of alternative ways to looking at the process of conveying information—by both machines and humans.

Perhaps the most influential of all existing models of communication of recent origin is that by Shannon (1948). Communication is viewed in terms of the direct transmission of information. Figure 3.3 depicts Shannon's Communication Theory model.

The model is self-explanatory in that it represents those elements assisting and to some extent interfering in information processing. This model was developed to describe a communication system, regardless of its complexity, in terms of a few essential elements. This universal communication system as described by Shannon (and later elaborated upon by Weaver to become the Shannon-Weaver Model) was meant to be useful to communication engineers who dealt more with the direct transmission of information through telephone wire, radio waves, and high fidelity phonograph or tape.

Another communication model that was forwarded about the same time that Shannon was developing his communication theory was that of the Lasswell model. This particular approach differs dramatically from Shannon's in that it is basically a verbal model of communication that consists of a series of questions. Developed as a means to analyze any information-sharing situation, it is unique in its simplicity. The Lasswell model is diagrammed in Figure 3.4.

This particular approach to the communication situation is not difficult to follow. The Lasswell model maintains that once the answers to these five basic questions are obtained, any communication situation can be explained.

Thus far we have concerned ourselves primarily with linear models of communication. To be complete in our discussion, the nonlinear explanations of the communication process must be mentioned.

According to Mortensen (1972) "the notion of communication as a linear, one-way event conflicts with the idea of complex activity in which the

89

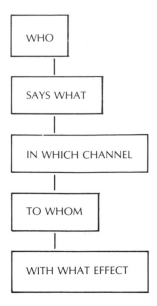

Source: Lasswell, H. The structure and function of communications in society. In L. Bryson, (Ed.), *The communication of ideas.* New York: Harper & Row, 1948, p. 37.

FIGURE 3.4   *The Lasswell Model of Communication*

respective parties are mutually dependent and where the degrees of freedom of choice are not fully known'' (p. 40). Certainly linear models of the communication process have made a significant contribution to communication theory, yet the notion that is conveyed in each linear diagram is that communication is, as Mortensen states, a ''one-way event.'' With respect to human interaction, this simply is not true. Communication encounters, however, appear to *require* a feedback component.

This lack of complete acceptance of the linear mathematical models of communication gave rise to a number of explanations for the communication process that are distinctly nonlinear in nature. Mortensen (1972) claims that Schramm's model of communication shown in Figure 3.5 was among the first of these nonlinear approaches to gain widespread acceptance.

In examining this particular approach to communication encounters, note the emphasis on exchange of ideas or messages that occurs between the encoder and the decoder. Inherent in this explanation is the assumption that each individual in the encounter can play both an encoder and a decoder role. Without this degree of commonality or overlap in ability, a successful communication encounter is highly unlikely.

To account for the operations that must be performed to transform a message received (decoded) into a message transmitted (encoded), Schramm incorporated an interpretation function into the model. Such an activity accounts for the complex processes that result in message sending and receiving.

Schramm's model, while useful as an explanation of most communication encounters, does not serve as an adequate explanation for situations that involve more than two people. Schramm's model seems to focus attention more directly on one-to-one interactions.

The literature dealing with communication theory contains still other nonlinear models—all of which attempt to represent still another dimension of the process. According to Mortensen, one can consider a mosaic model of communication (Becker, 1968) that depicts the interplay between "message bits, sources and receivers"; a cone-shaped functional model designed by Ruesch and Bateson (1951) that consists of four levels of interaction; and a systematic transactional model developed by Barnlund (1970) that is void of linearity, utilized spirals, and suggests that all meaning in a communication situation is assigned by the participants and is not just passively received. Each of these representations builds on the notion that the communication situation is extremely complex and must take into account numerous variables. The basic point to remember with respect to the nonlinear models is that the interplay that exists between participants (be there two or more) and the environment is a very crucial element in explaining the communication situation.

Both the linear and nonlinear communication models make it clear that the information sharing procedure is quite systematic in nature. In fact, both model formats have numerous features in common (see Figure 3.6). This commonality of features supports the notion of a real order and sequence to the events that comprise a communication encounter. An individual who possesses the appropriate understanding of the communication situation and exercises that knowledge can be a successful communicator.

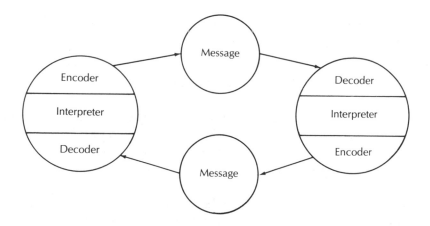

Source: Mortensen, C. *Communication—The study of human interaction.* New York: McGraw-Hill, 1972, p. 41.

FIGURE 3.5 *Schramm's Model of Communication*

91

Models

Common Features	Aristotelian	Barnlund (1970)	Becker (1968)	Byker & Anderson (1975)	Lasswell (1948)	Ruesch & Bateson (1951)	Schramm (1955)	Shannon (1948)
1. Destination identified	X	X	X	X	X	X	X	X
2. Feedback loop		X	X	X		X	X	
3. Inclusion of nonverbal elements		X	X	X		X		X
4. Interpretation function specified			X	X		X	X	
5. Identification of noise							X	
6. Linear in design	X				X			X
7. Message source	X	X	X	X	X	X	X	X
8. Nonlinear design		X	X	X		X	X	
9. Relay system described	X				X	X		X
10. Recognition of listener characteristics	X		X	X	X	X		

FIGURE 3.6 A Comparison of Common Features in Select Communication Models

Communication Models and the Classroom

The school is an arena of simultaneous activity. Within the confines of the public school, children and adults interact on a daily basis in a variety of situations. Given the range of possible activities, tasks, assignments, and exchanges of information that occur, there are few other environments that are as communicatively complex.

In a typical day, a school teacher on bus duty may greet students as they arrive at school, interact with the school principal prior to the opening bell on matters of budget requests, chat with fellow teachers over coffee in the teacher's lounge, place a series of telephone calls to parents who still have not scheduled a conference, give instructions to the unit aide who is anxious to take over the math learning center, advise the student teacher who is having problems with classroom discipline, explain to the custodian that the carpet in the reading center just has to be cleaned, and, finally, meet a class of inquisitive minds all seeking anwers to problems posed by today's reading assignment. To function effectively in this kind of environment, and to do so on a daily basis, requires a great deal of skill—skill in the communication arts.

In the classroom, the requirements for a successful communication encounter are almost identical to the exchange of information as described in Shannon and Weaver's mathematical model of the communication process. In the strictest sense, the teacher is concerned with the construction of a message, its transmission, and its arrival intact at a particular destination. It is realized, however, that in daily encounters with children and other adults in the public school environment, this one-way communication model will break down quickly since it becomes more important over time to maintain an *exchange* of ideas, not just a passing on of information. Thus, Mortensen's notion of communication with infinite number of choices by the participants becomes significant. The classroom *is* the arena in which the participants can and do exercise options on a daily basis and where information exchange alone *is not* of primary importance!

Recall that each communication model presented included a provision for an encoder of information, a channel for transmission, and a device or technique for decoding the information presented. It has been stated that the communicator must be aware of both verbal and nonverbal clues and cues in order to translate a message received or to construct a message to send. Within the classroom, both the teacher and the student must be sensitive to every item that is characteristic of a communication encounter. According to Miller (1966) the verbal, physical, and vocal stimuli are of equal importance in the construction and interpretation of a message. Within the classroom, the interplay among the three can be crucial in determining the degree to which participants interact. One must be aware that children, as well as other adults, will be attuned to the manner in which a message is constructed in all three of these areas. The teacher's tone of voice, stance, facial expression, rate of delivery, as well as vocabulary, sentence structure, and amount of elaboration are all significant ingredients in a communication encounter. In a situation involving a mildly handicapped child who may not be aware of the subtleties of gesture or facial expression or tone of voice, the probability of misinterpretation or communication failure is quite high (see Wiig & Semel, 1976, p. 303). It is impʋrtant then that the teacher be aware of and be sensitive to each of these items when interacting with children.

The communication models presented in this chapter relate to various areas of the language arts program. Figure 3.7 suggests a relationship among models and instruction in particular skill areas. As can be seen from this chart, communication theory can be a particularly useful basis for program decision making. Much of what is described in the arena of communi-

Models	Areas of the Language Arts Curriculum						
	Listening Skills	Oral Language	Handwriting	Composition	Spelling	Reading	Awareness of Non-verbal Clues & Cues
Aristotelian	X	X					X
Byker & Anderson	X	X	X	X	X	X	X
Lasswell	X	X	X	X	X	X	
Schramm	X	X	X	X	X	X	X
Shannon	X	X	X	X	X	X	X

FIGURE 3.7   Interrelationship of Communication Models to Various Language Arts Skill Areas

cation model building is in fact a rationale for language arts instruction. Throughout the remainder of this text, instructional programs in each of the language arts are based on our understanding of communication theory.

Becoming Sensitive to Personal Communication Styles

Hennings's (1975) text titled *Mastering Classroom Communication—What Interaction Analysis Tells the Teacher* provides numerous examples of ways to map personal communication styles. The following are examples of exercises and activities to heighten awareness of personal communication patterns. These examples have been borrowed from Hennings's (1975) text, Modules 2 and 6.

Developing Awareness of Verbal Stimuli

Am I using complex and compound structures?
Am I relying primarily on the simple sentence?
Am I drawing on imperative sentences, declarative patterns,
    rhetorical questions, complex and compound sentences? Do I
    repeat consistently a single pattern?

Am I using infrequently encountered words? Am I turning to words more commonly encountered in my interactions with children?

Do I draw on a large vocabulary? Do I restrict myself to a limited number of words?

Am I using a number of unnecessary words and sentences? Am I succinct? Am I overly brief?

Am I using formal English, esoteric forms, standard English, a nonstandard dialect?

Is my speaking style overly informal or formal?

Do I make use of questions that invite response and participation in group discussions?

In a communication encounter do I tend to structure the conversation rather than let it find its own direction?

Am I consistently a reactor only to the comments of others?

Do I respond frequently when spoken to, or when in a group situation in which comments are not directed to me personally?

Do I tend to solicit comments from other children or adults who are only by-standers in a communication setting?

Developing Awareness of Vocal Stimuli

Is my speaking voice monotonous?

Do I try to use expression when I read to a group of children?

Do I ever play with my voice? Have I ever tried to read a magazine advertisement or a recipe as if I were bored? Exasperated? As if this were the greatest? As if I were unhappy? As if I were in a hurry!

Developing Awareness of Physical Stimuli

Do I use gestures to speak for me?

Am I physically overactive in communicating? Underactive?

Do I make effective use of distance in my communication encounters? Do I demonstrate an awareness of space—intimate, personal, social, and public? Do I violate territorial rights and therefore create an uncomfortable atmosphere?

Do my body and my voice send the same message, or do they contradict each other?

Developing an Awareness of Interaction Patterns

The communication pattern of children in the classroom can also be a valuable source of information to the teacher. In situations where mildly handicapped children have been mainstreamed into the regular classroom, patterns of interaction can identify for the teacher those children who consistently initiate conversations, respond to other students, react to teacher inputs, or who frequently avoid communicating with peers. Interaction patterns can be a barometer of the mildly handicapped child's social acceptance by classmates.

Hennings (1975) has suggested that the interaction analysis procedure developed by Flanders can be a useful tool in determining communication patterns. By developing a recording sheet on which tallies of communication encounters can be entered, the teacher can determine over a short period of time the extent to which students are responding to other students or to the teacher. The tally form might look like this:

	Tallies of Student Statements	Totals
Responses to teacher, r/t		
Responses to other students, r/st		
Initiations, i		
	Total Tallies	

Source: Adapted from Hennings, D. *Mastering classroom communication*. Pacific Palisades, Calif.: Goodyear Publishing Co., 1975, p. 83.

Such a technique can be modified to consist only of a seating chart on which the teacher (or an observer) records an r/t for each response to the teacher, an r/st for each response to another student, and an i for each initiation that a particular student might make during the course of the observation period. Such a simple recording process of interactions can reveal quite quickly which students monopolize the conversation, which respond only to the teacher, and which respond most often to other students. The inclusion of the mildly handicapped child in the analysis procedure can provide some specific data on the child's degree of participation in class discussions and extent of interaction with other students.

Another procedure that departs from the Flanders interaction analysis technique and relies a bit more heavily on sociometrics is that of a simple grid arrangement. Here, on the vertical and horizontal axes the names of all the students in the class are listed alphabetically. With the record grid in hand, the observer simply checks each time a particular student responds to another student. For example, if Douglas were to respond to something Anthony said, a check would be placed in the block on the grid that corresponds to the names of these two boys. The grid then might look something like this:

	Student Names						
	Anthony	B	C	Douglas	E	F	G
Anthony							
B							
C							
Douglas	x						
E							

This process would continue until a topic had been fully explored or until a time limit had been exceeded. Regardless of the situation or the restrictions that are placed on the process, information regarding interaction patterns can be readily obtained.

Another technique using the same grid format incorporates the teacher into the interaction analysis. The extent to which the teacher dominates a discussion, contributes significantly, or responds to particular individuals can be determined. In this situation, the record grid is designed as follows:

Names	Communication Event									
	1	2	3	4	5	6	7	8	9	10
Teacher	x		x				x			x
Anthony										
B										
C								x		
Douglas		x		x		x			x	
E					x					
F										
G										

In this situation, the horizontal axis delineates the communication event while the vertical axis lists the class members and the teacher. In the hypothetical situation shown, the observer recorded each communication event with a check. In this case, the teacher initiated the conversation, Douglas responded, the teacher replies, Douglas responds, student E comments, Douglas reacts, the teacher intercedes, student C interjects a statement, Douglas defends himself, and the encounter is terminated by the teacher in the tenth exchange.

Note that these grid arrangements only focus attention on the *quantity* of interaction and not the *quality* of the exchange. It is another matter altogether to assess the effectiveness and success of communication encounters. Communication among children in numerous settings, at various points during the day, and with different partners must be encouraged before attention can be focused on quality.

The Mildly Handicapped and the Communication Process

Descriptions of mildly handicapped children often mention a language delay or disability. In some cases, the problem stems from a speech or articulation dysfunction and in no way is indicative of a serious processing deficit. In other situations, however, the referral and/or the ultimate diagnosis suggests that the mildly handicapped child in question is experiencing what is now referred to as a communication disorder.

Professionals seem to agree that there is more than a casual relationship between handicappism and difficulty in communication (Lloyd, 1976, p. xi). Perhaps, as the communication models have shown, it is that the process itself is so complicated. If this is the case, the teacher's awareness of the communication process as discussed here becomes even more important. In the language arts, a dysfunction in one area may or may not be found in another.

Sanders (1976) has written that:

The establishment of a communication system requires that the communication partners each:

1. Possess a set of referents or values.
2. Share a common set of tokens (symbols with which to identify those values).
3. Be familiar with generative rules governing the manner in which tokens may be used to construct patterns.

Through experience the partners learn to ascribe values to the different patterns. (p. 12)

Certainly, the communication processes as described in the various models all require the active participation of the parties involved. Where difficulties in communication occur, there is probably a failure on the part of one or the other of the participants to meet the minimum requirements of a communication system as described by Sanders.

The handicapped child in the classroom may have difficulty with the language arts curriculum due to an inability to either encode or decode information. Such a notion is entirely acceptable, since it has been established that all communication encounters, regardless of the model, involve information processing. The language arts curriculum as it is currently constructed focuses primarily on just such activity. Whether the concern is with communicating orally, in written form, or through gesture, the participants must be able to properly articulate the movement of the necessary speech organs; utilize hand and arm rotations to write, sign, gesture, and point; provide appropriate facial expressions to supplement meaning; and to organize both body posture and gross movements to reflect the communication intent (Sanders, 1976). Certainly, all the language arts involve one or more of these activities. It is quite apparent that in the case of the mildly handicapped child an inability to coordinate speech, movement, or expression, if coupled with a lack of primary understanding of the communication process, results in consistent failures to successfully communicate wants and needs. The degree, then, to which the mildly handicapped child can meet the requirements of the traditional language arts curriculum is reduced.

Barriers to Effective Communication

Knowing full well that many mildly handicapped children will experience some difficulty in learning the conventions of communication, it is appropriate to ask what some these specific difficulties might be. It can be anticipated that the mildly handicapped child will, in terms of learning to be a successful communicator, experience problems in some areas of the language arts curriculum. A child experiencing difficulty in communication may have errors in reading, spelling, handwriting, composition, oral expression, and listening skills, and misunderstandings or failures in production that are both bothersome and annoying to the classroom teacher and student alike. The diagnosed disability more than likely will determine the types of problems that must be dealt with; but, in general, the mildly handicapped child probably will have one or more of the following problems:

1. Difficulty focusing attention on the speaker.
2. Failure to respond to nonverbal clues and cues.
3. Trouble organizing thoughts for oral presentations.
4. Inability to attend to the subtleties of a conversation.
5. Failure to recognize shifts in topics or emphasis.
6. Production of unacceptable written work.
7. Use of speech patterns that are not understood (e.g., misarticulations, mispronunciations, inappropriate syntax, unacceptable vocabulary).
8. Stuttering.
9. Limited ability to converse on commonplace topics or items (e.g., not know names of household items).
10. Poor penmanship.

These are by no means the exclusive characteristics of a child with a communication disorder. The list only suggests the kinds of language arts problems most often experienced by the mildly handicapped child.

In addition to the difficulties specific handicaps cause with respect to communication success, there are three obstacles that often influence our own interactions with others—handicapped and nonhandicapped alike. Hennings (1975) has found that "at least three elements can block communication—masking, filtering, and wandering" (p. 33). Each of these deserves special mention in any discussion of communication because they occur so frequently. The following characteristics of each of these barriers to effective communication have been borrowed from Hennings (1975, pp. 33–43).

1. Masking can be characterized by:
   a. A slight hesitation that indicates a speaker is less than enthusiastic about doing something
   b. Gestures and facial expressions that contradict the spoken message
   c. Signs of irritation, anger, fear, unhappiness masked behind a calm exterior—shaking hands, blushing, tightening of the lips, heavy swallowing
   d. Tensions of the muscles that conflict with a calm voice
2. Filtering can be characterized by:
   a. The ego-based interpretation that is made of such commonplace occurrences as the failure of a superior to greet you as you pass in the hall
   b. The reading of meaning into casual physical contacts
   c. Reaction to dialectical differences
   d. Annoyance at the use of specific words, phrases, voice tone
   e. Displeasure with physical setting, dress, or the use of time by another individual
3. Wandering can be characterized by:
   a. Body signals that indicate a change of attention—eye focus, adjustment of bodily tensions
   b. Anticipatory behavior on the part of listeners
   c. Obvious digressions in conversations, lectures, or presentations

Each of these situations describes particular behaviors that could influence the outcome of a communication encounter. In most cases, the frequent occurrence of such obstacles results in a complete failure to communicate.

When working with the mildly handicapped, difficulties in communication may present themselves because of such behaviors on the part of teachers, nonhandicapped youngsters, and handicapped children alike. Everyone should be sensitive to these barriers to successful communication.

Encouraging Communicative Competence

Both the regular and special educator are responsible for ensuring that the mildly handicapped child achieves success with the language arts curriculum and thus with all communication encounters. Given the numerous problems that the handicapped child brings into the classroom, meeting this obligation is not going to be an easy task. Every tool, every skill, and every available opportunity to shape success in the language arts program must be tapped by educators to enable the mildly handicapped child to become a successful communicator.

Increasing Communication Competence with Oral Language

The need for awareness of communication models and communication behaviors is a prerequisite to the development of oral communicative competence. Once the teacher has become sensitive to the verbal, vocal, and physical aspects of the communication encounter and has begun to instill a similar awareness on the part of the children in the classroom, it is time to develop additional activities and lessons that stress communication success with oral language. According to Munkres (1959) "conversation is the most widely used of all forms of oral communication and one which does not wait on maturity " (p. 1).

Munkres suggests that every language arts program should incorporate numerous opportunities for conversing and discussing, storytelling, reporting, making speeches, dramatizing, and vocabulary and syntax skill development. The procedures used to develop these skills can range from before-school conversations, to in-class discussions, to imaginary stories, to real life experiences, to dramatization of prepared or original plays. Each teacher must construct activities that *provide the opportunities* for children to communicate with each other.

To develop communication skills through a language arts program that includes mildly handicapped children, errors in communication style must be tolerated. Munkres reminds teachers that it is essential to allow many errors to pass "in the interest of preserving spontaneity and encouraging expression of big ideas as well as choice of new and suitable words" (p. 3). It is the teacher's responsibility to decide, in view of the individual involved, how and when a particular communication problem should be handled. It is often best not to correct for communication inadequacies, but simply note the areas to attend to at a later date. The point is *to encourage* communication, since skill in oral language competence can only be achieved through supervised practice.

In the chapter on oral language development, additional games, activities, and instructional strategies will be provided to assist the teacher in the development of oral language communication competence. At this point, it is

101

essential to realize that oral language skill, and conversation in particular, is *the* medium for communication. It is within the confines of the language arts curriculum that skill in oral communication can best be developed.

Increasing Communication Competence with Written Language

Clark and Woodcock (1976) describe several graphic communication systems that have been developed over the years as alternatives to traditional orthography to assist the handicapped in becoming successful communicators with written language.

The following is a list taken from Clark and Woodcock (1976) of alphabetic and nonalphabetic systems that represent available alternatives to traditional orthography for the handicapped:

Alphabetic Systems

Traditional Orthography (T.O.)	
Controlled T.O.	Let's Read: A Linguistic Approach, Leonard Bloomfield (1961)
	Merrill Linguistic Reading Program, Charles Fries (1963)
	Miami Linguistic Readers, R. F. Robinett (1966)
Elaborated T.O.	Psycholinguistic Color System, A. Bannatyne (1971)
	Words in Color, Caleb Gattegno (1962)
	Colour Story Reading, J. K. Jones (1965)
Phonemic Alphabets	Initial Teaching Alphabet, Sir James Pitman (1959)
	Fonetic English, J. Rohner (1966)
	UNIFON, John Malone (1962)

Nonalphabetic Systems

Logographic Systems	Pictographic Logographs (rebuses)
	The Rebus Reading Series (Woodcock, 1965)
	Peabody Rebus Reading Program (Woodcock, Clark, Davies, 1968)
	Minnesota Early Language Development Sequence (Clark, Moores, and Woodcock, 1975)

From Clark, C. and Woodcock, R. Graphic systems of communication. In L. Lloyd (Ed.), *Communication assessment and intervention strategies*. Baltimore, Md.: University Park Press, 1976, pp. 552–599.

This apparent proliferation of alternatives to traditional orthography in written communication is indicative of the growing concern on the part of engineers, scientists, and educators to enable the handicapped to interact successfully with written language. The teacher of the mildly handicapped child must be familiar with as many practices and techniques as possible to ensure that the mildly handicapped child achieves success in the language arts program.

SUMMARY

This chapter has focused attention on the relationship that exists between the process of communication and the language arts. Those communication models that have served to shape current thoughts regarding the processing of information and the acquisition of skill in communication have been explored. Both linear and nonlinear models of communication have been examined. These models are useful in understanding the possible difficulties of the handicapped in attaining success in communication encounters. Such models can assist in the diagnosing of areas of information processing failure and may prove useful in predicting future performances. Various factors that inhibit success in communication were presented for consideration and consideration was given to procedures for encouraging the achievement of communication competence.

POINTS FOR DISCUSSION

1. In this chapter, considerable attention has been given to communication models. What are the advantages and disadvantages of viewing communication in a linear fashion? What about in a nonlinear manner?

2. How might you, as a teacher, make use of any of these models? What applications do you see to the classroom? To diagnosis? To the development of curriculum?

3. Can you develop your own model of communication that accounts for all the elements influencing the act? If so, what would it look like?

4. Observe an interaction between two or more individuals. Note the setting, time, purpose of the meeting, environmental characteristics, etc. When done, reorganize your notes to depict the exchange. Do you see your findings fitting into any of the descriptions presented here? If so, which ones? If not, why not?

5. Find a situation that places handicapped children into communication situations with nonhandicapped children. Take one of the models presented here and use

it as an observational guide. Describe your findings to a classmate. Just how successful was this encounter? How well did the model you selected serve as an outline of communication behaviors?

6. In this chapter, several obstacles to effective communication were discussed. Select one or more of them and design a situation that would assist a mildly handicapped child in overcoming that problem.

7. Using the concepts of masking, filtering, and wandering, devise a grid by which you can record "typical" examples of such behavior. Use this grid to chart the frequency or to list examples of such practices as you listen to a guest lecturer, to a television program, or to a new acquaintance.

8. It has been stated that the teacher has the responsibility to encourage communicative competence. Several programs and instructional alternatives for written language were presented here. Working in teams of two, investigate those alternatives that exist to oral language communication. Perhaps a film, chart, or actual presentation of these communication systems can be developed to demonstrate their effectiveness.

REFERENCES

Barnlund, D. *Interpersonal communication: Survey and studies.* Boston: Houghton Mifflin, 1968.

Becker, S. *What rhetoric (communication theory) is relevant for contemporary speech communication?* Paper presented at the University of Minnesota Spring Symposium in Speech Communication, 1968.

Bryson, L. *The communication of ideas.* New York: Harper & Row, 1948.

Byker, D., and Anderson, L. G. *Communication as identification.* New York: Harper & Row, 1975.

Clark, C., and Woodcock, R. Graphic systems of communication. In L. Lloyd (Ed.), *Communication assessment and intervention strategies.* Baltimore, Md.: University Park Press, 1976.

Flanders, N. *Analyzing teaching behavior.* Reading: Addison-Wesley, 1970. In Hennings, D., *Mastering classroom communications—What interaction analysis tells the teacher.* Pacific Palisades, Calif.: Goodyear Publishing Co., 1975, p. 80.

Hennings, D. *Mastering classroom communication—What interaction analysis tells the teacher.* Pacific Palisades, Calif.: Goodyear Publishing Co., 1975.

Lasswell, H. The structure and function of communications in society. In L. Bryson (Ed.), *The communication of ideas.* New York: Harper & Row, 1948.

Lloyd, L. (Ed.). *Communication assessment and intervention strategies.* Baltimore: University Park Press, 1976.

Martin, H., and Andersen, K. *Speech communication—Analysis and readings.* Boston: Allyn & Bacon, 1968.

Miller, G. A. *Language and communication.* New York: McGraw-Hill, 1963.

Miller, G. *Speech communication: A behavioral approach*. Indianapolis: Bobbs-Merrill Co., Inc., 1966. In Hennings, D., *Mastering classroom communication—What interaction analysis tells the teacher*. Pacific Palisades, Calif.: Goodyear Publishing Co., 1975, p. 4.

Mortensen, C. *Communication—The study of human interaction*. New York: McGraw-Hill, 1972.

Munkres, A. *Helping children in oral communication*. New York: Teachers College Press, 1959.

Pierce, J. *Communication*. San Francisco: W. H. Freeman and Co., 1972.

Ruesch, J., and Bateson, C. *Communication: The social matrix of psychiatry*. New York: Norton, 1951.

Sanders, D. A model for communication. In L. Lloyd (Ed.), *Communication assessment and intervention strategies*. Baltimore, Md.: University Park Press, 1976.

Schramm, W. How communication works. In *The processes and effects of communication*. Urbana, Ill.: University of Illinois Press, 1954.

Shannon, C. The mathematical theory of communication. In J. Pierce, *Communication*. San Francisco: W. H. Freeman and Co., 1972.

Wiig, E., and Semel, E. *Language disabilities in children and adolescents*. Columbus, Ohio: Charles E. Merrill Publishing Co., 1976.

4

Measuring and Evaluating Language Performance

A major challenge facing the teacher of the language arts is that of assessing child language ability. There is perhaps nothing more troublesome than attempting to make statements about a child's level of language performance. Language by nature is an extremely elusive substance. It is exceptionally difficult to collect language samples and to analyze them.

When confronted with a situation that requires language assessment, a teacher might legitimately ask how to go about assessing language ability. What obstacles need to be overcome when attempting to collect language samples? What specific instruments and techniques can be used to make meaningful statements about language ability? This chapter attempts to answer these and other questions regarding language assessment.

Problems Associated with Language Assessment

There are many difficulties associated with the language assessment process. Among those most frequently encountered by educators are realizing and understanding the influences of differences in background, that the course of language development is very uneven, that the data collection and transcription process is a difficult one, that the task the child is asked to perform will generate a particular speech sample, that sampling errors do occur, that children's role-playing tendencies will enter into the data collection process, and that children do respond to various listener characteristics. In this section, each of these factors is discussed.

Differences in Background

Children come to school with a wide range of experiences behind them. There is no question that for every child a teacher encounters there is a unique set of background experiences. While initially this may not seem significant, it does constitute one potential area of difficulty in the assessment of children's language.

Background experiences can influence a child's performance in a given language task situation. A child who has had exposure to national parks and museums, who has had extensive travel experience, and numerous encounters with individuals of various ethnic backgrounds may have developed an ability to respond verbally that appears to be superior to the language of a child lacking those experiences. The child with the experience-rich background may have developed a sense of confidence that results in superior performance. That child may have previously encountered the materials being presented or the places being discussed and could certainly perform verbally much better than a child without such exposure.

Uneven Normal Development

While the course of language acquisition and development is fairly sequential, the rate at which children acquire various skills may vary considerably. In terms of language assessment procedures, keep in mind that the rate of normal development is rather uneven. A child of four and one-half could have the language skills of a five year old. The order in which the four year old and the five year old acquired specific skills is probably identical, but the rate at which the skills were learned obviously varied.

Thus, assessing children's language requires a sensitivity to the differences that this uneven normal course of development can generate. Certainly it is not always possible to control for such subtle variations, yet they can be taken into account when any comparisons are made. Brown (1973) has stated that: "Though the order of acquisition of linguistic knowledge will prove to be approximately invarient across children learning one language and, at a higher level of abstraction across children learning any language, the rate of progression will vary radically among children" (p. 408). This statement, which is based on his extensive work with three children named Adam, Eve, and Sarah, reaffirms the notion that the language assessment procedure must take into account the rate variable.

Data Collection and Transcriptions

Imagine how difficult it is to collect samples of children's language for analysis. The entire child language assessment procedure rests almost exclusively on the teacher's ability to devise task situations that elicit appropriate language samples. While the task of recording a sample of children's speech may seem relatively simple, a child, a tape recorder, and a topic often do not produce the anticipated results. Generally, much time must be spent experimenting and familiarizing the child with the tape recorder and the data collector before a comfortable enough situation exists to permit the sampling of the child's speech.

Obtaining direct samples of the child's language requires patience. Certainly one cannot anticipate what will happen when a child is asked to respond to a series of questions, to a picture, or to an object when a tape recorder is in play. Some children take readily to this kind of task situation, others immediately become leery and quite shy. The situation should be as comfortable and as natural as possible to increase the child's adaptation.

Consider the speech of a child obtained from a picture stimulus. In this task situation, the child was presented with a card having half an image and a mirror and was asked to tell another child how to complete the figure. The following is the speech elicited by Figure 4.1.

Chris to Colvin—Mirror Card Stimulus
1. Take this
2. Try to make that a whole sun
3. You have to use the mirror to do it
4. And you have to put that down on the table
5. Put the card right next to the sun
6. Put the mirror on the card
7. No, not like that
8. Not like that
9. No, pick it up

109

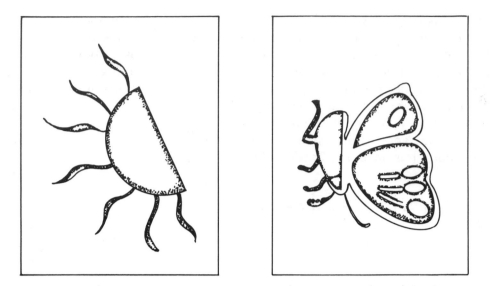

Source: Reproduced from the *Elementary Science Study Unit, Mirror Cards,* with permission of Education Development Center, Inc.

FIGURE 4.1   *A Picture Stimulus*

10. Put that on top of it with just one edge
11. Yeah, like that
12. You have the wrong side
13. There you made it
14. Put it on the other side of the card
15. No
16. This side
17. This side
18. Put it next to the body of that bug
19. Okay, push the mirror closer
20. Closer
21. Closer
22. Now pull it back a little
23. There
24. Now you have it
25. A butterfly
26. What else can you make
27. Put it on the other end where the red part is
28. Okay, push it a little more
29. More
30. There it is
31. You got it

Task and Situation Variables

It has been pointed out that the speech sample can be influenced by the complexity of the task situation. Krauss and Glucksburg (1969) emphasize that:

> In constructing a message a speaker must perform two rather subtle informational analyses; (1) he must consider the stimulus array to determine distinguishing characteristics and (2) of his listener, to formulate a message that is compatible with the listener's knowledge and capabilities. (p. 356)

Krauss and Glucksburg's work in concept complexity and its relationship to language has indicated that novel concepts are more difficult to express than familiar forms. When examining language samples, the task in which the child was involved becomes a significant factor to consider. The very game the child has been asked to play can influence significantly the speech that is generated. Krauss and Glucksburg (1969) and Glucksburg, Krauss, and Weisberg (1966) have confirmed that task selection is exceptionally important in data collection. In analyzing speech samples, one must be sure that the task used to stimulate the child was appropriate and did not involve too complex a concept. If speech adjustments and speech variations do occur, they should not be the result of task complexity. Task requirements must be controlled for across all subjects.

Sampling Errors

With respect to language samples, keep in mind that more than one sample of the child's speech is necessary before statements can be made regarding that child's performance. Sampling errors must be considered, because the language sample obtained may have been generated under circumstances that were less than optimal. Task requirements, setting, time of day, and other confounding variables may explain why the language elicited does not represent the child's normal speech.

To avoid this difficulty, several samples of the child's speech must be gathered prior to completing an assessment. These samples should, when possible, come from the child in a play situation, in an instructional setting, or in a home environment. Examining the child's speech in a number of situations ensures that the most accurate statements regarding the child's performance can be formulated. Sampling error occurs most frequently when referrals are done hastily, without taking enough time to collect adequate data. Both the regular educator and the special educator must understand that to make language assessments that yield reliable information, sufficient time must be allocated to collect and transcribe the speech sample.

Role-Playing Tendencies

Previous investigations have focused on the child's ability to make listener age adjustments in role-playing situations. The process of analyzing samples of children's language should consider the role-playing capabilities of the young child. Flavell (1968), Dale and Kelly (1972), and Sachs and Devin (1973) have demonstrated that the young child has the ability to make speech adjustments appropriate to the role they are requested to assume. Flavell (1968) constructed three experiments to test the child's ability to assume a listener's role. Even preschoolers were found capable of role-playing and adjusting to a listener. Dale and Kelly (1972) found that children in role-playing situations adjusted their speech to appropriately reflect characteristics of the speech expected from the role being imitated. Sachs and Devin (1973) reported that subjects likewise changed and simplified their speech when role-playing a baby. Their study concerned itself also with preschoolers.

Strong indicators do exist that young children attend to listener role characteristics and adjust their speech to suit the role being assumed. In an assessment of language, the child may not necessarily be providing the speech that is normally utilized, and may be assuming a particular role in order to successfully complete the task requirement. Role-playing capabilities of children, which have been shown to exist, complicate the child language assessment procedure and contribute significantly to the problems inherent in language assessment.

Responses to Listener Characteristics

An additional problem to complicate the child language assessment process is that of the speech adjustments which occur dependent on various listener characteristics. Young children adjust their speech according to such listener characteristics as age, emotional state, social class, and actual listener verbal responses. This fact needs to be taken into account whenever language assessment procedures are utilized.

For example, let us examine the speech adjustment that is made depending on the listener's chronological age. This aspect of speech adjustment has been discussed only recently in the literature, yet consistent findings seem to confirm that children adjust their speech depending on the age of their listeners.

Shatz and Gelman (1973) attempted to determine if the child as a speaker was capable of making speech adjustments similar to those made by adults. In an experimental situation, the ability of four year olds to alter their speech in response to different aged listeners, including adults, two year olds, and peers, was investigated. The four-year-old speakers were given the opportunity to converse with two-year-old children whose ages differed by several months. In similar play environments, the child speakers were recorded in conversation with peers. These play situations, with adults present, centered around the explanation of how a toy garage and an airplane were to be operated.

The speech samples obtained from these four year olds were recorded, transcribed, and subjected to analysis using mean length of utterance, type-token ratios of selected word forms, frequency counts of particular constructions (e.g., questions, exclamations, attention-getting devices, name calling), and the determination of pre-verb length.

Although the number of subjects involved was quite limited, Shatz and Gelman stated "that four year olds adjust their language in response to their listener's receiving capabilities" (p. 50). It was also reported that the younger the listener, the greater the tendency for the four-year-old speaker to use short, simple utterances, and to make obvious linguistic efforts to attract and sustain the listener's attention. In a similar study, Plaskon (1975) found that lower class seven-year-old children spoke differently to their peers than they did to five year olds on select variables. Children of low socioeconomic status (as defined by the Hollingshead and Redlich Index of Social Position) varied their use of syntax and adjectives as the listener changed from a peer to a five year old. This study provided additional support for the notion that some school-age children as well as preschoolers and adults adjust their speech according to the listener's chronological age.

Standard Language Assessment Procedures

Much discussion has been given to the problems associated with language assessment. However, the variables cited thus far do not preclude samples of children's language that are suitable for assessment and analysis. Beginning this chapter with a list of difficulties reminds us of the need for caution and consistency in any language assessment procedure.

Mean Length of Utterance

Perhaps the most useful standard assessment procedure is that of the mean length of utterance (MLU). This particular measurement technique is not difficult to use. The MLU is determined by:

113

1. Obtaining a sample of a child's speech. Approximately 100 utterances are recommended. An utterance is defined as any meaningful speech segment preceded and followed by a pause.
2. Transcribing those utterances (one utterance per line).
3. Counting the total number of utterances.
4. Counting each word or morpheme in the total transcription.
5. Dividing the total number of words or morphemes by the total number of utterances.

Figure 4.2 is an example of determining the mean length of utterance based on both word count and a morpheme count. The speech sample used

Chris (7 –11) to Carl (7)	Column A Word Count	Column B Morpheme Count
1. Okay, take a mirror card	5	4
2. No, take one of these too	6	6
3. And you have to try to make that like that	10	10
4. With the mirror	3	3
5. Okay, that does look like it	6	5
6. Yeah, that's it	3	4
7. Okay, take the next one	5	4
NOTE: New set of mirror cards		
8. Try these	2	2
9. Try to make that out of that	7	7
10. Put it up there	4	4
11. And there you have it	5	5
12. Don't put it on there	5	6
13. Take another one	3	3
14. Put it over there	4	4
15. No, that's not it	4	5
16. Put this side over this way a little more	9	9
17. That looks like it	4	4
18. Don't put it that way	5	6
19. This one's going to be a little harder	8	9
20. Put that	2	2
21. That one	2	2
22. Make it come up	4	4
TOTAL	106	108
MLU	4.612	4.909

FIGURE 4.2 Determination of Mean Length of Utterance Based on Word Count and Morpheme Count

1. Start with the second page of the transcription unless that page involves a recitation of some kind. In this latter case start with the first recitation-free stretch. Count the first 100 utterances satisfying the following rules.

2. Only fully transcribed utterances are used; none with blanks. Portions of utterances, entered in parentheses to indicate doubtful transcription, are used.

3. Include all exact utterance repetitions (marked with a plus sign in records). Stuttering is marked as repeated efforts at a single word; count the word once in the most complete form produced. In the few cases where a word is produced for emphasis or the like (*no, no, no*) count each occurrence.

4. Do not count such fillers as *mm* or *oh*, but do count *no, yeah,* and *hi*.

5. All compound words (two or more free morphemes), proper names, and ritualized reduplications count as single words. Examples: *birthday, racketyboom, choo-choo, quack-quack, night-night, pocketbook, see saw.* Justification is that there is no evidence that the constituent morphemes function as such for these children.

6. Count as one morpheme all irregular pasts of the verb (*got, did, went, saw*). Justification is that there is no evidence that the child relates these to present forms.

7. Count as one morpheme all diminutives (*doggie, mommie*) because these children at least do not seem to use the suffix productively. Diminutives are the standard forms used by the child.

8. Count as separate morphemes all auxiliaries (*is, have, will, can, must, would*). Also all catenatives: *gonna, wanna, hafta.* These latter counted as single morphemes rather than as *going to* or *want to* because evidence is that they function so for the children. Count as separate morphemes all inflections, for example, possessive [s], plural [s], third person singular [s], regular past [d], progressive [iŋ].

9. The range count follows the above rules but is always calculated for the total transcription rather than for 100 utterances.

Source: Brown, R. *A first language, the early stages.* Cambridge, Mass.: Harvard University Press, 1973, p. 54. Copyright © 1973 Harvard University Press. Used by permission of the publisher.

FIGURE 4.3   *Rules for Calculating Mean Length of Utterance*

in this example was taken during a data collecting session that involved a controlled task situation. These twenty-two utterances serve as an example of both the procedure by which transcriptions should be done and how length of utterance is determined based on word counts or morpheme counts.

While the determination of the mean length of utterance based on a word count is by far the most common means of determining the MLU, Brown (1973) describes the procedure that he and his associates made use of in determining the MLU of the speech of Adam, Eve, and Sarah based on a morpheme count. Figure 4.3 describes the criterion used by Brown in determing the mean length of utterance based on morphemes.

Using Brown's rules, the speech sample contained in Figure 4.3 has been examined in terms of a morpheme count. Column B compares the scoring of these same utterances in terms of morphemes over words. The slight differences in the final results can be seen clearly.

While the determination of the MLU is a commonly used measure, it is at best what Cazden (1972) refers to as "a superficial index of language maturity" (p. 252). Although there are difficulties associated in determining the mean length of utterance, be it based on a morpheme count or a word count, the measure is still made use of quite frequently. A sample of speech in excess of the one hundred utterances recommended by Brown may not always be available. Determining the MLU based on the five longest sentences in a transcription might provide information suitable for comparison. In addition, one may wish to also look at the mean number of words before the main verb in the sentence. This determination of what is called pre-verb length can also provide useful data in the analysis of the child's speech. Both of these particular variations on the determination of the mean length of utterance can be used effectively, and are in many cases desirable alternatives to the computation of the mean length of utterance based on either extremely lengthy or inadequate samples of children's speech.

Weighted Scales

Another procedure for analyzing children's language, weighted scales, involves the assignment of a particular value to various constructions. An obtained sample of speech can be analyzed by scoring each utterance according to the type of construction that occurs. This process of assigning particular values to various constructions is relatively convenient to use. One could decide in advance which categories will be scored. A value of one might be assigned to common nouns, two to proper nouns, three to adjectives, four to pronouns, five to adverbs, and so on.

Lee and Canter (1971) make use of a weighted scale in their Developmental Sentence Score, a measure of syntactic maturity. This analysis of a speech sample is based on the assignment of numerical values to particular constructions that use a developmental base. Lee and Canter maintain that the earlier occurring forms of personal pronouns, main verbs, negatives, conjunctions, and *wh*-questions all deserve a low numerical value; whereas the later occurring forms of these items deserve a higher numerical value. Figure 4.4 is an example of the scoring procedure utilized by Lee in a revised version of this syntax assessment technique. It demonstrates clearly the sequence and the rationale for the assignment of values to various constructions. (See Figure 4.4 on pp. 118–119.)

An analysis procedure such as Lee and Canter's demonstrates that the weighted-scale technique has considerable merit. It is possible to use a weighted scale effectively provided that a high degree of consistency is maintained throughout the analysis procedure.

Frequency Counts

Still another technique for analyzing children's language is that of frequency counting. All that is required is a sharp eye and a set of clear definitions. When doing a frequency count, the classroom teacher, special educator, or speech therapist simply decides which categories require tallies. For example, it might be decided to count all the adjectives; or a count might be made of all personal pronouns, adverbs, conjunctions, etc.

The frequency count procedure is direct and uncomplicated. It involves a predisposition, to some extent, to various grammatical constructions or word forms. In most cases the individual doing the analysis will have decided in advance on the items requiring examination or comparison. This preliminary planning is extremely helpful in terms of the child's total language program. Electing to do a frequency count, implies that a teacher suspects a dysfunction or a delay in learning to use particular word forms. The actual hand tallies are used to confirm initial suspicions.

Within the area of frequency counting, there is a great deal of flexibility in analysis techniques. Many options and alternatives are available to the classroom teacher or special educator who feels that it is necessary to analyze a child's speech sample. The list of constructions subject to tally is quite large. The following represent the basic areas in which frequency counts are often done:

1. Sentence types: Number of interrogatives, imperative, declarative, or exclamatory sentences
2. Dysfluencies
3. Repetitions
4. Single-word utterances
5. Imitations
6. Expansions
7. Attention-getting devices
8. Types of questions: Yes-no questions, indirect, tag, and *wh*-questions
9. Grammatic classes: Proper nouns, common nouns, adjectives, adverbs, personal pronouns, prepositions, conjunctions, and interjections.
10. Plurals

Certainly each individual situation warrants consideration of different variables. For example, specific omissions in a child's speech may confirm the

	INDEFINITE PRONOUNS OR NOUN MODIFIERS	PERSONAL PRONOUNS	MAIN VERBS	SECONDARY VERBS
1	it, this, that	1st and 2nd person: I, me, my, mine, you, your(s)	A. Uninflected verb: I see you. B. Copula, is or 's: It's red. C. is + verb + ing: He is coming.	
2		3rd person: he, him, his, she, her, hers	A. -s and -ed: plays, played B. Irregular past: ate, saw C. Copula: am, are, was, were D. Auxiliary am, are, was, were	Five early-developing infinitival complements: I wanna see (want to see) I'm gonna see (going to see) I gotta see (got to see) Lemme [to] see (let me [to] see) Let's [to] play (let [us to] play)
3	A. no, some, more, all, lot(s), one(s), two (etc.), other(s), another B. something, some-body, someone	A. Plurals: we, us, our(s), they, them, their B. these, those		Non-complementing infinitives: I stopped to play. I'm afraid to look. It's hard to do that.

4	nothing, nobody, none, no one	A. can, will, may + verb: *may go* B. Obligatory do + verb: *don't go* C. Emphatic do + verb: I *do see.*	Participle, present or past: I see a boy *running.* I found the toy *broken.*
5	Reflexives: myself, yourself, himself, herself, itself, themselves		A. Early infinitival complements with differing subjects in kernels: I want you *to come.* Let him [to] *see.* B. Later infinitival complements: I had *to go.* I told him *to go.* I tried *to go.* He ought *to go.* C. Obligatory deletions: Make it [to] *go.* I'd better [to] *go.* D. Infinitive with wh-word: I know what *to get.* I know how *to do it.*

Source: Lee, L. *Developmental sentence analysis.* Evanston, Illinois: Northwestern University Press, 1974, 134–135. Reprinted with the permission of the publisher and the author.

FIGURE 4.4 *Weighted Scales*

lack of obligatory words in the sample obtained. Are avoidance tactics employed in the child's speech so that the child does not have to use particular constructions, such as personal pronouns, when the sentence normally calls for it?

A variation on the frequency counting technique is the determination of type-token ratios. This measure of the occurrence of particular constructions is relatively easy to calculate. Once it has been decided which of the various parts of speech are to be analyzed, a count is made of all the occurrences of that particular form. To determine type-token ratios of adjectives, first examine the transcription, identify and count all the adjectives that appear, and total the number of adjectives. Then, classify the adjectives into either broad categories (quantitative or qualitative) or into specific areas (possessive, demonstrative, etc.) and determine the number of each kind. To arrive at a type-token ratio for each adjective category, divide the total number of adjectives of a particular classification (number of types/number of tokens). The resulting decimal figure is the type-token ratio.

These particular standard assessment procedures represent those most frequently used in child language assessment. The determination of the mean length of utterance, weighted scales, and frequency counting constitute the basis for most formalized assessment techniques.

Informal Language Assessment Techniques

While the teacher and speech therapist may recognize the importance of standard assessment measures, it may not always be feasible to complete transcriptions and to conduct the necessary analysis. In some cases, such analysis procedures are necessary and provide the only means to arrive at useful conclusions regarding the child's speech. However, if the determination of mean length of utterance, the assignment of weighted scales, or the use of frequency counts is not necessary, the teacher may wish to resort to a more informal language assessment procedure. The two techniques that follow are representative of informal data collecting devices that can be utilized effectively. These procedures are considered informal assessment techniques because of the ease with which they can be administered and scored and because they lack formalized field testing and normative data. Story retelling and an informal syntax assessment are examples that demonstrate just how easily an informal instrument can be constructed for use in a particular situation. Caution is necessary in interpreting the results obtained from devices of this kind, yet they do provide a structure by which the child's speech can be examined. Without instruments and checklists similar to these, statements regarding the child's speech are often very subjective. If upon administration they yield rather questionable results, additional testing may be required. Regardless of the situation, these direct, yet informal, data analysis techniques are satisfactory in most cases.

Story Retelling

Pickert and Chase (1978) suggest an informal language assessment technique based on the principle of story retelling. They maintain that the use of stories that are familiar to children is a legitimate basis for language assessment. The story retelling technique provides a means by which the classroom teacher can readily assess children's ability to comprehend, organize, and express language.

The procedure is relatively simple to utilize and to understand. The teacher simply tells a short story to each student, or to a select group of students individually. The student is asked to provide his or her version of the story. The story retelling is then taped and the taped version is transcribed for analysis. Pickert and Chase (1978) maintain that the following skills can be assessed from the story retelling:

1. Comprehension (understanding of grammatical forms and vocabulary words)
2. Organization (ability to integrate visual and auditory information and to recall sequence of events)
3. Expression (expressing the story in fluent, connected sentences, using correct grammatical forms). (p. 529)

The child's version of the story will probably provide insights into each of the areas listed above.

In terms of comprehension, the story retelling will demonstrate whether or not the child understood the original version. To comprehend an orally told story one must understand the grammatical forms that are utilized. If for some reason the story contains rather sophisticated syntactic structures that are unfamiliar to the child, comprehension will definitely be deficient. If the sentences in the original story were beyond the capabilities of the child, the results would show a lack of comprehension, a confused version of the story, or glaring inconsistencies. The words and concepts that the child uses will, depending on the degree of correlation to the original story, provide the teacher with some indication of the child's receptive language ability.

The second skill insight that the story retelling technique provides is that of word relations. The sequence of the events contained in the retold story will provide data regarding the child's ability to organize information.

The third area assessed by the story retelling procedure is that of the child's expressive language ability in terms of fluency and syntax. The child's rendition of the original story should be fluent, grammatical, and meaningful. In this situation, the language sample is being analyzed in terms of the child's expressive language ability. This category is quite broad and does not include specific constructions for examination. Instead, the teacher is merely

121

looking for consistency in the story retelling process. Most children will exhibit their tendencies to produce specific errors, to overgeneralize, and to imitate just as they might in a natural language setting, such as a conversation or play situation. While a high degree of correlation between the original version of the story and the child's version of the story is desirable, this particular area of assessment is more concerned with the fluency of the child's speech and the overall ability of the child to express thoughts intelligently.

The story retelling procedure is not meant to be an intensive language assessment process, rather it is a recommended technique to compare a child's speech against a given standard. The story used serves as a baseline against which the child's language can be compared. This particular technique, even with its inherent difficulties, focuses the classroom teacher's attention on the child's language in a structured situation. Figure 4.5 contains the short story that Pickert and Chase used in developing the informal language assessment technique. "This story was chosen because the plot was simple and the sentences were comprehensible, but too long to be memorized" (Pickert & Chase, 1978, p. 529). This table also contains children's versions of the story, including errors in comprehension, organization, and expression.

An Informal Syntax Assessment Procedure

A teacher is often concerned about the child's use of particular grammatical constructions. Perhaps, errors in forms of the verb "to be," plurals, personal pronouns, adjectives, and verb tense occur frequently enough to cause notice. In such situations, the teacher might wish to informally assess syntactic awareness.

An informal syntax assessment instrument can consist of a series of sentences that contain various syntactic constructions. The sentences may emphasize a particular grammatic form if one suspects a difficulty in a particular area. Figure 4.6 contains twenty-one sentences that exemplify the informal syntax assessment procedure. In this case, the sentences that the child is asked to repeat vary in terms of grammatical forms. As the sentences are presented and the child responds, notes are taken on which grammatical forms are incorrectly reproduced. For example, in sentence number one the child is expected to produce the noun form and the regular present of the verb "to run." If the child fails to produce the sentence "Mary runs" and says instead "Mary run," notation would be made that the regular present of the verb "to run" was not utilized. At the conclusion of the testing, a tally of errors is made to determine which forms were repeatedly misproduced. The information obtained from this informal assessment instrument assists the teacher in determining the next step to take with the child in question.

Original Story
This is a story about a grasshopper and an ant.
The grasshopper sat in the sunshine and played all summer long.
The ant was working hard gathering food for the winter.
When winter came, the hungry grasshopper asked the ant for food.
The ant said, "You played all summer, so now you must go hungry."

Errors in Comprehension
This is a story about a grasshopper and an ant.
The grasshopper was in the sunshine.
The ant need to carry food.
And the grasshopper played all winter long.
And the ant said, "You played all day and you must be hungry."

Errors in Expression
The grasshopper—an ant—look for food.
Working all day.
The grasshopper went into ant house.
Work all day.
Go for food.
Guess that's all.

Errors in Organization
Grasshopper standing on a rock, under the sun, playing his guitar.
And ant look for food.
And he worked all day.
And the grasshopper—he was hungry.
And he had worked all day because it was snowing.
And the ants don't like snow.
And the grasshopper went inside the ant's house.
And the ant said, "You had to go hungry."
Must have food, right?

Source: Pickert, S., and Chase, M. Story retelling: An informal technique for evaluating children's language. *The Reading Teacher,* 1978, *31*(5), 528–531. Reprinted with permission of Sarah M. Pickert, Martha L. Chase, and the International Reading Association.

FIGURE 4.5   Language Assessment Through Story Retelling

Formal Language Assessment Measures

There are a number of formalized language assessment instruments currently available. Most classroom teachers and special educators do not frequently use formalized language assessment inventories. School systems employ a communication disorder specialist or a speech clinician or therapist with whom the responsibility for formalized assessment rests. It is, however, becoming increasingly important that teachers be capable of interacting with

1. Mary runs.	reg. pres.; noun form
2. Twist her button!	imperative; pronoun
3. Bertha is hopping.	auxiliary verb
4. The dog chews on a bone.	reg. present
5. The house was built slowly.	past tense; adverb
6. The flowers bloom in spring.	plural; preposition
7. The teacher gave a test.	irreg. past; article
8. Martha typed her paper quickly.	reg. past; possessive pronoun; adverb
9. She did not think about the candy.	pronoun; negative, preposition
10. He didn't want any popcorn at the movie.	pronoun; contraction
11. Is the window open?	interrogative, reversal
12. Where did the monkey go?	*wh-* questions
13. Peter ate the biggest piece of cake.	irreg. past; superlative
14. Sue played with the puppies.	reg. past; preposition, plural
15. He wouldn't allow his cat to chew.	pronoun; conditional negative, possessive; infinitive

FIGURE 4.6   An Informal Syntax Assessment

the speech and hearing specialist in order to develop programs for remediation in the regular classroom. At one point or another, this entire process will involve the discussion by the teacher, and speech therapist of the particular tests that have been administered to the child in question. It is important that educators be familiar with the types of instruments that the speech and language specialist uses on a regular basis. It is not intended that teachers become qualified to administer these instruments, but they should be exposed to the formal assessment procedures currently available. Figure 4.7 provides a listing and brief description of the most common formal language assessment instruments. More detailed information regarding administration, scoring, normative data, and limitations of these testing instruments is presented in the appendix. Sample plates are provided where appropriate.

Utilizing Assessment Procedures in the Classroom

The language arts teacher has more occasion to use informal language assessment procedures than formalized assessment instruments. Comprehensive testing is usually completed by another professional in the school environment. To determine appropriate language assessment tools, the speech clinician, school psychologist, or related specialist often need information that has been gleaned from informal procedures. At this point the teacher can provide a considerable amount of input.

Assessment of Children's Language Comprehension (ACLC) (Foster, Giddan, & Stark, 1969, 1973)	This fifty-item test attempts to estimate a child's auditory comprehension level and to measure the extent to which a child can process (identify) increasingly complex sentences. The ACLC requires the child to identify items orally presented that vary from one element (horse) to four critical elements (horse standing under the tree). It does not require the child to produce or repeat language forms.
Carrow Elicited Language Inventory (CELI) (Carrow, 1974)	This assessment procedure involves the direct imitation of stimulus sentences. The test examines the child's ability to use the grammatical constructions of pronouns, prepositions, conjunctions, articles, adverbs, *wh-* questions, negatives, nouns, adjectives, verbs, infinitives, and gerunds. The CELI is scored on the basis of an error analysis. The five categories of error types are: substitutions, omissions, additions, transpositions, and reversals. Percentile scores and stanine-scale scores are provided for children ages three through twelve. The CELI can determine a child's performance relative to other children of the same age group.
Developmental Sentence Scoring (DSS) (Lee & Canter, 1971; Lee, 1974)	The DSS, another measure of syntactic ability, provides the examiner with both normative data and a standard technique by which values can be assigned to the forms that a child produces. The DSS requires the examiner to elicit utterances from the subject (fifty, complete, different, consecutive, intelligible, nonecholalic). Once a speech sample has been obtained, a transcription and analysis can be completed. The scoring of the constructions that appear results in a DSS score—an estimate of syntactic maturity. The grammatical categories examined are indefinite pronouns and/or noun modifiers, personal pronouns, main verbs, secondary verbs, negatives, conjunctions, interrogative reversals, and *wh-* questions.
The Illinois Test of Psycholinguistic Ability (ITPA) (Kirk, McCarthy, & Kirk, 1968)	Depending on the results obtained on screening instruments, a child might be given the ITPA by a speech pathologist. This comprehensive language assessment instrument is a diagnostic instrument that examines abilities in twelve inter-

FIGURE 4.7 *Descriptions of the Most Common Language Assessment Instruments*

Figure 4.7 (*continued*)

related areas: auditory reception, visual reception, visual sequential memory, auditory association, auditory sequential memory, visual association, visual closure, verbal expression, grammatic closure, manual expression, auditory closure, and sound blending. The ITPA must be interpreted with caution. Do not attribute specific behaviors to a child based on one administration of the ITPA and resultant scores. The inability to function in one subtest area (e.g., auditory reception) may be the result of a number of factors and should not be taken to mean that poor ability in this area is the cause for poor language performance. The ITPA examines many areas thought to be associated with language functioning. It can provide much useful information.

Peabody Picture Vocabulary Test (PPVT) (Dunn, 1959, 1965)

The PPVT is not strictly a language assessment instrument. It was devised to measure intelligence rather than receptive language ability. It does correlate highly with other measures of receptive language skills. The PPVT consists of 150 plates, each containing four pictures. A stimulus word is provided and the child is requested to identify the correct referent. Once the raw score has been determined, the examiner can convert it to an age equivalent (mental age) score, a standard score equivalent (intelligence quotient), or a percentile equivalent. The information regarding the child's ability obtained from the PPVT must be viewed in relation to other tests and assessment results.

The Northwestern Syntax Screening Test (NSST) (Lee, 1971)

This instrument is a screening device for use with children ages three to eight. The NSST provides the examiner with both receptive and expressive language estimates. The NSST consists of twenty plates for both sections. In each situation, the child is presented with a pen-and-ink drawing and is asked to respond by either pointing to a picture or by stating a given sentence that appropriately describes a picture. The comparative performance of a child can be isolated on the NSST by comparing the score obtained on either the expressive or receptive sections to those contained in the norm table. The NSST is not intended to be an in-depth

Figure 4.7 (*continued*)

	study of syntax nor is it meant to be a measure of a child's general language ability.
Verbal Language Development Scale (Mecham Scale) (Mecham, 1958, 1971)	This instrument examines children's ability in the area of listening, speaking, reading, and writing. It is to some extent a language inventory. For separate age groups it contains select language skills that the normally developing child would possess. The Mecham Scale simply codes the presence or absence of those skills.

In the sections dealing with informal assessment techniques and standard language assessment procedures, mention was made of the mean length of utterance, the determination of pre-verb length, weighted scales, frequency counting, story retelling, and syntax assessment. In many areas of the language arts, these assessment procedures can be used to modify language behaviors or to compare performance. The language arts teacher might find that an informal syntax assessment instrument is a valuable tool in composition instruction or that the frequency counting of particular phrases of a child's speech provides the information needed to change oral language behaviors. Figure 4.8 suggests the language arts areas in which informal assessment procedures may prove helpful. Note that in the subsequent chapters in this text, specific assessment procedures for each of the areas of the language arts are provided. This listing serves to demonstrate the manner in which the informal language assessment procedures delineated in this chapter can be applied to the various skill areas.

Nondiscriminatory Testing

In recent years, greater concern has been expressed for the use of testing procedures that do not discriminate against individuals with handicaps, who speak a dialect, who are culturally or economically deprived, or whose primary language is other than English. Every effort must be made to construct a testing situation that takes into account these particular factors. It is the teacher's obligation to ensure that test items, directions, and procedures for response are clearly understood by the child. When appropriate, alternatives to standard testing formats must be provided or developed for the handicapped child. In no way should the child be placed at a disadvantage from the onset due to a factor over which the child has had no control. In the case of language assessment, knowledge of cultural differences, socioeconomic

The Language Arts Skill Areas

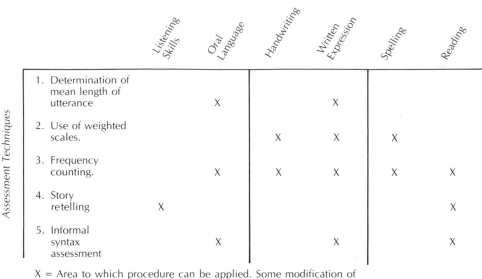

	Listening Skills	Oral Language	Handwriting	Written Expression	Spelling	Reading
1. Determination of mean length of utterance		X		X		
2. Use of weighted scales.			X	X	X	
3. Frequency counting.		X	X	X	X	X
4. Story retelling	X					X
5. Informal syntax assessment		X		X		X

(left side label: *Assessment Techniques*)

X = Area to which procedure can be applied. Some modification of the techniques suggested in this chapter may be required as cases may differ considerably.

FIGURE 4.8   Application of Assessment Procedures to the Language Arts

status, previous experience, and family history is often helpful in determining the testing procedures to employ. It is paramount that the teacher of the mildly handicapped or variant language speaker be concerned about fairness when language assessments are conducted.

Interpreting Test Results

The language assessment procedure is certainly a complex process. It is not easy to collect data, nor is it easy to transcribe spontaneous speech; yet, at the same time, this is the only means available to the teacher who is attempting to describe a particular language disability. By systematic analysis, particular disabilities can be isolated and language training programs devised.

In the discussion of the formalized instruments, the need for caution in interpreting test scores was pointed out. Regardless of the validity of the instrument used or familiarity with the subject, the information that is obtained must be viewed in light of other relative data. No one instrument will prove to be entirely satisfactory. No one testing situation can be viewed as representative of the child's true competence with language. The assessment procedure extends beyond the testing situation. It includes observation, continued collection of speech samples, and retesting at those points where new information is to be acquired.

No teacher is expected, even in light of PL 94-142 and the concept of mainstreaming, to be held entirely responsible for language assessment procedures. The teacher, however, will contribute more to the referral and diagnosis of a disability than in the past, since the teacher will be contacted much more extensively as a source of behavior and performance information. The teacher's participation in the referral, diagnosis, and program planning is necessary. Familiarity with these standardized language assessment procedures and techniques will prove to be valuable in interactions with other professionals.

There will always be a need for continued assessment to obtain new data. The teacher should be aware that in the language assessment process the intent is not to collect a series of scores; but rather to plot a pattern of language behavior in which the individual scores play a significant part.

The following case report provides an example of the assessment procedure utilized with a single child (Christopher) and clearly demonstrates the manner in which test scores are to be interpreted.

LANGUAGE ASSESSMENT – AN ILLUSTRATIVE CASE

A Summary Report on Christopher

Report of Examination

Behavioral Observations

Testing was conducted over three sessions, two one-hour sessions and one two-hour session. Chris's mother accompanied him to the testing room on the first day and left shortly after testing was initiated. Chris accompanied the examiners alone on the subsequent testing days.

Chris performed all required tasks on each of the three testing days. Very little spontaneity was evident in the first testing session; however, participation became more active in subsequent sessions.

Language

Analysis of language functioning was defined in terms of three processes: comprehension, the ability to recognize verbal and visual stimuli; association, the ability to relate, organize, and manipulate visual or auditory stimuli in a meaningful way; and expression, the ability to use verbal or manual symbols to transmit an idea.

Comprehensions

The Peabody Picture Vocabulary Test (PPVT) was administered to ascertain Chris's comprehension of single words.

Form A revealed a receptive vocabulary age of 3 + 2 years and Form B showed a receptive vocabulary age of 3 + 7 years. Responses obtained on Form B, which was administered on the third day of testing,

129

were judged valid. Scores obtained on both forms were within five months of each other and demonstrate Chris's comprehension of single words to be almost two years below the performance expected for his chronological age.

The receptive portions of the Northwestern Syntax Screening Test (NSST) were administered according to standardization to determine Chris's level of comprehension with syntactic stimuli. Chris scored fourteen correct responses which placed him below the tenth percentile for both his chronological age and for three year olds. This shows a significant discrepancy not only from the expected performance for his chronological age, but also from his performance with comprehension of single words on the PPVT.

Although Chris had demonstrated in examples that he understood what was expected of him within the receptive portion of the NSST, the examiner questioned task interference in Chris's performance and devised a format for administration controlling for the task. The examiners first controlled the auditory stimulus and readministered the receptive portion of the NSST presenting one sentence per stimulus item; i.e., "Show me the cat is behind the chair" (Chris points). This performance showed no appreciable gain from the standardized administration and demonstrated Chris's understanding of syntactic stimuli to be below the tenth percentile for his chronological age and for three year olds.

In an attempt to reduce visual as well as auditory stimuli, the expressive portion of the NSST, which presents only two pictures on each plate, was presented as a receptive task. Each of the twenty plates was presented consecutively twice through, first presenting each of the starred items as auditory stimuli, and then again presenting each of the unstarred items as auditory stimuli. Within this format Chris answered twenty-three of the forty items correctly. Although this performance still shows Chris's comprehension of syntactic stimuli to be significantly below his peers, it indicates that factors within the task may be adding to the comprehension difficulty.

In order to pinpoint the level at which syntactic units were breaking down, the Assessment of Children's Language Comprehension (ACLC) was administered.

Part A—Vocabulary—45/50. It is obvious that Chris possesses the single common identities necessary to complete the test. With the few concepts missed, prepositions "in" and "behind" and verbs, "eating" and "washing," instruction was provided to ensure his familiarity with these words. Chris met the requirement of forty-seven correct responses on Part A.

Part B—Two critical elements yielded a final accuracy score of 90 percent. The single error that occurred was with the first critical element.

Part C—Three critical elements. At this point, Chris earned a score of 80 percent. The two errors that occurred were both on the second critical element.

Part D—Four critical elements. At this point, Chris earned a score of 10 percent accuracy. It was apparent that the breakdown in syntactic units was occurring at the four-critical-element level. In analyzing the errors made on Part D, it is noted that of the nine errors, five were on the first critical elements, one on the third element, and three on the fourth critical component.

From his performance on the ACLC, Chris can be viewed as unsuccessful with utterances of four critical elements. In reviewing total test errors, it should be noted that of the twelve errors made, six of them occurred on the first critical component. Although errors occurred with all elements, in most cases, errors were made with first critical element.

Association

Two subtests of the Illinois Test of Psycholinguistic Abilities (ITPA) designed to assess the integration process which may be operating in the manipulation of visual or auditory stimuli were presented. These subtests were Auditory Association, which taps the child's ability to relate, organize, and manipulate concepts presented orally, and Visual Association, which assesses the child's ability to relate, organize, and manipulate concepts presented visually.

With the Auditory Association task, Chris received a raw score of 7 which yielded a scaled score of 23. This is thirteen points below the mean scaled score of 30 for the task and indicates a significant disability with integrating and manipulating concepts presented orally.

With the Visual Association task, Chris demonstrated eleven correct responses. This yielded a scaled score of 29, which is seven points below the mean scaled score of 36 for this task. This indicates a borderline disability with the integration and manipulation of concepts presented visually.

Chris is functioning below his peers in the ability to relate, organize, and manipulate concepts presented orally and visually. The greatest difficulty was demonstrated with orally presented concepts; however, the borderline disability with visually presented concepts is of concern as the tasks for assessment or auditory receptive functioning assume intact visual functioning. His difficulty deriving visual relationships may have influenced Chris's performance in the auditory reception tasks by adding a complicating factor to his auditory comprehension difficulty.

Expression

Chris's ability to use symbols to express ideas was assessed with manual as well as verbal symbols.

Verbal Expression

The expressive portion of the NSST was administered according to standardization in an attempt to measure Chris's ability to produce syntactically complete and appropriate responses.

Throughout the expressive section of the NSST, Chris responded only with single-word identifiers and in many cases, used the same word in response to both pictures. In no instance was a verbatim or grammatically correct and complete response given. Thus, the final score of the expressive items was zero.

Manual Expression

Chris's ability to use gestures to express ideas was assessed by the Manual Expression subtest of the ITPA. This task presents a picture to the child which the examiner names and asks the child to "show me what you do with a _____." The child gestures the function and the examiner scores points for specific gestures. Chris scored 26 points on this task yielding a scaled score of 45, which is nine points above the mean scaled score for this task. Using the criterion of a minimum upward deviation of ten points in the scaled score to indicate a special ability, and a seven-, eight-, or nine-point upward deviation to show functioning above the peer group that borders on a special ability, it can be seen that Chris is functioning above his peers in the ability to express ideas with gestures, and that his performance with this task borders on a special ability.

Impressions and Recommendations

Chris demonstrated difficulty in his ability to comprehend, organize, and use oral language. He is functioning significantly below his peers in all language skills and is showing a syntactic performance that is not only deviant from his peers, but also from children of a younger age. Verbal expression is additionally hampered by multiple sound omissions and substitutions, making Chris's speech unintelligible if the listener is not familiar with the topic.

Gross motor functioning and eye-hand coordination are commensurate with Chris's chronological age; however, some difficulty was demonstrated in his ability to relate, organize, and manipulate visually presented stimuli. This may have depressed some of the receptive measures; however, we cannot fully account for the difficulty demonstrated with the comprehension tasks.

Chris has demonstrated facility with semantic relationships (which are believed to underlie early language) and communication by gesture was above the expected performance for his chronological age. These suggest that Chris is enough aware of the world around him to have something to express, and that he is able to use symbols to communicate at a level at least commensurate with his chronological age in a nonverbal mode. The breakdown seems to be with auditory-vocal tasks.

Chris's behavior is representative of that seen in children with language disorders. It is recommended that Chris be enrolled for language therapy on a three-session-per-week basis. The management program should emphasize the following:

1. Expansion of vocabulary and auditory comprehension
2. Increasing of mean utterance length
3. Stimulation for production of subject-verb phrases and kernel sentences.

SUMMARY

This chapter has looked at problems associated with language assessment, standardized language assessment procedures, informal language assessment techniques, and formalized language assessment measures. The discussion of the problems associated with language assessment considered differences in background, uneven normal development, limitation of the data collecting procedures and techniques, task and situation variables, sampling errors, role-playing tendencies, and responses to listener characteristics. In the examination of the standard language assessment procedure, the tabulation of the mean length of utterance, of weighted scales, and of frequency counting was provided. After a detailed discussion of these standard language assessment techniques, their use in terms of formal language assessment techniques was demonstrated. Attention was given to two procedures that the teacher can use to effectively screen for particular language disabilities. The two informal language assessment procedures that were presented served as models of the types of assessment techniques that can be constructed with a relative amount of ease.

The Mecham Scale, the NSST, DSS, PPVT, the CELI, the ITPA, and the ACLC were presented to overview the formalized language assessment instruments used by speech clinicians. These instruments were not presented to develop the teacher's skill in their administration but, rather, to familiarize regular and special educators with the diagnostic tools they are most likely to encounter.

Because an effective language education program relies on the input of all professionals working with the child, it is necessary that all the educators involved have common understandings. Certainly, the ability to diagnose the disabilities and to interpret test scores remain the principle domain of the speech clinician, yet awareness of the limitations and problems associated with the language assessment procedure facilitates the design of effective programs for instruction.

POINTS FOR DISCUSSION

1. You have been recently hired as a regular classroom teacher in the Robertson Elementary School. You find during your first month on the job that you have a child whose language performance seems to be quite distinct from the other children in your third-grade class. Discuss with a colleague (a classmate) your plans for an informal assessment of the child to assist you in communicating your concerns to the speech therapist.

2. In this chapter, some of the problems associated with language assessment were discussed. Now that you have had a chance to consider the influence of uneven

normal development, background experience, difficulty of data collection and transcription, task and situation variables, sampling errors, role-playing tendencies, and listener characteristics, which of these stand out in your mind as being most significant? Which are of least importance to you? Explain why you feel the way you do to a classmate.

3. Using the transcription associated with Figure 4.1, calculate the mean length of utterance based on a word count alone. When you have completed this process, use Brown's criteria and determine the mean length of utterance based on a morpheme count. Compare the scores that you obtain with those of a classmate's. Were they different? Why? What might contribute to the similarity or difference between a mean length of utterance based on a word count and one based on a morpheme count?

4. At some point this semester you may have an opportunity to interact with children in the regular classroom or in a clinical setting. If it is within your means, try collecting a language sample from a child in a controlled setting. Once you have a data base, do a transcription of at least 150 utterances. Do more if possible. Once you have your transcription completed, use one or more of the standard assessment techniques to summarize the child's language performance. You might wish to do a frequency count, develop a weighted scale, or invent a pattern for describing the child's language, but be consistent!

5. Depending on your situation this semester, you may or may not be able to practice using informal language assessment techniques. If, however, you do have access to children (or to a child), you might want to use one of the informal language assessment measures discussed in this chapter. Perhaps you can administer and score one of these informal assessment instruments. You may even want to modify one of these to develop your own informal language assessment technique.

6. The informal language assessment instruments discussed in this chapter focus to a large extent on syntactic maturity. What are other characteristics of language that you feel an informal language inventory might do well to assess? If you were to develop an informal instrument to assess semantic ability, for example, what types of questions or tasks would you include? How would it be administered? Scored? Analyzed? Interpreted?

7. Formal language assessment instruments have the advantage of providing the classroom teacher or special educator with normative data regarding the child's performance. In addition, such instruments have generally been field tested and validated. In spite of these advantages, there are difficulties with formalized language assessment instruments. What are some of the problems that you see inherent in formal assessment instruments?

8. The language assessment process is not complete until the data that has been collected has been analyzed and interpreted. This is a most important aspect of the overall assessment process since the interpretation of the analysis is the basis for instruction. Review the summary report that was provided on *Christopher*. What

is your reaction to this case study? How would you have changed the summary? What deletions or additions would you have made? How would you change the report format? Share your impressions of this report with a classmate.

REFERENCES

Brown, R. *A first language.* Cambridge, Mass.: Harvard University Press, 1973.

Carrow, E. *Carrow elicited language inventory.* Austin, Tex.: Learning Concepts, 1974.

Cazden, C. *Child language and education.* New York: Holt, Rinehart and Winston, 1972.

Dale, P., and Kelly, D. *Language use and social setting: A suggestion for early education.* (ERIC microfiche, 1972, ED 071 757)

Dunn, L. *Peabody picture vocabulary test (PPVT).* Circle Pines, Minn.: American Guidance Service, 1959, 1965.

Flavell, J. *The development of role-taking and communication skills in children.* New York: John Wiley and Sons, 1968.

Foster, R., Giddan, J., and Stark, J. *Assessment of children's language comprehension.* Palo Alto, Calif.: Consulting Psychologist, 1969, 1973.

Glucksburg, S., Krauss, R. M., and Weisberg, R. Referential communication in nursery school children: Method and some preliminary findings. *Journal of Experimental Child Psychology,* 1966, *3,* 333–342.

Kirk, S. A., McCarthy, J. J., and Kirk, W. D. *The Illinois test of psycholinguistic abilities (revised edition).* Urbana, Ill.: University of Illinois Press, 1968.

Krauss, R., and Glucksburg, S. The development of communication competence as a function of age. *Child Development,* 1969, *40,* 255–266.

Lee, L. *Northwestern syntax screening test (NSST).* Evanston, Ill.: The Northwestern University Press, 1971.

Lee, L. *Developmental sentence analysis.* Evanston, Ill.: Northwestern University Press, 1974.

Lee, L., and Canter, S. Developmental sentence scoring: A clinical procedure for estimating syntactic development in children's spontaneous speech. *Journal of Speech and Hearing Disorders,* 1971, *36*(3), 315–341.

Mecham, M. *Verbal language development scale.* Circle Pines, Minn.: American Guidance Service, 1958, 1971.

Pickert, S., and Chase, M. Story retelling: An informal technique for evaluating children's language. *The Reading Teacher,* 1978, *31*(5), 528–531.

Plaskon, S. *An analysis of the speech adjustment of second-grade children to variations in age of listener.* Unpublished doctoral dissertation, University of Connecticut, 1975.

Sachs, J., and Devin, J. *Young children's use of age-appropriate speech styles in social interaction and role-playing.* Unpublished manuscript. University of Connecticut, 1973.

Shatz, M., and Gelman, R. The development of communication skills: Modification in the speech of young children as a function of listener age. *Monographs of the Society for Research in Child Development,* 1973, *38*(5, Serial No. 152).

5

Recording and Reporting Pupil Progress

The evaluation of the student's performance in the language arts is decidedly an issue that has to be dealt with by every teacher. In this text, we stress the need to design, implement, and evaluate an instructional program for the mildly handicapped child on the basis of pertinent performance information. We are the first to admit that such is not a simple task. Given the range of skills with which a competent user of the language arts must be proficient, the assessment process can be lengthy and detailed. In fact, the data collection process could become so cumbersome and awkward as to frustrate the teacher and be a negative rather than a positive ingredient in the instructional process.

The measurement and evaluation of a child's performance in the classroom is essential to the entire language arts program. Without information on the child's performance in spelling, in handwriting tasks, in composition, during conversation or oral language activities, as a listener, or as a reader, the teacher cannot appropriately construct an instructional program that is suitable for the child's level of achievement. The recording and reporting of pupil progress in the language arts is an integral part of the entire process.

Evaluation and Instructional Programming Models

To better understand just how essential this aspect of the educational process is, consider the instructional models in Figures 5.1 and 5.2 that have been drawn from two entirely different sources. Carefully examine the role that evaluation of student performance plays in each model and the point at which it occurs.

In Figure 5.1, the Instructional Programming Model developed by Klausmeier, Quilling, Sorenson, Way, and Glasrud (1971) states quite clearly that to design an instructional program for an individual child, evaluation must be an *integral part* of the process from entry to implementation of each level in an instructional sequence. No one teacher could move a single child through a skill sequence (be it language arts, science, or math) unless some data collection process was employed. Judgments about the student's entry skill behaviors, learning styles, achievement levels, attainment of objectives, and concept or skill mastery cannot be made unless there has been an on-going, active process for systematically recording and reporting the student's progress. Wiersma and Jurs (1976) have paralleled the instructional programming model with seven activities related to measurement and evaluation. They are as follows:

Steps in the IPM Model	Parallel Evaluation Stages
Step 1	Entry Evaluation
Step 2	Assessment measurement (Testing and other)
Step 3	Assessment
Step 4	Continuing evaluation
Step 5	Measurement
Step 6	Measurement (Testing and other)
Step 7	Evaluation decision point

In matching the seven steps of the Instructional Programming Model with seven measurement and evaluation stages, Wiersma and Jurs stress an evaluation process that is continuing in nature. In fact, they state that:

> The culmination of instructional programming consists of a decision point at which the various decision alternatives that exist must be judged. In order to make appropriate instructional decisions, teachers must have adequate information. Such information is collected and used throughout instructional programming, beginning with the statement of education objectives and the initial estimate of the range of objectives, through the decision on whether or not objectives have been attained. Thus, measurement, assessment, and testing become a part of evaluation. (Wiersma Jurs, 1976, p. 7)

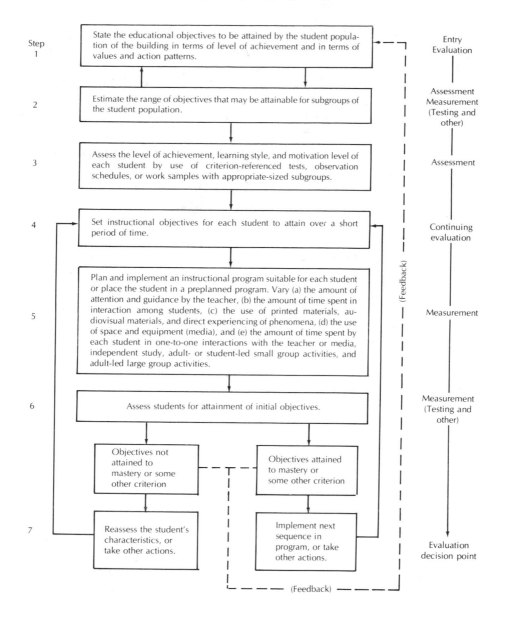

Source: Wiersma, W., and Jurs, S. *Evaluation of instruction in individually guided education.* Reading, Mass.: Addison-Wesley Publishing Co., 1976, p. 6. Adapted from H. J. Klausmeier, M. R. Quilling, J. S. Sorenson, R. S. Way, and G. R. Glasrud, *Individually guided education and the multi-unit school: Guidelines for implementation,* 'The IPM in IGE with evaluation emphasized at the appropriate steps.' Madison, Wisc.: Wisconsin Research and Development Center for Cognitive Learning, 1971. Reprinted with permission from H. J. Klausmeier.

FIGURE 5.1   Instructional Programming Model

Without considering such data, teachers cannot make appropriate decisions regarding a child's performance. The process, then, that one elects to use is *as important as* the skills that are being taught!

Figure 5.2 diagrams what has been referred to by Lerner (1976) as the clinical teaching cycle. Here, too, the role that evaluation plays in the entire instructional process is stressed. In this situation, one is working from a model that is directed toward the mildly handicapped child. Lerner indicates that the clinical teaching model differs from other designs for instruction because of its focus on the individual child. It is supposed that in the regular classroom setting instruction is geared to the "average child" and "to the class" (Lerner, 1976, p. 105). The clinical teaching model or cycle on the other hand is directed to that particularly special child requiring unique materials or procedures.

Whether or not this distinction still holds true given today's educational climate and the emphasis on mainstreaming the mildly handicapped child is another matter altogether. What is of significance is the role that the recording and reporting of pupil performance plays in a setting described as "clinical" in nature. In Lerner's model, Step 4 is the Evaluation stage, while Step 1, Diagnosis, implies a data collection stage. The diagnosis of learning disabilities assesses the lack of an ability to function in a particular manner or within a particular setting. It is in every sense an evaluative activity.

Source: From *Children with learning disabilities* by Janet W. Lerner, Copyright © 1976, 1971 by Houghton Mifflin Company. Reprinted with permission of the publisher.

FIGURE 5.2   *Diagram of Clinical Teaching Cycle*

The Teacher and Evaluation

Almost every teacher is confronted at some point early in the teaching career with the need to resolve the evaluation dilemma, or to at least decide how to handle the necessity of "grading" children. Consider the following example of the searching many teachers do in an attempt to clarify their stance in reporting progress. As you read through this actual justification for grading, written and submitted by a teacher to a school principal, think about your feelings regarding grades. Do you agree or disagree with the comments that are made? What would you say differently? Is the rationale for the assignment of grades A, B, C, and D appropriate and consistent? Does this explanation seem to make "good sense"?

The manner in which I grade my students involves a careful consideration of the following items. These particular qualities are *contributing factors* to a child's "grade." Since we do now use a system of letter grading, a child who consistently demonstrates a concern for these items is graded A; not so uniform B; satisfactory C; and so forth. In general, then, when "grading" a child, the thoughts foremost in my mind *regardless of the subject* are as follows:

A. *Participation*—How does the child respond to the particular lesson? Does he or she partake of the experimenting necessary to master a skill? Is a question researched to obtain an answer? Are specific assignments completed in the manner expected? Is material surveyed read and reviewed?

B. *Presentation*—How is the work handed in to me? What appearance does it take? Does a child take pride in his or her work? Is he or she visibly satisfied with it? How is the work done? Does it demonstrate care and concern for the quality and product? Is it complete? Is it an *honest* attempt on the part of the child to satisfy the requirement? (Here professional judgment is required and a knowledge of the child!) Is it an example of the child's ability level? Have directions been followed or altered with justification? Is the child aware of what he or she has done?

C. *Retention*—Does a child retain what he or she has been exposed to? Can he or she be questioned about work done and respond knowingly and intelligently? Can there be a time lapse and still a possession of knowledge? Do I know what the child has learned?

D. *Utility*—Does a child seem to use what he or she has learned? Does the child see the things he or she has learned in the present environment? How do I know that the child is a better person because of the exposure to the material that I have elected to teach?

These four areas constitute my major concerns when "grading" a child. Naturally, the answers to these questions are supplemented with daily performance records and specific grades per se on particular units. *Yet the emphasis rests on an interpretation of how the* child apparently participates, presents, retains, and utilizes information.

This example of the types of concerns that most teachers have regarding the grading process is by no means unusual. In fact, a number of insights are contained in the above memorandum sent from a teacher to a school principal on this very topic. You probably agreed with some comments and disagreed with others. But, we suspect, that much of this example reflects notions you may already have regarding the recording and reporting of pupil progress. You, as a teacher, must consider carefully just how *you* intend to assign "grades" to children in your charge. How will you handle the mildly handicapped child in your classroom who *is working* to the best of his or her ability? Where do you place *that* child on the grading continuum? Is your grade a comparison of that child to other children? Is it representative of the child's own performance? What do you do when the mildly handicapped child has been placed into the regular classroom where there will be a wide range of skills and abilities? Do we grade on a comparison basis to maintain the integrity of the system and thereby penalize the mainstreamed child? If not, how do we explain to the other children (and to their parents!) why a particular child gets an A or a B for work that is not nearly as good as that of the other children?

This issue of recording and reporting pupil progress is not easy to address or to resolve. The implications of proceeding in one manner over another are severe and numerous not just for a single child, but for the entire class. Each teacher is responsible for deciding, as in the example provided, just how to proceed. There are no simple answers. There are only data collection devices that can be employed as a basis for the decision making that ultimately confronts the teacher.

Observation and Record-Keeping Considerations

To develop an instructional program for a particular child and to determine the child's readiness to move to another level or next skill step, the teacher needs a structure for data collection and record keeping. Naturally, the vehicle a teacher elects is a function of the child or children in the class, the materials that are in question, the subject matter involved, and the degree to which the information will be used (e.g., referral, report cards, parent conference, staffing). Regardless of the function the record keeping and data collection will serve, the teacher should design a systematic, uniform, and regular technique for this evaluative process.

As indicated earlier, each teacher will have to begin this process by:

1. Confronting a number of pertinent issues.
2. Deciding on appropriate information sources.
3. Selecting a manner for sampling behaviors.
4. Developing a technique for record keeping.

Each step or element in the decision-making process has numerous characteristics and implementation alternatives. Let us examine just a few from each
category.

Confronting Pertinent Issues

Prior to the beginning of the school year teachers usually begin planning for the months to come. Most teachers seem to focus attention on the
classroom itself, the physical environment, and the in-coming class. Who are
these children? What have they already had? Where am I going to begin with
them? How will I determine who knows what in reading? Spelling? Composition? Handwriting? In terms of the classroom, the questions most often center
on the arrangement of furniture. Are there enough seats? Does the traffic flow
seem suitable for the kinds of activities I would like to have? Are there enough
work areas for small groups? For large groups? For individuals?

It usually is not until the children arrive that the teacher begins to
develop a question sequence revolving around specific children. This does
seem logical since many teachers do not know the children in their charge
until their arrival at the opening of school. In essence, teachers simply do not
know what they need to ask until they have had an opportunity to work with
a child or a class for a period of time. However, within a few weeks it
becomes quite apparent where more specific attention is going to have to be
focused.

Once a problem presents itself for a single child, the teacher needs to
consider three basic factors. In question form they are:

1. What do I *need to know* about this particular individual?
2. What specific *kind of information* do I need about this child in
    order to work with him or her?
3. What *is the problem* that I am seeking to solve?

At first reading, one may feel that there is considerable redundancy
between these basic considerations, but there are three distinct elements at
work here that require specific and unique information.

In the first question, determining what one needs to know about a
particular child, is just as significant as the means employed to obtain information. Here, we are considering whether or not information regarding frequency of contact with peers or select children is necessary information.
Maybe a teacher *needs to know* just how often a child is experiencing
frustration at completing assignments, or is misinterpreting information, or
failing to follow directions. Knowing what it is that one needs to know is just
as important as being able to select an appropriate technique for collecting
that information.

In the second instance, the focus is on the nature of the information itself. Here, we are asking specifically whether or not direct observation, time sampling, frequency counts, tests, or informal observations of interactions, for example, will provide the needed facts. Basically, one is stating that the results of these particular assessment procedures will be helpful in making a decision about a particular child. The results of a psychological or achievement test or the information obtained from a structured observation session or sequence will be the kind of information that is useful to the teacher in developing a program, making a referral, or reporting to parents.

Question three is perhaps the most difficult to answer even though it may appear to be the easiest to state. It seems logical to ask just *what* the problem is here, yet to do so intelligently and meaningfully is another matter altogether. The identification of the problem is a major step in the development of an instructional program that is suitable and appropriate for the child.

Deciding on Information Sources

Once these questions are answered, the teacher must consider the range of information sources that are available. It would be entirely appropriate, for example, to consider each of the following should the situation warrant:

- The child's entering behaviors
- The history of previous remediation attempts
- Family history
- Child's interests
- Previous test scores
- Formal or informal observation data
- Dated work samples
- Anecdotal records
- Skills checklists
- Activity checks
- Performance in other contracted situations
- Relationships with peers and other school-age youngsters

In most cases, however, the full range of information sources is seldom necessary. Many teachers select from those that are available and sample behaviors across a range of situations and settings. Yet, deciding on the source of information is a key ingredient in the overall decision-making process regarding any one particular child.

To illustrate the necessity of trying to focus attention on the most useful data, consider the consequences of selecting inappropriate information sources. If, for example, a teacher elected to stress performance on an achievement test in order to arrive at some conclusion regarding a particular child's misbehavior in class, there would be a clear mismatch between the information source selected and the information that the teacher needs to know about that particular child. In this hypothetical situation, some of the behavior problems associated with this child might be due to the child's poor academic performance, so chances are that focusing on this element alone will only contribute to the problem, thereby making it even worse! If instead of selecting achievement tests (and the related quizzes and reading scores), the teacher had elected to observe the child interacting with peers and sampled behaviors over a period of time, the teacher probably would have uncovered immature social skills or actual failures on the part of the child to engage others in conversations or in conflict resolution verbally. Here then, is a more appropriate match between the information source (observation and time sampling) and the information that the teacher needed to know (that the child does not know how to resolve conflicts verbally and/or is socially immature).

Information sources are often difficult to identify and to assess. Family histories, previous attempts at remediation, dated work samples, and anecdotal records are simply not available in many situations. When a child has been transferred from one school to another or has recently moved into the school district, many potentially valuable sources of information are no longer at the teacher's disposal. In some cases, it is possible to begin anew with anecdotal records, to reconstruct a family history, and to assume that a particular treatment or remediation program has been attempted, but doing so is often more difficult and time consuming than is practical. Therefore, the teacher must select from all *available* information sources those that will service both the teacher's and the child's needs most effectively.

Selecting and Sampling Behaviors

Most information collecting procedures require that the child's behavior be sampled over a period of time. Depending on the situation, the teacher may need to develop a technique that can be implemented alone, or one that utilizes an observer in the classroom. The sampling of the child's behavior need not be limited to just physical behavior as the term might imply, but can and does include academic performance, social interactions, and behaviors with materials. The process of sampling behaviors and collecting data can be extremely rewarding as it more often than not results in the isolation of information that is useful in effecting change.

Besides isolating information that should prove useful to the teacher working with the mildly handicapped child, the sampling of behavior throughout the year provides the teacher with information regarding progress over an extended period of time. It has already been pointed out that the sampling of behavior that takes place for a specific purpose needs to occur several times. Decisions regarding a particular child cannot be made on the basis of a single observation. We wish to emphasize here that this information-gathering process can be a year-long activity and can effectively note changes in behaviors that are significant to report at the end of a school year.

In speaking of sampling behaviors, a number of options and alternatives often come to mind. Included among these are the following:

- Time sampling
- Duration recording
- Frequency counting
- Planned Activity Checks (Plachecks)
- Checklists and rating scales
- Naturalistic observation

Pasanella and Volkmor (1977) discuss each of these activities in terms of the behavior samples that they are capable of providing.

Time Sampling

In this situation the teacher develops a grid that focuses on two different information sources:

1. The point in time at which an event occurs
2. The event under observation itself

In graph form, the time sampling procedure looks like this:

+ = in seat
− = out-of-seat

−	+	−	−	−	+	+	−	−	+
minutes 3	6	9	12	15	18	21	24	27	30

To illustrate the point, assume that a teacher has elected to focus attention on the child's behavior during a writing period. It seems as though every time the children in the class are engaged in a particular writing assignment, be it diary entries, composition, or creative writing, the child in question never seems to be seated. As a result, the child's performance in this aspect of the language arts is well below that of the class. It has become enough of a problem to warrant intervention. Before, however, the teacher approaches the special education personnel in the school, specific information was felt to be needed. Exactly how often is SueAndrea out of her seat? Is it as frequently as I suspect? When does it occur? Is it only during the morning? The afternoon? During language arts?

The time sampling grid and technique can assist the teacher in answering these questions. With baseline information of this nature, it will be possible to determine the extent to which any intervention program is achieving success.

In the example provided, the (+) symbol represented the times SueAndrea was observed to be seated and on the task. The (−) symbol was used to indicate positions other than seated. The bottom line indicates clearly the points in time at which the behavior was sampled. Here, a three-minute sequence was adhered to. Thus, there were ten observation points over a thirty-minute period of time. At this example indicates, SueAndrea was out of her seat six out of the ten times, resulting in an out-of-seat behavior 60 percent of the time.

Using such a time sampling technique over the course of several days helps to confirm or dispell suspicions regarding a particular child's behavior. If, in this case, continued observation of SueAndrea reveals similar patterns of behavior, the teacher's initial suspicions will have been confirmed. Unless just such a technique is employed, information about a child is based only on occasional notices of behavior.

Duration Recording

While the time sampling procedure may serve well when a child's particular behavior is subject to question, it is not always a good source of information when the desired activity cannot be observed as readily. In the example provided, the in-seat, out-of-seat behavior is quite easily monitored by time sampling procedures. In many classrooms, however, the focus of attention is not so much on physical position, but rather on the child's completion of particular tasks or assignments. This on-task behavior may comprise many elements that do not lend themselves to a (+) or (−) situation.

Duration recording permits the teacher to note over a period of time the extent to which a child is engaged in the appropriate on-task activity. In the language arts, a period of time each day is often devoted to peer-tutoring on spelling words or group work in dramatic play; and for some reason a particular child is observed to consistently fail to engage meaningfully in such activity. Since this is not in-group or out-of-group behavior, time sampling is not appropriate because the child is physically present. The focus of concern in this situation is the degree of continuous involvement or successful maintenance of attention on the activity.

In duration recording, the teacher simply predetermines the length of time the child should be engaged in a particular activity and observes over a period of several days (five or more) the amount of time the child is actively participating. This requires that a wall clock, wristwatch, or desk clock be available. The use of a stopwatch greatly facilitates the process as one can readily start and stop the watch as the child's behavior warrants. In either case, however, the objective is to determine over a set period of time (e.g., thirty minutes) the actual number of minutes that the child has spent "on-task."

The duration recording might look something like this:

Total Observation Time Per Day = 20 Minutes

Day	Time of Day	Total "On-task" Time
1	10:13–10:15; 10:18–10:21	5 minutes
2	10:00–10:04; 10:15–10:18	7 minutes
3	1:02–1:04; 1:11–1:14	5 minutes
4	11:15–11:19; 11:28–11:32	8 minutes
5	2:31–2:32; 2:40–2:42; 2:45–2:50	8 minutes
100 minutes total activity time		33 minutes

It would be quite clear to the teacher that the child in question was spending only about one-third of the assigned time in "on-task" behavior. Certainly if there were corresponding learning or academic deficiencies, the problem might be attributable to this failure to attend for an extended period of time to the task at hand.

Frequency Counting

As a method of sampling behaviors, frequency counting is the one most often engaged in by most teachers. In fact, at one point or another during the day teachers usually remark something to the effect: "If you do that one more time, I'll . . . !" The stern message that the teacher is conveying not only implies displeasure, but also that a counting of behaviors has been taking place and the frequency has increased too much.

Frequency counting is at times almost an intuitive behavior. Yet, used in a subjective fashion, it can be very misleading because it only *seems* as if the child has been doing something regularly when actually the behavior may not be as consistent as the teacher suspects. As a result, if the noting of the *number of times* a child does (or does not do) something is to be the basis for decision-making, it will also have to be systematic and precise.

In addition to the use of frequency counting as a measure of behavior, the teacher of the language arts will find that in spelling, handwriting, composition, and oral language and listening skills, the tabulation of academic performance is a necessary part of the instructional process. In each area of the language arts, error analysis, number of correct responses, approximations, and the occurrence of particular forms all require some degree of frequency counting. In this domain as well, the emphasis must be on accuracy and precision.

148

To achieve such a situation, the developed recording procedure should be convenient and simple to use. In fact, this method of sampling behaviors relies quite heavily on the recording process. We will discuss recording techniques for frequency counting later in this chapter.

Teachers should be aware that when frequency counting is introduced into the classroom, especially when mechanical counters are utilized, children's behavior changes abruptly. Time should be allowed to adjust to the constant monitoring that might be taking place. Children need time to adapt to the new procedure. A period of several days is sometimes necessary before a "true" measure can be taken.

Planned Activity Checks (Placheck)

The language arts teacher may wish to determine if the selected class activities themselves are typically enjoyed and attended to by the class, or by groups of children, rather than looking at individual student behaviors. In some settings, the behavior of a single student might represent discontent with the activity itself and not be an indicator of a learning or behavioral problem.

Perhaps the only way to judge the success or failure of an activity (or set of activities) is to systematically determine the extent to which the children are involved in whatever it is that has been planned. Pasanella and Volkmor (1977) describe the Planned Activity Check as follows:

Placheck (Planned Activity Check) is a recording technique originally developed by Risley (1971), which is useful for teachers interested in observing *groups* of students. As described by Hall (1971), the procedure is as follows:

1. The observer scientifically defines the behavior (planned activity) he wishes to record in a group of children.
2. At given intervals (e.g., each ten minutes) the observer counts as quickly as possible how many individuals are engaged in the behavior, recording the total.
3. The observer then counts and records as quickly as possible how many individuals are present in the area of the activity.
4. The number of pupils present can then be divided into the number of pupils engaged in the behavior. By multiplying the result by 100, the observer finds the percent of those engaged in the behavior at a particular time (p. 4). (In Pasanella and Volkmor, 1977, p. 92)

The Placheck technique is relatively easy to use and, with practice, it can serve as an effective and efficient tool for data collection. Of particular interest to the language arts teacher is the usefulness of this procedure in open-space or in totally individualized programs where a number of particular activities might be occurring simultaneously in the classroom. The Planned Activity Check can be an effective monitor of class behavior and can serve to isolate those activities that are consistently more popular and more often selected by children. A Planned Activity Check might work in the following manner:

A teacher has introduced into the room a learning center dealing with newspapers. In this center are numerous activities related to the daily paper. There are crossword puzzles, picture stories, tape recordings of new events, editorial cartoons, and comic strips. Because this classroom is totally individualized, the center was placed into the classroom for use by children wishing to develop a familiarity with the daily paper.

The teacher wishes to determine to what extent the children in the class are making use of this center. He decides that a Planned Activity Check would be a suitable means for collecting information about the center's use. Every ten minutes during the course of a one-hour period, the teacher quickly counts how many students are working in the newspaper center. He then determines how many students are present in the room. It might well be that of the 28 students in the class, 6 are in the center. The ratio would be 6/28. At the other five observation points, it is found that 4/28, 8/28, 3/28, 6/28, and 4/28 ratios are obtained. Converting these figures into percentages, it is found that 21, 14, 28, 10, 21, and 14 percent of the class population has been involved in the center at the various observation points. The average of these percentages indicates that approximately 18 percent of the class has used this newly introduced activity. The Planned Activity Check has enabled the teacher to determine with some degree of accuracy the extent to which this center has been incorporated into the daily class routine.

Checklists and Rating Scales

Perhaps a bit more conventional in nature, but still tremendously valuable to the teacher, is the use of checklists and various rating scales as a means by which behaviors can be sampled. The development of a checklist is not a complicated task and its ease of construction makes it a popular tool for assessing behavior and for data collection. In addition, the checklist format permits the language arts teacher to develop a chart that closely matches the activities, lessons, and subject matter. The checklist itself may be as simple as noting whether an activity has been completed or not, or it can be as complex as a specific skill continuum with spaces for noting the level of skill mastery.

The following is an example of a checklist of reading comprehension skills developed to record the progress of a fourth-grade student. It is a partial listing of comprehension skills and should serve only as an example of the manner in which a checklist can be constructed:

Comprehension Skills

A. Main Ideas

_____ Given a story paragraph and three statements of a main idea, the student will check the statement that best tells the main idea.

_____ Given a factual paragraph and three phrases, the student will check the phrase which best states the main idea.

_____ Given a story with a title and a list of four subtitles, the student will choose and write the two most appropriate subtitles.

B. Details

_____ Given a story and a set of multiple choice questions relating to time and place, the student will check the correct answer.

_____ Given a story and a stated main idea, and a list of details, some of which support the main idea, the student will check the details which support the main idea.

C. Sequence

_____ Given a short story with paragraphs in random order, the student will number paragraphs in the order in which they logically appear.

_____ Given a short biographical paragraph and a group of sentences related to events in the biography, the student will number the sentences in the order in which they happened.

Source: *Continuous Progress Materials,* Tuscaloosa City Schools, Tuscaloosa, Alabama. Checklist items adapted from grade 4-level 1 skill sequence.

In this situation, the teacher would simply note whether or not the child has demonstrated an ability in each of the areas specified. Here, a date, a tick mark, or a yes/no statement can be placed on the line appearing before each skill. In this manner, the teacher can keep track of a particular child's skill in developing reading comprehension abilities.

Rating scales do many of the same things that the checklist does, yet the focus for the rating scale is an evaluation of the quality of the work done. A checklist is primarily informative in nature in terms of quantity, whereas the rating scale is judgmental in terms of the quality of the work that has been done. In many settings, the teacher has elected to sample *both* the quantity and quality of the child's performance by combining elements into one chart. In these situations, the chart that is often displayed in the classroom indicates the level of skill achievement and includes a grade, notation, or a score as to how well the skill has been mastered.

These procedures for sampling children's performance are representative of those most commonly used in the classroom setting. Numerous variations exist for each of these and it is the prerogative of the teacher to adapt and to adjust them to suit each particular child, subject, or setting. What is standard, however, is the necessity of correlating the method of information gathering with the problem that one is attempting to solve.

Naturalistic Observation

One method or procedure for sampling children's behavior in the classroom that is now only beginning to be respected as a valid method of data collection is that of naturalistic observation. Observing children in their natural settings, school, play groups, at home, and interacting with materials and objects has been a commonly utilized data collecting form in psychology, sociology, and anthropology. In recent times, however, numerous educators have turned to naturalistic observation to more closely document what takes place in the classroom. Much has been gained from the use of this particular technique.

In the language arts classroom, many daily interactions cannot be readily recorded by conventional means. It is often impossible to gauge a child's ability to converse with peers, to introduce new topics into conversations, and to obtain social acceptance by time sampling, frequency counting, duration recording, or checklist keeping. It is quite appropriate to supplement information obtained through more traditional procedures with the insights that direct observation permits.

Naturalistic observation involves a process that employs several steps:

1. Identify the problem as best as you are able with the information at hand.
2. Take whatever time is needed to develop several different hunches as to what might be contributing to the difficulty.
3. Gather information through direct observation of the child (or children) in those settings that relate to the "hunches" you have developed.
4. Provide tentative solutions to the problem based on what you have observed.
5. Implement those solutions one at a time over whatever period of time seems to be suitable.
6. Gather information again through direct observation as to whether or not those tentative solutions are working.
7. Evaluate (make a judgment) as to the best of those tentative solutions you have experimented with.

There is no question that the naturalistic observation format is subject to interpretation and much imprecision. Yet, the focus on direct observation of the child coupled with an effort on the part of the teacher to develop tentative solutions to the problem can lead to effective resolution. Naturalistic observation can be yet another tool to assist the teacher of the mildly handicapped child in developing an appropriate instructional program. To ignore a potentially useful data collection technique on the basis of its non-behavioral orientation is to eliminate an information source that could possible serve in the improvement of instruction for a single child.

Developing Record-keeping Techniques

Without a system for recording the data that is collected in each of the procedures outlined in the chapter, the teacher's entire effort could prove fruitless. It is as important to develop a system for record keeping as it is to develop a technique for collecting the data.

This section presents a number of record-keeping devices that have been successfully used by teachers and have been cited in different sources. These devices which should serve as models for you to develop your own personal record-keeping system, include:

- Wall charts
- Sociograms
- Wristbands
- Mechanical counters
- Diaries and logs
- File cards
- Third-party observers and recorders
- McBee or Key sort cards
- Graphs and data grids

Wall Charts

As was mentioned, in a data collection process that uses a checklist or rating scale, teachers often develop a wall chart to display the activities completed and the quality with which the work was done. It is not unusual to find several different wall charts located around a classroom—each with a different focus. Wall charts are often developed to plot progress in reading (i.e., number of books read, number of skills mastered), or to note achievement level in writing, or to record the completion of spelling assignments. Take for example the following wall charts related to the language arts shown in Figures 5.3 and 5.4.

Wall charts are popular record-keeping devices because they can be adapted easily to each subject area and to groups of children in particular. Generally, wall charts are used to plot an *entire* class's progress rather than that of a single individual. Properly used, a wall chart can be an effective motivator for children who need a visual display of their performance in relation to other students.

Another decided advantage of wall charts is the accessibility of information for the teacher. It is simply no chore at all to record the children's completion of particular assignments at the end of the day or even during the class period. In some situations, the children themselves might be able to record the dates, times, or other particulars related to their own work at the time it is finished, thereby relieving the teacher of this responsibility.

Student Name	Letters of the Alphabet Mastered Capital Letters																									
	A	B	C	D	E	F	G	H	I	J	K	L	M	N	O	P	Q	R	S	T	U	V	W	X	Y	Z
1.																										
2.																										
3.																										
4.																										
5.																										
6.																										
7.																										
8.																										
9.																										
10.																										
11.																										
12.																										
13.																										
14.																										
15.																										
16.																										
17.																										
18.																										
19.																										
20.																										

FIGURE 5.3   Record of Progress with Cursive Letters

Wall charts can be quite attractive additions to any classroom. They may be colorful, decorated in numerous ways, and actual products of the class itself. A creative teacher can elect to make use of unusual shapes, sizes, designs, and even photographs, cartoons, and illustrations to make the wall chart a display center as well as a functional record-keeping device.

Sociograms

Throughout the chapters on each of the language arts skill areas we will emphasize the role that conversational expansion, stimulation, and varied experiences play in the development of language skllls. It has already been stressed in the chapter on language acquistion and development that children's contact with other children is perhaps one of the most important stimuli that children can have. It is imperative that the teacher of the mildly handicapped child notice the degree to which the child interacts with peers and the extent to which the child is engaged in conversation and verbal exchanges.

It is often difficult to know which children in a class interact most extensively with each other. In some situations the alert teacher can pinpoint with ease those children who are seldom included in discussions, question asking, and in verbal give-and-take sessions. In other cases, the teacher may not notice that a given child is seldom drawn into role-playing sessions, reading groups of an independent nature, or into exploratory projects. It is to the latter child that sociograms are directed.

When the problem at hand seems to be the exclusion of a particular child from numerous language arts activities that the teacher feels would benefit the child, the completion of a sociogram is recommended. There are several different types of sociograms that can be utilized. One that has been successful involves a simple plot of student preferences for other students. This sociogram can be displayed as shown in Figure 5.5.

This particular sociogram was developed on the basis of the choices of three best friends by a class of 14 girls and 17 boys. In this situation, the teacher requested that the students answer the question, "My three best friends in the class are: (very best friend) 1. _____, (second best friend) 2. _____, (third best friend) 3. _____." As each child completed the form, the results were taken and tabulated as shown in Figure 5.5.

To clearly understand the sociometric technique employed here, read carefully across row A. As you read across this row, you should note that in this case, Girl A chose Girl D as her very best friend, Girl C as her second best friend, and Boy c as her third best friend.

Now, read down column A to note just how often Girl A was chosen by the other students. Girl A was the first choice of three students (Girl D, Girl N, and Boy k), Girl A was the second choice of four different students

Student Name: _____

	Date Began	Author	Title	Date Completed
1.				
2.				
3.				
4.				
5.				
6.				
7.				
8.				
9.				
10.				
11.				
12.				
13.				
14.				
15.				

FIGURE 5.4 Example of Record of Reading Progress

Choices of Three Best Friends by a class of 14 Girls and 17 Boys

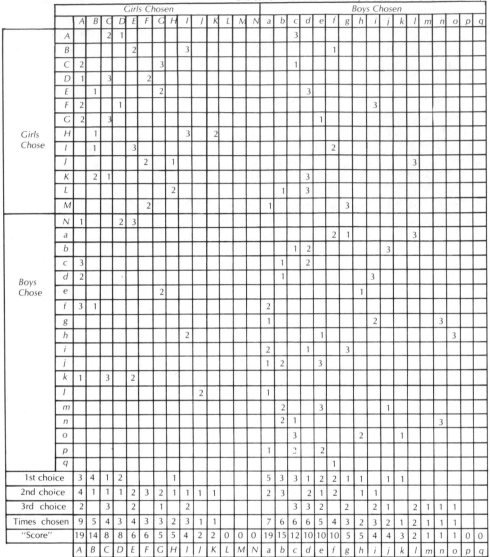

Source: Julian C. Stanley, Kenneth D. Hopkins, *Educational and psychological measurement and evaluation*, © 1972, p. 405. Reprinted by permission of Prentice-Hall, Inc., Englewood Cliffs, New Jersey.

FIGURE 5.5   A Grid-Type Sociogram Based on Choices of Three Best Friends

(Girls C, F, G, and Boy d), and Girl A was the third choice of two students (Boys c and f).

At the very bottom of the grid, the column totals are displayed in the rows labeled *1st choice, 2nd choice,* and *3rd choice.* The total number of times a particular student was selected is simply the sum of the three categories.

To arrive at a "score," the authors of this grid elected to score each first choice as being equal to 3 points, second choices as being 2 points, and third choices as 1 point. Girl A then received a score of 19 because of the sum total of the points she accumulated $(3 \times 3) + (4 \times 2) + (2 \times 1) = 19$. Naturally, the point values used are entirely arbitrary, but the assignment of such values enables the teacher to "score" each child. This method of data collection is more structured than other sociometric techniques, and clearly reveals lines of popularity and dislikes. Much can be learned from the final grid. Closer examination reveals those children seldom or never chosen, those who have only male or female selections of friends, and the concentration of popularity with a select group.

The sociogram is more than just a data collection procedure. When the results are plotted as in Figure 5.5, the teacher has a permanent record of a particular child's location in the social structure of the class. If attempts are made to involve a particular student in class discussions, or to alter the structure of particular groups, the effectiveness of the intervention can be judged accurately by comparing a plot done at a later point in time with the baseline information. The sociogram serves as both a data collection device, and a record-keeping form.

Wristbands and Mechanical Counters

Have you ever noted how often a particular child engages in an activity that you find undesirable? Consider just how often that very same child does a particularly appropriate thing. Which was the easier to remember? Was it the behavior that you disapprove of or the one you sanction? In all likelihood, if you are like most teachers, you probably answered that the negative behavior was easier to keep track of. Such is often the case. In collecting data that is based on frequency counts, it is quite easy to lose track of the number of behavioral occurrences, especially if it is a record of positive or appropriate behaviors. Such a situation would be enough to frustrate any teacher. Given the wide range of responsibilities, demands, and activities that the typical teacher engages in on a daily basis, the frequency counting method of data collection can be facilitated by the use of either a wristband or a mechanical counter.

Of these two techniques, the mechanical counter is probably the more familiar. It is simply the device information booth attendants, ushers, and sometimes ticket sales personnel utilize to record the number of contacts or sales that are made in a day, morning, or during a specific peak period. These counters have been introduced into the classroom to simply assist the teacher who needs to count the number of times a child does a particular thing—be it good or bad!

The wristband is not as common, but can be used to serve exactly the same purpose as the hand-held mechanical counter. The major advantage of the wristband is that it frees the teacher to use both hands for teaching activities and eliminates the need to tie the mechanical counter around one's neck, or to constantly be running back and forth to a desk or table to enter a tally.

The wristband is a counter (much like those worn by novice golfers) that is worn like a watch. It often consists of two separate dials, one for the units and another for the tens, that are turned as an event is counted. Teachers who cannot locate a golfer's scorekeeper sometimes adapt the principle to produce an inexpensive but effective wristband that accomplishes exactly the same thing. A piece of masking tape is wrapped around the wrist, and a pen, pencil, or felt-tipped marker is used to write on the tape. Each time a behavior occurs that should be noted, a mark is placed on the tape. At the end of the day or observation period, the tape is removed and the total number of marks is tallied. While certainly not as attractive as a golfer's wristband, the masking tape trick works quite well.

Diaries, Logs, and File Card Record-Keeping

The use of diaries, logs, and file card boxes by teachers is common. Many teachers summarize the activites of particular children at the end of a school day by making notations in a diary regarding performance or behavior. The diary method of record keeping is extremely open-ended and permits the teacher to record such factors as assignments given, the circumstances under which an activity or event occurred, and the outcomes. In some cases, a diary is kept to note the progress of a single student throughout a marking period, or it may be a record of the teacher's perceptions of the day, week, or unit that involves items related to the lesson, the class, and the materials utilized.

The logbook system is much like the diary keeping. The major difference is the fact that a log tends to be considerably more structured, with specific categories, or events requiring comment on a daily basis. The logbook approach to record keeping is valuable in settings that require information that has been collected systematically and regularly. In many cases, the log is nothing more than a structured checklist that specifies that an entry be made at the end of each day. The entry can be a check, a notation, a date, a score, or a symbol that represents the completion of a particular activity or the occurrence of a particular event.

Instead of becoming locked into the rigid nature of the logbook with its particular requirements, and instead of being as open-ended as the diary approach to record keeping, many teachers construct a file box of 3 × 5 or 5 × 8 cards with one card for each student. The file box is arranged alphabetically, and with a place marker for each student rather than just for the letters of the alphabet. In this manner, the teacher can enter as the need arises comments, notes, scores, conferences, or any other pertinent information that will prove helpful to the teacher as referrals or reports are made. The major advantage of the file box is the expandability of the records on those children who require the largest amount of data collection. It is often difficult to predict which children will need frequent and elaborate record keeping. The file box format permits the teacher to focus attention where it is most needed without upsetting the entire sequence or organization. In addition, file box notes can be drawn out and summarized readily without searching through looseleaf pages of diary entries for comments about a single child. In this situation, all the teacher need do is pull those cards on that single child. The method is efficient and effective as a means of record keeping both from the perspective of entries and utilization of the data obtained.

Observers and Recorders in the Classroom

Given the extensiveness of the activities that most teachers become involved in during the course of the school day, it is not uncommon to use third-party observers or record keepers in those cases where specific, accurate, and longitudinal information is required (here we mean over the period of several consecutive days). The use of a third-party observer permits the teacher to go about the normal daily classroom routine without having to interrupt the flow of events to note take or to make entries into a diary, logbook, or file box. In some settings, the third-party observer can record events that simply would go unnoticed by the teacher and that are relevant to the child in question.

Special resource personnel in the school, the speech pathologist, the reading specialist, the counselor, the school psychologist, and perhaps even the principal are all potential observers and recorders. The expertise that these individuals bring can be extremely useful in isolating procedures for the adaptation of materials and methods to better suit an individual child. It is quite appropriate for these individuals to meet with the teacher prior to the beginning of an observation period to cooperatively develop a form or checklist and to pinpoint behaviors and interactions that need observing. By structuring to some extent the information collection sessions, the effectiveness of the third-party observer can be enhanced tremendously.

McBee or Key-Sort Cards

A relatively unusual method of record keeping is that of the key-sorting process. Developed in conjunction with the Wisconsin Design for Reading Program (1972) for maintaining records of skill completion in each of the strands and skill levels in the program, the key-sort process is one that has seen much modification. The key-sort system operates by conforming to these characteristics:

1. Heavy-weight posterboard or cardboard is cut to approximately 6 × 8 inches.
2. The teacher lists those skills, activities, or items that are required for a particular subject or event.
3. The information is then printed on the card so that it is read clockwise around the perimeter of the card on one side and counter-clockwise on the other. Left-handed people can then

punch the card from one side and right-handed people from the other. See Figure 5.6.

4.   A ticket punch is used to perforate the card next to each skill or activity so that each skill has a single hole corresponding to it that appears on the outermost edge of the card. The teacher should

---

WISCONSIN DESIGN
FOR READING SKILL
DEVELOPMENT

© 1972—The Board of Regents of the University of Wisconsin System

WORD ATTACK

NOTE: Skills marked i are assessed by a performance test or teacher observation.

LEVEL A:

(1) Rhyming words
(2) Rhyming phrases
(3) Shapes
(4) Letters, numbers
(5) Words, phrases
(6) i—Colors
(7) Initial consonants
( ) All A skills

SKILL	RS	M	%C
C1 i Sight vocabulary			
C2 Consonant variants			
C3 Consonant blends			
C4 Long vowels			
C5 Vowel + r, a + l, a + w			
C6 Diphthongs			
C7 Long & short oo			
C8 Middle vowel			
C9 Two vowels separated			
C10 Two vowels together			
C11 Final vowel			
C12 Consonant digraphs			
C13 Base words			
C14 Plurals			
C15 Homonyms			
C16 Synonyms, antonyms			
C17 i Independent application			
C18 Multiple meanings			
D1 i Sight vocabulary			
D2 Consonant blends			
D3 Silent letters			
D4 Syllabication			
D5 Accent			
D6 Unaccented schwa			
D7 Possessives			

LEVEL C:

(1) i—Sight vocabulary
(2) Consonant variants
(3) Consonant blends
(4) Long vowels
(5) Vowel + r, a + l, a + w
(6) Diphthongs
(7) Long & short oo
(8) Middle vowel
(9) Two vowels separated
(10) Two vowels together
(11) Final vowel
(12) Consonant digraphs
(13) Base words
( ) Plurals
(15) Homonyms
(16) Synonyms, antonyms
(17) i—Independent application
(18) Multiple meanings
( ) All C skills

LEVEL B:

(1) i—Sight vocabulary
(2) i—Left-right sequence
(3) Beginning consonants
(4) Ending consonants
(5) Consonant blends
(6) Rhyming elements
(7) Short vowels
(8) Consonant digraphs
(9) Compound words
(10) Contractions
(11) Base words
(12) Plurals
(13) Possessives
( ) All B skills

MCBEE® SYSTEMS—ATHENS, OHIO Z54824X

LEVEL D:

1 i—Sight vocabulary
2 Consonant blends
3 Silent letters
4 Syllabication
5 Accent
6 Unaccented schwa
7 Possessives
All D skills

DATE	NO. OF SKILLS	GROWTH

Source: Wisconsin Design for Reading Skill Development Key-Sort Card. Copyright © 1977 by the Board of Regents of the University of Wisconsin System. Reproduced with the permission of the publisher, National Computer Systems, Inc., Minneapolis, Minn.

FIGURE 5.6   A Sample Key-Sort Card

notch the hole open to the edge of the card when a skill or activity has been mastered or completed.

5. All the cards are grouped together and arranged systematically in a file box or similar container. These cards can be mechanically sorted for instructional grouping. Simply face all the cards in the same direction. Insert a skewer through a common hole in all of the cards. Cards that fall off the skewer (those that have been notched) do not need instruction or to be included in the group being formed for an activity or lesson. Cards remaining on the skewer identify the students for instruction or grouping.

6. There is one card for each student placed into the box. This card will serve as the record of the skills completed by the student.

The key-sort system has been used to list and to identify interest groups, volunteers for special projects, and projects completed by students in the language arts (e.g., puppetry, newspaper work, plays, or pantomimes). The information contained on the key-sort card depends on the purpose that the teacher wishes to have the system serve. It can be made to correspond to a particular curriculum, subject area, or topic; to record information; and to be a means by which students can be grouped for instruction.

Graphs, Data Grids, and Pupil Profiles
In classrooms, the use of graphs, data grids, and pupil profiles is often limited to standardized tests or to science experiments. By far, the checklist, wall chart, and diary or logbook procedures are the more standard practices. However, do not ignore the more unconventional practices, especially when working with a mildly handicapped child.

It has been common operating procedure in a clinical setting, such as a speech and hearing clinic, or in a child development facility, to plot the progress that a child is making in skill acquisition. The resulting graphs indicate clearly the degree to which success in treatment or in instruction is being achieved.

In the classroom, the teacher can devise a graph to plot a particular child's performance. In the language arts, many situations require somewhat more precise information for determining the appropriate intervention program or whether a suggested adaptation of methods or materials is having the desired effect. Take, for example, the time lapse between the asking of a question and the student response. If oral language skills are to be developed, children, and the mildly handicapped in particular, have to be engaged in conversation and dialogue. One sure deterrent to conversational expansion is the failure to respond to a question, or the extensiveness of the time needed to respond. It might well be that in the classroom the teacher is attempting to change a pattern of behavior on this particular variable. To judge the effectiveness of the treatment program, the teacher must plot the pattern of be-havior exhibited by the child. Figure 5.7 is an example of how a graph might be utilized to assist in this data collection process.

A data grid is much the same as the checklist except that it con-tains specific scores or percentages. A checklist, as noted previously, is much more open-ended in its informational content. A data grid is a means to precisely display the degree to which success is being experienced in a skill area.

An example of a data grid for use in the language arts program with spelling words (sight vocabulary) is shown in Figure 5.8. In this situation, X and O symbols were utilized to indicate correctness or error in response for each word. It was possible, then, to gauge instruction over a two-week period of time for spelling words taken from a child's reading book. Once the criterion level of three correct spellings was reached, a new word was added to the list. Without such a system for record-keeping *and* for readily display-ing the progress that had been made, the task of providing appropriate in-struction for this child could be quite tedious.

Pupil profiles are quite well known to most teachers. They have been generated most frequently in connection with standardized test results in

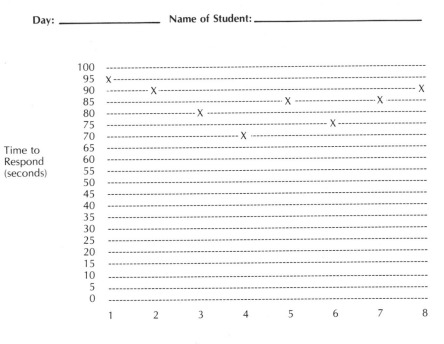

FIGURE 5.7 *A Sample Graphic Display of Response Time to Questions Asked*

Words to be Learned	Days of the Week									Review
	M	T	W	TH	F	M	T	W	TH	
COME	O	O	X	X	X	—	—	—	—	X
WERE	O	X	X	O	O	O	X	X	X	X
THINK	O	O	O	X	X	X	—	—	—	X
PLEASE	X	X	X	—	—	—	—	—	—	X
OVER	X	X	X	—	—	—	—	—	—	X
RECEIVED				X	X	O	X	X	X	X
BEFORE				O	O	X	X	X	—	X
AFTER						X	O	O	X	O
COULD						—	X	X	X	X
DEAR									O	O

X = correct response

O = incorrect response

— = word mastered after three consecutive responses and a new word added

FIGURE 5.8   A Partial Data Grid for Spelling Words

which several different subskills have been assessed. The Iowa Test of Basic Skills, for example, attempts to provide information regarding a child's ability in the areas of vocabulary, reading comprehension, spelling, capitalization, punctuation, and word usage as well as in mathematics and work-study skills. The results of the examination are displayed for the teacher in the form of a pupil profile as shown in Figure 5.9.

Pupil profile forms can be devised as the subject matter, skill areas, and informational needs warrant. They need not be just display formats for standardized test results. If a teacher is developing a language arts program for a particular child that involves each of the language arts skills of composition, handwriting, spelling, and reading (and the related subskills) a profile can be developed that matches the skills being taught. The child's performance in each of those areas might be plotted against the vertical axis of both date of completion and the achievement of a criterion score. The pupil profile form can be a useful and flexible record-keeping tool for those teachers who wish to make use of this particular form for charting pupil progress.

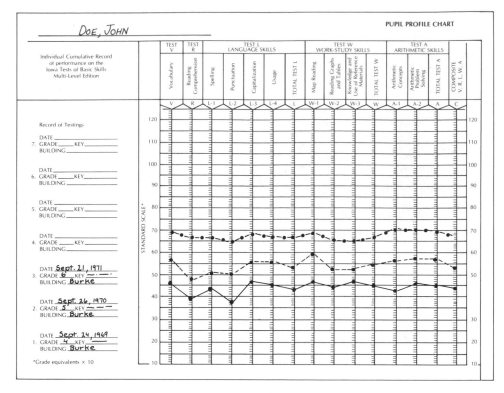

FIGURE 5.9   Pupil Profile Form

Communicating with Others about Pupil Progress

It is quite unlikely that the information that is collected concerning a particular child or even a class is going to remain solely in the hands of the teacher. The information that has been gathered is often to be shared with another party. Most frequently, that other party is the child's parents. In some cases, the other party consists of different professionals in the school (e.g., the speech clinician, the school psychologist, the principal, or team members). It is very important, then, that the information that is collected be in "usable form."

Now that PL 94-142 and the concept of mainstreaming has become a reality for parents and teachers of the mildly handicapped child, contacts with parents are more the rule than the exception. In fact, parent involvement in the development of the Individual Educational Plan (IEP) is *mandated* by the law. Teachers will have frequent contacts with parents that will require assessment information. Such meetings will not occur by chance, or by accident, or only at the conclusion of a serious incident in the school. Teachers of the mildly handicapped child will interact with parents in the development of instructional programs. The successfulness of such meetings depends to a great extent on the information that is brought to bear on the child and the skill area in question. In these meetings, the teacher will find other school personnel as well. The ability to communicate effectively and efficiently concerns, incidents, frequencies, and observations will contribute significantly to the design of the instructional program for the mildly handicapped child. Communicating with others about pupil progress will be one of the major roles and responsibilities of the teacher.

Let us examine information sharing with parents first. Periodic conferences are the best opportunities that the teacher has to comment on a particular child's performance. It is essential that:

1. The teacher prepare well in advance for the meeting.
2. An agenda be developed in order to focus attention on those items that are necessary to discuss.
3. A meeting time be agreed upon that permits both parties enough time to explore information fully.
4. The necessary information (e.g., graphs, logbooks, charts, or checklists) is readily available for reference and for documentation.
5. The teacher have a list of questions ready to ask the parents, as this is an opportune time to gather additional information and to clarify matters of concern.

It is our recommendation that parent conferences be held as frequently as the situation warrants. Experience has shown that those teachers who fail to involve parents early on in the information sharing process are the same teachers who have the greatest amount of difficulty in enlisting the parents' support for remediation and intervention programs.

Besides parent conferences, the use of notes, telephone conversations, and invitations to participate in class activities all serve to provide still other opportunities for information sharing. Certainly, inviting a parent into the class to participate in an art show or craft fair *is not* the time to engage in lengthy conferencing about a child, but casual conversation often focuses on items that do need attention and recognition by the parent. Such contact is surely desirable and is in fact recommended.

At report card time it is quite acceptable to provide a parent with a summary of data that may have been collected over the marking period or with a statement that explains the grades or marks that a child may have received. When letter grades are used, comments from the teacher are often essential to clarify why a particular grade was earned. Considerable grade comparison takes place in neighborhoods at the close of the marking period.

165

It is especially disconcerting to the first-year teacher to find that a group of parents are "up-in-arms" because of an apparent disparity in grade assignments among children—especially if the children are the best of friends.

Given the varied composition of the classroom in many schools, an explanation will be necessary as to how the teacher arrives at particular grades. A narrative, a comment sheet, or even a policy statement from the teacher accompanying each report card home can do much to alleviate this potentially uncomfortable situation. Consider, too, the problem of the mildly handicapped child in the regular classroom that was alluded to earlier in this chapter. Just how do you grade children who are working to the best of their ability? What do you say to those parents who realize that the A their child receives is not the same A that others in the class got since it is qualified by a lowered grade level score. There is no simple answer to this problem. What can be achieved, however, is a rapport and an understanding with parents that has been cultivated by frequent meaningful information-sharing sessions.

In communicating with other professionals in the school regarding the performance of a particular child, many of the same "rules" used with parents apply. It is the responsibility of the teacher to:

1. Provide pertinent, meaningful information to those special services personnel who have requested it.
2. Be organized in the manner of presentation.
3. Be able to document with clear evidence, comments, or statements made regarding a child in question.
4. Permit varying interpretations of the information presented as different opinions are expressed.
5. Allow for the collection of still more data or alter the data collection technique that has been used to date.

Any communications regarding a particular child should aim at improving services to that child or in adapting the materials and methods of instruction. Unless the teacher engages in communication exchanges with other professionals with this attitude, the entire purpose for the recording and reporting of pupil progress has been missed. It was stated in the introduction to this chapter that the ultimate goal of the measurement process was that of decision-making. To make the best possible judgment about the instructional program for a mildly handicapped student, the information that has been obtained must be shared with other personnel—especially with those whose services may be brought to bear on the child. This is only achieved through on-going communication and information sharing sessions.

SUMMARY

This chapter has looked at the role that evaluation plays in the development of instructional programming models for children in the language arts program. In any model for instruction, be it individualized or clinical in nature, the processes of diagnosis, assessment, and measurement provide needed information. The end result of any data collection is that of appropriate decision making regarding instruction for a particular child. It is imperative that evaluation of performance be an integral part of the programming for any child.

The teacher's role in appraising student performance is one of data collection, record keeping, and information sharing. Each teacher must decide how to approach the issue of "grades" or "marks." There are numerous factors to consider and many different conflicts to resolve. This chapter has tried to make you aware of some of them. It was pointed out that regardless of the approach ultimately taken, there will be numerous implications, not just for a single child, but for the entire class. No simple answers exist to the problems and questions of reporting and recording of pupil progress; there are only data collection devices to use as a basis for the decision-making that will ultimately take place. A familiarity with those particular techniques will help establish a firm foundation for developing procedures that result in improved language arts instruction for the mildly handicapped child.

This chapter has dealt with the issue of recording and reporting pupil progress from a general point of view. The methods chapters that follow will present *specific techniques* for assessing abilities in each of the language arts. Those ideas, procedures, and patterns for collecting and presenting data that have been discussed here are to serve as strategies for assessment of skills that can be made use of as one attempts to report progress in composition skills, handwriting skill development, spelling, reading, oral language, listening skills, and in active expression and nonverbal behaviors.

POINTS FOR DISCUSSION

1. The issue of "grading" the mildly handicapped child who is participating in the regular class program is a controversial one. Consider your own policy on the "grading" of mildly handicapped children. Prepare a five-minute presentation to be given before the class in which you defend your grading procedures or lack of them as the case may be.

2. Read each of the following hypothetical situations and decide which of the data collection techniques that have been presented in this chapter can be used to obtain the necessary information. You may need to combine procedures or to

modify the models you have just learned. In either case, decide on the most effective procedure.

> The teacher wishes to lengthen the amount of time that Sally and Willy engage in social interaction with their peers. It just seems to you, the teacher, that these two never interact with the group. What are you going to do?

> Sandra has really been acting up lately in class. The teacher can only record Sandra's behavior during one minute every half-hour in the school day. What should she do?

> The principal has asked for a description of all the incidents created by Billy on the playground during the coming week. You do not even have playground duty this week! What are you going to do to get the information that is needed?

> SueAndrea cannot seem to get her work done and is always behind the rest of the class. You decide to try and get some data before you call in a few other teachers to discuss the situation. What do you do?

3. Review the procedures for sampling behaviors that have been presented in this chapter and select any *two* of them that are of interest to you. With the permission of your instructor, utilize a class period to observe an activity or event. Follow the format that has been outlined for the behavior sampling technique you have selected and record your data.

4. Of all the sampling behavior approaches that have been discussed in this chapter, which appear to you to be the most effective? Which appear to be the most useful? Which appear to be easiest to implement? Which is the most difficult? As you answer each of these questions, be sure to elaborate on your answer. Discuss your comments with a classmate. Do you agree? Do you disagree?

5. Naturalistic observation was included as a technique for sampling behaviors. What advantages do you see in making use of this form of data collection? What are some of the disadvantages? In what types of situations would you elect to make use of this particular technique?

6. Working in teams of two, review the examples of wall charts that have been provided for you in this chapter. Select a particular style that is agreeable to you and devise a chart for a hypothetical class of children who will be doing independent reading. Your wall chart will be placed in a prominent spot in the room as an incentive for the class and as a means by which the children can keep track of the books, stories, or plays that they have read.

7. Meet together as a class and select a team to develop an experiment with a sociogram of this class. The team you select will be charged with the responsibility of devising a questionnaire, distributing it, and tabulating the results. A final copy of the sociogram should be given to each class member. It is suggested that the final plot of individual choices be coded to avoid singling out particular classmates. Your instructor will assist the team in the coding process.

8. Reporting to parents is an activity that every teacher will be engaged in at several points during the school year. Develop a letter, a narration, or a policy statement regarding your grading practices to be sent home with the report cards that you will be issuing. When you have completed your statements, have them duplicated and exchanged in class. Discuss those that are particularly good and make suggestions as to how those lacking in information might be improved upon.

REFERENCES

Klausmeier, H., Quilling, M., Sorenson, J., Way, R., and Glasrud, G. *Individually guided education in the multi-unit school: Guidelines for implementation.* Madison, Wisconsin: Wisconsin Research and Development Center for Cognitive Learning, 1971.

Lerner, J. *Children with learning disabilities* (2nd ed.). Boston, Mass.: Houghton Mifflin Co., 1976.

Pasanella, A., and Volkmor, C. *Coming back... Or never leaving— Instructional programming for handicapped students in the mainstream.* Columbus, Ohio: Charles E. Merrill Publishing Co., 1977.

Tuscaloosa City Schools, *Continuous progress materials.* Tuscaloosa, Alabama: Tuscaloosa City Schools.

Wiersma, W., and Jurs, S. *Evaluation of instruction in individually guided education.* Reading, Mass.: Addison-Wesley Publishing Co., 1976.

PART
III

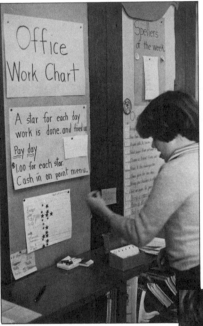

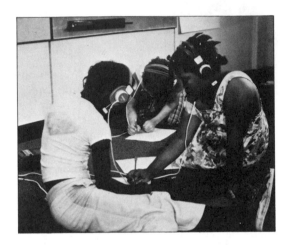

Teaching Language Arts Skills

6

Aural Skill Development

Of all the areas of the language arts, the development of aural language skills is by far the most neglected. Whether one is talking about the mildly handicapped child or the normal learner makes no difference. The amount of attention given to listening skills and to listening behavior is almost negligible. It has been reported by Kachur (1971) that in a typical classroom:

> Teachers fail to devote as much time to teaching listening as they say they do. This inconsistency may stem from the fact that teachers generally tend to rely heavily on textbook materials as a guide for instruction—and here again an inconsistency is prevalent between the acknowledgment of the importance of listening by publishers and authors, and their failure to include in textbooks any substantial amount of material designed to improve listening. (p. 19)

Burns and Broman (1975) report that the early research done by Rankin (1929) indicates that the listening skills of the typical adult and child are tapped on a daily basis. In general, an adult spends about 42 percent of the day in listening behavior. Certainly, compared with the 32 percent of waking time spent in conversation, the 11 percent in writing, and the 15 percent in reading, listening abilities take on new importance. More recent research (Flanders, 1970; Amidon & Flanders, 1963) suggests that the typical child, during the course of the school day, spends about the same amount of time—and possibly even more—in attending auditorily. Flanders (1970) has even gone so far as to suggest that upwards of 66 percent of the child's school day is spent in listening activity.

If it is known that such a great proportion of time is spent in situations that require an ability to process auditory inputs, greater emphasis should be placed on the development of this skill. Teachers should devote more of their instruction to the teaching of listening behaviors. Instructional materials should focus a proportionately greater number of activities and lessons on auditory skill development.

In all likelihood, an initial reaction would be affirmative to each of these statements. However, while teachers and publishers claim to be giving sufficient attention to this aspect of the language arts curriculum, it is not in fact happening. The responsibility for creating a clear focus on the development of good listening skills rests with the classroom teacher. Given that more and more hearing impaired and mildly handicapped children will be spending a greater amount of time in the classroom, considerably more emphasis is simply going to have to be given to the development of appropriate listening behaviors. Teachers will find themselves confronted with an entirely new set of problems, with new behaviors, and with new goals and objectives to be met with respect to the achievement of listening skills by both normal and mildly handicapped children. The concern now is not whether such a redirection should be given to the language arts curriculum, but rather *how* the classroom teacher can best meet the obligation of developing good listening skills.

The Role of the Listener in a Communication Setting

In chapter 3 a considerable amount of attention was given to the fact that all communication models and all information processing situations require a receiver or a listener, as well as a speaker or purveyor of information. The functions, roles, or responsibilities of the receiver or listener vary depending on the requirements of the communication encounter, but, in general, a number of characteristics are common enough to all listeners to describe as the skills a listener must possess to actively participate in an exchange of information.

The following represent just a few of the competencies required:

- An ability to attend to the speaker.
- An awareness of the value of nonverbal symbols in supplementing meaning.
- A sensitivity to the situation itself (i.e., time of day, room arrangement, light, heat, and context in which the encounter is taking place).

- An ability to assess the level of information processing of the speaker.
- An understanding of the pragmatics of the situation (i.e., where form and function do not coincide).
- An ability to determine to what extent the speaker requires participation, either verbal responses or nonverbal signs of attention.
- An understanding of the various kinds of listening: attentive, marginal, appreciative, analytic (Smith, 1971).
- A knowledge of the extent to which shifts in topic, focus, thrust, or orientation of the conversation can be made without inhibiting the speaker.
- An awareness of the extent to which the listener's attention can shift without loss of communication effectiveness.

Each of these skills is clearly essential to the communication encounter. The listener's role in determining success or failure is significant. By working with children throughout the elementary school years, their ability to engage in such exchanges can be influenced positively.

The Mildly Handicapped Child's Aural Skills

When dealing with the mildly handicapped child in the classroom, the teacher should keep in mind the characteristics that set the mildly handicapped child apart from the normal learner. Children, who in the past may have been receiving special services for the majority of the school day, now need to be dealt with in conjunction with children who are in a typical classroom setting. Such a situation probably requires an adjustment or modification of the curriculum to accommodate the special needs child.

The changes that may need to be made in the curriculum depend to a large extent on the characteristics of the mildly handicapped child. The mildly handicapped child's difficulty with listening may stem from perceptual, processing, or application dysfunctions. The following are some characteristics of the mildly handicapped child as a listener:

- Suffers mild hearing loss—between 20 and 40 dB.
- Uses a battery-operated hearing aid.
- Has difficulty with auditory attention.
- Does not identify commonly occurring sounds.
- Does not make gross sound discriminations.
- Has short attention span with respect to material presented orally.
- Fails to isolate particular passages, words, phrases that have occurred in orally presented materials.

175

- Has difficulty mentally organizing information presented through tapes, records, in-class demonstrations.
- Appears easily frustrated when confronted with tasks that require responses to oral questions, directions, or instructions.
- Does not enjoy oral reading—either by self or by teacher.
- Frequently misinterprets what is said.
- Fails to respond when called on.
- Does not repeat accurately simple digit spans.
- Does not make comparisons between comments that are made in a discussion or conversation.
- Frequently missequences information.
- Forms impressions of what is said that are distortions of the intended meaning.
- Fails to appreciate stories music, poems, for their rhythm, composition, etc.
- Appears to have little recall ability with respect to previously presented material.

Given the complexity of the skill area and the exceptionally wide array of possible skill deficiencies, the characteristics of the mildly handicapped child with respect to listening ability can be quite extensive. Those listed here appear to be the most frequently encountered in the classroom.

Depending on the situation, the teacher may find that the mildly handicapped child exhibits characteristics which commonly influence the aural learning environment. It may be that the child exhibits:

- A lack of sensory processing abilities
- A low tolerance for frustration
- A poor self-concept
- A short attention span, in general
- A below-average language ability
- A below-average ability to generalize and to conceptualize
- A play interest level below that of children of the same age

Adapted from Gearheart, Bill R., and Weishahn, Mel W.: *The handicapped child in the regular classroom,* St. Louis, 1976, The C. V. Mosby Co.

Such difficulties may be attributable to the overall disability or they may be symptoms of poor auditory processing skills. In either case, they are indicative of a situation that needs attention by the teacher.

If the child's difficulty is a direct result of a hearing loss and is not the apparent result of a cognitive deficiency, the teacher may observe that the child will:

- Display a lack of attention during class periods.
- Turn or cock head frequently.
- Have a real difficulty in following directions.
- Act out, be stubborn, or be withdrawn and shy.
- Be reluctant to participate in oral activities.
- Be dependent on classmates' for instruction.
- Display a disparity between expected and actual achievement.
- Have obvious physical problems associated with the ear (e.g., earaches, discharge, colds, and sore throats, and recurring tonsilitis).

Adapted from Gearheart, Bill R., and Weishahn, Mel W. *The handicapped child in the regular classroom,* St. Louis, 1976, The C. V. Mosby Co.

It is impossible to list all the situations that might be encountered in the classroom with respect to the mildly handicapped and listening disabilities. These particular features however, should serve to alert the sensitive educator to potential difficulties or to the need for curriculum modifications to accommodate the mildly handicapped child in the classroom.

Assessing Aural Skills

The teacher of the mildly handicapped child must constantly be on the lookout for signs that the child is not experiencing difficulty with aural language. One can determine the adequacy of a child's listening skills by designing simple informal assessment procedures or by plotting the child's performance on simple listening tasks over a period of several days. It should become apparent quite quickly whether or not the child's listening behaviors are satisfactory.

Perhaps the simplest technique available to the classroom teacher in terms of aural language skill assessment is the organized use of select activities as assessment tools. Here the classroom teacher selects a game, project, or task that can be presented to the child with the intent of examining or recording the results. The child's performance on the select task is of upmost concern. In the nonassessment situation, the emphasis is on the activity itself as a means of stimulating desirable behavior. In the assessment experience, the outcome is of significance.

However, remember in designing techniques for the assessment of auditory abilities, numerous variables may influence the testing situation. Vance and Hankins (1975) cite both Lerner (1971) and Fowler (1968) who have pointed out three inherent difficulties in the designing of auditory tests:

First, in both testing and teaching, each auditory subskill becomes contaminated with demands of the learning process. A second difficulty has been that some children who are successful in academic performance will fail certain auditory subtests. Third, the relationship between training in an auditory sub-skill and academic improvement has not yet been clearly established. (p. 70)

Keep in mind that even the best attempt to assess a particular child's auditory abilities, in fact, might have examined skills far removed from the auditory channel. The influence of prior learning and of other cognitive strategies the child might use to problem solve may conceal actual auditory difficulties. In those situations that warrant the use of an informal assessment technique, the teacher might find it useful to:

1. Assess short-term auditory memory by:
   a. Having the child listen, eyes closed, to the sound that the teacher makes (clapping hands, tapping foot, or humming a short tune) and repeat the pattern and sound.
   b. Having the child repeat digits, names of letters, words, sounds of letters, or combinations of these. Make each situation more difficult until a frustration level is reached. Make the task more complex by increasing the number of elements in a segment, by increasing the rate with which the items are presented, by diminishing the interval between task presentation and required response, or by introducing distractions or competing stimuli.

2. Assess auditory sensitivity by:
   a. Playing a sound effects record and asking the child to identify as many of the sounds as possible.
   b. Placing different coins into containers and asking the child to identify the coins.
   c. Playing a tape of common household sounds, (e.g., refrigerator door closing, silverware being placed on the table, dishes being done, the clothes dryer) and asking the child to identify them.

3. Test auditory discrimination by:
   a. Presenting two sounds in sequence and asking that the child distinguish one from the other. Perhaps, tap a pencil on a desk top, then a pen, and ask the child which sound was the pen and which was the pencil.
   b. Presenting different consonant sounds in one-syllable words in the initial, medial, or final positions and asking the child to identify the consonants. Examples are:

   c*at*–*f*at (initial)
   s*it*–s*at* (medial)
   ca*p*–ca*t* (final)

4. Test auditory recognition by:
   a. Identifying for a child a particular sound, such as the sound that /s/ makes in /snake/.

Inform the child that you will present a series of sounds and then you will include several times the /s/ sound. Each time the child hears the /s/ sound, a button or like object should be placed into a cup. At the end of the exercise, count the buttons to see if the child matched the number of occurrences of the sound.

5. Test auditory comprehension by:

   a. Using children's literature selections to determine if various points had been retained. After reading a favorite story to the child, ask specific questions that require the child to recall specific points, particular vocabulary words, or main ideas that should have been attended to during the oral reading. A variation on this activity would call for the presentation of the questions *prior* to the reading of the story.

   b. Requesting that the child follow a specific set of directions. Provide instructions for completing a simple puzzle, coloring a picture, designing an art project.

   c. Showing the child a set of photographs or pictures of familiar objects or places, describing one of them orally to the child, and asking the child to identify the one described.

Vance, H., and Hankins, N. Teaching intervention for defective auditory reception. *Academic Therapy*, 1975, *11*(1), 69–78. Reprinted by permission of Academic Therapy, San Rafael, Calif.

In each of these areas, additional tasks can be devised as individual situations demand. In some cases, the tasks should be considerably more complex than these examples. Sometimes, the activities will need to be simplified even further. Regardless of the situation, the assessment procedure needs to examine the five categories of auditory short term memory, auditory discrimination, auditory recognition, and auditory comprehension.

One might find that a child's skills in each of these major areas are more than adequate, yet there appears to be an attentional deficit with respect to the child's auditory abilities. In such cases, an informal checklist to help the teacher determine the child's overall listening behavior can be of considerable value. It may simply be a question of helping this particular child learn how to assume a better listening "posture." To collect the necessary information, the teacher might use a checklist such as the following:

A Simple Checklist of Listening Behavior

Name: _____   *Yes*   *No*

1. Does the child consistently request to have directions repeated?   ____   ____

2. Does the child appear to be easily distracted when presentations are being made in class?   ____   ____

3. Does the child appear to understand what is expected when assignments are given?   ____   ____
4. Does the child frequently participate in class discussions?   ____   ____
5. Is the child able to pick out inconsistencies in the conversations of others?   ____   ____
6. Does the child frequently complete the wrong pages in the workbook, or do inappropriate homework assignments?   ____   ____
7. Are requests, messages, or informational items orally presented to the child frequently misinterpreted resulting in misinformed parents or guardians?   ____   ____
8. Does the child not hear you so often that it has become annoying?   ____   ____
9. Are the other children in class complaining about the child's behavior in small group activities because the child does not seem to "listen"?   ____   ____
10. Does the child consistently have problems on the playground with peers because of misinformation regarding the rules for a particular game?   ____   ____

Depending on the answers to these questions, the teacher might find it appropriate to meet with the child to explain the need for closer auditory attention. Naturally, the session will be the first of many, but it might result in making the child a better "listener" in a wider variety of situations.

It might be possible to assist a child who has an attentional deficit by developing a personalized checklist that the child can frequently consult. The child might place such a chart or list on the desk just prior to a lesson, a storytime session, a guest speaker, or during show-and-tell as a reminder of what kinds of behaviors are expected. The actual design of the checklist should be developed with the child and be attractive, simple to read and to follow, and be durable enough to withstand numerous uses. Regardless of the final form the questionnaire takes, it should include questions of the following nature:

Getting Ready to Listen!

1. I have to remember now to get ready to listen. What are some of the things that I should ask myself to do?   Yes   No
   a. Am I comfortable?   ____   ____
   b. Am I in a location where I can see and hear?   ____   ____
   c. Should I move now so I will not be uncomfortable later?   ____   ____
   d. Am I ready to focus my attention on the speaker?   ____   ____
2. Am I ready now to concentrate?
   a. Have I really worked to push other thoughts out of my mind?   ____   ____
   b. Am I ready now to think about what the speaker is going to say?   ____   ____
   c. Am I going to listen carefully so I can ask questions when the speaker says things I may not understand or that I would like more information about?   ____   ____

    d. Am I ready to determine the main idea of the speaker's
       presentation?   ____   ____
3. Am I going to be able to evaluate the speaker's presentation?
    a. Am I going to take advantage of the speaker's clues (such
       as, first, second, on-the-other-hand, and in conclusion) to
       help me organize the presentation?   ____   ____
    b. When the speaker is done, and if there is time, am I going
       to be able to ask questions about the presentation?   ____   ____
    c. Am I going to be sure to make up my own mind as to
       whether or not I agree with the speaker?   ____   ____

      This checklist, which is a modification of a student checklist for listen-
ing behavior developed by Kopp (1967) could prove to be a useful tool in
developing good listening skills on the part of the unattentive child.
      In many instances, the teacher working with the mildly handicapped
child to develop aural language abilities, suspects that the difficulty in acquiring a facility with aural language to be the result of a cross-modal perception
dysfunction. Here, the mildly handicapped child is experiencing difficulty
with attentive listening or with auditory comprehension because of a failure
to integrate the images seen (e.g., the nonverbal expessions of the speaker;
the relationship of graphs, charts, illustrations, and pictures that might be
presented) with the comments being made. Such an inability to see necessary
relationships between graphics and spoken language can severely limit the
degree to which information is retained. Whenever cross-modal perceptional
dysfunction is suspected as the source of the mildly handicapped child's
problem, the teacher should devise informal assessment procedures to pinpoint the actual modalities involved. In these situations, it would be wise to
require that the child perform tasks that use two modalities in order to successfully complete the task. Vance and Hankins (1975) suggest the following:

In order to:	*Have the child:*
Assess visual to auditory abilities	Look at a pattern of dots and dashes and repeat it in rhythmical form on a drum.
Determine auditory to visual abilities	Listen to a rhythmical beat and select the matching visual pattern of dots and dashes from several alternatives.
Assess auditory to visual-motor skills	Listen to a rhythmical beat and transfer it to a visual form by writing out matching dots and dashes.
Determine visual to auditory-verbal abilities	Look at pictures and answer the questions: "Which begins with /f/? Which rhymes with coat? Which has a short /o/ sound?"
Assess auditory-verbal to visual skills	Discuss with you a picture you have described to the child and choose the picture you described from a set that includes the stimulus picture and some other similar pictures.

By developing additional tasks appropriate for each of the cross-modal categories cited here, an informal aural language inventory can be constructed which might prove useful in isolating a corresponding perceptual area that has been interfering with the child's overall listening abilities.

Regardless of the assessment procedure used, the teacher will find that time spent determining the child's abilities with respect to auditory memory, sensitivity, discrimination abilities, recognition, comprehension, and cross-modal capabilities will provide information valuable in constructing additional aural language activities. The basis for the aural language component of the language arts curriculum must be the child. By developing an informal assessment technique, the teacher can obtain useful information concerning a child's listening skills. The immediacy and relevancy of a locally constructed informal assessment inventory for aural language makes it an extremely valuable tool for the language arts teacher.

Emphasizing Aural Skills in the Classroom

Once the teacher has determined the extent to which listening skills need to be introduced into the curriculum, a pattern for instruction can be devised. It is important that each teacher introduce into the classroom a systematic program for instruction in listening skills. Many different elements and features might be incorporated throughout the year, but, in general, the language arts teacher who can successfully develop aural language skills is one who establishes and maintains a routine for instruction in listening skills.

Language arts teachers have traditionally experimented with listening centers, listening walks, listening time-outs, and similar aural-language-related activities. In many classrooms, especially at the primary level, listening skills are stressed at a particular time of the day. It is not uncommon to find that daily show-and-tell activities, regular storytimes, and beginning reading instruction are all directed toward developing an awareness of good listening skills. Frequently, teachers will stress listening skills during these regular activities by:

- Establishing a set of rules to govern behavior during these specific times each day.
- Focusing children's attention on a particular topic, story, or activity.
- Eliminating distractions in the room.
- Rearranging the physical environment for a short period of time each day during storytime, show-and-tell presentations, or reading instruction.
- Providing an incentive for "good listening," such as an extension of the activity time.

Many teachers find, too, that in addition to using specific periods each day, numerous opportunities to develop aural language skills occur as a regular part of each school day. The teacher may see these naturally occurring events as appropriate times to stress listening skills. These might include any of the following:

- Morning announcements over the P.A. system
- Opening classroom ceremonies
- Attendance taking
- Lunch and milk counts
- Collection and distribution of papers or completed work
- Preparation for travel through the school building
- Recreational activities on the playground or in the gym
- Direction giving for homework or assignments
- Individual conferences
- During spelling lessons, math, science, or social studies
- In the completion of special projects
- During closing activities such as room clean-up, furniture rearrangement, or line-ups

These and similar activities all serve to establish particular settings and situations in which aural skills can be emphasized. By regularly stressing listening skills during such periods, the classroom environment can become one that encourages good listening behavior.

The Listening Center

A listening center can be established in a classroom. Center teaching has become widespread recently and has been used successfully in all the content areas. In language arts, the aural language component of the curriculum lends itself well to learning center activities.

The center concept revolves around the individualization of instruction. Each center in the classroom is designed to function independently. If properly constructed, the center serves as a vehicle for introducing new ideas and activities into the classroom, and as a means for children to select specific skills on which to focus attention. In most centers, activities are self-correcting. Because learning centers do not require constant monitoring by the teacher, once they are established in a classroom, they can serve to supplement the instructional program.

Since the aural language skills by their very nature necessitate auditory attention, the teacher can construct a listening center to be used throughout the day. In a listening center one might include:

- a record player with headsets
- tape recorders
- pre-recorded cassette tapes
- blank tapes
- a collection of records, both old and new
- a radio
- an assortment of musical instruments
- mystery canisters (film containers filled with various objects)
- bottles with water at different levels
- the makings for home-made musical instruments
- scripts that can be read into the tape recorder
- newspapers for radio news casts
- a telephone
- an intercom
- walkie-talkies
- a movie projector with films
- materials for various art and craft projects that require direction giving
- booklets for recording sounds heard today, or favorite sounds, or unusual sounds
- stories, poems, or plays that can be read, or be recorded for others to listen to

These represent only a few of the many different items that could be introduced to a child through a listening center. Because of the open-ended nature of the center, a wide range of listening activities can be developed from the various materials placed there. By writing a set of instructional cards, the teacher can direct a child to focus attention on various listening skills (e.g., auditory discrimination, auditory retention, and auditory comprehension). These center activities can reinforce and supplement whatever formal instruction might be taking place in the classroom.

It is recommended that the number of children permitted to work in the listening center at any one time be limited. The teacher should determine how the available space can be best utilized and should establish guidelines regarding the maximum number of students in the center at any time. In addition, it is recommended that the listening activities be short in duration, and that a wide array be available for each listening skill area. There should be structured activities that require specific responses (e.g., "Listen for the sound of a horn and mark your copy of the story to show where you heard the horn.") as well as open-ended activities that permit creative responses. By developing a listening center and by making available many different listening activities, the teacher is providing multiple opportunities for children to develop skills in aural language.

Stimulating Aural Skill Development

Kachur (1971) has written that "a question examined in the 1955 and 1963 ASCD (Association for Supervision and Curriculum Development) reviews of research in the language arts—one that continues to receive attention from investigators—is whether skills in listening actually can be taught" (p. 19). When one considers that there is still some question as to the effectiveness of instruction in listening behavior, one might justly wonder whether or not time spent developing "good listening skills" is indeed time well spent. Perhaps listening skills can not be taught. Perhaps it is true that the ability to be a "good listener" is a unique personality trait that is possessed naturally by some people and is lacked by others. Fortunately, however, such is *not* the case. Research has shown that listening skills can be improved through instruction (Shane & Mulry, 1963; Lundsteen, 1964).

If it is quite likely that specific instruction in listening skills will result in improved abilities to respond to the spoken word, what are some possible alternatives for instruction, and what are some goals and objectives that can be established for this component of the language arts? The following objectives and activities are designed to stimulate the acquisition of listening skills. Each objective or goal is presented here as a framework for listening skill instruction. The accompanying activities are suggested ways in which the requirements of the objectives can be met. The framework for the selection of these activities and for the stated goals is taken from Smith's text titled *Creative Teaching of the Language Arts in the Elementary School* (1973).

Goal 1—*To teach children how to listen attentively in those situations that call for focusing of attention*

Suggested Activities	Instructional Strategies
1. Use as many "natural" situations as possible to reinforce attentive listening behaviors. Naturally occurring situations include: organizing the class into groups, recess activities, plays, assignment giving, attendance taking, group lessons, announcements, P.E. class activities, report giving, oral reading by the teacher or other students, and all audience style activities.	Teachers should plan to use these "natural" classroom events to explain the need for attentive listening. The teacher might point out specifics to be attended to, such as the order in which names are called, anticipation of one's own story being announced, or rules for a game.

185

Suggested Activities	*Instructional Strategies*
2. Use each situation in which directions are being given as an opportunity to "pay close attention."	A major portion of the day is spent in direction giving. Whether the situation involves behavior in the classroom, on the playground, in a new game, or during an art project, attentive listening skills can be taught in conjunction with direction giving. As in the previous activity, the emphasis is on *reminding* students of the need to pay close attention. It may be sufficient to simply refer to the use of some device such as the "putting on of your listening ears" to reinforce the attentive listening behavior. In other cases, as a preliminary to the direction giving, the teacher might want to review steps that have been discussed regarding "how to get ready to listen."
3. Use those reading assignments that involve oral reading.	Prior to reading to a group or the entire class, the teacher should reinforce the need for attentive listening skills by asking the children to listen for the answers to *specific* questions. The oral reading activity becomes a real opportunity to use attentive listening skills. These *specific* questions should be presented to the children at the beginning of the story and should involve character and plot references and characteristics of specific items in the story, such as, how many wings did the flying car have?
4. Use the classroom listening center specifically, for a period of time, for attentive listening skill activities.	If the classroom has a listening center, the teacher can introduce prerecorded tapes of particular environmental sounds that require very careful listening to identify. In much the same fashion, poems, records, and taped conversations or interviews can be made use of in conjunction with worksheets asking *specific* questions to develop attentive listening skills. The listening center may well be the best place in which to introduce activities that are unusual in nature (popular musical selections, for example) that do not necessarily fit into the other content areas.
5. Use a child's musical interest to develop attentive listening skills.	Children learning to play a musical instrument through the school music department or band program are constantly called on to attend carefully to notes, rhythms, and tones. By introducing musical instruments (i.e., simple, inexpensive rhythm instruments) into the classroom for all the children to use, the necessary lessons will all involve attentive listening.

Goal 2—*To teach children to identify those situations that call for appreciative listening behaviors*

Suggested Activities	Instructional Strategies
1. Use guest speakers in the classroom.	Reinforce appreciative listening skills by exposing the children to new and interesting concepts and ideas. One of the best vehicles is guest speakers. The teacher must prepare the class *prior to* the event by emphasizing the need to listen for new ideas, new topics, and overall themes.
2. Use music or story recordings as background for other classroom activities.	Appreciative listening is "taught" only to the extent that opportunities to listen to various selections *for their own intrinsic value to the listener* are provided. It is important to make selections frequently and to use them as purposeful background for related activities. By tying a musical selection into a writing or drawing activity, for example, students learn to appreciate the selection for the mood it can create, the activity it can stimulate, or the memories it can evoke.
3. Make greater use of audio-visual media in the classroom.	Often movies, slides, or filmstrips can be introduced into the classroom *not as a direct* supplement to the lesson at hand but rather as a vehicle for the teaching of appreciative listening skills. In these situations the audio-visual is presented for the pleasure and excitement it can generate.
4. Use choral speaking activities more frequently.	Choral speaking activities are still one of the best alternatives available to teach appreciative listening skills. The involvement choral speaking demands is instrumental in teaching children to appreciate the overall affect cooperative speaking activities can produce. It is essential in all choral speaking activities that the teacher record the event in order to provide feedback to the class.
5. Plan and take frequent listening walks around the school, both indoors and outdoors.	It is important to emphasize that appreciate listening behavior is not *only* for formalized settings. To have an effective appreciative listening skill development program, time should be taken to systematically "listen" to environmental sounds. Once the walk has been completed, children should be encouraged to comment on the sounds they heard and *how those sounds made them feel*. Such reporting should not be forced, but should be encouraged through writing, drawing, and conversation.

187

Goal 3—*To teach children the meaning of analytical listening and how to recognize situations that call for analysis of information*

Suggested Activities	*Instructional Strategies*
1. Use the other content areas to teach analytical listening skills.	More opportunities are perhaps available to the teacher to teach analytical listening skills than attentive, appreciative, or marginal listening. The reason should be obvious—most of what goes on in the classroom, be it mathematics, social studies, science, art, language arts, or reading, all require that the information or task at hand be analyzed.
	In *mathematics* instruction, for example, solving of word problems requires analysis of the components of the problem, especially when presented to the class orally. Some structure must be developed to organize information for computation. Here analytical listening is a prerequisite for the solution.
	In *reading* assignments, children are required to listen for specific events, specific information, supporting details, or conflicting facts. Such assignments should not presuppose that the children are capable of listening to the orally presented passage or story, but should include reference to the need to analyze what is heard systematically in order to answer the questions posed.
2. Capitalize on situations involving moral decisions or social matters affecting an individual, the entire class, or a community.	During the course of the year too, it is likely that discussions will take place concerning moral dilemmas or social problems. In each of these cases, whether they are based on classroom occurrences or on hypothetical situations, the teacher can capitalize on the need to listen analytically to the course of events or the circumstances in order to forward a solution to the problem.
3. Use the oral reports of other students as a basis for teaching analytical listening behaviors.	When children are requested to give oral reports, peers in the audience could assist in the "evaluation" process by listening analytically to determine the quality of the presentation in terms of sequence of events, supporting details, emotional impact, comparisons that are drawn, judgments that are made, inferences, and the extent to which information presented can be considered instruc-

Suggested Activities   *Instructional Strategies*

tional or useful. This process can be greatly facilitated by designing *with the class* a check sheet or evaluation form that would structure the audience's observations and reactions.

Goal 4—*To teach children to identify those settings that require only marginal listening behaviors*

1. Divide the classroom either temporarily or permanently into learning centers to reinforce and teach the importance of marginal listening skills.

In a classroom arranged into learning centers, children working on one task may need to listen only marginally to the other activity in the room. Such an environment can be artificially constructed by simply devoting one period during the day to small group activity. In these settings, the teacher can reinforce the need to listen to the activity in the room so that the small groups can judge their own activity levels.

2. Use dramatic presentations and the required rehearsals to teach marginal listening skills.

During the rehearsing for a play or dramatic presentation, characters must learn to listen for cues while attending to their own parts. Such activity is an excellent opportunity to explain the use of marginal listening, what it involves, and how a character in a play must depend on this ability for timing.

3. Use background music or story presentations again in the classroom, but without relating the music to a specific activity occurring in the classroom.

To develop children's awareness that many situations do not require attentive, appreciative, or analytical listening behaviors, the teacher should frequently expose the class to music as background. The music's object is *not* to serve as a direct stimulation for art or creative writing, but rather as something to be listened to sporadically. Attention is not focused on the background, but rather an ability to cope with the supplemental sounds is developed. Marginal listening differs from appreciative listening in terms of the degree to which attention must be focused. To appreciate something that is heard or seen, one must examine various characteristics carefully and make decisions about the arrangement of those elements, e.g., does it please me or not? Marginal listening does not require such decision making.

These particular goals and related activities might serve as a starting point for the listening component of a language arts curriculum. As the framework is implemented, the need for modification, adjustment, or expansion will become apparent. Each teacher will have to adapt Smith's categories of attentive, appreciative, analytic, and marginal listening behaviors to the particular class. In any event, these four elements can serve as the basis for programs and activities that develop listening abilities by both normal and mildly handicapped children.

The Teacher as a Listener

It has been suggested that a larger percentage of the child's day be spent in listening activities. The instructional strategy that has been presented in this chapter represents a procedure by which opportunities for aural skill development can be introduced into the classroom. Instruction in listening skills, however, is not sufficient to produce observable changes in a child's listening abilities. Any instructional program in aural language skill must be accompanied by reinforcement and modeling. The teacher's own listening skills need to be considered almost as carefully as those of the child's. For the listening skills component of the language arts program to be successful, the teacher must be a good listener, too. It is important that the teacher remember to:

- Show your interest in what the child is saying by commenting, asking questions, or verbally approving of the topic the child has elected to discuss.
- Avoid needless interruptions.
- Refer to situations that might be similar in nature to show that you are thinking about what the child said.
- Avoid distractions while in conversation with a child. Do not attempt to correct papers, make materials, or review projects while a child is attempting to communicate with you.
- Invite others to participate in the conversation. This expands the communication encounter to involve more people and indicates to the child that you as the teacher value what is being shared.
- Avoid unnecessary criticism of the child's comments.

Teachers often are unaware that they convey, either verbally or nonverbally, to young children the message that they are not listening. In verbal exchanges with children, teachers can become nonattenders, assumers, or word-pickers. Each of these characteristics of poor listeners interferes drastically with the teacher's ability to *listen* to what is being said.

Nonattending involves what might be referred to as daydreaming or wandering. In this situation, the teacher simply does not pay attention to what it is that the child is talking about. Nonattending is difficult for children to cope with because it may appear on the surface that the teacher is paying attention to what is being said, but in reality the teacher's thoughts are miles away. Such a communication encounter frustrates children because the teacher does not provide verbal reinforcement for the child's comments, yet the nonverbal clues are that the teacher is listening and is interested. It is only after some verbal dismissal or obvious change in the position of the body, facial expression, or physical location that the child realizes that he was not being paid attention to. The teacher should be careful to avoid becoming a nonattender.

The teacher as an assumer makes the mistake of answering questions, finishing comments, and making statements even before the child has finished speaking. In these situations, the teacher assumes the answer to the question or the response to the comment that the child is attempting to share even before the child completes a sentence. Teachers who are assumers are easily identified since they tend to dominate a conversation, to be aggressive in their verbal styles, and to interrupt the child more frequently than usual. Assumers generally believe that they are quick-on-the-draw verbally, "sharp" listeners, and "in-tune" with the speaker. These beliefs, however, are often the exact opposite of the real situation. Assumers simply *think* they know what is going to happen next verbally, and more likely than not are entirely wrong in their assumptions.

The word-picker focuses attention on specific words that appear in the speech of the speaker. The teacher who is a word-picker permits a child to only partially complete a sentence or to make a statement because of some one particular word that is used. In many cases, the word that is isolated by the teacher has been mispronounced or misused by the child. The entire exchange focuses only on the word that the child used (or attempted to use) and never deals with the topic or the issues raised by the child. The word-picker has a persistent approach to communication and seems to verge on being hyper-correct regarding word usage. This overemphasis on correctness interferes with the message relay process and serves to greatly inhibit the flow of conversation. Very young children will become reluctant to share experiences with a teacher who fails to appreciate what is being said and who picks apart statements they make.

The teacher needs to be aware that personal listening style greatly influences the behavior of children. It is unreasonable to expect that children will develop their own abilities as listeners, if the one individual with whom they interact most frequently fails to model good listening skills.

SUMMARY

O'Donnell (1975) in a review of recent research on listening skill development in the classroom cites Wolf's (1973) findings that:

> Most activities that take place in the classroom require the use of some listening and speaking skills, but they (the teachers) lack structure for the improvement of these skills. Such activities as 'Show and Tell,' storytime, giving directions, or explanation, large group instruction or small group discussion, could all be structured to teach important listening or speaking skills. (In O'Donnell, 1975, pp. 1080–1081)

It is apparent that the development of listening skills goes beyond the incorporation of activities into the language arts curriculum. As has been pointed out in this chapter, the selection, design, and utilization of aural language activities in the classroom are not extremely difficult to accomplish. While the task certainly does require creative behavior on the part of the teacher, the proliferation of materials and the ease with which activities that focus on auditory skills can be developed considerably reduces the time investment that might otherwise be required.

The classroom teacher must focus attention on the manner in which the activities are organized and the degree to which they have a real impact on the children's skill development. The only way such information can be obtained is through assessment. Without a procedure for determining the ability level of the child, the aural language component of the curriculum becomes nothing more than isolated activities employed only as the need arises. Listening skills must be integrated into the overall instructional day.

The teacher of the mildly handicapped child must be sensitive to those signs and signals that indicate a possible aural language deficit. The teacher may need to design a program and sequence of activities that best responds to a child experiencing a problem in auditory attention. Activities that require listening comprise the core of this component of the language arts curriculum. The structure within which they exist, however, and the goals that they define, provide the rationale for their inclusion into the curriculum. The teacher of the mildly handicapped child has to realize, that in many cases, the child's inability to integrate perceptual skills will influence significantly the kinds of activities that can be used, the level of complexity that is appropriate, and the degree to which variety can be introduced into the school day.

This chapter has established that children spend a considerable amount of the school day in listening activities, yet the amount of instructional time spent in developing listening skills is remarkably low. It has only been within recent years that a greater interest has been taken in the role auditory comprehension plays in learning. As a result, greater emphasis is being placed on this previously forgotten aspect of the language arts curriculum.

In summary, the following quote from O'Donnell (1975) seems appropriate:

> In incorporating listening activities in the classroom, Sam Duker, in "Goals of Teaching Listening Skills in the Elementary School," alerts the teacher to four key principles that should be kept in mind by anyone interested in attaining the goals of a good listening program:
>
> 1. Listening activity in the classroom should be a pleasurable rather than a threatening experience.
> 2. Daily class activities should be so planned that the amount of listening required of children is not overpoweringly and impossibly great.
> 3. Listening in a classroom situation should not be confined to listening by the children to the teacher.
> 4. Classroom listening should be "for" rather than "at."
>
> (In O'Donnell, 1975, p. 108)

POINTS FOR DISCUSSION

1. Recent studies by Flanders and others have indicated that the amount of time children spend in listening activity approaches almost 66 percent of the school day. Working with a classmate, try to develop an observation schedule similar to those found in the chapter on communication that plots interaction patterns over a short period of time. Your analysis/observation format should be aimed at the frequency with which conversation is directed at children.

2. While it is recognized that activities require structure to be useful in the teaching of listening skills, they are still the keystone of the listening program. Look again at those activities included under the four goals for listening instruction included here and add several new activities to those present.

3. In this chapter, practical activities for listening skill development were organized around Smith's framework for teaching listening skills. Can you delineate other approaches to listening that are equally as valid? In your design of alternative frameworks, you may include aspects of Smith's goals for listening skill development.

4. It has been said that the greatest amount of emphasis on listening skill development needs to be placed at the primary level. Examine again the activities that have been included in this chapter and adapt them for use at the grade level you are most interested in teaching. You might wish to emphasize at the primary level more reading readiness listening activities for example. Exchange your suggestions with a classmate.

5. The assessment of a child's listening behavior is an activity extremely important to the overall success of the language arts program. In this chapter suggestions were provided as to how the teacher could design informal assessment inventories utilizing basic listening activities. One area of particular interest is that of

cross-modal perceptual abilities. Develop at least two additional testing situations for each of the five cross-modalities discussed.

REFERENCES

Amidon, E., and Flanders, N. *The role of the teacher in the classroom.* Minneapolis, Minn.: Paul Amidon & Associates, 1963, p. 44. In D. Hennings, *Mastering classroom communication: What interaction analysis tells the teacher.* Pacific Palisades, Calif.: Goodyear Publishing Co., 1975, p. 80.

Burns, P., and Broman, B. *The language arts in childhood education.* Chicago: Rand McNally & Co., 1975.

Duker, S. Goals of teaching listening skills in the elementary school. In H. Newman (Ed.), *Effective language arts practices in the elementary school: Selected readings.* New York: John Wiley & Sons, 1972, pp. 214–220.

Flanders, N. *Analyzing teaching behavior.* Reading, Mass.: Addison-Wesley, 1970. In Hennings, D. *Mastering classroom communication: What interaction analysis tells the teacher.* Pacific Palisades, Calif.: Goodyear Publishing Co., 1975, p. 80.

Fowler, R. The evaluation of auditory abilities in the appraisal of children with reading problems. In H. Smith (Ed.), *Perception and reading.* Newark, Delaware: International Reading Association, 1968.

Gearheart, B. R., and Weishahn, M. W. *The handicapped child in the regular classroom.* St. Louis, Mo.: C. V. Mosby Co., 1976.

Kachur, D. Having ears they hear not. In Shane, M., Walden, J., & Green, R. *Interpreting language arts research for the teacher.* Washington, D.C. Association for Supervision and Curriculum Development, 1971.

Kopp, O. W. The evaluation of oral language activities: Teaching and learning. *Elementary English,* 1967, *44,* 117. In Burns, P. & Broman, B. *The language arts in childhood education.* Chicago: Rand McNally & Co., 1975, p. 126.

Lerner, J. *Children with learning disabilities.* New York: Houghton Mifflin, 1971.

Lundsteen, S. Teaching and testing critical listening skills in the fifth and sixth grades. *Elementary English,* 1964, *41, 743–747.* In Shane, H., Walden, J., and Green, R. *Interpreting language arts research for the teacher.* Washington, D.C. Association for Supervision and Curriculum Development, 1971, p. 20.

O'Donnell, M. ERIC/RCS Report: Are you listening? Are you listening? *Language Arts,* 1975, *52,* 1080–1084.

Rankin, P. *Listening ability.* Proceedings of the Ohio State Education Conference, 1929, Ohio State University, pp. 172–183. In Burns, P. & Broman, B. *The language arts in childhood education.* Chicago: Rand McNally & Co., 1975, pp. 100–101.

Shane, H., and Mulry, J. *Improving language arts instruction through research.* Washington, D.C.: Association for Supervision and Curriculum Development, 1963. In Shane H., Walden, J., & Green, R. *Interpreting language arts research for the teacher.* Washington, D.C.: Association for Supervision and Curriculum Development, 1971, p. 20.

Shane, H., Walden, J., and Green, R. *Interpreting language arts research for the teacher.* Washington, D.C.: Association for Supervision and Curriculum Development, 1971.

Smith, J. A. *Creative teaching of the language arts in the elementary school* (2nd ed.). Boston, Ma.: Allyn & Bacon, Inc., 1973.

Vance, H., and Hankins, N. Teaching intervention for defective auditory reception. *Academic Therapy,* 1975, *11*(1), 69–78.

Wolf, R. *A curriculum guide for the teaching of listening and speaking skills to the primary grades in the public schools of Madison, Connecticut.* M. S. Press, Southern Connecticut State College, 1973.

195

7

Oral Language Skill Development

It seems as though everyone knows which student in the class is the "best" at expressing ideas, answering questions, or leading discussions. Teachers, administrators, and children alike seem to have an affinity for classmates who can hold their own when it comes to oral communication. How very often do teachers find themselves commenting on the verbal ability of a particular child? How frequently do conversations in the teacher's lounge center on that one seemingly precocious child who dominates each and every conversation throughout the day?

By the same token, it is quite likely that in the very same class, in the very same school, there are a very large number of children who simply do not distinguish themselves at all when it comes to oral reporting, conversation, discussion, or idea sharing. This section of the school population tends to also be the topic of numerous teacher-to-teacher conferences. Here, however, rather than focusing on the real "pleasures" of teaching, and the "joy" of having so-and-so in class, the dialogue revolves around just what can be done to improve the oral communication skills of these children.

Facilitating Oral Language Development

Most schools place some emphasis on the development of oral language skills. In the primary as well as in the middle grades, there are usually some activities that engage children in dialogue, conversation, question asking or answering, or a form of oral reporting. Yet, the degree to which oral language in the classroom is encouraged and is made a regular part of the school day is, in our opinion, far too limited.

To arrive at some technique to facilitate the development of oral language skills in terms of both *quantity* (the extent to which oral language activities are employed) and *quality* (the impact exchanges and encounters have), the teacher should to consider the following:

1. How can I adapt the classroom environment to promote oral language?
2. How sensitive am I to my own "teacher talk," both the verbal and nonverbal characteristics of my actions?
3. How able am I to cope with disabilities and to improve the speech of the mildly handicapped child?
4. What kinds of opportunities and stimuli do I provide that encourage communication encounters among children in the class?

The teacher *can* influence significantly the degree to which oral language skills are made use of during the school day. The degree to which success is achieved depends primarily on how the teacher answers these four questions.

Adapting the Physical Environment

How does a teacher begin to respond to the question concerning the adaptation of the physical environment? One possible approach that could be taken involves the separation of classroom management skills from the development of oral language skills. Such an attitude, however, is not recommended. What one is capable of doing in the classroom with respect to oral communication *is* a function of how one elects to arrange the furniture, schedule the day, assign the students, and manage their time. Oral language activity is to a great extent actually determined by these organizational considerations.

Consider Figure 7.1 which depicts a typical elementary school classroom. As you examine this diagram, ask yourself the following questions:

1. How does this classroom encourage communication among children? How does it inhibit it?
2. What does the teacher's role seem to be in this setting? What types of encounters does this situation seem to call for? How could it be altered?
3. What opportunities exist here for the introduction of new and unusual stimuli?

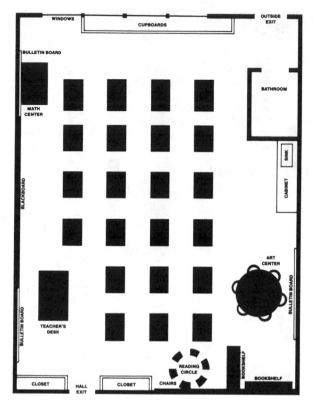

Source: Blackburn, J., and Powell, W. One at a time all at once—The creative teacher's guide to individualized instruction without anarchy. Pacific Palisades, Calif.: Copyright © 1976 by Goodyear Publishing Co. Reprinted by permission.

FIGURE 7.1   The Classroom Environment

4. To what extent can these children experiment with their environment? How can they influence the degree to which they interact with their peers?

5. How flexible does this classroom appear to be in terms of shifting to meet the needs of handicapped students? Unusual instructional programs? Displays or demonstrations?

It should be obvious from the majority of your answers to these questions that this particular classroom setting is not designed to encourage interaction. It is quite likely that the responses that occur are elicited primarily by the teacher and *not* by the other children.

Now examine Figure 7.2 and ask yourself the same questions applied to Figure 7.1. In this situation the following is quite likely:

1. The emphasis on teacher directed behavior is reduced considerably.

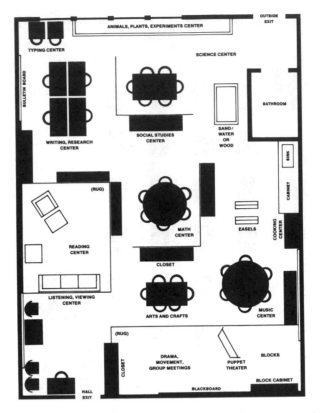

Source: Blackburn, J., and Powell, W. *One at a time all at once—The creative teacher's guide to individualized instruction without anarchy.* Pacific Palisades, Calif.: Copyright © 1976 by Goodyear Publishing Co. Reprinted by permission.

FIGURE 7.2   A Modified Classroom Environment

2.   There are numerous opportunities for interaction among children and that conversation is more likely to take place.

3.   There is a built-in degree of flexibility in this classroom that permits reorganization, depending on the instructional activities planned or occurring.

4.   Children have a greater number of opportunities to select both working locations and partners.

5.   New stimuli can be readily introduced into this setting without upsetting the balance of the organizational pattern.

There are probably a dozen or so other observations that can be made about this particular classroom environment in terms of the manner in which it can serve to facilitate oral language. Any teacher who wants to improve oral communication skills must consider the physical organization of the classroom.

The Mildly Handicapped Child and the Classroom Environment

The models presented here have focused on classroom environments in general. One must consider now how these particular room arrangements affect the mildly handicapped child. What might the possible effects be of having a mildly handicapped child in the classroom described in Figure 7.1 as opposed to Figure 7.2? How might the oral communication patterns among children differ when a mildly handicapped child is introduced into the classroom depicted in Figure 7.1 as opposed to Figure 7.2? How might the teacher respond to the mildly handicapped child in terms of oral language encounters in the Figure 7.1 classroom as opposed to the Figure 7.2 classroom?

These are just a few of the many questions that can be raised with respect to oral language, the classroom physical environment, and the mildly handicapped child. They are representative, however, of the overall concern teachers should have for the oral language development of the mildly handicapped child as affected by the physical environment.

Consider Figure 7.3 which is a modification of the traditional classroom depicted earlier. In this situation, the triangle represents the mildly

△ = Mildly handicapped child

FIGURE 7.3   The Classroom Environment and the Mildly Handicapped Child

handicapped child. Do you realize that in this setting, if a teacher is not sensitive to interaction patterns, the following could very well be true:

- The mildly handicapped child will be isolated from all but a small number of students in the class.
- Unless the teacher is consciously aware of the mildly handicapped child in the classroom during the majority of the day, many opportunities to engage the child in dialogue will be missed.
- The mildly handicapped child has no flexibility in selecting classmates with whom to interact.
- Other children have no freedom to elect to converse with the mildly handicapped child.
- The mildly handicapped child cannot choose when to become a member of a group discussion or conversation.
- All interactions between the mildly handicapped child and the other children are a function of the teacher and do not occur at random.

In contrast to this particular situation, the classroom environment that is built along more informal lines and models more closely the modified classroom shown in Figure 7.2 is going to provide the teacher and the mildly handicapped child with more alternatives. The degree to which interactions can be encouraged, the extent to which exchanges can take place, and the freedom the child has to select working companions is generally much greater in such a setting.

Consider now Figure 7.4 which depicts the mildly handicapped child in the modified classroom setting. In considering this situation, the teacher should realize the following:

- There will be multiple opportunities for children to engage in conversation, discussion, and problem solving with each other, and therefore, with the mildly handicapped child.
- The teacher will be able to group, organize for instruction, and modify materials or presentations for the mildly handicapped child as a natural course of action. Such "changes" would not single out the mildly handicapped child and would be more a part of the daily class routine.
- Implied in the room arrangement is the freedom to move about as assignment, topics, and activities warrant. Mildly handicapped children can readily select working partners or those individuals with whom they easily relate and do so in an unobtrusive manner.
- Resource personnel, other adults, or other professionals can observe, interact, and implement intervention programs *within* the classroom environment because the built-in flexibility for rearrangement, regrouping, or modification of the environment.

$\triangle$ = Mildly handicapped child

FIGURE 7.4   *The Modified Classroom Environment and the Mildly Handicapped Child*

There are still other possible ways in which the modified classroom environment can influence the teacher and the mildly handicapped child. Those that have been listed should demonstrate the numerous advantages in terms of communication skill development to be derived from such a classroom arrangement. It is simply a matter of teacher choice as to whether or not this very important natural resource is tapped.

In addition to the furniture arrangement in the classroom, the sensitive teacher also takes into account the manner in which the mildly handicapped child is integrated for instruction, small group meetings, or discussions. The following are seven grouping patterns for discussion that are variations on the total group discussion model dominated by the teacher or group leader.

Model 1	*Model 2*
Total group discussion is guided by the teacher or a student leader. This type of discussion generally allows for less participation by any one person. It may give the teacher	With most of the group acting as one group, a small group can spin off from the total group to discuss. At the end of the discussion, the large group and the small group

a clearer idea of what has been covered.

Teacher

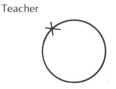

can share the results. Sometimes teachers find this technique useful in introducing the idea and responsibility of independent, small group work.

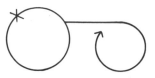

Source: Fitzgerald, S. Teaching discussion skills and attitudes. *Language Arts,* 1975, *52*(8), 1094–1096. Copyright © 1975 by the National Council of Teachers of English. Reprinted by permission of the publisher and the author.

Model 3

Two or more spin-off groups can be used to meet certain interests or needs that will contribute to the total group topic.

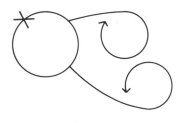

Model 4

In a fishbowl technique, one group of students discusses a topic while the rest of the class sits and listens. This pattern requires that children be comfortable in front of their peers, and it should be used when the teacher is sure the children are ready to volunteer for this exposed type of discussion.

Model 5

An open chair (or two) gives a variation on the fishbowl technique. Any student from the observer group who wants to ask a question or make a statement can join the inner circle temporarily and then return to his/her seat.

Model 6

A panel discussion may be a more formal type of reporting with some, but more limited, discussion among the panelists and limited response from the listeners when the panel is finished.

Model 7
Small group work probably allows the most interaction by the most students. It requires that the children have a clear understanding of goals and processes.

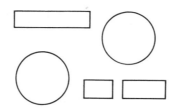

The alert teacher should realize that these patterns for grouping all have particular advantages for the mildly handicapped child. Consider how these suggested arrangements can possibly impact the teacher and the mildly handicapped child:

Model   *Possible Impact*

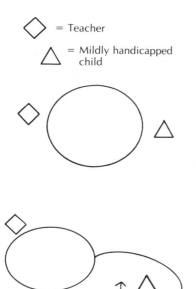

◇ = Teacher

△ = Mildly handicapped
    child

Model 1
In large group discussions, the teacher can place the mildly handicapped child within the direct line of sight. Attention can be focused on the child, behaviors can be monitored, and the teacher can encourage participation by the child in the large group discussion—something that might not happen independently.

Model 2
The teacher can select a group of children to explore a topic further and can consciously include the mildly handicapped child. A degree of independence is encouraged, yet it has been structured for success.

205

Model	Possible Impact

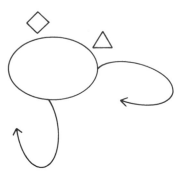

Model 3
If the topic under discussion generates a great deal of interest, more than one spin-off group might be necessary. It could be appropriate to maintain contact with the mildly handicapped child to continue to encourage involvement and interaction.

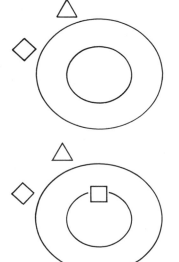

Model 4
It is not recommended that the teacher place the mildly handicapped child in a situation that might inhibit interaction. The fishbowl technique requires that a select group of students be chosen to discuss a topic under the observation of the remainder of the class. It might be wise to place the mildly handicapped child on the outside circle as an observer of the interactions until there is evidence that the child can be successfully placed in the discussion ring.

Model 5
When the teacher decides that an open chair can be introduced into the discussion pattern, the mildly handicapped child should be given the option to occupy or to not occupy the chair. Depending on the degree to which the child has been interacting and has expressed an interest in the topic, a decision can be made to include the child in the discussion circle. It might be best, however, to let the child decide whether or not to occupy the vacant seat. Because a single open chair might be rather intimidat-

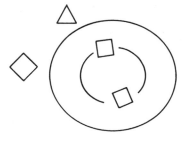

ing to the child, including another seat gives the child the option to participate even though someone else may have elected to go first. In fact, seeing other children, and possibly a friend, in the open chair might encourage the child to participate. The double open chair concept can be utilized very effectively.

Model 6

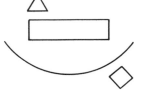

Certainly, the panel discussion is a much more formalized procedure for encouraging interactions. It can and should be used occasionally to familiarize students with the technique. The teacher can elect to include the mildly handicapped child on the panel or in the audience as the topic demands. One should not make the mistake of thinking that the mildly handicapped child cannot be a panel member.

Model 7

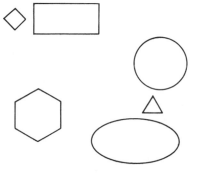

The small group pattern for discussion has already been dealt with in terms of the overall classroom arrangement. What is reinforced here is the fact that the mildly handicapped child can be integrated easily into any of the small groups that might be constructed as the result of a particular presentation or activity.

In practice then, it is possible to alter the classroom physical environment to encourage oral communication. Both the room arrangement and student grouping patterns can be effectively manipulated by the teacher who is sensitive to the role played by such factors.

Developing a Sensitivity to Teacher Talk

By far one of the most significant ingredients in the development of oral communication skills in children is that of the role of the primary caretaker. It is the teacher who serves as the primary model in many children's lives. Given that a very large percentage of the child's waking hours are spent in the teacher's care, consideration has to be given to the role that the teacher's own oral communications play in shaping the child's ability to express and communicate ideas.

What then should the teacher become sensitive to, verbally speaking? What is it about the speech of the teacher that should be examined most closely? Where should the emphasis be placed when one speaks of becoming sensitive to "teacher talk"?

Hennings (1975) believes strongly that the teacher's procedure for question asking, both the manner in which questions are asked *and* the manner in which they are constructed, is one major area of "teacher talk" that should be examined closely. Question asking according to Hennings (1975), "is a significant component of teaching" (p. 135). Since it occurs so frequently and is such an essential ingredient in instruction, the teacher must realize how questions influence the communication encounters that occur in the classroom.

With mildly handicapped children, the manner in which the question is asked is important. Many special needs youngsters need to have their attention focused prior to the asking of a question. When dealing with the mildly handicapped child, one should preface a question with the child's name. This alerts the child that attention is required, and the probability of achieving success with the oral interaction is increased dramatically. The respondent-question format guarantees that the question will be attended to.

In some cases, one might wish to focus the child's attention after the question has been posed. Here the question-respondent format calls for the teacher's forwarding of a question and then naming a child to respond. When encouraging the mildly handicapped child to participate in oral exchanges, the question-respondent format is a device that elicits a response from the mildly handicapped child who might not otherwise comment. Certainly, one would not want to constantly follow questions with specific names, but in some situations doing so results in the involvement of *all* the children in the class.

Questions do not always have to call for a single child response. Unison answers allow special needs children to participate even though they may not know specifically how it is they should be responding. The mildly handicapped child in this situation is afforded the opportunity to model the behaviors of the other class members and thereby not feel excluded. The benefits to be derived from this tactic should not be underestimated. Such an approach is highly recommended when concepts are being initially learned or practiced. It is not, however, a technique one would wish to utilize when assessing individuals.

Sanders (1966) maintains that classroom questions need to be structured in such a fashion that they involve various thinking processes. Sanders utilized the taxonomy of educational objectives developed by Benjamin Bloom (1956) as a basis for describing classroom question-asking techniques. Figure 7.5 is a representation of the manner in which Sanders adapted the elements of Bloom's taxonomy of educational objectives in the cognitive domain to describe those operations that can serve to guide the teacher in the question-asking process.

This particular representation of the thinking process implies that teachers, by virtue of the questions they ask, require students to perform particular mental and/or verbal operations. The seven categories of thinking found in Figure 7.5 stipulate, according to Sanders, that the following activities occur:

Categories	Related Activities
Memory	The student recalls or recognizes the information.
Translation	The student changes information into a different symbolic form or language.
Interpretation	The student discovers relationships among facts, generalizations, definitions, values, and skills.
Application	The student solves a lifelike problem that requires the identification of the issue and the selection and use of appropriate generalizations and skills.
Analysis	The student solves a problem in the light of conscious knowledge of the parts and forms of thinking.
Synthesis	The student solves a problem that requires original thinking.
Evaluation	The student makes a judgment of good or bad, right or wrong, according to the standards he designates.

Source: Specified material from p. 3 in CLASSROOM QUESTIONS—WHAT KINDS? by Norris M. Sanders. Copyright © 1966 by Norris M. Sanders. Reprinted by permission of Harper & Row, Publishers, Inc.

It should also be apparent to the teacher that the various levels of thinking delineated in Figure 7.5 correspond to the overall learning process. In Sanders's model it might be said that those questions focusing on memory, translation, and interpretation correspond to initial learning activities— perhaps skill or concept development; that the application, analysis, and synthesis questions focus on retention and reinforcement of concepts or skills learned; and that the final level of question asking, evaluation, is in fact a stage of learning that stresses maintenance and review of concepts.

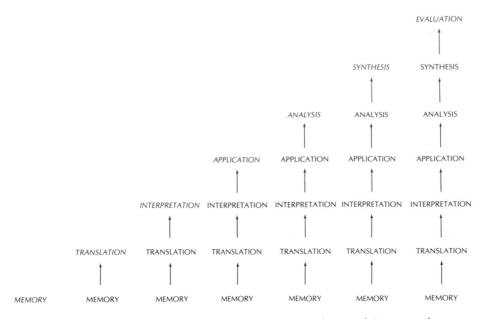

FIGURE 7.5   The Seven Categories for Question-Asking and Correspond-ing Mental Operations

While the cognitive activity of the child is determined by posed ques-tions, there is also a relationship to the verbal responses that the child is capable of making. A question that focuses on pure recall requires a consid-erably different oral response from a child than a question involving evalua-tion. The teacher who is committed to the development of oral language skills is responsible for consciously varying the types of questions asked to encourage responses that involve several different mental operations.

In addition to being aware of how questions are used, teachers can become sensitive to how they respond in a communication encounter, either with peers or with children. When placed in a setting that requires verbal exchanges, such as a discussion, meeting, or instructional program, what kind of posture does one tend to take verbally? Hennings (1975) maintains that the work of Bellack (1966) has shown that in the classroom the teacher plays a communication "game" in which moves are made to structure, so-licit, respond, or react to what has been said or done. Each of these particular activities can be described in the following manner:

In the role of	The teacher
Structurer	Tries to organize the conversation or exchange. The teacher might always seem to be saying, "O.K., let's get started here!" or "All right, that's enough of this, let's go on to something else." Generally speaking, the teacher as a structurer is concerned about the topic and about achieving closure.

In the role of	The teacher
Solicitor	Tries in a conversation to get students involved. The teacher seems to be interested in helping others express themselves and does not focus on structuring the conversation. As the solicitor, the focus is on the exchange of information by all the parties involved.
Responder	Behaves in much the same manner as the solicitor, except that the comments made now are generally replies to another's solicitation. The teacher as a responder could be thought of as one who does not initiate a conversation, but who volunteers information when spoken to and who will raise new and interesting points at the request of others. The teacher as the responder is pleasant, always answers sincerely, but does not take the lead.
Reactor	Moves to modify, adjust, rate, correct, qualify, and evaluate what students have said. The teacher as a reactor does not generally initiate a conversation, nor structure it. All the teacher in this role does, it seems, is *react*.

In the classroom the teacher moves constantly from one role to another. Depending on the situation, the topic, and the students, the teacher selects one role over another in order to engage children in conversation. However, it is important to realize that the maintenance of one role to the exclusion of another will result in the inhibiting of oral language exchanges. It is paramount that the teacher recognizes each of these postures and controls encounters by effectively moving between them as the situations demand.

Teacher Sensitivity to Nonverbal Aspects of Communication Encounters

It would certainly be an error to emphasize only the verbal aspects of teacher behaviors in facilitating children's oral language abilities. It has been noted that the teacher's attitude, as well as spoken behaviors, contributes to the quality of classroom interactions. Wilkinson (as found in Destefano & Fox, 1974, p. 64) reports that:

> Several American studies indicate that the attitude of the teacher may have considerable influence (on the language growth of children). Vocabulary growth was significantly greater under teachers whose pupils rated them high on a "warmth" scale (Christensen, 1960). On the other hand, authoritarian methods of teaching have been found to discourage talk and participation in discussion. (Lippitt & White, 1958; Ryans, 1961)

Such information leads one to suspect that care must be taken to convey to children that a sincere interest is being taken in their comments. The attitude of the teacher that says clearly to the young child, "I respect what you have to say and I want to hear you tell me about it" is bound to be considerably more productive than the "Don't bother me—I'm too busy attitude" that so often describes adult-child interactions.

The nonverbal elements of teacher behavior consist of quite a bit more than mere attitude. The use of gesture, the posture assumed, the tone of voice used, the distance maintained, and the forcefulness of eye contact are all factors that serve to inhibit or to facilitate a message. Teachers should be aware that the display of nonverbal signs that contradict or are in conflict with the spoken message are picked up by young children and are interpreted accordingly. A successful facilitator of oral language must manipulate the nonverbal as well as the verbal aspects of an exchange.

In a review of research related to the sensitivity of deviant populations (learning disabled, educable mentally retarded, deaf individuals, and psychiatric patients) to nonverbal aspects of the communication process, Thomas (1978) found evidence to support the contention that there are varying degrees of abilities to perceive nonverbal clues and cues in a communication encounter, and that nonverbal behaviors are an important and necessary ingredient in the communication system. Given this information, it should be clear to the teacher that mildly handicapped children as well as normal youngsters respond to nonverbal elements of a message.

Teachers should be aware of:

1. Their use of gesture, facial expressions, and tone of voice when interacting with children.
2. The need to be sensitive to the mildly handicapped child who may not perceive as easily as the normal youngster those signs that are intended to supplement a message.

It is perhaps equally as important that the teacher of the mildly handicapped child take time to emphasize through pantomime, dramatic activity, or role playing just how important nonverbal aspects of a communication encounter are. Here a teacher might focus on facial expressions, tone of voice, and eye movement to convey anger, suspicion, jealousy, envy, greed, or almost any other emotion. Such efforts, especially with the mildly handicapped child, should result in a noticeable improvement in communication effectiveness. Naturally, the best approach to take is to serve as a model and to focus attention on one's own actions as appropriate for instructional purposes.

It is not possible to modify teaching style or behaviors overnight—both verbal and nonverbal. It is understood that the process of becoming sensitive to these elements of "teacher talk" is a slow and deliberate one. However, to have a significant impact on the child's ability to develop oral language skills to provide an optimal environment for the utilization of such skills, the teacher's attention must be given to these characteristics of a communication encounter. By considering how attention can be focused on "teacher talk," a major step can be taken toward a heightened awareness of the teacher's role in the development of oral language skills.

Coping with Disabilities and Improving the Speech of the Mildly Handicapped Child

In earlier chapters, we attempted to point out some of the distinguishing characteristics of the mildly handicapped child. Figure 7.6 recaps those characteristics and suggests how they might possibly manifest themselves in terms of oral language abilities.

These particular characteristics can be helpful in identifying the child who may experience learning problems. However, in terms of assisting the teacher with the child's oral language development, they contain little instructional advice. To improve the oral communication ability of the mildly handicapped child, the teacher must be familiar with more specific aspects of the speech of the mildly handicapped child.

The speech of the mildly handicapped child is not always different from the speech of the normal youngster. It is not a forgone conclusion that, if a child is mildly handicapped, oral production will also be a problem. With the mildly handicapped child, one is more likely to be confronted with problems in *communication* that may include articulation disorders, dysfluencies, voice disorders, stuttering, and language and processing difficulties. In some situations, the teacher may deal with a child whose disability is clearly one mentioned (e.g., articulation or stuttering). In other cases, however, a combination of problems may result in an inability to organize and express ideas and information. These situations are considerably more complex and require more comprehensive treatment.

Since the teacher may be confronted with one, two, or possibly all of these contributors to an oral communication disability, it is necessary to examine each of them in a bit more detail. Before considering these difficulty areas, however, it is wise to heed the advice of Gearheart and Weishahn (1976) who state:

A question that must be considered before reviewing the major types of speech problems is—"When is a *difference* in speech sufficiently different or significant to consider it a *handicap?*" The various authorities appear to agree that a speech problem may be called a handicap if (1) it interferes with communication, (2) it causes the speaker to be maladjusted, or (3) it calls undue attention to the speech (as opposed to what the

With the characteristic of	There might be this impact on oral language
A low tolerance for frustration	The mildly handicapped child's low tolerance for frustration may result in frequent "flare-ups" when engaged in discussions or conversations. Such displays may discourage other children from involving the mildly handicapped child in group work, games, or activities. Thus, numerous opportunities for oral language usage are eliminated.
A poor self-concept	Mildly handicapped children who do not think highly of themselves will not readily engage in communication exchanges. The very fact that the child feels inadequate, inferior, or unable to function as well as other children may be enough to result in the self-elimination from situations that normally would be beneficial to the child.
A below-average ability to generalize and to conceptualize	Because the mildly handicapped child has difficulty relating some information to other situations, overall problem-solving abilities may suffer. This would result in the child's inability to respond to situations that are similar to those previously experienced, to contribute to discussions, group work, or activities that are the result of previously encountered information. The child is basically described as being "lost."
Having a play interest below those of peers	Certainly the ramifications of such a characteristic in terms of language development can readily be seen as the result of this particular characteristic. By simply not being interested in the games, activities, and sports of the peer group, the mildly handicapped child is automatically restricted from a number of out-of-school or out-of-class activities that serve to solidify relationships and to reinforce contacts made in school. As a direct result, the child is unable to story tell, to report, and to relate to those topics that comprise a large percentage of the conversations among peers.
A short attention span	This particular characteristic would result in the child's inability to engage at length in a topic of conversation with a peer or with an adult. A short attention span means, too, that the child is not able to learn from topics of prolonged interest to classmates. This inability to focus attention would reduce considerably the array of items about which the child could effectively talk. It could mean, too,

With the characteristic of	*There might be this impact on oral language*
	that the child's class behavior and the child's ability to respond to questions is below that of the peer group. Such recognizable traits would only serve to exclude to an even still greater extent the child from daily communication exchanges.

FIGURE 7.6   *Characteristics of the Mildly Handicapped Child and Possible Impact on Oral Language Abilities*

speaker is saying). Stated another way, if the speech causes communication problems (for example, unintelligibility) or if it causes negative reactions on the part of the speaker, or the audience, it is a speech problem. (From Gearheart, Bill R. and Weishahn, Mel W.: *The handicapped child in the regular classroom.* St. Louis, 1976, The C. V. Mosby Co.)

It is our contention that those children in the public schools who have difficulty communicating *for whatever reason* need attention. Since it is no longer possible to refer children to the speech clinician as extensively as in the past, the teacher is going to have to become comfortable working with the mildly handicapped child in the classroom. The following are descriptions of the most commonly occurring communication disorders as found in McCartan's text *The Communicatively Disordered Child.*

Articulation Disorders

Omissions	The child omits a sound in all or some words, phrases, or sentences. For example, the child may omit all "f" sounds.
Substitutions	The child produces one sound in place of another sound. For example, substituting a "p" for "f."
Distortions	The child produces an approximation of the correct sound. For example, the child may produce the sound "fp" for "f."

Voice Disorders

Problems of respiration	Voice disorders of this type result from abnormal breathing patterns during speech. Some characteristics of this type of voice disorder are insufficient intensity and shortness of breath.
Problems of phonation	These voice disorders are symptoms of difficulty in the larynx, resulting in faulty sound

Voice Disorders

production. These types of voice disorders are characterized by: breathiness, hoarseness, monotone, and inappropriate pitch.

Problems of resonance

Voice disorders of resonance are characterized by impaired quality of sound. These problems occur in the oral and nasal cavities and may result in a nasal or denasal voice.

Stuttering

Repetitions

The speaker rapidly produces repeated sounds, syllables, or words; these repetitions occur on initial sounds.

Prolongations

The speaker fixes on a sound, syllable, or articulatory position for an abnormally long period of time.

Other behaviors

These may include lip and jaw tremors, eye movements, head jerks, and changes in pulse and breathing rates.

Communication Disorders

An inability to understand or use a wide variety of words

Occasionally children demonstrate that their understanding and use of words are below expectations for their chronological age.

Omission or incorrect usage of grammatical structures

In these situations, the child may misuse pronouns, past tense verbs, plurals, future tense verbs, prepositions, auxiliary verbs, adverbs, and conjunctions.

Inability to respond appropriately to questions

This may manifest itself in three ways: (1) no response to questions or (2) repeating a segment of or the complete question without apparent understanding or (3) responding with clearly inappropriate answers.

Source: The communicatively disordered child: Management procedures for the classroom. by Kathleen McCartan; edited by Thomas N. Fairchild, Ph.D.; and illustrated by Daniel B. Fairchild. Boston, MA: Teaching Resources Corporation, 1977, pp. 3–8, 28–34, 50–52, 84–88.

Having become familiar with the general features of speech problems often associated with the mildly handicapped child, strategies for coping with such disabilities need to be developed. The causes of communication disorders, articulation difficulties, stuttering, or problems with voicing are often difficult to determine. In many cases, one simply is aware that something is wrong in this situation, yet what it is specifically remains a mystery. Basically, causal factors cannot always be determined. It is sometimes more profitable for the teacher to focus on procedures for helping the disabled child to communicate more effectively than it is to spend precious time attempting to diagnose a disability. In the case of the child experiencing a communication problem, most teachers recognize quite readily whether or not the child in question is having a problem in articulation, voicing, is a stutterer, or is experiencing serious problems in processing.

With respect to problems in articulation, the knowledgeable teacher can make use of the generalizations suggested by Gearheart and Weishahn (1976) in developing an approach for dealing with articulation errors. The basic principles that must be considered are:

1. Children must first of all *hear* the error they are making. The instructional program at this point focuses primarily on what is commonly referred to as "ear training."
2. Attempts should be made to reduce or to eliminate "known causal factors." Here, reference is made primarily to the providing of good models for the child at home and at school. In some cases, the articulation error in question is more a result of lack of motivation on the part of the parents or siblings, failure to reinforce correct pronunciations, or failure to provide good speech models for the child.
3. Children, once they have learned to hear the differences between correctly produced and incorrectly produced phonemes, should be taught to produce the sound in question correctly.
4. Once sufficient instruction has been provided in production in isolated situations of troublesome phonemes, children should be encouraged and tested in the use of the newly acquired sound in familiar and commonplace settings. At this point, the teacher is looking for accurate production 95 to 100 percent of the time.

Adapted from Gearheart, Bill R., and Weishahn, Mel W.: *The handicapped child in the regular classroom*, St. Louis, 1976, The C. V. Mosby, Co.

Naturally, it is understood that whatever the teacher is doing in the classroom is complimentary to the recommendations of the speech clinician's care. As Gearheart and Weishahn aptly state:

... *if the child is being seen by a speech clinician, the teacher should consult with the specialist to be certain that any special efforts in the classroom are complementary, not contradictory, to the efforts of the speech clinician.* (From Gearheart, Bill R., and Weishahn, Mel W.: *The handicapped child in the regular classroom*, St. Louis, 1976, The C. V. Mosby Co.)

Often, the articulation error that the child is making is one common to most primary age children. Teachers should keep in mind that some phonemes are not fully acquired by the child until after the age of seven (see Figure 7.7).

Age of Mastery	Phonemes
3 years	/b/, /m/, /n/, /f/, /w/, /h/
4 years	/p/, /d/, /g/, /k/, /y/, /l/, /t/
5 years	/v/, /s/, /z/, /š/, /ž/
5½ years	/č/, /r/
6 years	/ǰ/
6+ years	/θ/, /ð/, /ŋ/

Paula Menyuk, *The Acquisition and Development of Language.* © 1971, pp. 78–79. Reprinted by permission of Prentice-Hall, Inc., Englewood Cliffs, New Jersey.

FIGURE 7.7   *Children's Mastery of Phonemes, According to Age.*

One needs to carefully consider the age, socioeconomic background, and IQ of the child before making a decision to work on the remediation of an articulation difficulty. The child may simply grow out of the misarticulation in due time.

With respect to the other three areas—voice disorders, stuttering, and communication disabilities or dysfluencies—an entirely different set of recommendations are necessary. Mowrer (1978) has suggested that the teacher take the following action for each of these problem areas:

Problem Area	*Teacher Role*
Stuttering	If you subscribe to the notion that stuttering is a learned behavior that has occurred because of previous traumatic experiences, your role as a teacher is to reduce the anxiety level of the student. This calls for careful observation on your part to determine which settings and events in the classroom result in the child's stuttering. Once situations have been identified that result in stuttering, the teacher can avoid placing the child into such settings until the child's level of confidence has been increased.
	If, however, you as a teacher maintain that it is the child's self-image and personal adjustment that is of greater importance than fluent speech, you might take the tactic that improving the child's image of himself or herself is of greater importance than a particular speech pattern. In this case, you might even tell the child that stuttering is perfectly all right!

Problem Area	*Teacher Role*
Voice Disorders	Most teachers are quick to learn that the majority of voice disorders are the direct result of vocal abuse more than anything else. Here, according to Mowrer, "the classroom teacher can be of great aid in the treatment program. By pointing out to the child those occasions on which he uses his voice to imitate cement trucks or machine guns, the teacher can help the child become aware of how he is misusing his voice and thus help him reduce these instances of abuse" (1978, p. 37). Basically, the instructional strategy with respect to voice disorders is minimal. One is seeking to reinforce modification in the use of the voice and the avoidance of vocal abuses.

Other voice disorders, i.e., nasality or denasal voice quality are generally not capable of being dealt with in the classroom. The teacher's role in these situations is one of referral. |
| Communication Disorders | In this case, the role of the teacher will vary depending upon the particular difficulty being experienced by the child. Since the various communication disorders can range from vocabulary development to an inability to respond to questions, the role of the teacher will by necessity have to hinge on the child. In general, there is no "easy one-two-three step solution to the problems language deficient children have" (Mowrer, 1978, p. 37). The best service the teacher can provide is the identification of the child who is experiencing a communication disorder. It is only after an examination by a communication order specialist or speech clinician that a program for remediation can be arrived at. It is quite probable, however, that the teacher will be encouraged to modify his or her instructional practices for the child in question; to change the levels of expectation; be a model for good speech; and to create numerous situations during the day in which the child can experience successful interactions. |

Source: "Speech problems: What you should do and shouldn't do" by Donald Mowrer. Reprinted by special permission of *LEARNING, The Magazine for Creative Teaching,* January 1978 © 1978 by Education Today Company, Inc.

Child's Name _____

Grade _____ Date _____

INVENTORY OF SPEECH PROBLEMS

1. Is voice:
    a. loud?   _____
    b. too low?   _____
    c. nasal?   _____
    d. hoarse?   _____
    e. monotonous?   _____
    f. pitched abnormally high?   _____
    g. pitched abnormally low?   _____

2. Is rate of speech:
    a. too slow?   _____
    b. too rapid?   _____

3. Is phrasing poor?   _____

4. Is speech hesitant?   _____

5. Is there evidence of articulation difficulties such as:
    a. distorting sounds?   _____
    b. substituting one sound for another?   _____
    c. omitting sounds?   _____

6. Is there evidence of vocabulary problems such as:
    a. repetition of phrases?   _____
    b. limited vocabulary?   _____

7. Is there evidence of the child's attitudes toward oral
    communication such as:
    a. does not engage in discussions or conversations?   _____
    b. does not volunteer to give a talk or oral report? _____

Source: From *Teaching elementary language arts* by Dorothy Rubin. Copyright © 1975 by Holt, Rinehart and Winston. Reprinted by permission of Holt, Rinehart and Winston.

FIGURE 7.8   An Informal Speech Assessment Inventory

It is often possible for a teacher to isolate a problem area through the use of an informal inventory. The suggestions that have been described thus far have been in terms of particular disabilities. For the teacher of a mildly handicapped child with a speech or language problem in the classroom for the first time, it is often difficult to know into which category the child's behavior fits. Until a more comprehensive workup can be completed, a teacher can provide a valuable service by completing one or more informal inventories over the course of a few weeks.

Included in Figure 7.8 is an example of just such an instrument. In some cases, it is entirely appropriate to develop one's own informal assessment tool if those available lack the specific categories appropriate to the child in question. Assessment instruments are basically nothing more than observation schedules. It should be understood that their use *does not* constitute a diagnosis of the problem! Usually, informal inventories are helpful in completing a referral, in clarifying for the teacher the basic concern, and in assisting the speech clinician in developing a program for remediation.

Encouraging Communication Encounters

Regardless of the composition of the class, the major role of the teacher is the providing of numerous opportunities for interaction. It is perhaps this area of the language arts curriculum that is the most exciting and the most stimulating for both the teacher and the class. When it comes to the development of new materials, the implementation of ideas, the introduction of games, activities and learning centers, the creative talent of almost every teacher seems to take charge. The development of oral language skills is no exception. In fact, the teacher may have the greatest amount of flexibility of all in this area because of the almost unlimited number of ways in which children can be encouraged to interact.

It is fairly common knowledge that a discussion of oral communication skills and procedures for stimulating their development, leads to focusing on one or more of the following:

Discussions	Message Giving and Writing
Conversations	Direction Giving
Oral Reporting	Explanations
Storytelling	Oral Reviews of Books,
Drama	Movies, Television Shows
Movement	Telephone Use
Characterizations	Introductions and Social Courtesies
Improvisation	Conducting of Meetings
Literary Dramatization	Interviews
Puppetry	Debates
Choral Reading	Panel Discussions
Announcements	

Generally speaking, most teachers are not hard pressed to generate ideas and situations in which to develop oral language skills. It is most likely that the basic procedures for engaging children in oral interactions can be readily accounted for.

Why, then, do so many classrooms take on the characteristics of a college lecture hall in terms of opportunities for conversation, dialogue, and idea exchange? Could it be that while the procedures for oral communication are easily recognized, a mechanism for implementing them is sadly lacking? Could it be that most teachers simply do not know how to incorporate conversation, discussion, debate, and improvisation into the daily classroom routine?

The answer to these questions is an unqualified yes. Conversation after conversation with both pre-service and in-service teachers has revealed that while most are familiar with oral language activities, they *are not* made use of on a widespread basis for the following reasons:

> "Many of my special children need to spend their time on reading and mathematics. They come to school with language already, but they lack these other skills."
>
> "There is simply too much other material that needs to be covered in the language arts curriculum. I can't take time out for 'talking' activities when the children should be reading or writing."
>
> "The children who are referred to me come for specific skill work—be it word-attack skills, phonics, word problem solving, computation, or because of behavioral difficulties. Oral language skill work is seldom the case in point."
>
> "The only time I work with a child on oral language skill development is when the classroom teacher has referred him or her to me because of an articulation difficulty. And this is about the extent of my work—articulation and not language."

These are typical responses on the part of a large number of educators. It seems that the overriding concern here is control and order, rather than conscious decision making about what constitutes a good language arts program.

When a teacher becomes familiar with a mechanism for integrating oral language activities into the curriculum, the overall attitude toward conversation in the classroom changes dramatically. It is almost as if, until it is tried, it is not liked!

One technique for structuring oral language activities in the classroom is that of webbing. This particular strategy for conversation, dialogue, debate, discussion, and oral reporting has been used most widely in curriculum development. The concept, however, is readily applicable to the language arts curriculum.

Basically, webbing requires that some particular theme, topic, idea, product, issue, or situation be selected and agreed on by the class as warranting the focusing of attention. It may be necessary (or even appropriate) for the teacher to select the topic and to simply *inform* the class that such-and-such is going to be explored in greater detail. Regardless of the manner in which the topic is arrived at, doing so is the first step in the process. Once the main idea has been decided upon, the building of the "web" can begin.

The teacher, or discussion leader, writes the issue, topic, or point for discussion on the blackboard or on a large sheet of easel paper. A circle is generally placed around the topic to establish the center of the "web." From this point forward, all related points, concerns, and possible areas for exploration are tied into the central theme. Each new subcategory can then be further expanded upon as related ideas are proposed.

Figure 7.9 is an example of a web that has been generated for the topic "water" (Norton, 1977). It should be obvious from this illustration just how the web is constructed. Here, the central theme has been broken down into the related areas of oceans, experimentation, water cycles, fresh water, and water power (read the topics clockwise around the center). As the children's interest in the theme developed, further issues related to each subcategory were listed. Naturally, as the conversation develops, there is bound to be overlapping of ideas and interrelation between items. Such correspondence can be shown by interconnecting lines (see, for example, the subcategory oceans). Figure 7.10 is an example of a web of interest constructed for a class of primary age children on the topic of the "Family." Here the same pattern of organization has been made use of—a central theme, subcomponents, and related issues or topics. It is important to realize that the webbing process can be utilized across the elementary grades and that it is equally as effective as a structuring device for primary age children as it is for junior high schoolers.

Now that you have an idea of what a web is and how it can be built, you might be wondering how such a process can be of value in the development of children's oral language abilities. Moreover, you may also be wondering how this concept can serve as a vehicle for increasing oral interactions among students.

It is possible to expand Norton's web procedure to highlight specific classroom outcomes. For instance:

1. As you introduce the idea, you will have to, by necessity, engage your class, small group, or individual student in a conversation and discussion about the possible topics that can be explored. Use of motivators such as pictures, models, and stories are helpful in providing mildly handicapped child with the necessary background and vocabulary. (Outcome 1—Immediate Adult-Child Interaction)
2. When a topic is decided on debate, dialogue, and idea sharing will be needed. Each participant in the activity will need to justify, explain, and elaborate upon the reasoning behind the subcategories suggested. (Outcome 2—Child-to-Child Interaction)
3. As the number of related topics begins to be expanded upon, relationships among them will need to be clarified, pointed out, and explored. (Outcome 3—Indirect Oral Reporting on Topics of Special Interest to Some Students)
4. If this web is being built by a student leader, there will be multiple opportunities for the leader to organize the comments of others, to

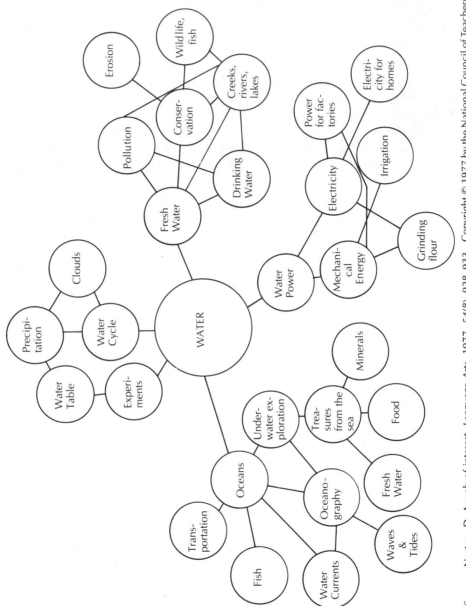

Source: Norton, D. A web of interest. *Language Arts*, 1977, 54(8), 928–933. Copyright © 1977 by the National Council of Teachers of English. Reprinted by permission of the publisher and the author.

FIGURE 7.9   *A Web of Interest Using the Central Theme of Water*

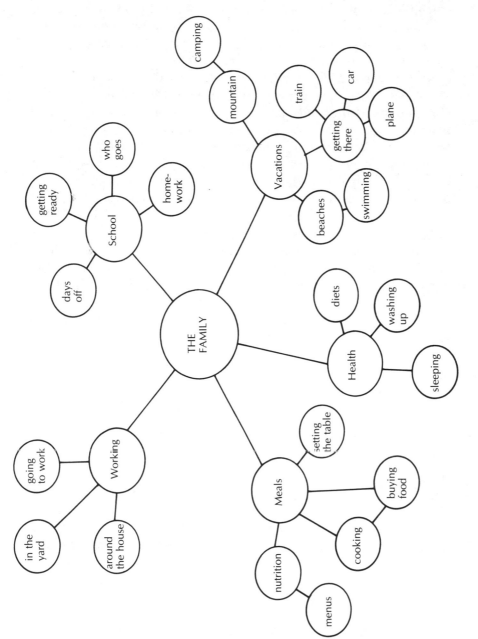

FIGURE 7.10 Web of Interest on the Topic of "The Family"

engage in decision making orally, and to actively select those elements that are essential to include in the web. (Outcome 4—The Development of Group Meeting Skills) Naturally, even when the teacher dominates the discussion and web building process, the participants are engaging in a group meeting and are learning how to conduct themselves in such situations.

5. Once the web is constructed, it is not discarded. It is meant to serve as a basis for continued instruction. When a topic has been fully explored and participants have agreed that all areas of interest have been exposed, information gathering tactics can be developed. The teacher may key into the particular skills, interests, learning styles, or even resources possessed by particular children. At this point, it is desirable to have the class, group, or child decide what aspect of the topic to study in more depth. (Outcome 5—The Assignment of Particular Tasks and Integration of the Language Arts into Other Subject Areas, in this case, science and social studies)

6. Besides moving the class to investigate a topic in greater detail by assignment of tasks, the teacher or group leader must delineate (or help the child or small group) decide how to report back the information they uncover. In this case, the web serves to structure the reporting mechanism *and the use of the other language arts* that are often the sole emphasis of the curriculum, e.g., composition, vocabulary development, reporting, handwriting, and book reports. One might be surprised to observe how elaborate and creative the suggestions for reporting back to the class become. The entire process is so open ended it seems to encourage rather than discourage children. (Outcome 6—The Utilization of Related Language Skills)

7. After a period of time, the class will be ready to engage in a presentation of the material culled together on a topic. This particular activity might be confined to a single class or be extended to include an entire grade level, unit, or school. Depending on the topic and the point at which it occurs during the school year, parents might even be the invited audience. Regardless of the composition of the receiving group, the web started weeks before is responsible for the overall presentation being planned. (Outcome 7—Formal Presentation to a Specific Audience Utilizing Varied Media to Culminate the Activity)

Naturally, an individual teacher will have numerous other outcomes for a project of this nature depending on the age/grade and ability level of the children, the resources available, and the topic finally agreed upon. It is exciting, however, to realize that such a significant set of activities can be incorporated into the daily classroom routine over an extended period of time by such a simple mechanism. A "web of interest" can and does serve as a vehicle for the development of oral language skills in the classroom as well as integrating the language arts into other content areas.

Another technique for oral language development that has been effectively used in the past with mildly handicapped children (Buchan, 1972) is that of role-playing. In general, role-playing activities have been directed toward the development of appropriate social behaviors. There is nothing, however, to prevent the alert teacher from using a proven technique to more than one end—it is quite possible to work on the shaping of appropriate social skills *while stressing* oral language development.

The teacher who is interested in tapping children's role-playing tendencies in order to facilitate oral language should consider the following:

- Do I have a situation in mind that the children can easily identify with? (e.g., asking for lunch money, learning to play a new game)
- How will I engage the other children in the class in the activity? Will they be observers? Evaluators?
- Am I prepared to intercede in a role-playing situation that appears to be breaking down or is becoming uncomfortable for a child— especially a mildly handicapped youngster who might be taken advantage of in a particular situation.
- To what extent will I construct role plays that focus attention on known difficulties or problems of specific students in the class? (e.g., dealing with a speech problem or coping with a physical handicap on the playground)

Once these and related issues have been resolved, the teacher can proceed to incorporate into the language arts program role-playing activities. There might be a time each day, or during the week, that is devoted exclusively to this activity. Each activity period can be used to teach a specific skill, to highlight a particular problem (thereby serving as a vehicle for discussion), or to pinpoint a problem area that will require more interaction to resolve. Role-playing can be an effective vehicle for teaching:

- Use of the telephone
- Interview techniques
- Introductions
- Basic problem solving (e.g., being overcharged in a supermarket)
- How to apply for a job
- How to ask for a favor
- Procedures to follow in an emergency
- How to handle an embarrassing moment
- Dealing with an angry person

• Asking directions
• Locating information in a library, store, or museum
• Extending an invitation

In each of these settings, an exchange of information is required. How well the role is played is a function of how well the requirements of the situation, both verbally and socially, are understood. Such a tactic has a twofold benefit: an opportunity to use language is provided and a socially acceptable pattern of behavior is taught.

Single-session activities are often selected by teachers to stimulate oral language. The activities included here have been taken from different sources and should serve as examples of the *type of stimuli* that can be successfully utilized in the classroom. These particular items are representative of the approach that maintains a speaker needs opportunities to construct and to convey a message to a varied audience.

Single Instructional Activities

Selected from: Colvario, M. The development of classroom workshops in oral communication. *English Journal,* December 1974, pp. 55–61.

The Interview
This activity requires that each class member interview every other classmate. The instructions are relatively simple: each interviewer must obtain *one fact* about each interviewee and must record that fact on a class record sheet. Obviously, this activity requires much interaction. This can help children get to know each other.

Usually it will take an entire class period (or maybe two) for the interview process to complete itself. Once this has been accomplished, each interviewer will be required to report to the class on the "facts" that he was able to obtain.

Nonverbal Considerations in Communication
In this case the teacher, or even other classmates, provide each other with a list of feelings, e.g., affection, anger, and anxiety. The task is to determine the manner in which the feeling can be expressed nonverbally. Students should first discuss how such feelings are expressed nonverbally and then demonstrate, if possible, how such emotions might manifest themselves.

A variation in this activity would involve the use of note cards that have printed on them a particular emotion. The students select a note card, act out the emotion, and the audience attempts to determine what emotion is being portrayed.

228

Speaking Before a Group—Prelude to Oral Reporting
This activity requires that a number of communication skills be incorporated into them. It is quite possible, too, for the teacher to unleash a bit of the old creative talent as the activity is constructed.

A list of statements that are commonly heard on television, in the movies, or on the radio are typed and numbered on a sheet of paper that is placed on a lecturn or desk at the front of the room. Such statements should be those that can easily incorporate gestures: "He tripped over his own two feet." "When I make a move, I move with clout!" Those students participating in this activity should randomly select a number. When a student's turn is up, he or she is to go to the lecturn at the front of the class and find the sentence that corresponds to the number chosen. The sentence is then read silently at first, actions selected, and then presented to the class along with the statement. The activity is designed to help students become more comfortable speaking before a large group and reinforces the need to make use of gesture when giving oral reports.

Selected from: Tiedt, S., and Tiedt, I. *Language arts activities for the classroom.* Boston: Allyn & Bacon, 1978, pp. 155–159, 176.

Storytelling and Dramatization
Have the children collect numerous pictures from various magazines. All the photographs, or even the magazines themselves, should be given to the students to select from and to arrange to tell a story. The completed story, along with the pictures that tell it, can be told to the entire class, or it can be put on tape and placed, along with the photos, in a listening center.

Developing Speaking Skills—Impromptu or Planned
Figure 7.11 contains 150 topics that fall into 15 different categories that are suitable for use in developing oral communication skills. These topics for discussion can be made use of in numerous ways by the teacher. Some may be selected for improvisational speaking, for interviews, for oral reporting, or for role-playing, or acting. The variations that occur are a function of the age/grade level of the students.

Still other approaches can be taken to encourage children to communicate orally. In fact, the list of techniques and activities can be rather extensive. It is the responsibility of teachers to determine the approach to oral language development that they want to pursue and guide them in their instructional programming (i.e., a theme or web of interest approach versus a single activity approach) and then to develop the activity to the level that it can be implemented in the classroom.

Providing opportunities and stimuli for oral language need not be limited to paper and pencil activities. It should be realized that while the ideas and suggestions selected as examples in this chapter were of a particu-

Amusements

1. Reading the Sunday funnies
2. Playing hide and seek
3. Popsicle from the ice cream truck
4. Chinese checkers with a friend
5. Swinging in a hammock
6. Going to a movie
7. Watching a kitten play
8. Riding a Ferris wheel
9. Playing in the sand
10. Going to a school dance

Education

1. Why Government?
2. A good teacher
3. More schooling or work?
4. The value in experience
5. A well-rounded education
6. Does business want bright students?
7. A practical education
8. The value of art and music
9. Preparing for responsibility
10. Education for fun

Customs

1. Prayers at mealtime
2. Saluting the flag
3. Celebrating holidays
4. Shaking hands
5. Honking horns after a wedding
6. Learning new dances
7. Ladies carrying purses
8. Sunday drive
9. Birthdays
10. Shopping on Saturday

Friends

1. Friends for life
2. I wonder what happened to . . .
3. The beauty of friendship
4. So comfortable to be with
5. We're on the same wavelength
6. A friend in need
7. The art of being a friend
8. The friends I miss the most
9. She never gave advice unasked for
10. My dog, Scottie, is always there

Hobbies

1. Photographing wildflowers
2. Hobbies are relaxing
3. Profitable hobbies
4. My hobby helped me meet people
5. Building strange kites
6. Sharing a hobby
7. Inexpensive hobbies
8. Outdoor hobbies
9. Collectors' items
10. Animals are interesting

Manners

1. Going out to eat
2. Waiting for a man to open the door
3. Manners at home
4. Are good manners needed?
5. Courtesies are appreciated
6. Remembering a sick friend
7. What are good manners?
8. How manners can make a difference
9. A time when *please* helped me
10. Things I am thankful for

Home

1. Picking out a new house
2. Wedding in the spring
3. Family discussions
4. Sharing experiences
5. Planning for a holiday
6. A new brother or sister
7. Home-making as a full-time job
8. Father likes to go to the beach
9. Mother enjoys working
10. Learning responsibilities

Sports

1. Women in sports
2. Enjoying the Olympics on TV
3. Jogging
4. I'd rather go sailing
5. Bicycle trips
6. Understanding football
7. Water ballet
8. Tennis fanatics
9. Archery for the whole family
10. Sportsmanship

Nature

1. What is a biologist?
2. Classifying wildflowers
3. Understanding ecology
4. Dolphins and porpoises
5. Underwater creatures
6. Growing a garden
7. Hiking in the forest
8. Edible plants
9. Bee language
10. Mountain trout fishing

Occupations

1. I want to be a pilot
2. Going on a job interview
3. Work can be fun
4. Working with people
5. Scientific research
6. Working in a foreign country
7. I like the outdoors
8. My career is marriage
9. My paper route
10. Teaching is rewarding

Organizations

1. What is a Democrat?
2. Charitable organizations
3. Are unions necessary?
4. Businessmen's groups
5. Wildlife preservation
6. Social clubs
7. I'm a nonconformist
8. Senior citizens
9. Religious membership
10. Magicians

Pets

1. Animals have personalities
2. Training a dog
3. Cats are night creatures
4. Parakeets are clowns
5. Dogs can be protective

6. Problems in raising exotic pets
7. Unusual pets
8. Keeping your pet healthy
9. Annual visitors
10. Trust and wild animals

Morals

1. Cheating on tests
2. My personal philosophy
3. Respect for law and order
4. Gambling problems
5. Being self-reliant
6. What is an honor code?
7. Morals in the business world
8. Are chaperones needed?
9. Attending church
10. Is honesty the best way?

Reading

1. My favorite stories
2. Reading for recreation
3. Learning from biographies
4. Story hour at home
5. Appealing adventure stories
6. Books my teacher read
7. My favorite character
8. Magazines on newsstands
9. Comic book collections
10. Funny and sad poems

Travel

1. Discovering new cultures
2. Exploring America
3. Coastal cruises
4. Historical American Indian dwellings
5. Trips for camera buffs
6. Sailing the Mediterranean Sea
7. Hazards of traveling
8. Communication problems
9. Hitchhiking through Europe
10. A good traveling companion

(*Source:* Tiedt, S. & Tiedt, I. *Language arts activities for the classroom.* Boston: Allyn & Bacon, 1978, pp. 155–159.) Reprinted with permission.

FIGURE 7.11 *Suggested Topics for Discussion*

lar variety, there are numerous ways in which audio-visual materials can be introduced into the oral language program. Films, filmstrips, cassette tapes, records, radio, overhead transparencies, and slides can all be adapted and utilized as vehicles for conversation, discussion, and dialogue.

Clearly, we believe strongly in the need to provide mildly handicapped children with opportunities to practice using their language. It is only by speaking that one learns how to speak. It is not a skill that can be developed in isolation.

SUMMARY

This chapter focused on the manner in which the teacher can facilitate the development of oral language skills. To impact the child's ability to use oral language, the teacher must be able to:

1. Adapt the classroom environment to promote opportunities for interaction.
2. Become sensitive to "teacher talk" and its related characteristics—both verbal and nonverbal.
3. Be able to cope with disabilities and to improve the speech of the mildly handicapped.
4. Provide numerous opportunities and stimuli that encourage communication encounters and oral language.

In each of the subsections, suggestions, ideas, and procedures to assist the teacher in meeting their obligations in oral language development were explored. Opportunities for experimenting with language in a number of varied and different settings as essential ingredients in developing oral language skills was emphasized.

This chapter has demonstrated that the mildly handicapped child, while possibly having distinguishing speech characteristics, can be dealt with in the classroom. Certainly, it may be necessary to modify instructional procedures, materials, and/or the physical environment, but these demands should not be viewed as difficult ones to respond to. The mildly handicapped child will need more opportunities to speak, to engage in conversations, to become involved in discussions, to respond to questions, and to role play. In general, however, if the teacher of the mildly handicapped child works to include the child in the daily interactions of the class by developing a planned oral language program, it is our contention that noticeable changes will occur in the entire class's deliberations and daily exchanges. The very tone of the classroom is determined not just by those who people it, but by the combination of the people and the freedom they have to express their ideas.

POINTS FOR DISCUSSION

1. The classroom environment is not always thought of as being readily modified to encourage oral communication. This chapter stated that a typical classroom could be transformed into a more suitable environment for communication by rearranging the instructional space. One example of how a classroom's physical environment could be altered was provided. Using as a basis for change the classroom shown in Figure 7.1, design several alternative learning environments. Remember, you will have to justify the changes that you make. Be sure you consider what curricular changes might also occur as you alter the physical environment.

2. In the discussion that focused on the classroom environment, seven models for interaction were presented. Working with a friend, devise still other patterns for grouping children that would serve to facilitate discussion? Refer to the models discussed in this chapter and develop your own technique for grouping children.

3. Sanders has categorized those questions most frequently asked by teachers. Check back through this chapter and find those seven categories and construct one question for each of them. Ask a classmate your questions and have your partner determine the category of your question rather than trying to answer it specifically.

4. The information that has been presented on the roles teachers take when they engage in classroom communication encounters suggests that a great deal of interplay exists between the "moves" of structuring, soliciting, responding, and reacting. Observe a peer in a microteaching setting and try to determine which of the four "moves" are brought into play and what percentage of the teaching time was devoted to each. If microteaching is not a part of your program, observe a teacher in a local school if it can be arranged or plot your own instructor's behavior on these variables.

5. Assessment of speech and language disorders is not an easy task and the isolation of difficulties in oral communication is no exception. It has been suggested that the teacher use an informal inventory to assist in the completion of referrals and in the description of a particular child's problem in communication. Using the information that has been presented in this chapter, develop an informal oral language assessment instrument similar to the one shown in Figure 7.8. You may adapt this inventory to include areas of particular interest to you.

6. The concept of webbing was discussed as a vehicle for structuring oral language encounters. An example of a web was provided to demonstrate how easily such an activity can be used in the classroom. Select a single topic, and in a small group (seven or less) develop a web of interest using the model contained in this chapter as a guide. When you have completed exploring all the related aspects of your topic, discuss just which of the language arts you could possibly integrate into the activities and subtopics generated by your web.

7. The use of isolated activities in the development of oral language skills is not inappropriate at times. In fact, it may well be that a single activity has more value

and is of greater use to you in the classroom than a fully developed theme or web. Without getting too elaborate, develop at least five separate activities related to oral language instruction. Each of these activities should be ready to introduce to group of children. You will need to keep in mind the need for instructional materials that are durable, attractive, permanent, adaptable to individual learning styles, and easily and inexpensively constructed. Plan to display your materials in your class along with those constructed by other students.

8. Oral language activities are so often closely related to aural language skill development. Work with a classmate and relate the information in this section of the text to that found in the chapter on aural language skill development. Develop a table or chart that shows the correspondence between oral and aural skills. Similar characteristics? Differences? Relationships? Contrasts? See just how complete you could be in your delineation of these two distinct, yet complementing, language skills.

REFERENCES

Bellack, A. The language of the classroom. New York: Teachers College Press, Columbia University, 1966. In Hennings, D. *Mastering classroom communication: What interactional analysis tells the classroom teacher.* Pacific Palisades, Calif.: Goodyear Publishing Co., 1975.

Blackburn, J., and Powell, W. *One at a time all at once—The creative teacher's guide to individualized instruction without anarchy.* Pacific Palisades, Calif.: Goodyear Publishing Co., 1976.

Bloom, B. *Taxonomy of educational objectives, Handbook I: Cognitive domain.* New York: David McKay Company, Inc., 1956.

Buchan, L. *Roleplaying and the educable mentally retarded.* Belmont, Calif.: Fearon Publishers, 1972.

Christensen, C. Relationships between pupil achievement, pupil affect-need, teacher warmth, and teacher permissiveness. *Journal of Educational Psychology,* 1960, *51,* 169–174.

Colvario, M. The development of classroom workshops in oral communication. *English Journal,* December 1974, 55-61.

Destefano, J., and Fox, S. *Language and the language arts.* Boston: Little, Brown and Company, 1974.

Fitzgerald, S. Teaching discussion skills and attitudes. *Language Arts,* 1975, 52(8), 1094-1096.

Gearheart, B., and Weishahn, M. *The handicapped child in the regular classroom.* St. Louis, Mo.: C. V. Mosby Co., 1976.

Hennings, D. *Mastering classroom communication: What interaction analysis tells the classroom teacher.* Pacific Palisades, Calif.: Goodyear Publishing Co., 1975.

Lippitt, R., and White, R. An experimental study of leadership and group life. In Maccoby, E. (Ed.), *Readings in Social Psychology.* New York: Holt, Rinehart and Winston, Inc., 1958.

McCartan, K., Fairchild, T., and Fairchild, D. *The communicatively disordered child: Management procedures for the classroom.* Austin, Texas: Learning Concepts, Inc., 1977.

Mowrer, D. Speech problems: What you should do and shouldn't do. *Learning Magazine,* January 1978, pp. 34-37.

Norton, D. A web of interest. *Language Arts,* 1977, 54(8), 928-933.

Rubin, D. *Teaching elementary language arts.* New York: Holt, Rinehart and Winston, 1975, p. 116.

Ryans, D. Some relationships between pupil behavior and certain teacher characteristics. *Journal of Educational Psychology,* 1961, *52,* 82-90.

Sanders, N. *Classroom questions, what kinds?* New York: Harper & Row, 1966.

Thomas, C. *An investigation of the sensitivity to nonverbal communication of learning disabled and normal children.* Unpublished doctoral dissertation, University of Virginia, 1978.

Tiedt, S., and Tiedt, I. *Language arts activities for the classroom.* Boston: Allyn & Bacon, 1978.

Wilkinson, A. Oracy in English teaching. In Destefano, J. and Fox, S. (Eds.), *Language and the language arts.* Boston: Little, Brown and Company, 1974, pp. 64-71.

8

Handwriting Instruction

Handwriting instruction is one of the oldest areas of continuous academic concern. Throughout educational history, attempts have been made to teach children to write legibly for the purpose of efficient communication. Writing, as we know it today, developed through the centuries, originally forming letters only by hand and later through printing and increasingly complex mechanical techniques. The manuscript style so commonly used in reading and printed material is a variation of past Italian and English script—a form derived for its ease and clarity. The practice of writing from left to right stems from the Roman preference and has been maintained throughout the western world.

The continuance of handwriting instruction has increasingly become a topic for discussion among educators, futurists, and parents. Educators complain that the writing of American children today is less legible and that this deterioration results from a lack of direct instruction in handwriting skills at the lower grades. Futurists have in some instances claimed that the need for handwriting skill may eventually disappear as society becomes more and more technological. Although American adults do use less handwritten correspondence today than in the past, the likelihood of the need for this skill disappearing completely is extremely slim. As the educational system moves toward the establishment of minimum competency levels, many parents have become more vocal over the need for their children to receive direct instruction in the "three Rs—reading, 'riting, and 'rithmetic." As a result, teachers will once again be asked to provide daily instruction in both functional communication and handwriting.

Handwriting is still a very necessary skill in business and interpersonal communication and it is the schools' responsibility to teach each child its effective use through systematic instruction. In addition, the development of a legible handwriting is an aid to reading and spelling. Indeed, in many academic programs these skills are taught simultaneously as interrelated tasks. It is hard to separate reading, spelling, and writing skills from each other due to their functional dependency. That is, you cannot really write without spelling and what is written and spelled correctly can be read! However, for instructional purposes, it is possible and, especially during the early learning stages, it is necessary, to distinguish between the specific skills of handwriting and other academic subjects and teach them somewhat in isolation.

Handwriting can be defined as a communication tool consisting of visual markings representing spoken language. Written expression is often acknowledged as the most advanced and difficult form of language. To master an important component of written communication, such as handwriting, the mildly handicapped child needs direct instruction. The principle objective of the handwriting skills program is to help the child learn to write legibly and with reasonable speed. Speed is a secondary objective to be focused on only after accuracy in letter formation has been accomplished.

Handwriting Disabilities

Proficiency in handwriting involves the integration of a variety of psychomotor processes including visual perception, visual memory, hand-eye coordination, and motor ability. The mildly handicapped child may experience difficulty in handwriting due to a disability in any of these processes. Satisfactory development in writing skills depends on accurate assessment of the child's handwriting problem, and the development of appropriate remedial programming.

The proliferation of educational programs for children with visual-perceptual problems has not resulted in immediate solutions. Such programs as those developed by Kephart (1960) and Frostig (Frostig & Horne, 1964) rely on geometric forms as the focus of the instructional plan. The assumption is that a child who completes the series of prescribed exercises will be able to transfer the trained perceptual skills to other visual-motor activities. Unfortunately, in many cases this has not been true. The weakness of such programs may be in their failure to recognize that many mildly handicapped children have difficulty transferring general principles, and they are unable to make the transition from the perceptual exercise to the academic task of letter writing.

When a child is experiencing difficulty in developing handwriting skills, the problem may become apparent in any of the following ways:

1. Illegible letter forms
2. Improper spacing of letters, words, or sentences
3. Extreme pressure (too light or too heavy) on the writing tool
4. Extremely slow movement and lack of completion of the writing task
5. A disinterest in writing and an unwillingness to approximate the standard forms

Children who display these behaviors may actually be experiencing difficulties in specific areas. The most common writing disabilities are *dysgraphia* and a *problem in revisualization*. Dysgraphia is a visual motor disorder characterized by an inability to copy or write words and numbers. The child with a revisualization problem can recognize and read words and symbols but is unable to revisualize them in order to write without following a model. In essence, this is a visual retention problem, since the child performs satisfactorily when a model is present. A more definitive list of writing difficulties which may result in an illegible handwriting includes:

1. Inability to retain visual forms
2. Poor hand-eye coordination
3. Inadequate fine motor skills
4. Physical or psychological illness
5. Unestablished dominance (hand and/or eye)
6. Poor visual acuity
7. Distractibility
8. Inability to sequence shapes and movements
9. Inability to function at the automatic level
10. Spacial disorientation.

Many mildly handicapped children are inadequate incidental learners and as such will not be able to acquire new skills or alter existing ones without receiving specific attention. The teacher who is aware of this fact will realize the importance of planning for each new learning segment. It is up to the teacher to properly identify the cause of the child's difficulty and to develop an individualized handwriting program. To achieve this objective the teacher must provide systematic instruction which will teach step-by-step procedures for handwriting acquisition.

Handwriting Readiness

In their eagerness to appear grown-up, to please their parents, and to demonstrate their developing skills, many preschoolers begin to write prior to the development of necessary motor control and perceptual ability. The emphasis on early acquisition forces the child to "do the best he can" and often results in the establishment of unsatisfactory writing habits, which may interfere with later instruction and are often difficult to correct.

Although handwriting readiness has been acknowledged to be "as important as a sound readiness program in reading" (Barbe & Lucas, 1974, p. 209), it has not been given appropriate attention in instructional programs. In particular, the learning problems displayed by many mildly handicapped children point to the need for an organized writing readiness program.

Maria Montessori, a well-respected early educator of young children, believed that children need intelligence, motor development, and a variety of experiences before they can write. This was later interpreted by Donoghue (1975) to mean:

> A child acquires mental readiness through experiences that reveal the value of handwriting and promote interest in learning to write. He attains motor readiness through activities that enable him to learn to hold the writing tools and to perform the simple movements required. (p. 332)

Many of the young child's play activities provide necessary motor development. A child who stacks objects, digs in a sand box, paints, helps mother bake and father hammer, is continuously experiencing activities that increase visual-motor integration. Although home environments differ, the teacher can make use of a variety of experiences and materials with which the child is already familiar. Once the child enters school, other more instructionally appropriate training activities can be structured to increase handwriting readiness. With the proper sequencing of readiness activities the teacher can guide the child's progress to a legible handwriting pattern.

Prior to implementing the handwriting program the teacher needs to establish the child's readiness. Children vary in their rate of development and in their readiness for handwriting instruction. Not every child is ready to write at the same time. There is no clear consensus of which mental age level is most appropriate for beginning instruction. Hanson (1976) suggests that the lower age limit may be 5 or 6 for the average child, while Donoghue (1975) believes a child should have a mental age of approximately 6-6 before the formal handwriting program is begun. Even for the normal child, however, the complexities of writing tasks are such that many children experience initial difficulty and should not receive formal instruction until they exhibit increased readiness skills and awareness of the function of writing. Children should also evidence a desire and facility for writing. This may be expressed by an interest in writing one's name, making letter forms while drawing or painting, and imitating the writing posture of holding a pencil and "writing" on paper. The chart (Figure 8.1 on p. 242) presents the readiness areas necessary for handwriting development as well as specific subskills and related informal assessment methods.

Laterality is defined as "the initial awareness of the two sides of the body and their difference, which later becomes the basis for concepts of direction in space" (Hammill & Bartel, 1978, p. 357). This awareness is central to the competency of spacial relationships and an appropriate body image. Some children experience difficulty writing across the body's imaginary midline. For instance, children may not be able to draw a line from one end of the paper to the other if it means reaching across their body to do so. In such cases, they may switch hands with the writing instrument at the midline and continue to draw the line. This difficulty is the result of poorly established laterality and should be remediated through prescribed exercises which encourage midline crossings.

For instance, ask the child to rotate his arms in large circles in front of his body or draw a large X directly in front of him on the chalkboard (do not allow him to switch the chalk from one hand to another).

The *left-to-right directionality* followed in English must be taught and practiced as a prerequisite orientation to mature writing. Although written many years ago, research has not disputed Hildreth's (1936) statement that:

> . . . young children with little writing training can write in either direction equally well. . . . The apparent ease of writing from "left-to-right" as opposed to "right-to-left" direction in mature writers may be due more to training and practice than to any inherent difficulty in the direction. (p. 224)

Unless the child can establish *handedness and eye-dominance,* writing proficiency will be limited. Eye-dominance is necessary for determining a good body posture advantageous to the writing task which will reduce eye strain. The child's hand preference is important for determining specific aspects of the instructional program. Most children have a commonality of eye-hand preference. However, in cases of mixed dominance, left-eye/right-hand or right-eye/left hand, the child may experience problems and writing discomfort characterized by fidgeting with the paper and frequently changing writing position.

Readiness Activities

The mildly handicapped child may require more attention than normal in the handwriting readiness program. Activities should be designed to

241

Skill Area	Subskill	Informal Assessment Technique
1. Visual Ability	Visual acuity	Test the child's ability to read the eye chart at the prescribed distances. While seated at a table in the center of the room, have the child name objects and people located at different distances.
	Visual discrimination	Ask the child to identify which object does not belong in a series of objects.
2. Motor Development	Small muscle coordination	Have the child string a series of beads of varying sizes. Have the child color in the center circle in a set of two concentric circles.
3. Visual-Motor Integration	Left-right progression	Ask the child to point to and name a series of different objects across a row from left to right.
	Eye-hand coordination	Ask the child to draw a line across the page from the sun to the moon. Using a wide felt-tip pen ask the child to draw a line through a series of dots.
	Copying ability	Divide a paper in half and on one half draw a happy face. Then ask the child to draw the same thing on the other half. Do the same task again using simple forms.

Skill Area	Subskill	Informal Assessment Technique
		Using pipe cleaners, make a simple model for the child to observe and reproduce.
4. Visual Memory	Revisualization of shapes and symbols	On the chalkboard draw a series of large dots. Cover the dots and ask the child to draw the same configuration on paper.
5. Laterality	Hand dominance	Chart the child's hand preference when reaching for an object, holding a paint brush, and throwing a ball. Ask the child to stack a pile of blocks. Note which hand picks up the blocks and which is used for placing and steadying the blocks.
	Eye dominance	Cut a small hole in the center of a 3 × 5 card. Ask the child to look through the hole with both eyes open and to focus on a distant object. Have the child close one eye at a time. If the child can still see the object through the hole with the left eye closed, the right eye is dominant, and vice versa.
6. Language Maturity	Receptive language ability	Record whether the child can follow simple directions.
	Expressive language ability	Note whether the child can answer simple questions, make wants known, and express feelings through language.
	The concept of words as written language	When a story is being read from a book, observe whether the child looks at the words as well as the pictures. Note if the child has ever asked the pronunciation or name of a letter or words, or how to write his own name.

FIGURE 8.1   Readiness Chart

reflect the various skills related to developing handwriting ability. The following tasks are examples of activities to increase the child's readiness for formal handwriting instruction:

1. Have the child practice arranging objects in a left to right progression.
2. Provide the child with a variety of tracing forms. Templates can be used on the chalkboard or on large sheets of paper.
3. Allow the child to practice holding crayons, chalk, and pencils.
4. Develop dot-to-dot pictures and simple paper maze tasks for the child to complete.
5. Have the child reproduce pegboard designs to develop visual memory skills.
6. Combine language and motor activities by asking the child to describe what he is doing and how he is feeling.
7. Make up simple story statements to correspond with the basic manuscript strokes. The child can then draw the picture as the teacher says the story and shows the model. For example:

   a. Here is the flag. Can you draw the pole?

   b. The road is very long and flat. Draw a road.

   c. The teeter-totter goes up and down. First make it go this way and then that way.

   d. The sun is nice and round. Draw the sun.

   e. Sometimes the moon looks like this.

      Can you make half of that moon, ?

   f. There are times when the moon looks as though it faces the other way . Now make half of this moon

Issues in Handwriting

Manuscript versus Cursive

The manuscript form of writing was introduced to the American educational system in the early 1920s. Prior to that time all children learned cursive in the initial writing stages. The manuscript method spread quickly and today the traditional handwriting program is based on the premise that manuscript is an easier developmental form and, therefore, should precede instruction in cursive writing. When manuscript writing is taught initially, cursive is generally introduced between the second and third grades. Although almost all school-age children are given beginning writing instruction in manuscript, the issue of which writing form is most advantageous is still being debated. Most recently the discussion has centered on the application of each method for mildly handicapped populations. The arguments are convincing on each side and deserve the attention and consideration of the teacher who is responsible for developing the mildly handicapped child's instructional handwriting sequence.

The continuance of manuscript as the introductory writing system is based on a belief by the large majority of educators that manuscript is superior to cursive for the following reasons:

1. The young child is developmentally better equipped to handle the muscular demands of manuscript. The beginning writer is required to master only three essential forms, the straight line, the circle, and the half circle.

2. The formation of individual letters affords the child a rest period. The continuation of joined letters found in cursive demands a sustained period of control of the hand and arm movements which is a difficult task for some young children.

3. Manuscript more closely resembles the printed letter form which the young child is learning to read. This allows the child to relate what has been learned from two approaches and provides reinforcement for each.

4. Manuscript writing is the easier form to master and legibility in this approach leads to more rapid acquisition of cursive. Cursive is built on the general forms of manuscript letters with the addition of connecting links.

The proponents of beginning handwriting instruction with the cursive form provide arguments which run counter to those for manuscript. A great deal of support for the use of cursive as the introductory handwriting method has centered on mildly handicapped children with neurological difficulties. The advantages of cursive are considered to be:

1. Cursive is the accepted adult writing form. There is little enough time to teach all that is required in the curriculum during the school years. Early instruction eliminates the duo-system of handwriting instruction.

2. In cursive, each word consists of a rhythmic flow of letter forms. A continuous, unbroken line is used except when a word includes the letters i, j, t, and x (these need to be dotted and crossed). Manuscript, on the other hand, requires children to frequently pick up their pencils as they start and stop a temporal sequence of isolated

245

movements. For instance, the letter *K* consists of three distinct lines pieced together in the proper order.

3. The forms of cursive letters assist directionality through temporal sequencing. This reduces the likelihood of the child making letter reversals, transpositions, and omissions.

4. In cursive the spacing between letters is controlled by the slant and form of the connective strokes. This avoids the difficulty of inappropriate spacing within a word which often occurs in manuscript.

5. Cursive allows the child to see the totality of the word form instead of focusing on isolated letters. The child can monitor kinesthetic feedback of the whole word. This image will assist the child in reading and spelling programs.

6. Cursive is for most people a speedier, more efficient writing method which allows the child to function at the automatic level. This means that the child can generalize movement patterns without directly thinking about them. The whole word pattern becomes the goal, and as a result the child makes fewer writing errors.

Research related to the manuscript versus cursive issue has been inconclusive. The accepted practice of teaching manuscript prior to cursive may be more the result of traditional programming than sound theory. However, until data is collected which justifies one program over the other, the decision to teach either method will have to be based on individual needs. An awareness of the advantages of each approach and the diagnosed writing difficulties of the child will assist the teacher in this decision.

Handedness

Which hand a child prefers to write with has not been determined to result from any single clear factor. Some professionals believe hand-dominance is the result of hereditary factors, while others claim early practice determines handedness. Regardless of the cause, hand-dominance is expressed in the majority of children prior to school entrance. A teacher should observe the child's hand preference in general activities as well as in specific structured tasks, such as picking up a toy, throwing a ball, coloring with crayons, and taking an object from another person. If there is a clear preference for one hand over the other, the child should be encouraged to write with that hand. There is no evidence to suggest that a left-handed child should be made to switch to the right hand for writing purposes. In fact, a great deal of testimony has been given to the difficulties encountered by attempting to change children from a left- to a right-handed preference. Some children may show mixed-handedness (no clearly established preference), while others are ambidextrous (nearly equal facility with both hands). In either case, the teacher may encourage the child's use of the right hand as a matter of convenience. Since desks in school, scissors, and most educational programs are designed for the right-handed child, it will actually be easier for the child, in the long run, to have strengthened coordination of the right hand.

Manuscript Instruction

A systematic approach to manuscript instruction requires specific periods during the school day for handwriting development. During this time the child will acquire skills in individual letter formation, spacing, and word writing. Remember that the paper is placed directly in front of the child so that downstrokes produce vertical lines. The basic strokes in manuscript are the straight line, circle, and parts of circles. These can be subdivided into seven easily practiced forms as shown in Figure 8.2.

Letter Formation

As students show readiness for direct instruction in handwriting skills, the teacher must give specific guidelines for forming manuscript letters. These include:

1. All letters begin at the top. There are no upstrokes in the manuscript form. All vertical lines in a letter are formed before horizontal lines in the same letter.
2. Each stroke is made separately with a slight lifting of the pencil between strokes. No stroke is retraced at any point.
3. Letters consist of straight lines, circles, and parts of circles. Circles and parts of circles for letters a, c, d, e, f, g, o, q, s are made counterclockwise from a two o'clock position preceding left. Letters b, h, m, n, p, r are made with the part circle beginning at the ten o'clock position and preceding to the right.
4. All except five letters end at the baseline. These five are g, j, p, q, y.
5. Capital and tall letters are proportionately two spaces high, while small letters are only one space.

Source: From Markoff, A. M., Teaching low-achieving children reading, spelling and handwriting, 1976. Courtesy of Charles C Thomas, Publisher, Springfield, Illinois.

FIGURE 8.2   Manuscript Practice Forms

6. Spacing varies between letters according to letter shape. Two consecutive vertical letters take more space between them than a circular and vertical letter located next to each other. For example, in the word, *sell,* the last two letters are spaced farther apart than either the *s* and *e,* or the *e* and *l.*

Commercial handwriting programs occasionally vary on the number or order of strokes within a letter. These differences are not major however, and the teacher should be more concerned with the consistency of formation, size, and spacing. The manuscript handwriting alphabet in Figure 8.3 provides information as to stroke sequence, direction, and size.

For the purpose of instruction many teachers find it effective to group letters that are similar in type and direction of stroke. The manuscript grouping chart (Figure 8.4) organizes capital and small letters which can be taught together to increase skill generalization.

Source: Used with permission from *Expressional growth through handwriting.* Copyright © 1969 Zaner-Bloser, Inc., Columbus, Ohio.

FIGURE 8.3   *Manuscript Alphabet*

Sequence	Group Members	Representative Strokes
1	L, E, F, T, I, H	straight lines
2	O, C, G, Q	circles straight lines
6	o, c, e, d, a, g, q	counterclockwise circles straight lines
7	b, p, r, n, m, h	straight lines clockwise circles part circles
4	v, w, x, y, z, k	straight lines slant lines
3	t, i, l	straight vertical lines straight horizontal lines
5	V, N, M, W, K, A, Z, X, Y	straight lines slant lines
9	s, u, j, f	straight lines half circles
8	D, P, B, R, J	straight lines half circles
10	S, U	half circles

FIGURE 8.4   Manuscript Grouping Chart

Common Manuscript Errors

During the beginning stages of learning all children make errors in formation, direction, and spacing. Reversals and omissions are characteristic of many young children's writing samples. Problems exist when these errors continue to persist over time. Lewis and Lewis (1965) in an error analysis of manuscript samples written by first-grade children found the eight most common errors in the formation of letters were:

1. Letter size, specifically with descenders g, j, p, q, y.
2. Reversals of letter forms N, d, q, y.
3. Partial omission of letters m, U, l.
4. Letters C, k, m, y, q were given additions.
5. Incorrect stroke relationship, especially in letters k, R, M, m.
6. Incorrect line position, especially with descenders.
7. Most frequently miswritten letters were j, G, J.
8. Most difficult letter forms were those consisting of curves and vertical lines.

Understanding common stroke errors and their possible causes will provide the teacher with further insights for remediation and modification of the instructional program (Figure 8.5).

Many of the mistakes that children make during the initial writing stages are inadvertently reinforced by teachers. The following example demonstrates that a child's confusion can be partly due to the teacher's correction

Problem	Causation	Example
Excess in stroke: 1. Heaviness	Too much pressure on pencil from the index finger Incorrect writing instrument	 nice
2. Lightness	Pencil held too straight Incorrect writing instrument	 we
3. Straightness	Arm held too close to the body Finger too close to pencil nib Pencil guided by index finger only Incorrect paper position Fingers too stiff Writing tool held too tightly	 Susan
4. Slant	Writing too close to the body Fingers too far from writing tool point Incorrect paper position Misunderstands direction of stroke	 come
5. Size/width	Lacks understanding of proportion Hand and arm movement too slow Inflexible movements	 house
6. Spacing	Pencil moves too fast or too slow Misunderstands purpose of spacing (e.g., between letters, words, etc.)	 c ar

FIGURE 8.5   Error Chart

strategy which provides the child with irrelevant information for the task and confusion as to the correct letter symbol. For instance:

Child: writes *d* for *b*
Teacher: (pointing to *d*) "This is not a *b*, this is a *d*. Write *b*."
Child: writes a *d* again.

When providing correction be careful to focus the child's attention on the specific task of the letter form or word desired and give only the necessary information. In the example given above the teacher should have said, "This is not a *b* (pointing to *d*), this is a *b* (writing proper letter form for child to imitate)." In this instance the child is given only the relevant information and can model the teacher's response.

The Instructional Program

Handwriting is generally taught through group instruction and is often allocated the least amount of instructional time of any of the language arts. As a result, many children develop illegible handwritings or experience difficulty in written expression due to difficulty in reproducing letter forms. The child's handwriting ability, that is legibility and speed, will influence the achievement of many other academic skills. Handwriting instruction should be given for at least 15–20 minutes a day with specific objectives planned for each lesson. Stated goals will increase the effectiveness of the instructional period and allow for later evaluation of student progress. For many problem learners individual instruction in early skills is most beneficial.

Copying letter forms has been shown to be a more effective teaching method than repeated tracing of individual letters. Even when tracing has been combined with a backward fading technique, a gradual removal of the end of a stroke first, followed by preceding strokes, the ultimate result is not as legible as written letter samples of children who were given copying exercises. Copying provides the child with practice in visual memory, increasing the likelihood of the child achieving the final objective, writing from memory, without additional stimulus support.

During the beginning writing stages the student should be given ample opportunity to practice on the chalkboard, unlined newsprint, and large paper sheets. Unencumbered by lines and limited space the child can develop the kinesthetic feel of the letter form and established a clear visual image.

A multisensory approach should be used to teach letter formation and can be developed in a sequence similar to the one suggested below for each letter as it is introduced into the program.

Instructional Sequence

1. Introduce the strokes by writing them on the chalkboard or a large piece of paper. Name each stroke as it is written.
2. Demonstrate the complete letter form while naming it.
3. Have the child name the letter as another model is written.
4. Discuss the letter form.
5. Let the child develop the kinesthetic feel of the letter by using sandpaper letters, sunken letter forms, and salt boxes.
6. Ask the child to write the letter while looking at the model. Eyes should be on the model, not the writing hand.
7. Compare the child's and the teacher's letters. Let the child discuss likenesses and differences.
8. Provide auditory cues as the child rewrites the letter while again looking at the model.
9. Direct the child to look at the model then look at the paper and write the letter.
10. Compare the model and the child's letter sample. Discuss.
11. Repeat steps 8–10 until the child is able to satisfactorily make the letter.

The mildly handicapped child should recognize handwriting as a skill necessary for success in and out of school. Practice exercises should consist of relevant materials which avoid undue repetition and unstimulating drill. Handwriting practice should include writing personal letters, invitations, business letters, greeting cards, announcements, and applications.

Cursive Instruction

The Transition from Manuscript

The cursive writing program is usually begun in the third grade after the child has had two years of manuscript writing. The child's transfer from manuscript to cursive should depend, however, more on the child's readiness to master this new writing form than on a grade-level curriculum. Even while learning cursive, the child should not be forced to use it at all times. When other competencies are being examined, such as spelling practice, test answers, and filling in forms, the child should be encouraged to use whatever writing style is most comfortable.

A child is ready to transfer to cursive when the teacher observes proficiency in manuscript writing from memory, an interest in reading and imitating the cursive style, and increased muscular development. Cursive writing, although related to manuscript, does demand that the child learn new habits related to:

1. Positioning the paper
2. Letter slants
3. Connecting letters
4. Extension loops on specific letters
5. Unique letter forms (b, e, f, r, k, s, z) and spacing

Letter Formation

The transition to cursive can be assisted by helping the child recognize the relationship between manuscript and cursive letter forms. The transitional program should include writing letters and short words first in vertical manuscript then slanted manuscript. Once this is achieved the child may join the slanted manuscript letters and gradually introduce slanted cursive letters. This slowly developed program (Figure 8.6 and Figure 8.7) will give many problem learners the opportunity to recognize the relationship between manuscript and cursive writing and to transfer their learning from one form to the other.

The student can be given the following guidelines for developing a legible cursive style.

1. Remember to join the letters of each word. Do not lift your pencil until the word is completed.
2. Cursive writing has a uniform slant to all letters.
3. Spacing between cursive letters is related to letter slant and the joining or connecting of strokes.
4. The paper position for cursive writing is a slant to the right for left-handed students and to the left for right-handed writers.
5. Letters i, j, t, x are dotted or crossed at the completion of the whole word.

As in manuscript, many teachers find it advantageous to group letters for introductory cursive writing lessons. A basic classification system centers on

Step 1: vertical manuscript— can
Step 2: slanted manuscript— can
Step 3: joined manuscript— can
Step 4: cursive— can

FIGURE 8.6 Transition from Manuscript to Cursive

253

a combination of the type of connecting stroke used to join letters and the immediately following stroke. Sample groupings would include:

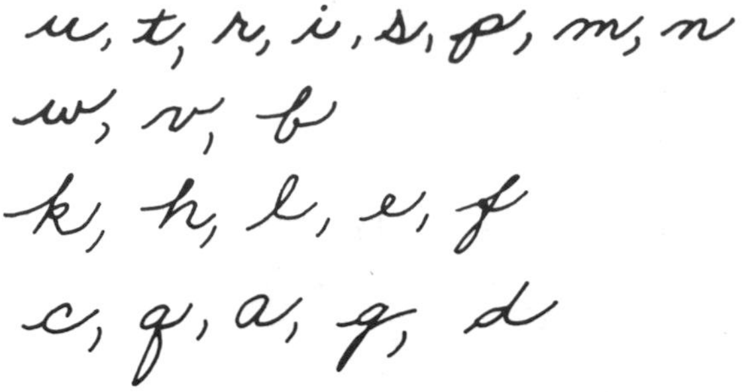

u, t, n, i, s, p, m, n

w, v, b

k, h, l, e, f

c, g, a, q, d

Each letter should be taught separately and then gradually illustrated with connecting strokes. Cursive letter instruction can be given following a teaching program similar to the one suggested for developing manuscript writing. Once again, the teacher should be aware of the importance of a multisensory approach and the use of a copying method to increase visual memory.

a c d g h i j l m

a c d g h i j l m

a c d g h i j l m

n o p q t u v w x y

n o p q t u v w x y

n o p q t u v w x y

b e f r k s z

b e f r k s z

a clown doll

a clown doll

a clown doll

Source: Anderson, P. S. *Language Skills in Elementary Education.* New York: Macmillan Publishing Co., Inc. 1972.

FIGURE 8.7 Transition Alphabet

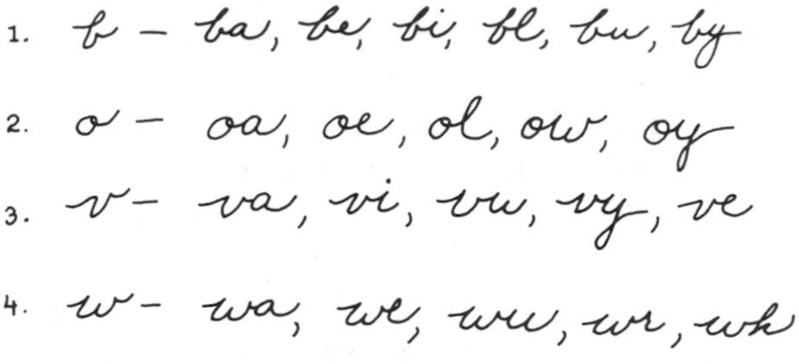

1. *b* – *ba, be, bi, bl, bu, by*

2. *o* – *oa, oe, ol, ow, oy*

3. *v* – *va, vi, vu, vy, ve*

4. *w* – *wa, we, wu, wr, wh*

FIGURE 8.8   *Difficult Letter Combinations*

It is also necessary to develop cursive writing lessons for joining letters since this is a significant new aspect of the adult style. Many children have difficulty joining specific letter combinations (Figure 8.8) and as a result produce an inappropriate word form. Letters *b, o, v,* and *w* are the most difficult to join as they connect at the top of the next letter and not at the baseline. In the early stages of cursive writing the child should join only lowercase letters, leaving capitals separate. After all letter forms have been mastered, the child can be given instruction in joining capital and lowercase letters.

Common Cursive Errors

In an extensive research study involving over 2000 writers, ranging from elementary school children to adults, Newland (1932) determined that a very small number of frequently occurring errors accounted for over 50 percent of all illegibilities in cursive writing. Newland concluded that the ten most common cursive writing errors are:

1. Lack of letter closings (*a, b, f, o,* etc.)
2. Closed top loop (*l* like *t* ; *l* like *i*)
3. Inappropriate looping (*i* like *e*)
4. Replacing rounded strokes with straight up-strokes (*n* like *u*, *c* like *i*)
5. Inappropriate stroke ending (not brought up, or down or left horizontal when it should be)
6. Too short a top (*b , d, f, h, k, l, t*)
7. Forgetting or improper crossing of *t*
8. Letters too small
9. Improper closing of such letters as *c , h, u, w*
10. Omission of letter parts

Writing Materials

The selection and use of writing materials vary according to the handwriting program established in the school and the individual teacher's preference for methods and materials. However, materials such as chalk, chalkboard, paper (unlined and lined), crayons, pencils, pens, and commercially produced handwriting books are generally used in basic handwriting programs. Most instructional designs call for beginning with chalk and large primary pencils. The use of these early writing instruments provides a thicker writing line which can be easily seen and which provides better visual feedback. The larger diameter of the instrument allows firmer control for young children who have less developed fine motor skills. Although paper is often assigned by grade level, the teacher should ensure that several types of paper be available within the classroom so that paper can be designated according to the child's competence and needs. The following guide to writing materials establishes the progression of paper and writing instruments that will be used during the instructional program (Figure 8.9).

The teacher should model the proper pencil position, give verbal directions, and frequently check to see that the writer is maintaining the appropriate hold. Check to see that the child has the index finger placed on top and one inch back from the point with the thumb placed against the pencil to hold it high and near the large knuckle of the index finger.

Writing Posture and Paper Position

To write most efficiently the child should be seated at an appropriately sized table or desk to ensure a comfortable posture. The child can adjust to the proper head distance from the paper by putting the elbow of his writing hand

Paper	Writing Instruments
1. Large unlined paper (newsprint)	1. Large crayons, paint, or chalk
2. Chalkboard	2. Large soft lead pencil
3. Lined paper, 1 inch between writing rows with ½ inch markings	3. Smaller soft lead pencil (the lower the number, the softer the lead)
4. Lined paper, 1 inch between lines	4. Small No. 2 lead pencil
5. Lined paper, ½ inch between lines	5. Ballpoint pen (medium point)
6. Lined paper, ⅜ inch between lines	6. Ballpoint pen (fine point)
7. Stationery	

FIGURE 8.9   Writing Materials

on the table and placing a clenched fist under the chin. It is helpful to have a slope of 20° on the writing surface (Figure 8.10).

The paper is positioned perpendicular to the desk's edge during manuscript writing. Once the child begins cursive instruction, the paper is slanted according to the writing hand. For the right-handed child the paper is tilted to the left at a 45° angle. The child's head is also tilted slightly to the left to allow him to see the written image and to assist in hand-eye coordination. The left-handed child slants both paper and head toward the right. Appropriate positioning for the left-handed child avoids the "left-handed hook" which results when the paper is improperly slanted and the child must compensate in order to perceive his written form.

The Left-Handed Child

Left-handed individuals represent approximately 10 percent of the population and in a world designed for the right-handed person constitute a definite minority. The school environment and the demands of the learning situation often place the left-handed child at a disadvantage. For instance, although left-handed desks and scissors are available, their quantity is often limited within a particular class and many times the child must use ones designed for right-handers. Perhaps, the most important and difficult task is for the left-handed child to learn to write from instructions given by a right-handed

Head position above the paper should be the length of the forearm with fist clenched. It helps to have the desk slope about 20° as shown.

Source: Consilia, M. *The non-coping child.* Distributed by West Georgia CESA, LaGrange, Georgia, 1974, p. 99.

FIGURE 8.10   Head-Paper Position

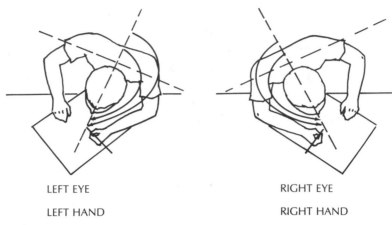

LEFT EYE   RIGHT EYE

LEFT HAND   RIGHT HAND

Source: Consilia, M. 1974, p. 100.

FIGURE 8.11   Paper Slant

teacher. The child must learn writing skills without the advantage of an exact model. The teacher must assist the child to adapt the instructional program in order to be aligned with the left hand.

The major area of concern is the proper positioning of paper and body. Early guidance is necessary to ensure that the child does not develop a backward "hooked" writing slant and an awkward body posture. The left-handed child who follows directions intended for his right-handed peers will evidence a hook position. Therefore, individualized instructions are necessary and should begin with reassuring the child that being left-handed is not odd or a fault to overcome.

There is no one position or paper slant that should be followed for all left-handed children. The recommended paper position for cursive writing is a tilt to the right; however, the child should have flexibility in adjusting the paper to meet individual comfort needs. Rather than insisting on a slant similar to that of the right-handed writer, the teacher should help the left-handed child develop uniformity of slant whether it is to the right, straight up and down, or slightly to the left.

Special considerations may be given to the left-handed child during the writing program in order to assist the child's acquisition of writing skills.

1. Allow the left-handed child additional writing practice and the opportunity to verbalize the tasks (e.g., letter form) as they are done. This provides additional feedback and helps the child's self-instruction.
2. It may be advantageous to the left-handed child to delay the transition from manuscript to cursive writing longer than usual or until the child has developed greater muscular control.

3. Soft pencils, crayons, and many ballpoint pens smudge easily. Provide the left-handed writer with a harder lead pencil or a pen that will not smear.

4. Provide the left-handed child with an appropriate writing desk. In cases where chairs with attached writing arms are used, be certain that the left-handed child has a chair with an arm on the left. If this is not possible, arrange for a table to be used for writing activities.

5. Do not insist that the left-handed child's writing slant match the writing samples established for right-handed children.

6. When a group of children are writing, drawing, or painting at a table, position the left-handed child at the left corner of the table edge. This avoids unnecessary interference from a right-handed person and allows each child appropriate space in which to work.

Evaluation

By examining a writing specimen and evaluating specific aspects of the student's penmanship, the teacher is able to determine remediation needs and to plan appropriate corrective methods. It is important to keep in mind that there is no one *right* way to form letters and by which to ultimately judge handwriting. Rather, the goal is to have each child achieve a level of penmanship which falls within an acceptable range of legibility and speed. The purpose in evaluating handwriting skills is not to eradicate individuality, but, quite the contrary, to assist the child in developing a writing style that is both personal and practical.

Legibility in handwriting can be broken down into the smaller elements of size, slant, form, spacing, line quality, and alignment. Each of these can be informally assessed either by the teacher or the student. Based on the analysis of these components the teacher and student can determine goals for future handwriting lessons.

Size

In both manuscript and cursive writing it is easy to determine if letters are of a proper and consistent size. Using a short writing sample, draw a line across the tops of the letters to see if they are uniformly made. In manuscript, uppercase and tall letters are generally one space high, while lowercase letters are one-half space. Cursive varies according to the particular letter form with capitals being one space high, small letters one-fourth space high, descenders one half space below the line, and ascenders three-fourths of a space high.

Slant

In manuscript the slant is a vertical line for all writers, however in cursive the slant leans toward the right. In assessing the slant of the writing sample, consistency is once again the key. Lines, either vertical or uniformly slanted depending on the written form being used, should be drawn through each letter in order to determine which letters are not slanted properly.

Form

Letter form can be checked against a commercially prepared or teacher-made alphabet. This comparison can be simplified by using a standard transparency which can be placed over the child's letter specimen and judged according to closeness to the standard.

Another technique commonly used for verifying proper letter form is to cut a hole, slightly larger than the child's letter, in a small card. As the hole is moved over individual letters, the child can focus on the form and note illegible letters.

Spacing

Spacing varies according to the sequence of letters within a word. The general rule requires a space the size of one small *o* between each letter. Slightly larger spaces should be used between words and sentences. When checking spacing, look for consistency throughout the writing sample.

Line Quality

Line quality refers to the evenness of the pressure exerted on the writing instrument. An equal amount of pressure should be applied throughout the specimen and should be heavy enough to leave a firm quality.

Alignment

The base of all the letters should be touching at the same level in order for the specimen to be well aligned. This can be checked by using the line on the paper or by drawing a line along the base of the word to determine if all letters begin at the baseline.

even *even*

Handwriting Scales

Several commercially produced handwriting scales, sometimes referred to as *merit scales,* are available for classroom use. The quality of the student's handwriting is determined by comparing the child's writing sample to a scale sample with pre-established grade level value. The evaluation scales (Figure 8.12) produced by the Zaner-Bloser Company are excellent examples of general merit scales. Manuscript samples are available for grades 1 and 2 and cursive for grades 3 to 9. Samples with ratings of excellent, good, average, fair, and poor are used as the standard for comparison.

It is worth mentioning that, although handwriting scales can be used for grading, this is probably not their most advantageous use. Grades based upon merit scales may create too much pressure to conformity. The child may feel that the intent is to exactly reproduce the scale sample or else fail. On the contrary, individuality should be encouraged and students should use the scales only as a means of comparing their own writing to make decisions for improved legibility.

Checklists

A final means of handwriting evaluation is the development of a handwriting checklist. Checklists also provide a record-keeping procedure by which the child and teacher can chart continued progress. The teacher can

Example 1—Excellent for Grade One

I wrote my name
upon the sand.

Example 2—Good for Grade One

I wrote my name
upon the sand.

Example 3—Average for Grade One

I wrote my name
upon the sand.

Example 4—Fair for Grade One

I wrote my name
upon the sand.

Example 5—Poor for Grade One

I Wrote MY name
UPONthesand.

Example 1—Excellent for Grade Three

Look in a book
and you will see
words and magic
and mystery.

Example 2—Good for Grade Three

Look in a book
and you will see
words and magic
and mystery.

Example 3—Average for Grade Three

Look in a book
and you will see
words and magic
and mystery.

Example 4—Fair for Grade Three

Look in a book
and you will see
word and magic
and mystery.

Example 5—Poor for Grade Three

*Look in a book
and you will see
words and magi
and mystry .*

Example 1—Excellent for Grade Six

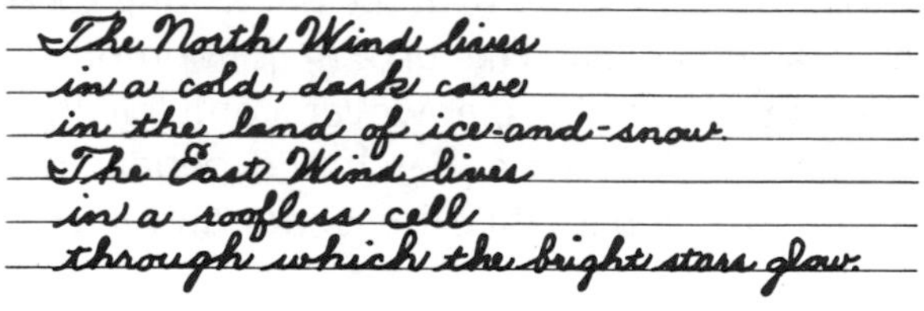

*The North Wind lives
in a cold, dark cave
in the land of ice-and-snow.
The East Wind lives
in a roofless cell
through which the bright stars glow.*

Example 2—Good for Grade Six

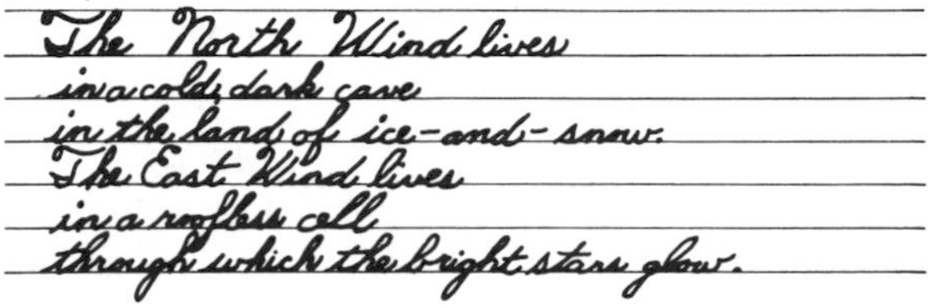

*The North Wind lives
in a cold, dark cave
in the land of ice-and-snow.
The East Wind lives
in a roofless cell
through which the bright stars glow.*

Example 3—Average for Grade Six

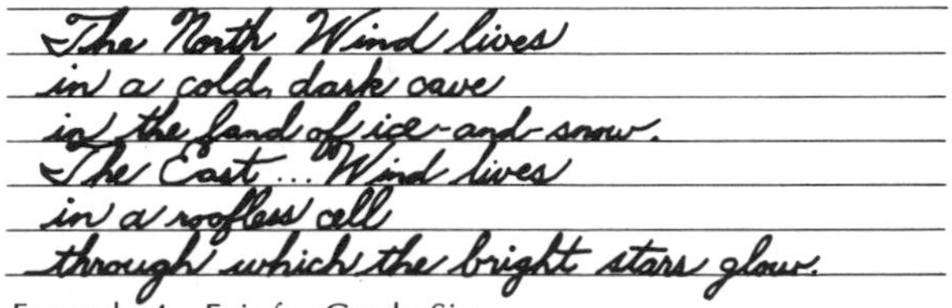

*The North Wind lives
in a cold, dark cave
in the land of ice-and-snow.
The East ... Wind lives
in a roofless cell
through which the bright stars glow.*

Example 4—Fair for Grade Six

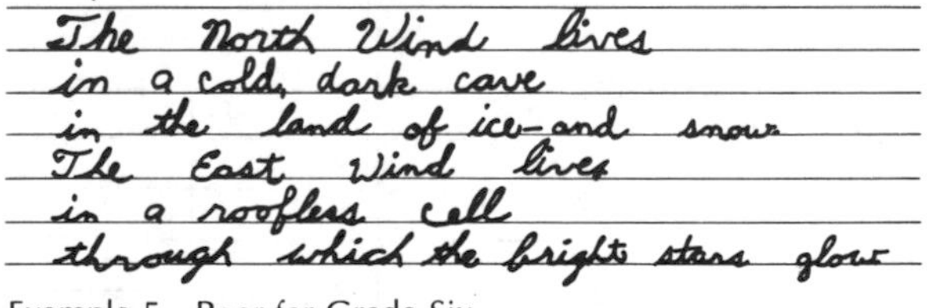

*The North Wind lives
in a cold, dark cave
in the land of ice-and snow
The East Wind lives
in a roofless cell
through which the bright stars glow*

Example 5—Poor for Grade Six

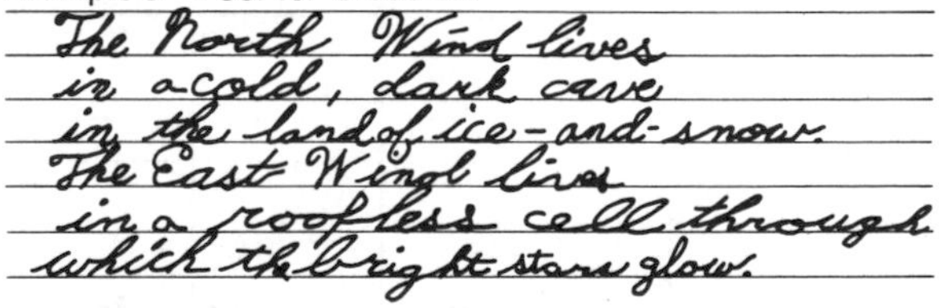

*The North Wind lives
in a cold, dark cave
in the land of ice-and-snow.
The East Wind lives
in a roofless cell through
which the bright stars glow.*

Source: Used with permission from *Creative growth with handwriting,* 2nd ed. Copyright © 1979 Zaner-Bloser, Inc., Columbus, Ohio.

FIGURE 8.12   *Handwriting Evaluation Scales*

devise a checklist based on the handwriting program objectives or can adapt the most common error lists given earlier in this chapter for manuscript and cursive writing. The following chart (Figure 8.13) is a simple self-evaluation checklist by which the student can record growth and assess future needs.

Speed

Many problem writers show extremes in writing speeds. Some are so slow that a written assignment can take up a major portion of the day, leaving little room for other subjects. Others, however, complete the task quickly but the writing is illegible. In either case the child experiences difficulty in producing a proper writing sample while in school and later as an adult. The

Rate: 1. good—for each of the following categories unless otherwise indicated
2. average
3. fair
4. poor

	Oct.	Dec.	Feb.	April	June
I. Neatness					
a. Appearance of work					
b. Cleanliness of paper					
c. Organization of margins					
II. Legibility					
a. Size					
b. Slant					
c. Form					
d. Spacing					
· Letters within words					
· Between words and sentences					
· Paragraphs					
e. Line quality					
f. Alignment					
III. Rate of writing					
[mark (s) slow or (f) fast]					
IV. Writing Position					
a. Posture					
b. Pencil grip					
c. Slant of paper					

FIGURE 8.13   Self-Evaluation Chart

program objectives should be ordered to develop accuracy, that is, legibility first and speed second. Once the child can make acceptable letter and word forms and does so on a fairly consistent basis, the teacher should establish time limits for completion of the task. By gradually reducing the allotted amount of time, the teacher can structure an increase in the child's writing speed. If, however, the child loses legibility, it is probably because the writing time was reduced too quickly. In such a case the teacher should note the changes and return to the shortest time limit which still provided legibility.

Handwriting speed can be recorded using a rate measure. To find rate, the teacher should divide words (letters, sentences) the child has completed by the amount of time required for the task. That is:

$$\text{handwriting rate} = \frac{\text{number of words written}}{\text{minutes of total task}}$$

Adapting the Handwriting Program for the Mildly Handicapped

Some mildly handicapped children may experience problems in developing appropriate writing skills. Once the teacher has assessed the child's difficulty, the next step is to modify the program to meet the child's needs. Adaptations can be made to the writing tools, the child's positioning, and the task itself. Figure 8.14 breaks these areas down into their component parts and provides adaptations for each. The teacher should not be limited to the suggestions given here but should use these as a guide for further remediation.

Typing

Recently writing programs designed for mildly handicapped children have been extended to include instruction in typing skills. The rationale behind this trend is to help the child achieve self-expression without undue effort being placed on the production of a legible handwriting. For those children who have been unable to develop a clear and efficient writing style, the use of typewriters for assignments related to other academic skills is a positive alternative and one that should be instituted before the child experiences failure for too long. Being able to type test responses and written assignments may relieve the pressure that some children perceive when trying to conform to an acceptable handwriting style. The child may be able to approach the learning task positively and achieve success in other academic skills.

A note of caution is necessary, however. There will always be occasions when the child must hand write a word, note, address, phrase, or phone number. Typing skills cannot and should not substitute completely for hand-

Adaptation of grip	Wrap the writing tool with tape, clay, styrofoam, rubber bands, or commercial holders to enlarge the area and allow the child with poor muscular control to hold firmly.
Adaptation to paper	To help some children write between the lines, provide additional guides by pasting string or yarn to act as lines. Heavy lines of Elmer's glue when dry can also provide boundaries. Emphasize lines by using different colored markers or folding the paper. Newspaper columns, such as classified ads, make excellent practice sheets.
	To help children develop a left-to-right progression with appropriate margins, use start and stop signals on the sides of the paper. For instance, a green line on the left and a red line on the right could be easily drawn prior to beginning the writing tasks.
Adaptation of time	Some children are too slow, laboring over each letter form. Use a kitchen timer to help them speed up their writing. Other children seem to be racing an unknown clock and need to slow down in order to write legibly. A timer would also help these children to pace themselves.
Adaptation of task	For those children who have trouble copying off the board, provide a desk model for practice exercises.
	Allow the child to develop the kinesthetic feel of the writing task by writing in sand or salt boxes, or place the paper over a board covered with sandpaper.
	Many children will self-correct errors once they become aware of them. Provide the child with materials that emphasize visual feedback, such as dark colors on lines, heavy markers, and spacing guides.
Adaptaton of letter forms	To help make the transition from manuscript to cursive form, have the child write oval rather than round manuscript letters, teach slant manuscript and/or give instructions in making manuscript letters with a continuous stroke.
	To sharpen the visual image, instruct the child to increase both the letter size and the space between words.
Adaptation of grades	The use of letter grades for handwriting evaluation may not be appropriate. Corrective feedback is preferable as a means of achieving legibility within a range of acceptable performance.

FIGURE 8.14 Handwriting Program Adaptations

writing competence. The child should be encouraged to continue practicing writing in either manuscript or cursive according to personal preference while learning to use the typewriter.

Resources

1. Many objects commonly found around the school and house can be used in the handwriting program. For instance:

    a. Use newsprint to practice both manuscript and cursive letter forms. Turned sideways the columns found in the classified ads provide an inexpensive ruled writing paper. (Figure 8.15)

    b. Tape a sheet of medium grade sandpaper over the cardboard

FIGURE 8.15 *Newsprint Used to Practice Handwriting Skills (double letters—t, j, k, l, etc.—go into two columns).*

forms found in the center of a bolt of cloth. This material will serve as a writing desk which provides multisensory feedback to the writer. (Figure 8.16) The child should use a large soft pencil or a crayon while writing on the sandpaper surface.

2. Examination of the following list reveals the diversity among programs and illustrates the need for a teacher to carefully select handwriting materials. Many commercially produced handwriting programs are suitable for mildly handicapped children. In some cases it may be necessary for the teacher to make adjustments to the instructional program in order to match the specific needs of individual children.

    a. Barbe, W. B., Lucas, V. H., Hackney, C. S., and McAllister, C. *Creative Growth with Handwriting.* Columbus, Ohio: Zaner-Bloser, Inc. 1975. The handwriting program is directly related to the total language arts curriculum. The goal is to teach handwriting concurrent with other communication skills.

    b. Noble, T. C. and Handwriting Research Institute. *Better Handwriting for You.* New York: Noble and Noble Publishers, Inc. 1971. Four distinctive features make this program suitable for individualized instruction: the student paces and evaluates his own work; emphasis is given to common writing errors; letter writing and spelling are integrated; and letters are sequentially introduced according to strokes.

    c. King, F. M. *Palmer Method Handwriting.* Schaumburg, Illinois: The A. N. Palmer Company, 1976. Handwriting is viewed as a physical skill and emphasis is placed on the freedom of the arm movement. Provides drill in letter formation to help develop correct movement habits.

    d. Enstrom, E. A. *Adventures in Handwriting.* Stone Mountain, Georgia: McMillan Publishing Co., Inc., 1975. Reduces the need for frequent teacher supervision by providing *colorgraph,* a step-by-step, color discrimination method for guiding letter and number formation.

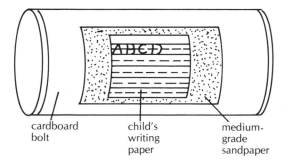

cardboard bolt   child's writing paper   medium-grade sandpaper

FIGURE 8.16   Sandpaper Writing Desk

268

e. Skinner, B. F., and Krakower, S. *Handwriting with Write and See.* Chicago: Lyons and Carnahan, Inc. The child benefits from immediate feedback given to correct responses due to special line ink in the workbook. Independent work habits are fostered, allowing the teacher freedom to provide additional remediation when necessary.

3. *D'Nealian Handwriting* (Scott, Foresman and Company, Tucker, Georgia, 1978) is a commercially produced program that appears to have a great deal of potential for mildly handicapped children. *D'Nealian Handwriting* was designed to eliminate many of the inconsistencies (e.g., letter size and spacing) found in traditional handwriting programs. It teaches a simplified manuscript alphabet which more directly leads to cursive writing. Each manuscript letter (except *i, j, f, t,* and *x*) is made from one continuous stroke which is slanted and reduced in size (½-inch ruled paper) from the beginning. As a result, the child is able to more easily make the transition to cursive writing.

An advantage of the D'Nealian method is that it minimizes the perceptual problems of some mildly handicapped children who are unable to connect the noncontinuous strokes in traditional manuscript. D'Nealian emphasizes legibility within flexible standards of form, size, and slant. The lack of rigid models allows a range of individual differences to be appreciated.

SUMMARY

Handwriting continues to be an essential communication skill and one that deserves direct instruction within the general curriculum. Teachers who are often familiar with the behavioral manifestations of writing disabilities need to become more knowledgeable of the causes of these difficulties and specific techniques for remediation. This chapter provided information regarding the development of a handwriting program for mildly handicapped children. Procedures for instructing and evaluating both manuscript and cursive writing styles were discussed. These methods were consistent with the diagnostic-prescriptive framework advocated throughout this text.

In developing the handwriting program the teacher should be aware of issues regarding the use of a duo-writing system (manuscript and cursive), handedness, and the use of typewriters for writing disabled students. Each of these topics was discussed in relation to the needs of the mildly handicapped. Finally, the chapter offered suggestions for adapting the handwriting program and a review of current handwriting materials on the market that are suitable for disabled learners.

POINTS FOR DISCUSSION

1. As a teacher your handwriting will serve as a model for your students. It is therefore important that you develop a legible style. For practice, write your favorite poem or song lyric in manuscript and then cursive. Repeat this type of exercise whenever you have a chance. Then write on a chalkboard, since this will undoubtedly be where your students will see your writing most often.

2. Try to discover what it is like to be *reverse-handed*. If you are a right-handed person try to cut, sew, or bat a ball modeling from a left-handed person. What problems did you encounter? Try to delineate the techniques that are helpful in teaching a left-handed child.

3. Develop a handwriting bulletin board or learning center. Collect and display such things as class autographs, a list of things that must be written neatly (addresses), a list of things that can be casually written (notes, diary), and different letter forms found in printed books. Develop activities that will help children realize the importance of handwriting and the range of differences among individuals.

4. Gather writing samples from children of various ages and friends. Use error analysis to determine any consistent problems. Compare and contrast differences in style and try to relate styles and errors to purpose of the written sample.

5. Keep a folder of your own handwriting samples. Analyze your own errors. Develop a program to correct your mistakes and keep a record of your progress. Self-teaching can be an excellent learning experience if you clearly describe and adhere to your established program.

6. Use handwriting scales to evaluate several different children's writing. Practice doing this at various grade levels and on different types of writing samples. Does the purpose of the writing sample influence legibility?

7. Develop a collection of writing activities and materials to help children develop writing skills. Put all materials together in an appropriate sequence and develop a management system for their use and recording progress.

8. In class discuss why you think many successful adults are illegible writers. For example, the doctor who writes illegible prescriptions is well-known for this characteristic and no one seems concerned. In fact, it is often an assumed trait.

9. Discuss the relationship of handwriting and other school subjects. Do you think the importance of handwriting instruction is understated in American schools today?

10. Discuss the use of the typewriter in programs for mildly handicapped children. Do some investigation in the schools in your area. Try to find out when typewriters are used (grade), by whom, and for what purposes.

11. Examine several different handwriting programs now on the market. What differences are evident in the programming? Do any of these handwriting programs provide modifications for problem writers?

12. Select a commercially produced handwriting program and examine it for use with mildly handicapped children. Suggest adaptations which would make the program more appropriate to this population of learners and try to field test your ideas.

13. Discuss whether you feel it would be useful to give instructions in handwriting to left-handed students separately from the rest of the class. Perhaps all left-handed students in a grade level should be grouped for this purpose. Would it be advantageous to have left-handed children learn handwriting from a left-handed teacher? Is this practical?

REFERENCES

Anderson, P. S. *Language skills in elementary education*. New York: Macmillan Publishing Co., Inc., 1972.

Barbe, W. B., and Lucas, V. H. Instruction in handwriting: A new look. *Childhood Education*, 1974, *50*, 207–209.

Consilia, Sister Mary. *The non-coping child*. Distributed by West Georgia CESA, LaGrange, Georgia, 1974.

Donoghue, M. R. *The child and the English language arts* (2nd ed.). Dubuque, Iowa: W. C. Brown Company, 1975.

Frostig, M., and Horne, D. *The Frostig program for the development of visual perception*. Chicago: Follet, 1964.

Hammill, D. D., and Bartel, N. R. *Teaching children with learning and behavior problems* (2nd ed.). Boston: Allyn & Bacon, Inc., 1978.

Hanson, I. W. Teaching remedial handwriting. *Language Arts*, 1976, *53*, 428–431.

Hildreth, G. *Learning the three R's*. Minneapolis: Educational Publishers, 1936.

Kephart, N. C. *The slow learner in the classroom*. Columbus, Ohio: Charles E. Merrill Publishing Co., 1960.

Lewis, E. R., and Lewis, H. P. An analysis of errors in the formation of manuscript letters by first-grade children. *American Educational Journal*, 1965, *2*, 25–35.

Markoff, A. M. *Teaching low-achieving children reading, spelling and handwriting*. Springfield, Ill.: Charles C Thomas, Publisher, 1976.

Newland, T. E. An analytical study of the development of illegibilities in handwriting from the lower grades to adulthood. *Journal of Educational Research*, 1932, *26*, 249–258.

9

Developing Skills in Written Expression

Written expression is one of the more difficult of the communication arts to master. The process of putting one's thoughts into written form involves the integration of all the areas of the language arts: oral expression, reading, handwriting, spelling, vocabulary, and writing conventions (capitalization, punctuation, and organization). Difficulty in any one of these areas reduces the degree to which the written product effectively communicates the message.

Written composition develops gradually as the child progresses through stages of development, self-expression, and skill achievement. The writing sequence as shown in Figure 9.1 begins with initial writing experiences when children understand that language can be written down for others to read. Motivation increases along with experience, and a natural desire for clearer expression and better communication leads to *skill development*. Vocabulary, organization, and the mechanics of writing take on importance when applied to written products. The final stages in the sequence are achieved when children begin to *refine* their writing by first proofreading for conventional errors and clarity and then developing a personal style.

For mildly handicapped children the development of writing abilities is essential for later independence as adults. The child must learn to communicate personal needs and thoughts. Society demands that many experiences be put into written language, such as in writing a letter to a friend, taking a written test, or completing a homework assignment. The mildly handicapped child, who as an adult can perform these daily tasks will avoid attracting attention and will ultimately achieve greater independence.

Writing can also serve a therapeutic purpose for the mildly handicapped child who is often confronted with frustrating and problematic experiences. Writing can be a private and intimate exercise in which the child feels free to reveal personal concerns. "One may communicate effectively in writing without the necessity of the face-to-face confrontation that oral communication requires" (Cramer, 1978, pp. 53–54).

Expressions of personal feelings of some mildly handicapped children are shown in Figure 9.2. After readings these accounts the teachers gained some additional insights into the individuals in their classes and were able to relate on a more personal level with each child. Expressive writing of this kind serves two distinct purposes; it allows the children to communicate with those around them as well as with themselves (Cramer, 1978).

These examples also serve to highlight the integration of the various language arts skills. Notice the handwriting, spelling, and vocabulary level of each statement.

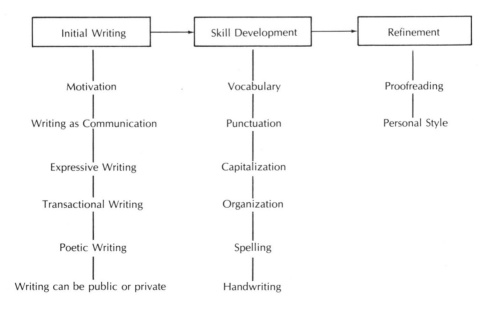

FIGURE 9.1   Sequence of Written Expression

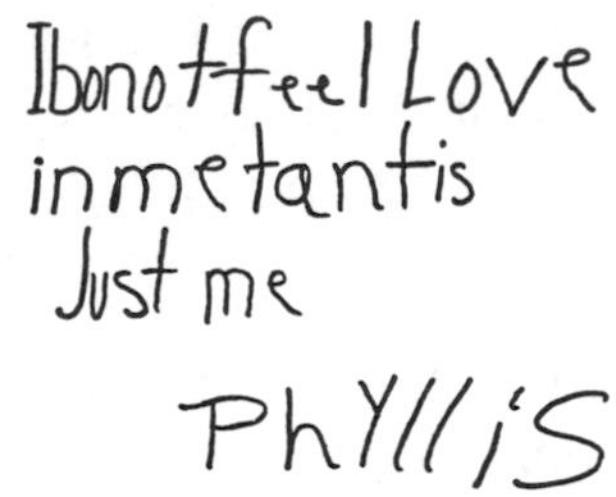

Ibono tfeel Love
in me tantis
Just me

PhYlliS

(I DO NOT FEEL LOVE IN ME THAT IS JUST ME)
(age 8)

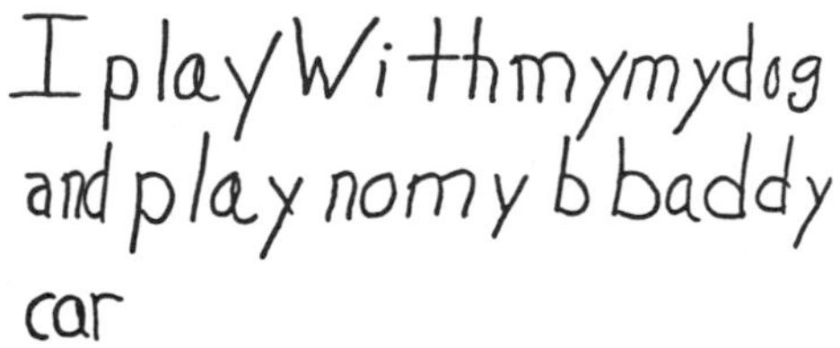

I play Withmymydog
and play nomy b baddy

car

(I PLAY WITH MY DOG AND PLAY ON MY DADDY'S CAR)
(age 9)

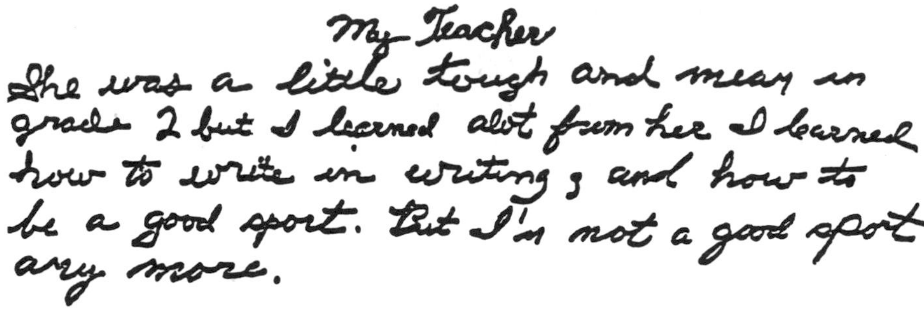

My Teacher

She was a little tough and mean in grade 2 but I learned alot from her I learned how to write in writing; and how to be a good sport. But I'm not a good sport any more.

(Greg—grade 4)

FIGURE 9.2

Writing Instruction—A Question of Approach

Most mildly handicapped children are classified as such because of the specialized support services that they receive during their school years. Generally the predominant philosophy of special services emphasizes the teaching of the basic skills through highly structured programming. Where successful remedial techniques have been developed, they become a significant element in the instructional procedures. Often such an approach pays off and problem learners show academic gains to verify the emphasis on basic skills. However, written expression may be an area which takes exception to this general philosophy and educators may need to reexamine their goals and methods for teaching written composition.

275

To write effectively, children eventually need to understand that correctness in spelling, punctuation, capitalization, and variety in vocabulary is desirable. But is it necessary to formally instruct the child in rules prior to allowing large-scale experimentation in writing itself? Or is it possible that Blake (1971) is correct when he says, "Children learn to write by writing?"

The question of whether we should have children write before we teach them basic rules and conventions, or instruct them first and have them write later (i.e., write to learn or learn to write?) needs to be considered. The debate is appropriate to the planning of instruction for the mildly handicapped as it directly relates methodological approach to instructional goals. General education would postulate that a focus on writing skills does little or nothing to improve written communication and that provisions for expressive writing are the significant factors in writing achievement (Blake, 1971; Davis, 1976; Evertts, 1974). While on the other hand, special educators have either ignored the issue, or followed a more structured approach toward functional skill development, believing that special children need to learn acceptable behaviors. Since there is little research in the area of written expression for exceptional children, the position one takes is often arbitrary or based on research from other populations.

In fact, it may be preferable to reconcile these two points of view. Spontaneous written expression may be one of the most effective means of teaching mildly handicapped children conventional skills. Using the child's own writing samples as a base, a program of gradual skill introduction can be developed where the imaginative and the practical are successfully teamed. The central core of a writing program for mildly handicapped children should be to have each child *write something everyday*. The objective is for the child to comfortably express ideas and feelings and to generate materials which are then used as the basis for skill development.

Creative writing is thought of by some as original composition reflecting both experience and imagination in an extremely personal manner. In common practice the term is, more often than not, used when speaking about fictitious story writing, poetry, and other personal expressions. The term creative is seldom applied to the more mundane tasks of writing letters, reports, and announcements, all of which, however, require the author to put thoughts into words and sentences. Such functional writing is sometimes referred to as "realistic writing" because of its expository nature.

Creative writing and functional writing are not in complete opposition and one should not supersede the other in the writing program. The mildly handicapped child can learn and grow considerably from opportunities for personal expression. With nonhandicapped students writing is used to increase vocabulary and cognitive development as well as modify effective behavior. There is no reason to believe that this is not true with most special children also.

The integration of creative and functional writing can take place if the teacher develops a philosophy which redefines the terms somewhat. A more positive definition of creative writing given by Cramer (1978) is: "The act of recording one's ideas in words and sentences." This conceptualization applies the term to any writing in which the writer expresses an element of himself. It does not matter whether the written piece serves a practical or fanciful purpose. A carefully planned writing program incorporates a variety of writing experiences, blending creativity and functionalism.

Initial Writing

Motivation

The instructional program begins with motivating the child to write. Posturing or developing a positive attitude toward writing is essential. The child must recognize that writing is synonymous with communication and that communication is a life-long necessity.

Before beginning to write, a nurturing environment must be established which will promote the acceptance of the child's ideas. Unless the child feels comfortable in self-expression, it is highly doubtful that "creativity" will emerge. It is also a good idea, especially with mildly handicapped children, to hold an oral discussion of the topic and related subtopics before assigning the writing activity. By sharing ideas, children are often spurred on to convey their own thoughts. The teacher should not only lead the discussion but also participate in it, offering suggestions and expansions when appropriate.

Several authors offer suggestions on how to create environments which encourage children to write. The ideas listed below are an incorporation of the views of Blake (1971) and Cramer (1978).

1. *Promote oral expression as often as possible.* Give the children the chance to talk about things and share their ideas.
2. *Read to children often* using a variety of literary formats. Enthusiasm for writing begins with good models.
3. *Relate to the children's experiences.* Help them to express areas of interest and concern.
4. *Provide many varied experiences* in which the children can participate. Children can only write about what they have experienced.
5. *Be sensitive to oral and written expressions.* Let it be known that you value what has been said.

6. *Arouse the students' awareness* of things around them (colors, shapes, sounds, objects, etc.).
7. *Provide a purpose for writing.* Help the children understand the rationale behind effective communication.
8. *Provide "warm-up" activities* prior to having children begin writing. These warm-ups (discussions, experiences, readings), will motivate children and help them focus on the main points of the writing.
9. *Integrate writing into the rest of the curriculum.* Writing should be an active part of learning.
10. *Follow through on writing activities* so the children see the products of their efforts. Completed compositions should be praised and shared.

Motivation to write, as we define it, extends beyond the establishment of a positive environment. It includes a fundamental understanding of what writing is and the functions it can serve.

Writing as Communication

Written language is a symbolic means of representing our world. A comprehensive view of children's writings, formulated by James Britton is currently gaining a great deal of acceptance. Britton (1972) classifies writing according to the purpose of the communication and the audience. Children's writing formats exist along the following continuum:

Transactional ← Expressive → Poetic
1   2   3   4   5

Expressive writing represents the child's earliest and most common writing attempts. Expressive writing tells a great deal about the writer by revealing personal experiences, feelings, and reactions. For instance, a child may write about a family activity, what happened at the carnival, or how it felt to feed a baby sister for the first time. Expressive writing is an effective form of communication when the reader either has a common experiential base or is very familiar with the writer.

Utilitarian writing is *transactional* in nature. Transactional writing contains elements of factual information and practical application. The audience is required in some way to participate in the communication by responding or interpreting the information for appropriate use. Examples of transactional writing include letters, notices, applications, book reports, histories, and greetings.

At the opposite end of the continuum from transactional writing is *poetic writing* which represents the formal literary style. Included in this category are the story form, poetry, fables, and tall tales. The reader is a spectator to the images and ideas portrayed.

Britton's continuum shows transitional stages between expressive and the transactional or poetic poles. Most children, and the mildly handicapped in particular, are not fully capable of the more extreme forms and their writing includes elements of either expressive-transactional or expressive-poetic styles. A transitional stage of writing is evident in composition about inflated personal adventures (expressive poetic) or writing a message about yourself to be placed in a time capsule (expressive-transactional). In each case, however, the children's writing is aimed at communication of their own thoughts and words.

Expressive Writing

Initial writing begins with expressive writing. In fact, children's first experience with written expression occurs when they excitedly scribble or draw a picture and ask the parent to look at their story. In many cases the child accompanies the art work by a verbal description. This early involvement with "pretend writing" show's the child's emerging understanding of writing as communication.

Early writing within the school setting begins when children dictate a story to the teacher who in turn writes it down and reads it back to them. Very often this initial writing activity starts during preschool and is continued until the child can independently manage the necessary multiple writing skills along with self-expression. As the dictated story format is repeated, the child becomes familiar with the elementary components of writing and of communicating one's own thoughts to others.

Children, like all of us, are most comfortable talking about things they know, have done or have felt themselves. For this reason the *experience story* is an excellent mechanism for early writing. The name experience story means just that, the expression of a personal occurrence. Topical areas which can be developed include:

- Field trips
- My family
- School life
- Holidays
- Pets
- Science activities
- Favorite things

By dictating the language script to the teacher or into a tape recorder, the child is freed of the burden of handwriting, spelling, punctuation, and other conventional factors. The primary purpose of dictated experience stories is to assist the child in organizing personal expression. The teacher, through a series of questions, can lead the child toward a logical presentation. Sample questions related to organization are:

> *How shall the story start?*
> *What is the first thing that happened?*
> *What happens next?*
> *Can you give some details?*
> *How does this story end?*

Other questions may lead the child to think about the expressive aspects of the story. For instance:

> *Can you think of another way to say that?*
> *Do you think your message is clear?*
> *Do you feel good about the story?*

Experience stories in writing parallel the language experience approach to reading and adopt the same rationale. Simply stated it is:

> *What I can think about, I can talk about.*
> *What I can talk about can be written.*
> *What can be written, I can read.*
> *I Can Read What I Write! (Van Allen, 1976)*

In the beginning the experience stories should reflect the syntactic forms used by the child. As writing and language skills are introduced they should be incorporated into the composition when appropriate for the written expression. Capitalization, for instance, should be used correctly once sufficient instruction has been given.

Experience stories may be developed individually or by a group process. Transcriptions from the child's speech to written compositions can be made by the teacher, an aide, an older child, or a parent volunteer. Children's stories can be reproduced and distributed, put on charts and displayed, bound as a book, or kept as an individual record of progress. In any case, they provide a rich medium for early expression.

As the child's writing and language skills increase, more spontaneous writing can occur. The child will become more independent, although many mildly handicapped children may need some continued structuring in the form of a warm-up activity or discussion. A good point to remember is that the more interaction (experience) children have with a topic, the better they can write about it. If the task, therefore, is to write about what it is like to be president, then the child should be exposed to stories, films, pictures, and discussions about the presidency.

Transactional Writing

Children need a variety of writing opportunities. Purposeful writing related to actual experiences will be most advantageous and will be recognized by children as something they need to learn to do. The more "real" and concrete the retionale behind a writing task is the more likely that the child will understand it.

There is generally a greater expectation of achievement related to transactional writing due to the insistence upon acceptable forms and the utilization of specific writing conventions. This is due to the insistence on acceptable forms and the utilization of specific writing conventions.

The reality of certain writing tasks does not preclude incorporating many basic instructional principles, specifically motivation/stimulation, receptiveness, and reinforcement. For instance, a trip to the post office may proceed a unit on letter writing and may be followed by the creation of class penpals.

Situations which can appropriately be considered transactional writing activities have been suggested by Burns and Broman (1979) and are listed below with some modifications.

1. Letters: friendly letters; business letters; social notes of thanks, invitation, sympathy, or congratulations; and letters of complaint
2. Card writing and postcards
3. Reports in content subjects
4. Announcements and notices of events: articles for the school newspaper; items for the bulletin board; and class exhibits
5. Records of class plans; class activities; events; clubs; room histories; or diaries
6. Forms such as registration slips; applications; requests

Transactional writing is a skill a child should have prior to leaving school. However, the notions that such functional writing must be repetitious or uniform are nonsense. For instance, children should not be required to copy "standard" letters from a textbook or the chalkboard. Instead, they should be taught the basic writing conventions (see Figure 9.3) and given natural practice exercises in which they are encouraged to be original, i.e., creative.

281

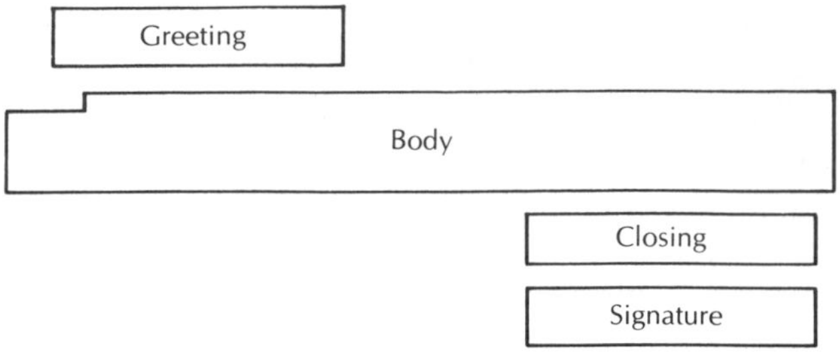

FIGURE 9.3   An Example of a Writing Convention Friendly Letter Format

Activities for practicing transactional writing include:

1. Establish a post office in the classroom. Encourage children to send notes to the teacher and their peers throughout the school day. Set the model by using the postal system to send feedback on class assignments, behavior, and attitude.
2. Create a class newspaper reporting class activities and happenings about school.
3. Collect forms from businesses around town. Have children (intermediate level and up) complete them including sections on "Why I returned this item" or "Why I want this job."
4. Have students design greeting cards and send them to each other for birthdays, holidays, or illnesses.
5. Have each child write a medical or a social autobiography, including as many of the actual facts as possible.
6. When a new student enters the class have the group develop an announcement of the new arrival.

Functional writing tasks should be judged for content and convention. However, children cannot be expected to know rules or skills they have not been taught. Attend to only those features which you expect to be accomplished. As in other writing, content should always be valued. Suggestions as to content or mechanics can be given in a positive light encouraging another attempt if necessary.

Poetic Writing

Several poetic writing programs have been successfully instituted with mildly handicapped children (Cady, 1975; Rich & Nedboy, 1977; Nathanson, Cynamon, & Lehman, 1976). In each program, time was given to preparing the students for the writing task by discussions and either reading material related to the subject or presenting an exciting stimulus. In each case, special provisions were also made to minimize the effect of the handicapped students' learning problems on their written performance. Ideas included:

1. Having the students dictate the story or poem to a teacher.
2. Presenting each child with an audio-dictionary which included all words listed during a brainstorming session on the topic. The audio-dictionary consisted of a set of language master cards (one word on each card) arranged in alphabetical order. If uncertain of a word, the child could locate it in the card file, put in on the language master, and hear it spoken and explained.
3. Children were told not to worry about writing conventions during the initial writing activity. Later, each composition was reviewed in a personal conference between the student and the teacher and corrections were made on a one-to-one instructional basis.
4. Poetry was developed by a group process so that each child felt his ideas were accepted and encouraged by his peers.
5. Children's writings were read expressively by the teacher to the class. This eliminated the discomfort of children who are not good readers or are hesitant to read their material. It also presented the writing in the most positive light, receiving the full range of expression, so the author and others could value it appropriately.

Creative writing activities which can be used with mildly handicapped children do not vary greatly from ones developed for nonhandicapped children. Modifications which reduce frustration are always in order.

The use of a story frame which stimulates initial thinking and motivates the child to complete the tale is a creative writing stimulus technique. A sample story frame may be:

"You have been walking down a winding, narrow street when suddenly _ _ _ _ _ _."

or

"Pretend you are a door (or car, chair); where do you lead to? What would happen if someone went through you?"

Pictures and films are very useful in fostering writing. Pictures may be cut from magazines, coloring books, or comic books and their uses are limited only by the teacher's own imagination. Figure 9.4 shows the combi-

FIGURE 9.4   Creative Writing Ideas

nation of two sets of drawings which might be used in a creative writing situation where children are told:

> *"You have been asked to catch strange creatures who are known only by their descriptions. Name each creature and write a report about it for a popular adventure magazine."*

Films or slides are also quite stimulating. Children can be asked to write a script for a particular story or slide sequence. After the script has been written, the next step is to tape it and present the show to an appreciative audience.

Poetic forms can be fun. Many mildly handicapped children have never written a poem. In some cases they are unsure as to what a poem is exactly. Contrary to what some would think or say, almost any form, rhyme, or meter is acceptable. "Trains and Stuff" in Figure 9.5 is a poem written by delinquent boys in New York working as a group. Notice the many personal feelings attached to the poetic symbol, the train.

Poetic forms which can be easily taught to children and which many will enjoy are:

1.   *Alliteration*—Sassy Susie says, "So long."
2.   *Couplets*—My cat's so pretty.
           She's just a kitty.
3.   *Limericks*—(Many children know some popular ones and are excited to write their own or change the ending of one they know.)

> *There was an old woman named Ell*
> *Who lived way down in the Dell.*
> *She counted her sheep,*
> *When she couldn't sleep.*
> *But how many she had she won't tell.*

Children also enjoy being expressive about themselves. For older children especially the writing program can include biographies, diaries, and descriptive personal fantasies. Activities such as these can act as vehicles for children to express their own likes and dislikes, desires, fears, and frustrations. The affective expression can offer insight to the teacher and comfort and pleasure to the child who has written it.

Writing Is Public or Private

Writing is for communication; communication with others and/or with oneself. Schools have a tendency to declare all property of children as

Trains an' Stuff

A train feels he don't like to get stepped on no more
A train feels burned
A train hates to be pushed
We feel great but the train feels bad
The train gets mad
Once in a blue moon they clean it
The train wishes he was a human being
The train wants revenge
We have the B train, the D train, the N train, and the RR
    train
The train likes the tunnel
It takes care of the snow and rain
Keeps it off his back
The train don't have no mouth but he has two eyes and a
    horn
The train blows his nose
The train looks like a bus.

The train doesn't feel like running everytime
Whoever was a train, if they were a train, would want
    nobody writing on them
The train feels awful
The trains sees the tracks
Miles and miles long
Oh yea
They go across the country
People be going to their home, to work, and visiting aunts
    and uncles
They go on trips
In the summer we went to Governours Island but the train
    didn't go there
He was mad.

Source: Rich, A. and Nedboy, R. Hey man—we're writing a poem. *Teaching Exceptional Children,* 1977, 9, p. 93.

FIGURE 9.5   *Trains an' Stuff*

public domain, however, it is not necessary for all writing to be shared. In fact, children need to be aware that some writing is too personal to be shared. Allow the children to select what writing samples they wish not to open to review. Respect their right to do so and allow those written compositions to remain private. Encourage private writing by setting aside time for personal expression throughout the school year.

At the same time establish that most writing serves a function when it is passed on to others. Let the child know that her work will be shared with others in the same way that theirs will be to open to her. Only "public" writing is qualified for assessment purposes and for instructional diagnosis. By establishing this rule, a more comfortable and natural writing environment will be created.

There are an endless number of ideas for writing activities. A list of possible writing topics, which was generated by mildly handicapped boys enrolled in a writing program, is given in Figure 9.6. The topics are of expressive, transactional, and poetic writing substance. By no means is this list finite. Depending on your class level, you may choose to present no more than two or three topics at one time for children to select their focus from or you could use a large list such as this to structure the writing program. Remember, however, that topics alone will not generally excite children at the beginning of the writing program. Present a visual enactment of a topic, provide supporting experiences, or begin the writing as a group, discussing and sharing ideas to develop interest.

Skill Development

The mechanics of writing: *vocabulary, organization, punctuation, capitalization, spelling,* and *handwriting,* make communication clearer. They are mastered as a social courtesy to the reader and are part of the conformities created by society.

Writing exercises that focus on a specific mechanical skill will foster communication. The goal is for the child to be able to understand and use the writing convention whenever appropriate. Some educators are highly critical of placing too much attention on writing mechanics, believing that it will interfere with the goal of fostering written expression of individual ideas. It has been suggested that teachers spend less time on conventions and more upon the development of creative thought. The error is in believing that one excludes the other. Imaginative teaching can lead to a satisfactory balance between skill development and personal expression. For instance, children may tape, transcribe, and punctuate their own stories or letters to a friend in one exercise, and in the next session capitalize wherever necessary.

For the student who has learning difficulties and who is just acquiring

The following is a partial list of topics used in the creative writing project at Cove School. Use *your* creativity to add to it.

1. Loneliness.
2. What will you be doing in 1991?
3. Pollution: What is it? Why? What can we do about it?
4. What would you do if you were invisible for 48 hours?
5. Love.
6. Happiness.
7. Fight.
8. War.
9. Peace.
10. I am a raindrop.
11. I am a snowflake.
12. Death.
13. What is your favorite sport and why?
14. Describe what it is like to be fog. How does it change things?
15. What bugs you?
16. Describe someone you like. Why?
17. Write a spooky Halloween story.
18. Describe television commercials, one you like and one you don't.
19. Excitement is.
20. Be an animal.
21. What is your favorite television show? Why?
22. 'Twas the night before Christmas and you were in a haunted house.
23. You are a checker.
24. You are a shoe. Where have you been and what have you seen?
25. What scares you?
26. Pretend you are a yo-yo.
27. Pretend you are a flower.
28. Pretend you are the wind.
29. A day in the life of an ice cream cone.
30. A day in the life of a lollipop.
31. A day in the life of a pencil.
32. A day in the life of a balloon.
33. Pretend you are a magician.
34. You wake up and you are the only one left on earth.
35. A day in the life of a cup of coffee.
36. Pretend you are 20 years old.
37. Pretend you are a book.
38. Pretend you are a bank.
39. Pretend you are a teacher.
40. Pretend you are a leaf.
41. Pretend you are a television.
42. Pretend you are a pumpkin.
43. Pretend you are a skeleton.
44. How could you make someone happy?
45. How can you make the world a better place to be?
46. I am a tough kid.
47. I am a smart kid.
48. Sometimes I have trouble remembering things.
49. A day in the life of a hot dog.
50. I am a toad.
51. I am a scarecrow.
52. I am invisible.
53. If I were president.
54. If I were a python.
55. If I were a dolphin.
56. How a snowman feels when he melts.
57. If I were a star.
58. If I were being attacked by an octopus.
59. If I were a frogman.
60. If I were a caveman.
61. If I were a hunter.
62. What I see when I look out the window.
63. Tell about a fight.
64. If I were weightless.
65. Describe a classmate and have the class guess who it is.
66. Describe a funny made up animal and draw it.
67. Invent a new invention.

68. You are an inventor. What did you invent? What does it do? How does it work?
69. A new labor saving device—what it does, how it works.
70. An advertisement.
71. A treasure chest.
72. Ouch!
73. I can fly.
74. I am an old man.
75. Wow!
76. I am a doctor.
77. Look out!
78. Don't.
79. It was midnight.
80. The mysterious stranger.
81. An old wooden bucket.
82. It was as big as a _____.
83. My greatest wish is to _____.
84. I am the proud owner of _____.
85. You have just become champion of _____. How did it happen? How do you feel?
86. A great day for a turtle.
87. It was an autumn day. I was burning leaves when _____
88. The time you thought something terrible might happen to you.
89. That special day.
90. The day I climbed the mountain to see the volcano.
91. A shipwreck.
92. An African safari.
93. A strange night.
94. Fire!
95. It was a dark, foggy night.
96. Have you ever spent a night on the desert?
97. A tall tale.
98. Lost!
99. When dinosaurs lived.
100. A caterpillar won't hurt you, or will it?
101. A camping trip.
102. The train wreck.
103. You spent the night in a cave. How did you get there? How did you feel? How did you get home—or did you?
104. To soar like an eagle.
105. Life in a shell.
106. Hey! Wait a minute.
107. Why I think I'm great.
108. What I want to be.
109. The exciting night when the grizzly bear came.
110. I am a quarter.
111. An adventure story.
112. A day in the life of a Big Mac.
113. From the tallest tree I can see _____.
114. Inside a bottle.
115. Pretend you are a gumball.
116. A day in the life of a hand.
117. A tack.
118. Sweetie, the all day sucker.
119. A drop of glue.
120. A hot rod racer.
121. A message in a bottle.
122. Cartoons.
123. A mystery.
124. A funny thing that happened.
125. A wug is _____.
126. The Loch Ness Monster.
127. A doorknob.
128. Motorcyclist.
129. Motorbike.
130. Pilot.
131. The wild, wild west.
132. A candy bar.
133. A made up word.
134. Darkness.
135. Robin Hood.
136. I am a zipper.
137. Where teachers go after school and what they do.
138. How do you get up on a Saturday morning?
139. A bucket of chicken.
140. A fly is in my soup.
141. A soft drink.
142. A hammer.
143. Hey look! I'm a drum.
144. Ugh!
145. Watch out for that bucket of paint!

Source: Cady, J. L. Pretend you are an author. *Teaching Exceptional Children,* 1975, 8, p. 30–31.

FIGURE 9.6   A List of Topics

specific skills, structured writing exercises can be sequenced by small increments. Step by step, through direct teaching, the child is able to attain the skill and is given opportunities for transfer. Knowing and using fundamental skills will prevent the mildly handicapped child's learning problems from interfering with communication. The child who can complete written assignments, write a note to a friend, or express feelings in a story with minimal or no mechanical writing errors will be more acceptable in the mainstream of society.

This section focuses on vocabulary, punctuation, capitalization, and organization. Spelling and handwriting which have been included in other chapters are also important elements for clarity in written composition. Each of these skills can be taught separately, however, their application essentially involves integration with other skills. In written expression, the whole is greater than the sum of the parts. In other words, the effectiveness of written communication is partially based on writing conventions, but the result is richer than the division of the skills (Figure 9.7).

Capitalization

During early reading and handwriting instruction, children learn the differences between upper- and lowercase letters. However, the selective use of the appropriate letter form is often not taught until later in the writing program.

Some children will often mix upper- and lowercase letters throughout their writing. In many cases this is the result of poor writing habit rather than a reflection of any confusion in the mechanics of capitalization. Direct instruc-

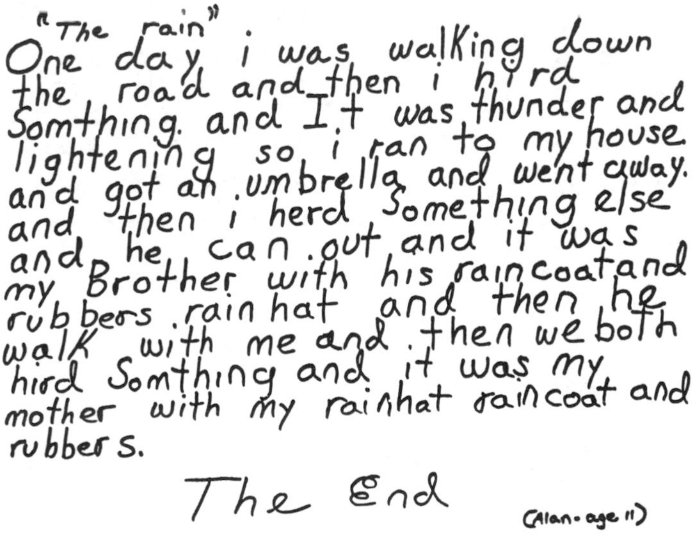
"The rain"
One day i was walKing down
the road and then i hird
Somthing. and It was thunder and
lightening so i ran to my house
and got an umbrella and went away.
and then i herd Something else
and he can out and it was
my Brother with his raincoat and
rubbers rain hat and then he
walk with me and then we both
hird Somthing and it was my
mother with my rainhat raincoat and
rubbers.
The End
(Alan - age 11)

FIGURE 9.7

tion in capitalization usage and activities focused on eliminating unnecessary capitalization will help put an end to such poor habits. Confusion, resulting in unnecessary capitalization, may also occur when the child is not given a clear understanding of *when to capitalize*. This problem is compounded by conflicting models of written letter forms found on the bulletin boards, chalkboards, and experience charts around the classroom. The teacher should check all examples of written expression found around the class and be certain they follow the correct capitalization format.

Figure 9.8 illustrates a ten-year-old child's use of inappropriate capitalization. There appears to be no standard use of capitalization other than at the beginning of a sentence. The many unnecessary capital letters are randomly placed and show the student's confusion in the use of the writing convention.

Systematic instruction of appropriate capitalization conventions begins when children start to copy words and sentences. The use of capitalized letters should be pointed out and simply explained so that children are aware of the differences in the letter forms they copy. The earliest instructional example of capitalization usage occurs when the children learn to write their names (Michael begins with a capital *M* because it is a name). This is followed by experiences with sentences and words found on charts, on bulletin boards, and in printed material.

As soon as the child begins independent writing, the teacher should observe the use of capital letters. If consistent errors are made, reteach the application and provide practice exercises. When errors are due to carelessness, allow the child to state the capitalization rule and correct the mistake.

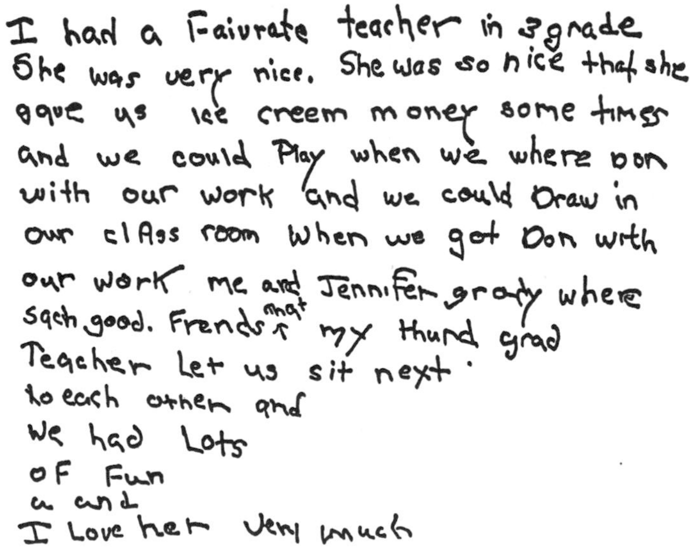

I had a Faivrate teacher in 3grade. She was very nice. She was so nice that she gave us ice creem money some times and we could Play when we where pon with our work and we could Draw in our clAss room When we got Don with our work me and Jennifer groaty where sach good. Frends that my thurd grad Teacher let us sit next to each other and We had Lots oF Fun a and I Love her very much

FIGURE 9.8

290

The following list of standard uses of capital letters is sequenced according to the suggested order of introduction in the writing skills program. Attention should be given primarily to the content, not the sequence of the list since curriculum will vary according to the purpose of the writing program. Words which are to be capitalized are:

1. A person's first name
2. A person's last name
3. The first word of a sentence
4. The word *I*
5. The date
6. Proper names: holidays, months, places, days of the week
7. Names of streets and cities
8. Titles of compositions and books
9. Title names: *Mrs., Ms., Mr., Miss, Dr., President* Washington
10. Mother and Father, when used as proper names
11. First word in the salutation of a letter
12. First word in the closing of a letter
13. Names of organizations and clubs
14. Geographical names
15. Names of states
16. Commercial product names
17. First word of a quotation
18. Race and nationality

A wide variety of activities can be used to teach capitalization. Some suggestions are:

1. *Capital Word List.* Develop a class list of all words (other than sentence beginners) that the children found capitalized in their books and assignments.
2. *Capital Hunt.* Have each child read a passage that has no capitalized words. The child must "hunt" down each incorrect word and capitalize it.
3. *Capital Word Classifications.* Make lists of words for common classifications which begin with capital letters. For example "Important People," "Name the Place," and "Today is."
4. *Capital Dictation.* Read a passage to the class and have the children write the dictation using capitalization whenever necessary.
5. *Storyland.* Write a story using as many proper names as possible. Include people, holidays, cities, states, countries, and so on.
6. *Guess Who.* Have children invent new names for themselves or people in the class or school. Allow them to be creative using names that express positive elements about each person.

7. Have children do a variety of activities which highlight capitalization rules, such as: make a calendar, write a class list, write down names of places that have been visited, and write the names of important people in the school.

Punctuation

Punctuation mistakes are often the most common writing errors made by children. The continuation of punctuation errors across the grade levels suggest that:

1. The items are regarded by the children as of little importance.
2. The teaching has been inadequate.
3. There has been insufficient review and use of the items to establish their uses.
4. Insufficient opportunity has been given for their use in genuine writing situations. (Petty, Petty, & Becking, 1976, p. 200)

The difficulty in learning appropriate use of punctuation may also relate to the fact that children do not associate written and spoken language. They fail to see that punctuation influences written composition in much the same way that gestures, intonation, facial expression, and pauses affect speech. Instruction should begin with this parallel and proceed to the mechanical aspects of punctuation usage.

Although familarity with a broad range of punctuation usage is important and is the ultimate goal, emphasis should be placed on the most commonly used punctuation forms. Remember that many punctuation practices are arbitrary and flexible and are not essential for satisfactory written performance.

The following list of punctuation should be included in the instructional program. The uses for each element are sequenced according to the suggested order of presentation in the writing program.

1. Period
   a. At the end of a sentence
   b. Following a command
   c. After an abbreviation
   d. After numbers in a list
   e. Following an initial
   f. After numerals and letters in an outline
2. Comma
   a. In dates (between the day of the month and the year)
   b. In addresses (between the name of the city and state)
   c. After the greeting of a friendly letter
   d. After the closing of a friendly letter
   e. Between words given in a series
   f. To set off appositives

  g. After "yes" and "no" when they are used as parenthetical expressions

  h. After the name of a person being addressed

  i. To separate a quotation from the explanatory part of a sentence

  j. After a person's last name when it is written before the first name

3. Question Mark

  a. At the close of a question

4. Quotation Marks

  a. Before and after the direct words of a speaker

  b. Around the title of a story, poem, or an article

5. Apostrophe

  a. To establish a possessive noun

  b. In a contraction

6. Exclamation Point

  a. At the end of an exclamatory sentence

  b. After a word or group of words showing surprise or strong feeling

7. Hyphen

  a. In compound words

  b. In compound numbers (e.g. telephone numbers)

  c. Separating syllables of a word that is divided at the end of the line

8. Colon

  a. Between the hour and minutes in the time of day (e.g. 3:25)

  b. After the salutation in a business letter

Punctuation marks are aids to communication and should be taught as often as possible within natural writing situations. However, for the mildly handicapped child, direct and systematic teaching of each punctuation element is essential. Direct teaching begins with an introduction of the punctuation mark and its most common usage. The child must be able to identify the punctuation, recognize when it should be used, and apply it in new situations.

A suggested teaching program for teaching the initial use of the *period* is:

1. *Teacher:* This dot at the end of this statement is a period.
       Example: My name is Steve.
       What is this dot called?
   Child: A period.
  Teacher: Correct.

2. *Teacher:* A period tells us to stop reading.
       What does a period tell us?
   Child: To stop reading.
  Teacher: Good.

3. *Teacher:* A period comes at the end of a statement.
Where does a period come?
Child: At the end of a statement.
Teacher: That's right.
4. *Teacher:* Look where I placed a period. Am I right?
Example: This is my house.
Child: Yes.
Teacher: Good.
(Repeat using several more examples)
5. *Teacher:* Look at these examples. Where should a period go?
I like cake
Some balls are big
You are my pal
The red ball is not here
This book is good

Repetition and small instructional sequences are very important for the child to learn appropriate use of each punctuation component. Direct instruction along with supplemental activities such as the following will provide the basis of the teaching program.

Activities for teaching punctuation:
1. Reproduce a passage missing some or all punctuation. Tell the children the type and number of punctuations to be added. Provide an answer key for self-correction.
2. Reproduce a child's own tape recorded story minus the punctuation. Have the child listen to the tape and put in the punctuation.
3. Have children make up stories about punctuation marks and what they would be like if they were alive. For instance, one story might be about the puzzled question mark who counld not find an answer.
4. Have the children develop mnemonics about punctuation marks; excitable exclamation, curvey comma, etc.
5. Play sentence anagrams and add punctuation cards also.
6. Develop a bulletin board showing examples of punctuation marks and their uses. This will act as a cue for children who are still acquiring the convention's application and need additional help.

Vocabulary Development

Language is all around us. The average child entering school has large speaking and listening vocabularies and can communicate with others in an exchange of ideas, emotions, and needs. The major factor in vocabulary growth is experience—those daily activities that involve language. The more opportunities children have to be involved, to feel, touch, do, and learn, the greater the potential increase in their vocabulary development.

The child's greatest facility with words is in the area of listening comprehension. This is followed by speaking, reading, and writing vocabularies, respectively. Although there is some tendency to use different sets of words for each of these language areas, a great deal of overlap does exist and an increase in one area will usually influence the others. For example, improvement in oral vocabulary will most likely result in improvement in written expression.

Cartwright (1969) delineated the importance of vocabulary for written expression when he stated:

> Adequate written expression in any form, whether it is letter writing, a composition assignment, or an answer to an essay question, depends a great deal upon the variety of words known to the writer. (p. 99)

Mildly handicapped children may find it extremely hard to effectively express themselves in written form. Part of the difficulty may be due to a limited vocabulary of highly functional words. The child may not understand how to increase writing fluency by:

1. Adding prefixes and suffixes to change word meanings
2. Using descriptive words
3. Developing and using expressions
4. Appropriately using synonyms

Instructional attention to word meanings and direct teaching (i.e., meaningful interaction with objects and concepts) are necessary for the child to gain knowledge of words and to use them productively in writing.

A precautionary note is in order regarding written composition and vocabulary development. It is important to realize the value of a smaller accurately used vocabulary over a larger imprecisely used one. Although the objective is to expand the child's facility with words it must not be gained at the expense of writing fluency. A functional goal of providing mildly handicapped children with word skills which allow them to successfully manipulate a limited core of words is advisable. An honest selection of words which fit into the total language pattern and allow for the greatest multiplicity will be most effective.

Vocabulary development implies operationalizing concepts, appropriate selection of alternative word choices and the development of expressive units. Planning instruction around a conceptual framework which will heighten word meaning and increase the likelihood of their use is preferable. By teaching clusters of words, centered around instructional themes, the teacher can introduce new vocabulary and develop concrete learning situa-

295

tions. The following word clusters may be used to teach vocabulary for more effective written composition.

1. Naming Things
   a. Everything has a name (people, places and things).
   b. Some things have more than one name (kitten-cat; Tom-he; Ms. Smith-teacher).
   c. Some names change when there are more than one (child-children; tree-forest; mouse-mice; bird-flock).

2. Describing Things
   a. Everything can be described (big, green, plaid, shady, soft).
   b. Many different words can be used to describe the same thing (a table is hard, brown, flat-top).

3. Activity Words
   a. Some words tell about movement (run, jump, swing, roll).
   b. Some words tell things we do (cut, think, sew, write).
   c. Some words show things we feel (cry, laugh, smile, frown).

4. Word Pairs (subject–verb pairs)
   a. Some words work in pairs (he-is; we-are; you-are, it-is, children-are, the-child-is).

5. Time Words
   a. Special words are used for time concepts:

day	January	hour
week	February	minute
Sunday	season	second
Monday	summer	holidays
month		

6. Facts About Me
   a. Words can tell about a person:

birth date	height	first name
age	sex	last name
address	weight	hair color

7. Prefixes
   a. A prefix added to the beginning of a word changes the word's meaning:

dis – not (disbelief)	re – again (rewrite)
in – not (inappropriate)	over – above (overhead)
un – not (unable)	under – below (undercurrent)
non – not (nonverbal)	anti – before/against (antiroom/
mis – wrong (misdeed)	antibody)
	il – not (illegal)

8. Suffixes
   a. A suffix added to the end of a word affects the word's meaning:

   able, ible - fit to (wearable)
   er, or - one who acts (player)
   ant, ent - agent in (servant)
   ed - past tense marker (wished)
   ing - in the act of (painting)
   ish - like (girlish)
   like - like (childlike)
   ful - full of (wishful)
   ous - full of (outrageous)
   ness - state of (sweetness)
   ship - state of (friendship)
   er - comparative adjective (bigger)
   est - superlative adjective (biggest)

9. Synonyms
   a. Many words mean the same thing:

   bumpy - rough
   smooth - slick
   road - street
   girl - female
   movie - film
   teach - instruct
   draw - sketch
   woman - lady
   man - gentleman
   restroom - bathroom

10. Expressions
    a. Certain words put together have a special meaning

    sweet as honey - pleasant
    good as gold - worthy

    b. Different expressions can mean the same thing:

    Speed
    - quick as a wink
    - fast as lightning
    - before you can blink an eye
    - before you can say, "Jack Rabbit"

    Annoyance
    - a bone to pick
    - a bee in her bonnet
    - sour grapes

297

Depending on the focus of the instructional cluster, the teacher may choose a variety of activities to teach vocabulary. As the child practices word clusters and becomes more familiar with the words he is more apt to include them in written composition. Activities such as the following are appropriate for vocabulary instruction.

1.   Keep class charts of synonyms, words that begin with a certain prefix, or end in a specific suffix. Allow the children to add to the list as they come across new words. Develop activities to discuss the words and then to use them in a writing activity.
2.   Present the child with a written passage in which certain words or phrases are underlined. Ask the child to substitute a different word or expression for each underlined element.
3.   Brainstorm word clusters or thoughts to be included in a letter or story. Allow each child to add to the collection and then write a composition using as many of the brainstormed words as appropriate.
4.   Develop a series of crossword puzzles centered around differing themes (Christmas, furniture, automobiles, careers). Have the child complete the puzzle and then use the words in a written story. As children do crossword puzzles, they begin to understand that a word can be represented by another word or phrase.

Organization

All written expression is effective only to the extent that it makes sense. That is, the message must be clearly and logically constructed. The focus of instruction should be on the development of sentences that can be sequenced to form paragraphs and completed manuscripts.

The mildly handicapped child often experiences problems in ordering language—both oral and written. For this child teaching strategies that help organize the thoughts to be written will ultimately improve communication.

Organization in written performance is based on an understanding of sentence building, sequencing, and paragraph development. Organized expression can be developed through practice of structured exercises which emphasize these areas. The more opportunities for writing the child has, generally, the greater the improvement in expressive quality. However, for the mildly handicapped child to benefit from the writing experience the focus of teaching must be on the content of the expression. Direct teaching helps the child construct clear sentences and then logically sequence sentences into paragraphs.

Sentences

Instruction in sentence building should begin early. Children need to understand that a sentence is basically a means of expressing an idea. A sentence must make sense. A practical approach to sentence building is most helpful. A sentence can best be defined structurally as commonly having a noun phrase and a verb phrase.

In most language arts programs, sentences are classified by purpose (declarative, interrogative, exclamatory, and imperative) or by structure (simple, compound, and complex). Such categorization may be useful in a grammatical sense, but may only serve to confuse the mildly handicapped child if the terminology is stressed. The instructional program for the problem learner need not include such formalized classification, yet it still can maintain the essence of sentence development.

Teaching questions can be phrased in such a manner that they promote sentence development. Using experience stories and charts is an excellent means for achieving this objective. For example, after a class has gone on a trip to a farm, the following exchange between a teacher and a child may occur:

Teacher:	Tell me something you saw at the farm.
Child:	I saw animals.
Teacher:	Good, can you name one of the animals that was at the farm?
Child:	There were cows at the farm.
Teacher:	What type of cows did the farmer say they were?
Child:	He said they were dairy cows.
Teacher:	That's right. What do dairy cows do?
Child:	Dairy cows give milk.

The teacher in the above situation has designed the questions to help the children organize their expression of the experience. There will often be many answers to such questions. When all the answers are recorded, the teacher may help the class decide on which responses to select, or how to organize the responses for the final composition.

Another early sentence development technique is to have a child dictate a sentence about a stimulus (a drawing, magazine picture, or object) which is recorded by the teacher. Again, the teacher must assist the child and reinforce each successful effort. Slowly the child will move from a single sentence to a two- and three-sentence composition.

As children learn the general concept of a sentence, they can be taught that there are different types of sentences. Some tell things, some ask questions, and others exclaim about something. Each type of sentence ends in a unique punctuation mark and serves a specific function. It is important that the child recognize these differences.

As children get older, the percentage of run-on and choppy sentences increases along with the desire to write more complex sentences (Bear, 1939). Also, during the intermediate school years many teachers notice what is commonly referred to as the *and* fault in children's writing. These difficulties may be associated with linguistic and intellectual growth and can not be expected to be remediated quickly. However, concentration on exercises that build sentence sense can help correct the problem.

Many activities can be constructed to help the mildly handicapped child use complete sentences. The following suggestions can be varied according to individual needs.

1. Using a set of stimulus picture cards and a set of sentence cards have the child match an appropriate sentence for each picture.
2. Have the child tape record a story and then listen to where his voice drops at the end of a group of words; the end of a sentence. Transcribe the tape and have the child punctuate the sentences.
3. List a series of different types of sentences on the board. Have the child tell whether they state something, ask a question, or exclaim. Punctuate accordingly.
4. Give a list of declarative sentences and have the child rearrange each one to ask a question.
5. Present the child with phrases written on strips of tagboard. The task is to match two phrases that can combine to make a complete sentence.

Once the child understands the function and development of a sentence, it is necessary to learn to sequence a series of thoughts. The mildly handicapped child may have difficulty expressing a thought because of a failure to organize the expression. The child must be taught to recognize relationships, and this can be done prior to actual writing experiences. Activities such as the following will help the child understand relationships such as grouping and sequencing before beginning to write paragraphs.

1. Sequence picture cards to tell a story.
2. Put together puzzles which have relationship pieces (a puzzle of a face, animal, or house).
3. Group a series of objects according to different classifications (function, color, size, or material).
4. Retell a story retaining the proper sequence of events.
5. Sort picture sentences according to common ideas.
6. Read several sentences one at a time aloud to the child. Have the student tell whether each is appropriate for a specific picture stimulus.

Sentence Combining

When the child successfully demonstrates an understanding of grouping and sequencing, the next step is to apply these concepts to sentence building. O'Hare (1973) and Hunt (1969) describe a technique which teaches syntactic maturity. *Sentence combining* allows the writer (or speaker) to embed one statement within another. For example, "John was early for school," and "John was the first one at school today," can be combined to read, "John, who was early, was the first one at school today."

The purpose of teaching sentence combining is to give the child alternative ways to say the same thing. Embedded sentences are also less "boring" to attend to than a series of short, overly simplified ones. Studies by O'Hare (1973), Hunt (1969), and O'Donnell, Griffin, and Norris (1967) have determined that children tend to embed more sentences as they grow older and this tendency continues to grow into adulthood. Furthermore, a relationship seems to exist between sentence embedding and IQ, with students of higher IQ levels achieving a larger number of sentence combinations. However, the research was designed to compare high IQ subjects with average IQ subjects and should be interpreted loosely when referring to other populations.

Sentence combining techniques can be successfully taught to children. In fact, training in sentence embedding can be helpful in developing syntactic maturity and memory strategies. As O'Hare (1973) states:

> A further attraction of sentence combining practice is that it forces the student, as he embeds the given kernels into the main statement, to keep longer and longer discourse in his head. (p. 31)

Some sentences may be combined by simply adding a relevant element to one of the sentences. In other cases, certain words are used as connectors when two related thoughts are combined into one sentence. Possible connector words are *when, because, and, after, before, if, until, however, then, where, but,* and *there.* After demonstrating how to combine sentences, the teacher should present a series of sentence pairs with which the child may practice combining strategies:

The big lemon.
The yellow lemon.

This is a funny book.
This is a hard book to read.

We are going to the airport.
At the airport we will see the planes land and takeoff.

The green grass.
The grass is high.
The grass needs to be cut.

I like cake and ice cream.
I like birthday parties.
At birthday parties you get to eat cake and ice cream.

Many children require a considerable amount of practice in sentence building before they are comfortable with it. Providing numerous practice opportunities, presenting good models and reinforcing successful attempts will help mildly handicapped children attain the skill.

Paragraph Development
In the initial writing stages the child hears and tells stories that are arranged in short paragraphs. The child's earliest writing generally consists of only one or two sentences. As the child's communication needs and experiences grow, writing becomes more extensive and instruction must then include paragraph development.

A paragraph is a convention for organizing related sentences. All sentences in a paragraph tell about one topic and are arranged to follow a logical sequence. An introductory or topical sentence is generally found near the beginning of the paragraph, followed by sentences which explain or support the topic. Although not all paragraphs have topical sentences, they are used often enough as organization devices to warrant teaching. Areas of study for learning about paragraphs are:

1. Finding the main idea/topic.
2. Arranging sentences in logical sequence.
3. Locating key words.
4. Listing details about the topic.

The instructional sequence for teaching paragraph development should include the following points;

1. A paragraph should deal with a single topic.
2. A paragraph generally has a topic sentence.
3. A paragraph develops a topic.
4. Sentences in a paragraph are related to each other.
5. A long, self-contained expository paragraph should be concluded or summarized with a general sentence related to the topic or beginning sentence. The last sentence of one paragraph may lead into the next paragraph. (Burns, 1974)

When teaching children to organize their writing into paragraphs it often is helpful to teach outlining skills. Outlining can be a particularly functional skill for mildly handicapped children who need structure in order to gather information, plan what they want to say, sequence several thoughts, and organize supporting sentences. Tell the child that all writing can begin with an outline which helps focus on the main topic and related subtopics. Outlines may be brief and informal. To stress formal outlining is not advantageous with the problem learner who may be frustrated by such an overly rigid format. The instructional emphasis should be that outlines will provide guidance in planning what the writer wants to say. Provide the child with examples. Call the child's attention to the importance of planning the main points and ordering the series of ideas, even in a business letter.

Children can begin outlining by developing guides for class activities (What needs to be done before a class trip?), or planning work schedules. These organizational plans will help focus attention on the need to structure and order events. Later, activities can be used to illustrate the main elements of an outline—topic, detail, and sequence—which the child should learn to organize. Some suggestions are:

1. Read a short story to the class and have them decide what the main topic is and what subtopics there are.
2. Using magazine pictures, have children classify them according to a given topic. Then, reverse the activity and have the children examine a group of pictures and tell what is the main idea they illustrate.
3. Present an object or picture to the group and state one important element of the stimulus. Then, have the class provide details that support the teacher's statement.
4. Present a series of tagboard strips, each with a different but related idea, to the class. Ask the children to sequence the strips in a logical order to form an outline.
5. Using the ideas in the activity above, have the children write a sentence for each strip. Then, put the sentences together to form a paragraph.
6. Help the child create outlines for writing by asking questions such as: Why are you writing this composition? Who will read it? What do they need to know to understand your point?
7. Have the children examine comic strips for sequencing, and then develop their own comic strip stories. (This can easily be done by cutting comics from the newspaper. Cover the captions with masking tape and make a ditto master. Children can then write their own story lines.)

Using an outline the child will be better able to develop well organized paragraphs. As in the other writing skills, a great deal of practice is necessary. Success at this level will entail assisting the child to develop thinking strategies which conform to writing conventions. Emphasis during

303

skill development should always be placed on effective communication, not length, variety, or innovation.

Refinement

Once the child has acquired the basic writing skills included in the previous section it is necessary to turn attention to refining the writing process. Two specific aspects of this instructional stage are *proofreading* and developing a *personal style*. The goal is to refine each written product until it conforms to an acceptable standard of quality and conveys the message in the most effective form.

Standards of quality refer to the correct application of writing conventions. A child learns to proofread written compositions and to edit (i.e., locate and correct) any writing mistakes. Proofreading is an onerous task for the mildly handicapped child but it is very important. The student must learn to independently locate and revise any error that may impede communication. Proofreading strategies will benefit the writer throughout life.

A child receives the greatest advantage from editing his own work. It is not sufficient to remind the child to proofread material. Unless the child understands the purpose of proofreading and knows what to look for, the edit will be futile. To ensure success, the teacher should guide the child through the proofreading process by establishing specific elements to be looked for, such as:

- Is the first word in every sentence capitalized?
- Do sentences end with punctuation marks?
- Have you indented the first word of the paragraph?
- Are all proper nouns capitalized?
- Have you used commas in the appropriate places?
- Can sentences be combined?
- Have you conveyed the message clearly?

Guidelines such as these may be posted on the bulletin board for easy reference after each writing exercise. Early in the proofreading process it may be preferable to present one guideline at a time according to the child's level of skill development. First, the child should attempt to edit alone. Later working in a conference format, the teacher and student can review and locate any area of great difficulty which needs correction. The child who can "catch" mistakes has acquired the skill, but needs more practice.

Mistakes on drafts are quite common, even with professional writers. The mildly handicapped child should be aware of this so as not to become too frustrated during the editing procedure. Proofreading should be used primarily with functional writing in which writing conventions apply most directly. The typed note in Figure 9.9 was written by a sixteen-year-old special education student upon resigning from a newspaper route. Had Ben been taught to proofread more accurately the receiver would have been left with a more positive impression of Ben's capabilities.

A *personal style* develops when the student understands the purpose of the writing task and can clearly express the message in a individualized way. The importance of fostering individual expression is evident in the following account of a special education teacher who after teaching for three years moved to another state.

> For the past two years I have been receiving letters from my former students. When they were in my special education class I taught them to write friendly letters. I did my job well and each student learned to write informal notes. From the many letters I've received, I've realized that I only taught them a standard form and not how to express themselves as individuals.
>
> Each one of their letters begins with, "Dear Mrs. Tally, How are you? I am fine" and ends with "I miss you. Your friend, _____." In between are one or two very formalized personal thoughts such as, "I am doing well in school". Although these children did learn a standard procedure, I never taught them to go beyond the level of conformity to express themselves as individuals.

This teacher's perceptions about writing instruction for the mildly handicapped are all too accurate. Very often the instructional program has concentrated on standardization and has never progressed to the level of

```
Dear, customer

    I am sorry to say that this is my last week on the
route, Yes, Iam quiting(not because of bad paying or
anything like that) the reasons vary such as school,
relaxation etc. I ask that you have money on time.
                    P.S. You've really
                         made the job worth
                         while.


                                        THANKS

                                   Ben Williams
```

FIGURE 9.9   *An Example of a Lack of Proofreading*

allowing students to refine and personalize their writings. As a direct result, children reporduce the models they have been given and their writing is stilted and uncreative.

Writing skills should be taught through a variety of activities and children should be given numerous models from which to learn. After a period of skill acquisition, the teacher must provide opportunities for individual expression by demonstrating alternative strategies for presenting similar ideas. The activities given below will help children develop a personal style. These are only a few suggestions. The teacher should think of as many additional exercises as possible.

1. Brainstorm lists of alternative sayings; for instance, different ways to say "I miss you":
    It's been a long time since I've seen you.
    I wish you were here.
    I was thinking about you today.
    It would be nice to see you again.
2. Write letters to four different friends. Make sure that each note is different throughout (except possibly for the salutation). Have the children exchange their ideas for beginning and closing the letter.
3. Ask the children to keep a diary. The entries may be simply one line that expresses something nice that happened each day. Have the class read back through their own diaries to appreciate how each day has been somewhat unique.
4. Distribute a comic strip to each child with only the last caption written in. Have every student write a story line and share it with the class. The focus of discussion should be on variety and how many different stories can be developed.
5. Give the child a "label" (vacation, rainstorm, or king) and have him describe himself so others can guess what he is).

In developing a personal style, the child begins to more precisely express personal ideas and feelings. Creation of personalized writing does not exclude using conventional forms, it only allows the child to go beyond them. No writing program, even one that emphasizes functional writing, is satisfactory unless it attends to the development of the child's personal expression.

A Note on Writing Instruction

The instructional suggestions offered throughout this chapter are appropriate for mildly handicapped children as well as their "average" peers. This commonality between the components of the instructional program for the mildly handicapped and those for the regular education child should be stressed. A difference exists in the need for the teacher to analyze the task into more and more easily comprehended segments and to provide learning experiences which compliment one another and reinforce achievement. Ultimately, differences in instruction for the mildly handicapped student will vary according to emphasis and the method of evaluation. The amount of necessary instructional time, the need for continuous practice, and generalization training will alter the focus of the writing program for the problem learner. In addition, the maintenance of rigid standards and grading procedures will not be beneficial to this type of child. Using measures of corrective feedback for specific writing elements is preferable. The children should be told when they are writing for public review and what convention or element will be examined. In this way attention is sharpened to the pertinent feature and they can apply their best effort.

Assessing Written Expression

Debate over the evaluation of written composition has generated a great deal of controversy and confusion among educators of the language arts. "Some educators rail against the practice on 'Humanitarian' grounds, asserting that it stifles creativity, disregards individuality, and has assorted other nasty consequences" (Hogan & Mishler, 1979, p. 142). Many authorities complain that because writing is multidimensional, judgments on written expression are fraught with psychometric problems, such as unreliability, lack of standardization, and invalidity. Yet, in recent years the demand to return to the basics has produced a public outcry for accurate evaluation of student writing. The issue of assessing a child's written products is complex and must be examined from several directions.

To evaluate student written performance, the teacher must be aware of:

1. The purpose of evaluation
2. The components of written language to be assessed
3. The variety of assessment techniques available

The teacher must approach the evaluation process with a positive attitude, believing that it is possible to judge the quality of written composition and to plan instruction accordingly. Finally, it is necessary to appreciate the differences between the child's attempts at public communication and private writing.

The objectives for assessing written language parallel those of assessment for all the language arts: to identify students who are experiencing problems; to chart individual child progress; and to identify a student's strengths and weaknesses. The mildly handicapped child who experiences written language problems is generally not identified until second grade or later. Prior to second grade, academic attention is placed on beginning reading, handwriting, and spelling as isolated skill areas. Writing difficulties emerge at the time the child is expected to integrate the various language components in written composition.

The question of when it is appropriate to evaluate a student's written work can be simply answered by a examination of the objectives for evaluation. Assessment implies diagnosis with the goal of instructional planning. Therefore, the judgment of a child's writing ability is a prerequisite for instructional decision making. In seeking information regarding a child's skill level, expressive ability, or understanding of standard conventions, the teacher should, by all means, assess the child's written performance. If, however, the writing exercise is a creative endeavor or an activity chosen by the child for personal expression and enjoyment, feedback should always be given but should be nonjudgmental. Evaluation, by means of constructive comments, can be given without being reflected in grades.

Assessment of written language can be divided into the many interrelated components of writing itself. Specifically these include: vocabulary, punctuation, capitalization, sentence and paragraph development, and expressive content (a more complete analysis would also include handwriting and spelling skills, chapters 9 and 11). Of all the components, punctuation and capitalization are the most easily evaluated because they are rule-oriented. Vocabulary use and sentence and paragraph development are open to more interpretation and are therefore considered more subjective. Analysis of expressive content is judged to be the most difficult because of the lack of normative data. However, Hogan and Mishler (1979) showed that experienced elementary school teachers, who evaluated 1000 written essays for clarity and content, achieved reliability coefficients of .79 to .90 with a median of .87. The implication is that there is some consensus of what is a "good" written composition. Teachers who evaluate written expression should be able to communicate the elements of acceptable writing to their students and to judge progress fairly.

Formal Assessment of Writing Disorders

Standardized tests in written language are usually designed to provide only a general estimate of achievement level. The intent is to provide comparative data to determine if a child is functioning up to his peer group. Most scores are given as grade equivalents or percentiles and offer little or no diagnostic information.

Tests	Components Assessed	Grade Levels
Comprehensive Tests of Basic Skills (CTB/McGraw-Hill, 1968)	Word usage, mechanics,[a] and grammatical structure	1–12
California Achievement Tests (Tiegs & Clark, 1970)	Word usage, mechanics, and grammatical structure	3–12
Stanford Achievement Tests (Madden & Gardner, 1972)	Mechanics and grammatical structure	3–9
Iowa Test of Basic Skills (Hieronymus & Lindquist, 1971)	Word usage and mechanics	1–9
SRA Achievement Series (Thorpe, Lefever, & Nasland, 1974)	Mechanics and grammatical structure	2–9
Metropolitan Achievement Tests (Durost, et al., 1970)	Word usage, mechanics, and grammatical structure	3–9

[a] Mechanics includes punctuation and capitalization.

Source: Wallace, G., and Larsen, S. *Educational assessment of learning problems: Testing for teaching.* Boston: Allyn & Bacon, Inc., 1978, p. 406.

FIGURE 9.10   Achievement Tests with Written Expression Sections

The majority of standardized tests employ a contrived writing format. Skills such as capitalization, punctuation, and word usage are presented in isolation. For example, the student is asked to look at a sentence which may or may not be correctly punctuated. The task is to indicate any errors and to punctuate the sentence correctly. Each item is designed to test a specific element in isolation from a general written product and no attempt is made at evaluating the acceptability of a child's own written composition.

Figure 9.10 lists the most common achievement tests which have written language sections. Not all components of written expression are included in each test. The teacher should be cognizant of what elements the test is assessing and how the information is generated.

In using standardized tests, such as those listed in Figure 9.11, two basic assumptions are made about the child's abilities. First, that there is a high correlation between the student's performance on the contrived measure and his actual writing proficiency. Second, that the student is able to read at or near grade level. For the mildly handicapped child who may have a reading disability such tests would not provide a valid measure of writing skills.

Diagnostic Tests of Written Ability

Three diagnostic tests of written expression have been constructed and marketed for widespread use. Each of these test supplies basic information usable for instructional purposes; however, they differ in content, format, and reliability. Basic information about the *Test of Written Language, Picture Story Language Test*, and *Sequential Test of Educational Progress* is presented in Figure 9.11. As is the case with achievement tests, standardized diagnostic measures may not yield an accurate assessment of the mildly handicapped child's writing skills. Therefore, the teacher is reminded to be cautious in interpreting the test results. Wallace and Larsen (1978) recommend that diagnostic tests, such as the ones cited above, be used primarily as observation tools to verify information gained from informally constructed procedures.

Informal Assessment of Written Expression

Initial evaluation of a child's written language abilities begins with observation of general language performance, work habits, and written work samples. The teacher should ask if the child:

- Completes written assignments?
- Expresses personal ideas and feelings?
- Interacts verbally with peers?
- Initiates conversations?
- Attends appropriately to a task?
- Follows directions given orally?
- Shows an interest in writing?
- Enjoys having stories read aloud ?

Recording observations may help to focus attention on specific areas of difficulty. The teacher must then proceed to additional measures of assessment based upon accumulated written work samples. The child's own writing is the most accurate tool for judging writing skills. The child should have an opportunity to edit the writing prior to being evaluated. However, there are times when the teacher may wish to contrive a writing situation in order to pinpoint certain difficulties. Just remember that appropriate use of a written convention in contrived situations does not always transfer to more natural writing experiences.

The establishment of standards within the writing curriculum provides criterion-referenced measures for assessment and allows for the direct application of diagnostic information to the writing program. Checklists based on predetermined criteria can easily be developed for certain writing

Test Name	Subtest	Format	Comment
Test of Written Language-TOWL (Hammill and Larsen, 1978)	· Handwriting · Thought-units · Spelling style · Word usage · Vocabulary · Thematic maturity	Spontaneous and contrived measures	A highly reliable measure suitable for individual and group administration. The test is designed to yield grade equivalents and scaled scores which are helpful in determining long-term objectives.
Picture Story, Language Test (Myklebust, 1965)	· Productivity · Correctness · Meaning	Spontaneous writing	The reliability and validity of this measure have been seriously questioned. However, as an informal observational technique it can provide information pertaining to content, mechanics, and clarity.
Sequential Test of Educational Progress-STEP (Educational Testing Services, 1958)	· Organization · Conventions · Critical thinking · Effectiveness · Appropriateness	Contrived writing situations	The contrived format is based on actual writing specimens of children. It provides normative information as well as analysis of specific error patterns which are useful in establishing learning programs.

FIGURE 9.11 Diagnostic Tests of Written Expression

Student Name	Period	Comma	Question Mark	Quotation Mark	Apostrophe	Exclamation Point	Hyphen	Colon

Directions: Record the date that each child successfully demonstrated the use of a specific punctuation mark.

FIGURE 9.12   Punctuation Checklist

skills. Checklist specificity is flexible according to the diagnostic needs for each student. Figure 9.12 illustrates a general checklist for punctuation skills, whereas Figure 9.13 is much more specific for capitalization usage. In the punctuation checklist, the teacher records the date the child successfully demonstrated the use of a particular punctuation mark. To do this the teacher would need to keep a continuous record of progress for each column heading (e.g., period, comma . . .). The capitalization checklist can be used in the same way or as a record of capitalization used for any one writing sample. Although each checklist represents a group recording form, it is a relatively simple matter to adjust them for individual use.

When recording information on the writing ability of one child, a form that can show continuous progress is advantageous. The general pro-

Student / /Date												
beginning a sentence												
first name												
last name												
"I"												
the date												
proper names												
streets												
cities												
titles												
first word in salutation												
first word in closing												
states												
race/ nationality												
commercial products												

FIGURE 9.13 *Capitalization Checklist*

313

gress profile for written expression (Figure 9.14) can be used for repeated assessment. In addition, this observation form focuses on both the expressive content and the mechanics of writing. The scoring procedure includes differential skill assessment which more accurately reflects writing progress.

Vocabulary, because of its slightly less objective nature, is difficult to assess whithin a checklist format. Therefore, it is necessary to use other evaluative measures. *The type-token ratio* determines the variety of words used in the written product. In effect the ratio represents the number of different words used (types) over the number of total words (tokens) (Johnson, 1944). In the sentence, "The book is on the table in the dining room," there are eight word types (*the* is used three times) and ten tokens. Thus:

$$\frac{8 \text{ types}}{10 \text{ tokens}} = .8 \text{ (type-token ratio)}$$

The lower the type-token ratio, the more vocabulary redundancy. This might be indicative of an inadequate vocabulary needing further attention. The ratio may be used as a technique to assess one child's progress or to compare several children if it is based on a standard number of words (e.g., first 50 or 100 words of a written piece).

The *index of diversification* is another method of determining vocabulary variety. Originally developed by Carroll (1938), it has been modified by Cartwright (1969) for easier calculation. "Simply divide the number of words in the composition by the number of "the's," or by the number of occurrences of the most frequently used word" (p. 100). The higher the value, the broader the vocabulary.

A final channel of assessment for writing ability is to examine the child's fluency, measured by the *average sentence length*. A simple analysis of average sentence length is done by:

1. Counting the total number of words in the writing sample
2. Counting the number of sentences
3. Dividing the word total by the sentence total

As the child matures and learns to write more clearly sentence length will increase (Cartwright, 1969).

A positive approach to the assessment of written expression is to provide feedback during teacher-student conferences. Within this structure both the teacher and the students have a chance to evaluate the writing samples. Once students recognize their errors, they can make immediate corrections. This procedure is helpful in developing the children's proofreading skills.

Systematic instruction of written expression is based on observation, assessment, and record keeping. The teacher should establish procedures

Student _____

DATE	Writing Sample Description	Content			Mechanics		
		Expression	Sentences	Paragraphs	Vocabulary	Punctuation	Capitalization
		Main idea is clearly stated and logically supported	Expresses a complete thought	Adequately developed paragraphs consisting of closely related sentences	Varied and appropriate word choice	All punctuation appropriately placed throughout writing	Appropriate use of capital letters

Scoring: + satisfactory skill   (+) skill is evident but confusion exists
− unsatisfactory skill   NA—skill is not attempted

FIGURE 9.14 General Progress Profile for Written Expression

which are of the greatest diagnostic benefit. Careful analysis of these measures will result in the creation of necessary writing objectives for each child.

SUMMARY

A persistent problem among many mildly handicapped children is the inability to transfer thoughts into written communication. Yet, writing is an essential skill for children to acquire while in school. Society demands that the adult be able to convey thoughts, needs, and personal information in written form.

Of the several current writing positions discussed in this chapter, the first deals with the question of whether to teach writing rules and conventions before allowing the child to write, or to encourage writing first and teach the mechanics later. The authors contend that the mildly handicapped child should be stimulated to express himself freely and as often as possible. Direct teaching of writing conventions should be based on the child's spontaneously written compositions. After each convention is taught, it should be used in later writing.

The second issue, the emphasis on functional writing for the special child, was considered to be too narrow a focus and limiting to the child's potential for growth. A narrow definition of "creative" relating only to original compositions and poetry was discarded for a broader one focusing on any writing done in one's own words and sentences. This new definition now makes it possible to merge functional and creative writing endeavors.

The final area of concern relates to the assessment of a child's written work. A distinction must be made between public writing (written expression which is to be shared with others) and private writing (penned only for oneself). Public writing can and should be evaluated whenever there is a direct need for diagnosis and instructional planning. Specific suggestions for assessing written expression were presented. These included formal achievement tests, diagnostic tests, and informal observation and recording procedures.

Initial writing, skill development, and refinement represent the continuum of written expression. Each of these areas was analyzed and discussed according to its component parts. Motivation included presenting a rationale for writing as communication and for the different types of written expression. Skill development was subdivided into vocabulary, capitalization, punctuation, and organization. Refinement, the final stage, includes proofreading strategies and developing a personal style.

Throughout the chapter suggestions were given for instructing the mildly handicapped child in written expression. In particular instruction should:

1. Always be built on the child's experiences.
2. Include warm-up procedures for motivation.
3. Encourage acceptance of expressed ideas and teach appropriate skill development.

POINTS FOR DISCUSSION

1. Several significant issues were mentioned at points throughout the chapter. For each of the issues listed below select a position, either pro or con, and be able to defend your stance.
   a. Mildly handicapped children should have a primarily functional writing program.
   b. Creative writing is not compatible with the precepts of functional experiences.
   c. Writing should *always* be assessed for instructional purposes.

2. Many times signs, chalkboard assignments, charts, and bulletin board titles are written in a manner that can confuse the problem learner. For instance, this learning center title is inappropriate. Discuss why.

The Reading Corner

3. Read a paragragh (or a short story) with a small group of children. Ask them to rewrite the paragraph by first substituting as many synonyms as they can and then combining sentences so that the passage contains the same content but reads differently.

4. Reread the children's writing found in this chapter. Try to analyze the vocabulary by use of a type-token ratio.

5. Spend some time examining children's writings. Interview the authors and try to find out what they think writing is all about and how they feel about their own writing. Ask the children if they have ever written anything only for their own pleasure. Was it a worthwhile experience?

6. Try to arrange to spend some time with younger children for the purpose of developing an experience story. Provide a motivating experience that all the children can share. Prepare a series of focusing questions to lead the development of the story.

7. Look around for pictures, objects, stories, and music that are appropriate motivators for written expression exercises. Inexpensive sources are contest coupons in which the entrant must complete a jingle or sentence, old functional objects such as an oil lamp or a worn pair of boots, and unusual musical sounds. Organize your materials so that they are readily available when you need them.

8. Read collections of children's writings such as *The Me Nobody Knows* (Joseph, 1972) and *Wishes, Lies and Dreams,* (Koch, 1970). Record your reactions first to the content and then to the mechanical aspects of the entries. Use these readings to sensitize yourself to the feelings that children so often reveal in their writings.

9. Do you agree with Britton's classification of children's writing? For each classification (expressive, transactional, and poetic), develop three teaching activities to stimulate a specific type of writing.

REFERENCES

Bear, M. V. Children's growth in the use of written language. *The Elementary English Review*, 1939, *16*, 312–319.

Blake, H. E. Written composition in English primary schools. *Elementary English*, 1971, *48*, 605–616.

Britton, J. *Language and learning*. Norwich, Great Britain: Penguin Press, 1972.

Burns, P. C. *Diagnostic teaching of the language arts*. Itasca, Ill.: Peacock Publishers, Inc., 1974.

Burns, P. C., and Broman, B. L. *The language arts in childhood education*. Chicago: Rand McNally College Publishing Company, 1979.

Cady, J. L. Pretend you are . . . an author. *Teaching Exceptional Children*, 1975, *8*, 27–31.

Carroll, J. B. Diversity of vocabulary and the harmonic series law of word-frequency distribution. *Psychological Record*, 1938, *2*.

Cartwright, G. P. Written expression and spelling. In R. M. Smith, *Teacher diagnosis of educational difficulties*. Columbus, Ohio: Charles E. Merrill Publishing Company, 1969, pp. 95–117.

Cramer, R. L. *Writing, reading and language growth*. Columbus, Ohio: Charles E. Merrill Publishing Company, 1978.

Davis, D. Teaching writing, the 20 year (or longer) crisis. *English Journal*, 1976, *65*, 18–20.

Evertts, E. Dinosaurs, witches and anti-aircraft: Primary composition. Found in DeStefano, J. and Fox, S. *Language and the language arts*. Boston: Little, Brown and Company, 1974, pp. 387–396.

Hammill, D. D., and Larsen, S. C. *Test of Written Language – TOWL*. Austin, Texas: Pro-Ed., 1978.

Hogan, T. P., and Mishler, C. J. Judging the quality of student's writing: When and how. *The Elementary School Journal*, 1979, *79*, 3, 142–146.

Hunt, K. W. Teaching syntactic maturity. In G. E. Perren and J. L. M. Trims (Eds.), *Applications of linguistics*. New York: Cambridge University Press, 1969.

Johnson, W. Studies in language behavior, A program of research. *Psychological Monographs*, 1944, *56*, 2.

Joseph, S. M. *Me nobody knows: Children's voices from the ghetto*. New York: Avon-Discus Books, 1972.

Koch, K. *Wishes, lies and dreams.* New York: Random House, 1970.

Myklebust, H. R. *Development and disorders of written language.* New York: Grune & Stratton, 1965.

Nathanson, D., Cynamon, A., and Lehman, K. Miami snow poets: Creative writing for exceptional children. *Teaching Exceptional Children,* 1976, *8,* 87-91.

O'Donnell, R. C., Griffin, W. J., and Norris, R. C. *Syntax of kindergarten and elementary school children: A transformational analysis.* National Council of Teachers of English Research Report No. 8, Champaign, Ill., 1967.

O'Hare, F. *Sentence combining: Improving student writing without formal grammar instruction.* Urbana, Ill.: National Council of Teachers of English Research Report 15, 1973.

Petty, W. T., Petty, D. C., and Becking, M. E. *Experience in language: Tools and technique for language arts methods.* Boston: Allyn & Bacon, Inc., 1976.

Rich, A., and Nedboy, R. Hey man . . . we're writing a poem. *Teaching Exceptional Children,* 1977, *9,* 90–92.

Sequential test of basic skills. Palo Alto, Calif.: Educational Testing Service, 1958.

Van Allen, R. *Language experiences in communication.* Boston: Houghton Mifflin Company, 1976.

Wallace, G., and Larsen, S. C. *Educational assessment of learning problems: Testing for teaching.* Boston: Allyn & Bacon, Inc., 1978.

10

Spelling Instruction

A *good speller* is someone who can produce letter patterns in such a way that they form words. There is only one correct way to spell a word, and all other attempts, even close approximations which are readable, must be considered incorrect. For the mildly handicapped student with learning difficulties, this right or wrong element can be the source of great frustration. Appropriate letter arrangement (i.e., correct spelling) implies a knowledge of phoneme-grapheme (sound-symbol) association. Yet, as any English speaker and writer knows, the language contains phoneme-grapheme inconsistencies which are a concern for all learners.

The inconsistencies of the English language (such as the *k* sound symbolized by *k, ck, c, lk,* and *ch*) reflect historical and geographical influences. The first attempts to record the language occurred when our Anglo-Saxon ancestors used Latin as the basis of written expression. The Latin phoneme-grapheme associations used for writing the English language were centered upon an alphabetic system. To transcribe the various Anglo-Saxon dialects, a modified Latin was developed and many inconsistencies in word spellings appeared. Spelling the same word differently was an acceptable practice at the time and was of little concern to anyone.

The irregularities in phoneme-grapheme relationships increased with the Norman conquest of 1066 when the French language and culture were introduced. Although the French and Anglo cultures eventually merged, the irregularities in spelling continued with writers spelling words as they preferred to pronounce them, regardless of other spellings.

The development of printing is often credited with bringing about

321

spelling reform and imposing uniformity on the written word (Fries, 1963). The practical demands of printing a common language form created a "regularity" in English spelling which persists today. The student of English orthography must meet the demands of acceptable spelling in order to communicate in written language.

Linguists have long debated the question of whether English orthography follows a generally consistent pattern with predictable grapheme-phoneme associations. Hanna (Moore, 1951) examined the 3000 most fre-

Grapheme	Phoneme	Example
Vowels		
a in all positions	/ă/	cat
i in all positions	/ĕ/	bit
o in all positions	/ŏ/	ton
u in all positions	/ə/	but
e in medial positions	/ĕ/	set
a in syllable final—but not word final position	/ā/	placate
e in syllable final—but not word final position	/ē/	legal
oy in word final position	/oi/	boy
ow in all positions	/ou/	how
Consonants		
b in all positions	/b/	boy
ch in all positions	/ch/	chart
d in all positions	/d/	dog
f in all positions	/f/	few
h in all positions	/h/	here
wh in all positions	/hw/	when
x in all positions	/ks/	mix
qw in all positions	/kw/	queer
l in all positions	/l/	lamp
le in all positions	/l/	able
m in all positions	/m/	man
n in all positions	/n/	new
p in all positions	/p/	push
r in all positions	/r/	run
s in all cases	/s/	say
t in all positions	/t/	toe
th in all positions	/th/	thing
v in all positions	/v/	vet
w in all positions	/w/	wet

FIGURE 10.1   *Examples of Grapheme-Phoneme Relationships*

quently used words in children's writings and found that the grapheme-phoneme associations were consistent almost 80 percent of the time. In a later study, Hanna (Hodges & Rudorf, 1966) expanded his research to include 17,000 words. Again, the results showed a high percentage of consistency when phonological factors, such as position in syllables, internal constraints, and stress, are considered.

Consistent grapheme-phoneme relationships are detailed in Figure 10.1. These major sounds provide stability in the production of spelling forms and are useful in spelling unfamiliar words. Yet, as Hillerich (1977) points out, " . . . no one can be assured of the correct spelling of a word that has not been examined specifically for spelling. It is simple to come up with phonetic possibilities, but impossible to be certain of the "correct spelling" (p. 301).

Let us examine the word *know*. According to acceptable grapheme-phoneme association it is possible to phonetically spell the *kn* phonemes as *n* (no), *gn* (gnaw), *pn* (pneumonia), or *mn* (mnemonic). The *ow* sound at the end of the word may be spelled *oe* (hoe), *o* (go), or *ough* (through). The implication is that knowledge of linguistic generalizations will not assure correct spelling of an unknown word.

Based upon research in spelling, several approaches for assessing and instructing spelling will be discussed in this chapter. Spelling difficulties experienced by many normal children are compounded by the learning problems of the mildly handicapped. The approach selected for spelling instruction should be based upon an understanding of the child's learning style, language competence, and communication needs.

Spelling Difficulties of the Mildly Handicapped

Due to the complexity of the spelling process, it is often difficult to isolate the factors that are the direct cause of poor performance. The language deficiencies manifested by many mildly handicapped students play a significant role in hindering the acquisition of spelling skills. Several generalizations about handicapped learners and the causes of their spelling problems given by Stephens (1977), are summarized below:

1. Poor spellers often have lower intellectual ability. Spelling is a cognitive function that depends on multisensory skills, such as visual and auditory acuity, discrimination, imagery, and motor adequacy.
2. Poor spellers often have revisualization problems and are unable to reproduce word patterns. The ability to visualize a word in one's mind is an effective means of improving spelling through self-correction.

323

3. Poor spellers have difficulty in using phonetic skills to learn sound-symbol associations.
4. Poor spellers may mispronounce words when speaking and then spell them as they are said. Examples are: acount (account), probly (probably), and telphone (telephone).
5. Poor spellers may rely solely on phonetic rules and be unable to spell irregular words. Although many words are spelled as they sound (sit, when, and slip), many are not (laughter/laffter and knee/nee).
6. Poor spellers may be unfamiliar with word meanings and as a result may have difficulty spelling words which sound alike but are spelled differently (knead/need, red/read, die/dye).

An examination of the reasons why some children are poor spellers establishes the close relationship of spelling and the other language arts. Although spelling words can be learned from word lists, they must be applied within the communication framework. That is, the child must be able to translate spoken language or cognitive thought (subvocalized language) into written language. To do this, a complete sequence of communication skills has to be achieved. A problem in any process or language related area may be reflected in the child's spelling performance.

The Spelling Process

Recent research is providing evidence that spelling ability may develop in a pattern similar to language ability. Children seem to follow a general sequence in learning to spell (Beers & Henderson, 1977; Beers, Beers, & Grant, 1977), beginning with early inventions of spelling as they seek to understand the relationships of sounds, letters, and written language. Children create their own spelling strategies to meet their early writing needs during the preschool and early primary years.

Children's first spelling words may be at a prephonetic or phonetic stage in which they test a personal theory of grapheme-phoneme associations. Such a spelling system is based on a knowledge of phonology. As a result a vowel sound is represented by a letter whose name is closest to the sound (*tip* for *type*). Although incorrectly spelled, these written word attempts are as relevant in the learning sequence as the child's early attempts at language ("cookie," "give cookie").

As children progress, their invented spelling can be associated with five identified strategies. In line with the developmental nature of the spelling process, children progress at varying rates of achievement and may fluctuate between an advanced strategy for high-frequency words and a less sophisti-

Brian Kindergarten Deviant	Angela Kindergarten Prephonetic	Chris Grade 1 Phonetic	Joyce Grade 2 Transitional	Lorraine Grade 2 Correct
IMMPMPM	J	CHRP	CHRIP	CHIRP
2PMPBMN	SB	SAP	STAMP	STAMP
BPRIM	AT	EDE	EIGHTEEY	EIGHTY
MPRMRHM	J	GAGIN	DRAGUN	DRAGON
BDRNMPM	P	PRD	PURD	PURRED
BRNBMM	TP	TIP	TIPE	TYPE
PMIMRN	T	CHUBRL	TRUBAL	TROUBLE

From: Gentry, J. R. Early spelling strategies. *The Elementary School Journal*, 1978, 79, 2, 88-92.

FIGURE 10.2   *Classification of Spelling Strategies Used by Five Children*

cated strategy for low-frequency words. Examples of children's spellings for each of these strategies appear in Figure 10.2. Figure 10.3 contains the phonetically spelled sentences of a five year old and of a mildly handicapped nine year old.

With exposure to written language and opportunities for spelling performance, young children make the transition to standard spelling. During transition the children must be able to compare their spellings with standard form. A self-discovery method (self-checking) allows children to refine and generalize their understanding. The transition to standard spelling is generally completed by the third grade when, as a "correct" speller, the child employs a knowledge of basic English orthography (Gentry, 1978).

Research in spelling is heavily oriented toward the production of written word forms by nonhandicapped children, but the application of these findings is not limited to the "normal" population. The teacher of the mildly handicapped must be aware of the growing evidence that children need opportunities to systematically examine words and to compare their self-generated forms with standard spellings. However, it is possible that older children who manifest a large number of aberrant spellings, do not follow the developmental pattern and may only achieve through a very structured, direct program. Further research is necessary before a clarification of this point will be achieved.

Spelling Variables

Spelling ability depends on the interaction of many skills. These have been identified by Westerman (1971) as auditory skills, visual skills, motor skills, and integration abilities. Figure 10.4 contains a more detailed listing of

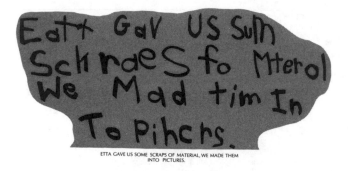

ETTA GAVE US SOME SCRAPS OF MATERIAL, WE MADE THEM
INTO PICTURES.

I rod mi bick

it is fon t or i d mi bick

(I rode my bike. It is fun to ride my bike.)

FIGURE 10.3   Phonetic Spelling of Two Children

the spelling skills. Emphasis is clearly on the auditory channel input, however, the interrelatedness of the other channels is evident.

Each of the abilities in the task analysis must be adequately developed for written spelling to be achieved. The prerequisites of these
abilities deserve attention in that they are the cornerstone of the child's
formal spelling performance. Deficiencies in two or more prerequisites at the
time that spelling instruction begins results in the development of poor spelling habits and frustration in an unsuccessful task. Six prerequisites to spelling

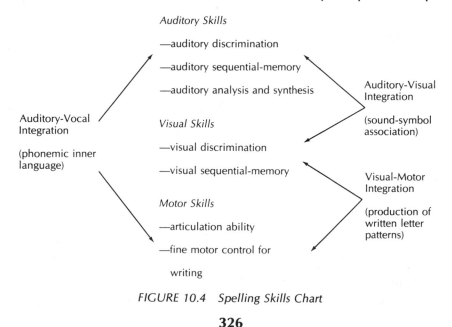

FIGURE 10.4   Spelling Skills Chart

Prerequisite	Justification
1. Adequate vision and hearing ability.	1. The child must be able to visually and auditorally discriminate letter patterns and sound sequences
2. Satisfactory fine motor skills.	2. Spelling performance can only be judged in close relation to handwriting and writing skills within the final product.
3. Ability to pronounce sound sequences.	3. Phoneme-grapheme association skills allow the child to correctly spell many previously unlearned words.
4. Knowledge of letter identification.	4. Naming the letters in the word increases visual and auditory memory of the spelling sequence.
5. Understanding of word meaning.	5. Understanding the function of a word increases both the chance of its use and the need for rote memory of the word pattern.
6. Desire to communicate successfully.	6. Understanding the importance of correct spelling and of written communication motivates the child to acquire good spelling habits.

FIGURE 10.5   Spelling Prerequisites

and a justification of their importance to the spelling process are detailed in Figure 10.5.

Spelling Program Goals

Learning to spell words in isolation is often a boring and difficult task. Most poor spellers also experience difficulty in other areas of the language arts. Students who are fluent in reading and speaking and are able to express ideas in writing are seldom poor in the rudiments of spelling. Spelling, in comparison to the other language arts, is not in and of itself considered an academic subject, such as written expression and reading. It is therefore important, and possible, to teach spelling within the context of broader language skill development aimed at bettering communication. Direct spelling instruction should be closely related to meaningful units of written language expression, such as vocabulary and reading achievement.

The major aim of the spelling program for the mildly handicapped is to develop writers who will not make themselves conspicuous through spelling errors. Spelling is a skill often used to judge education, intellectual ability, and concern for self-presentation. A good number of errors are necessary before a piece is considered unreadable. (This fact was verified in the letter written to Dr. Fonerden originally published in the *American Journal of Insanity* (1850) and presented in chapter 1.) The frequency and type of spelling errors that are made influence the reader's acceptance of the message and view of the writer. The example of a mainstreamed mildly handicapped child's writing in Figure 10.6 illustrates the effect spelling errors can have on the reader's comprehension of the passage. In the first sentence it is unclear whether the writer likes fourth grade "because we dissect bugs" or "because we discussed drugs."

The mildly handicapped child whose written work presents a positive image will have a better chance for achievement both in and out of school. Precisely stated the objectives of the spelling instructional program for the mildly handicapped child are:

1. To accurately spell the most frequently used words that the child needs to write now and in the future.
2. To develop self-correction skills for adjusting spelling errors.
3. To develop the ability to locate the correct spelling of unfamiliar words.

Each of these objectives is directed toward establishing ease and confidence in spelling written words. Mastery of spelling skills will aid the child by:

1. Increasing self-concept
2. Allowing better communication
3. Aiding the acquisition of related language abilities

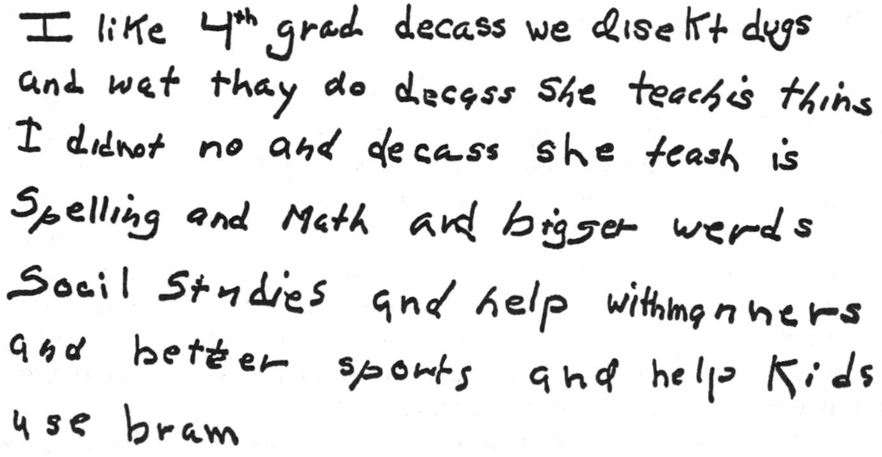

FIGURE 10.6

Assessment of Spelling Abilities

Difficulties in spelling, as in any other language arts skill, should be systematically assessed to locate the source(s) of the problem and to outline sequential steps for remediation. There are several test options available to the teacher who is seeking information about a child's spelling ability. Many standardized achievement tests have sections related to spelling which provide an objective means of obtaining age and grade level norms. Unfortunately, these are little more than gross estimates of the child's spelling ability, specifically, whether or not the pupil is spelling above or below the average child. This information is of little use for the remediation of spelling difficulties.

Standardized achievement tests which include spelling sections are listed in Figure 10.7. As the chart indicates there are essentially two techniques used to measure spelling ability. The *dictated-word* format requires that the child write words dictated by the examiner. The word is first given orally, then used in a sentence, and then given in isolation once again. The second approach, *proofreading,* presents the student with a series of words that may or may not be correctly spelled. The child must decide whether or not a word is acceptable. A variation of this approach asks the student to select the correctly spelled stimulus word from several possible spellings of that word (e.g., Peabody Individual Achievement Test).

One standardized spelling test of achievement that does provide accurate information regarding the child's spelling level, as well as focusing direction on areas of difficulty, is the Larsen-Hammill Test of Written Spelling (TWS), 1976. The test words, selected because they appeared in ten commonly used basal spelling programs, are presented with validity coefficients and difficulty levels.

The TWS was constructed to accommodate the two beliefs that:

1. Mastery of a certain number of rules and generalizations is necessary to be able to spell the many new words one encounters.
2. Certain words that do not conform to such rules must be learned through memorization.

Reflecting these hypotheses, the test words are classified as either *predictable* or *unpredictable* and scores are given for each subtest as well as total achievement. Although the authors recommend the TWS be given individually, it can be adapted for group administration and scoring, and interpretation is easily accomplished.

Administration of the TWS provides a general estimate of spelling achievement and indicates areas of possible concern needing further diagnosis. However, the TWS is not sufficient as a single diagnostic tool and the teacher must use additional informal assessment strategies prior to planning and initiating a complete program of spelling remediation.

Test	Procedure for Assessing Spelling	Grade Levels
Test of Written Spelling (Larsen & Hammill, 1976)	Dictated-word	1–8
Comprehensive Tests of Basic Skills (CTB/McGraw-Hill, 1968)	Proofreading	2–12
California Achievement Tests (Tiegs & Clark, 1970)	Proofreading	1–12
Stanford Achievement Tests (Madden & Gardner, 1972)	Proofreading	1–9
Peabody Individual Achievement Test (Dunn & Markwardt, 1970)	Proofreading	K–12
Iowa Test of Basic Skills (Hieronymus & Lindquist, 1971)	Proofreading	1–9
Metropolitan Achievement Tests (Durost, et al., 1970)	Dictated-word Proofreading	2–4 4–9
SRA Achievement Series (Thorpe, Lefever, & Nasland, 1974)	Proofreading	1–12
The Gray-Votaw-Rogers General Achievement Tests (Gray, Votaw, & Rogers, 1963)	Dictated-word Proofreading	1–3 4–9
Wide Range Achievement Test (Jastak & Jastak, 1965)	Dictated-word	3–12
The Iowa Test of Educational Development (Lindquist & Feldt, 1959)	Proofreading	9–12
McGraw-Hill Basic Study Skills: Spelling (Raygoz, 1970)	Proofreading	9–12

Source: Wallace, G., & Larsen, S. Educational assessment of learning problems: Testing for teaching. Boston: Allyn & Bacon, Inc., 1978.

FIGURE 10.7   Achievement Tests with Spelling Sections

Informal Spelling Assessment

A variety of informal techniques for diagnostic spelling assessment tend to be more useful than the standardized achievement measures. Diagnostic spelling instruments which can be either commercially or teacher produced are generally designed to reveal specific spelling skills that need further mastery and general error patterns. A careful interpretation of these instruments can yield information that is vital to a systematic remediation of spelling deficits.

Initial spelling assessment should begin with careful observation of a student's written and oral work habits. Appropriate examples of a child's ability can be gathered during reading activities, writing assignments, and spelling lessons. Since a wide range of abilities are integrated within the spelling task it is pertinent that the teacher scrutinize a spectrum of skills. The systematic observation guide provided in Figure 10.8 is appropriate either as an initial screening device or as a record-keeping procedure for notation of continuous progress.

The systematic observation guide can be used as a means of focusing on general areas of difficulty that need further diagnosis. An example of a more detailed analysis is Partoll's (1976) comprehensive checklist for the identification of specific spelling skill weaknesses. The checklist, provided in Figure 10.9, can be applied to any written work or test sample in which the student has relied on his own spelling ability. Periodic use of the checklist will establish a record of the child's progress in spelling achivement.

In some instances a teacher may feel the need to construct a checklist which more closely follows the spelling program implemented within the classroom or devised for an individual child. Wallace and Larsen (1978) recommend the use of the skill sequence specified in the basal spelling series being used within the school. Through simple modification of a record form from the basal series, the teacher may construct a criterion-referenced checklist which is appropriate for determining the child's:

1. Level of functioning in that series
2. Skill deficiencies
3. Rate of individual progress
4. Attitude toward spelling

Another possible means of assessing spelling ability is through an informal spelling inventory (ISI). Like other informal inventories the purpose of the ISI is to establish a child's spelling deficiencies. Informal spelling inventories are teacher constructed instruments and are generally based on the basal spelling program. Mann and Suiter (1974) suggest the following procedure for developing an informal spelling inventory.

1. Using a basal spelling series, select a random sample of words from each book. For grade one choose 15 words and for grades two to six 20 words.
2. A random sampling is developed by dividing the number of words in each book's word list by the number of words desired on the final ISI list (e.g., 250 words, divided by 20 means you would select every twelfth word for your test sample).
3. Begin the testing at approximately two grade levels below the child's actual grade placement. For first and second graders begin at level 1.

331

Systematic Spelling Observation Form

Student _____

Date _____

	Consistently good performance	Inconsistent performance	Consistently poor performance
I. Analysis of General Work Habits **a.** Attention **b.** Follows directions **c.** Completes assignments **d.** Approaches new learning systematically			
II. Analysis of Written Work **a.** Legibility of handwriting **b.** Errors in written expression **c.** Uses a range of vocabulary **d.** Knowledge of writing conventions or rules **e.** Able to reproduce a visual form or letter sequence			
III. Analysis of Oral Work **a.** Pronunciations **b.** Dialectical speech **c.** Articulation **d.** Ability to repeat a short sentence heard orally **e.** Sound-blending			
IV. Analysis of Spelling Work **a.** Knows phoneme-grapheme associations **b.** Uses a visual memory approach to new words **c.** Spells by syllables **d.** Spells one letter at a time **e.** Spells in whole word units			

FIGURE 10.8   Systematic Spelling Observation Form

Checklist for Specifying Spelling Errors

_____ 1. Consonant sounds used incorrectly (specify letters missed)
_____ 2. Vowel sounds not known
_____ 3. Sounds omitted at beginning of words
_____ 4. Sounds added at the beginning of words (e.g., a blend given when a single consonant required)
_____ 5. Omission of middle sounds
_____ 6. Omission of middle syllables
_____ 7. Extraneous letters added
_____ 8. Extraneous syllables added
_____ 9. Missequencing of sounds or syllables (transposals like "from" to "form")
_____10. Reversals of whole words
_____11. Endings omitted
_____12. Incorrect ending substituted ("ing" for "en" or for "ed")
_____13. Auditory confusion of *m/n, th/f, s/z,* or *b/d* or other similar sounds
_____14. Phonetic spelling with poor visual recall of word appearance
_____15. Spelling laborious, letter by letter
_____16. Poor knowledge of "demons" (e.g., one, iron, forecastle)
_____17. Spells, erases, tries again, etc., to no avail
_____18. Reversals of letter shapes *b/d, p/q, u/n,* or *m/w*
_____19. Spelling so bizarre that it bears no resemblance to original; even pupil cannot read his own written words
_____20. Mixing of upper and lower case letters
_____21. Inability to recall how to form either case for some letters
_____22. Spatial placement on line erratic
_____23. Spacing between letters and words erratic
_____24. Poor writing and letter formations, immature eye-hand coordination
_____25. Temporal disorientation: slowness in learning time, general scheduling, grasping the sequence of events in the day
_____26. Difficulty in concept formation; not able to generalize and transfer readily to abstract "the rules and the tools"

Source: Partoll, S. F. Spelling demonology revisited. *Academic Therapy,* 1976, XI, 339–348.

FIGURE 10.9   Spelling Error Checklist

4. The testing procedure for each word is for the teacher to *say the word, use it in a sentence,* and *say the word again.*
5. The student should be encouraged to attempt to spell each word by putting down any sound he knows in the word.
6. Stop testing at the level at which a child misses seven words in the list.
7. The inventory may be given in several sittings so as to avoid boredom and frustration.

Construction of an ISI offers the advantage of relating directly to the spelling program and the chosen basal series. However, if a teacher does not choose to develop an ISI, there are preconstructed ones, such as the Mann-Suiter Developmental Spelling Inventory (1974), which are designed to accommodate those students who are being instructed in any basic spelling program.

Modality Preference Testing

Modality preference refers to the favored receptive/expressive processing channel by which the child interacts with his external world. Understanding the child's modality preference may help the teacher to match instructional procedures to the child's individual style. Westerman (1971) has delineated a modality testing procedure that attempts to determine the combination of input/output channels which produce a child's best spelling performance. The five channels are:

1. *Auditory-vocal channel.* The child hears the word spelled aloud, then spells it orally to the teacher. The word is never presented visually.
2. *Auditory-motor channel.* The child hears the word spelled aloud, then writes the word on paper.
3. *Visual-vocal channel.* In this method, the words are presented on flash cards, identified (i.e., "this word is 'carpet.'"), but are never spelled aloud. The child looks at the word, then spells it back orally to the teacher.
4. *Visual-motor channel.* Again, the word is presented visually on a flash card and identified. The child looks at the word, then writes it on paper.
5. *Multisensory combination channel.* In this method, the child looks at the word on a flash card while it is spelled aloud, then spells it back orally and writes it on paper (p. 40).

The instructional sequence for each of these channel combinations is provided in Figure 10.10. Westerman suggests that the best evidence of the child's modality preference can be gained by teaching 10 unknown but "learnable" words each day, 2 for each input/output channel. After a day's instruction, test all 10 words. On Friday, after 40 words have been taught, a cumulative test is given. The teacher should record delayed recall and error patterns for each modality.

An adaptation to this procedure for the mildly handicapped may include reducing the total number of words by testing only 15 words taught within a three-day period. In this, as in other assessment techniques, the

334

teacher must be certain the performance outcomes are properly interpreted and are not confused with the child's other learning problems.

Not every child demonstrates an obvious modality preference, but for those who do, the teacher needs to tailor the spelling program to their learning style. Westerman's testing procedures can be easily altered for instructional purposes. A child who clearly is a visual-motor learner, for example, should be given repeated opportunities to look at a word and write it, look at it, write it, look, write, look, write, and so on. Whereas, a child who appears as an auditory-vocal learner will need to use a tape cassette, study carrel, or some other classroom arrangement that would allow practicing spelling words aloud.

Recently, the use of a strength-oriented approach (providing instructional activities according to a child's perferred modality) has been seriously questioned. In a thorough review of the modality research related to reading instruction Tarver and Dawson (1978) were unable to find any interaction between modality preference and teaching method. The authors suggested that other learner variables may also be important to the learner-task match and that perhaps more attention should be given to assessment of the task. Although this review does bring forth many relevant points, modality preference cannot be disregarded. First, major research in this area has not been done in academic subjects, such as spelling; and second, many practitioners feel that attention to modality preference is a useful instructional aid.

Spelling Test Strategies

When one mentions a spelling test we typically conjure up an image of the Friday morning dictated spelling exam. The *dictated test,* in which the teacher gives a series of words, each one said in isolation followed by its use in a sentence, is the most common testing strategy. Dictated spelling exams take little preparation, are easy to administer to a group or individual, and can be analyzed for spelling errors. Because of these advantages many teachers do not often seek alternative testing strategies.

The learning difficulties experienced by the mildly handicapped child may be reflected by, or be increased as a result of, a specific testing procedure. The teacher is responsible for experimenting with alternative strategies to gain as much information as possible about the child's learning style and skill development. Keep in mind that a child may have some knowledge or skill, but may be unable to express it in the required test mode. Smith (1969) presents at least three additional testing procedures other than dictation which are appropriate for spelling assessment:

1. Cloze procedure
2. Proofreading
3. Free writing

	Auditory-Vocal	Auditory-Motor	Visual-Vocal	Visual-Motor	Multi-Sensory
TEACHER	1. Say word ("This is the way to spell 'chart'") 2. Spell word aloud (c-h-a-r-t) 3. Say word again ("chart") 4. "Say the word and spell it for me."	1. Say word. 2. Spell word aloud. 3. Say word again. 4. "Write the word I have just spelled."	1. Show word on card. 2. Name word (do not spell orally) 3. "Look at the word, say it, then spell it for me."	1. Show word on card. 2. Name word. 3. "Look at this word and write it on your paper."	1. Show word on card. 2. Name word. 3. Spell orally. 4. "Look at this word and spell it for me." 5. "Now write it on your paper."
PUPIL	1. Say word ("chart") 2. Spell aloud (c-h-a-r-t)	1. Write word on paper.	1. Say word. 2. Spell orally. 3. Say word again.	1. Copy word from flash card. 2. Cover sample. 3. Write word again—check back and forth until spelled correctly.	1. Say word. 2. Spell orally. 3. Write on paper.

	TEACHER	PUPIL
	1. If error in student response, say "Almost, Bob— you try it John." Then go back to Bob. 2. After everyone has spelled back word correctly 4 times, say "Now everyone write 'chart'"	1. Write word on paper from memory. 2. Hold paper up for correction. DO NOT SHOW FLASH CARD.
	1. Repeat spelling orally for correction. 2. After writing word correctly 4 times, say "Turn your paper over and write ___"	1. Write word on paper from memory. 2. Hold paper up for correction. DO NOT SHOW FLASH CARD.
	1. After each child response, take word away. 2. Ask each student to spell from memory. 3. After 4 correct responses from each child, say "Everyone write ___"	1. Write word on paper from memory. (Correct with flash card.)
	1. After 4 correct response, tell children to turn paper over and write word from memory.	1. Write word on paper from memory. (Correct with flash card.)
	1. After each child has responded, cover card. Ask students to spell orally from memory (2 times); then write from memory (2 times). 2. "Now turn your paper over and write ___"	1. Write word on paper from memory. (Correct with flash card.)

From Beery, K., Westerman, G. S., & Wilkinson, A. Sensory modality preference testing. In G. S. Westerman, *Spelling and writing*, Sioux Falls, South Dakota: Adapt Press, Inc., 1971, p. 40.

FIGURE 10.10 *Sensory Modality Preference Testing*

The *cloze procedure* has been used more commonly in reading and is a successful means of visually examining spelling abilities. The cloze task requires the student to complete a sentence or phrase by filling in the missing word or letters of a word. For example, the sentence may appear like this, "The girl's _____ was Susan" or "The girl was reading a b__k." Items presented in this way can test general spelling ability or can be controlled to assess specific areas of concern. For the latter, the teacher may devise sentences with the omitted words focusing on a consistent rule or generalization, such as plurals, doubling final consonants, or irregularly spelt word forms.

A variation on the cloze procedure is to provide the student with two or more options for sentence completion.

"The clown made the girl _____."
                    laff, laugh

"The sk_____ is blue."
        i, ie, y

Since the cloze procedure is so visually oriented, it is wise to use it in conjunction with other techniques. The more avenues used to evaluate a mildly handicapped child's learning skills the more appropriately matched the learning program can be.

Proofreading is another technique by which the child can associate visual word patterns within a language context. The assessment strategy is to ask the child to read a passage and to mark any incorrectly spelled words. By controlling the word errors in the story, the teacher can test for knowledge of certain spelling rules.

Finally, it is possible to examine the spelling errors a student makes in *free writing* a composition. For free writing analysis to be beneficial for assessing spelling, it is necessary that the teacher systematically record all errors and note possible patterns across time. Student profiles or class profiles can be developed from forms such as the checklist of errors in Figure 10.9. Continuous record keeping of student progress will verify program effectiveness.

Caution must be exercised in the assessment of spelling as an isolated endeavor. A spelling program based entirely on the weekly spelling list will not help the mildly handicapped conceptualize the role of spelling within the communication process. As Zutell (1978) clearly states:

> In many such programs children interpret the spelling task as one of rote memorization. The results are inefficient processing, boredom or frustration, the development of a strong dislike for writing in general, and a lack of carry over from the teaching-testing situation to their own written products. . . . (p. 848)

The problems resulting from an isolated spelling program can be avoided by integrating both spelling instruction and assessment into the general language arts curriculum. The testing procedures suggested here will allow the child to examine his ability in generalizing spelling knowledge.

Approaches to Spelling Instruction

There is little conclusive evidence as to the best method for teaching spelling. Research in spelling and spelling instruction for nonhandicapped learners have provided findings that suggest:

1. Word lists are the most efficient and effective means of presentation for spelling. Instructional time is shortened, while retention and transfer are increased for words learned from a list.
2. A pretest of new spelling words which is corrected immediately by the student allows the child to study only those words he does not know. The student can recognize the areas of difficulty and focus on the appropriate spelling. This has been found to be the single most important element in successfully teaching spelling relative to the allotted time.
3. Spelling must be taught in a direct, systematic manner. Poor spellers need to be instructed on how to study a word. The teacher should be careful not to just point out errors but to provide a corrective program.
4. Phonics instruction is supplemental to, not a substitute for, spelling. Teaching a few essential rules can be beneficial, but only those generalizations that apply to a large number of words should be stressed.
5. Less than 300 words account for more than 50 percent of the words used in children's writings (Fitzgerald, 1951). A properly selected list of 2500 will account for 96 percent of all words used in adult writing (Horn, 1924). The implication is that the beginning speller should learn the most frequently used words first. Individual experience will dictate the selection of additional words.

Most basal spelling programs incorporate these findings into their instructional scheme. However, the teacher who is developing a spelling plan without the assistance of a commercial program should note them carefully.

The child's own learning style and immediate spelling needs should be carefully considered in the selection of words. Remember that the most frequently used words are generally easier to learn. Although word lists are considered an efficient means of learning spelling words, the mildly hand-icapped child may need added practice in spelling words in context. The teacher should plan for the transfer of spelling skills to ensure the child's success. Keeping in mind the integration of spelling ability in the total written communication process, it is important to practice spelling words in sentences.

Transfer refers to the child's ability to apply knowledge and response patterns learned in one situation to a new situation (Smith, 1974). In spelling transfer occurs when a child learns to spell a word from a list and uses it appropriately in a sentence. Another transfer situation is when a child learns the final *t* sound in "sa*t*" and, without additional instruction, applies it when spelling "be*t*." Some mildly handicapped children will have difficulty trans-ferring information, and the teacher will need to plan the curriculum in such a way that they will begin to generalize their knowledge.

To help the mildly handicapped child transfer spelling (or any other) skills the teacher should first sequence the instructional task, establishing small segments of learning. Concrete materials and manipulatives are helpful when learning the response pattern. The child may need assistance in under-standing relationships between old and new situations before he can apply the information he has learned. Plan for success, reinforce the child on every early attempt, and finally, provide numerous opportunities to practice the newly learned behavior pattern in a variety of settings.

Recent work with mildly handicapped children has shown that con-tingent imitation of a child's spelling error can be used to effectively reduce the inappropriate response. (Kauffman, Hallahan, Hass, Brame, & Boren, 1978). The study, consisting of two separate experiments, compared the effectiveness of two methods of providing a child (who has made a spelling error) with a correct model versus imitating the child's error ("this is how you spelled the word") and then giving a model ("this is the right way to spell the word"). In each case the child was required to rewrite the word. The Imita-tion Plus Model technique was the most effective, especially, when used with errors made in nonphonetic words. Kauffman et al. speculate that the results are due to the learning principle of providing examples of "not concepts" when teaching basic concepts. As Becker, Engelmann, and Thomas (1975) noted, providing a negative concept example followed by a positive example is the appropriate teaching sequence. Therefore, showing a child the mis-spelled word followed by the correct model achieves better results.

Linguistic Approach

A linguistic approach to spelling is based on the predominant consis-tencies in the English language and may be taught to mildly handicapped children as they learn grapheme-phoneme associations. Although the utility of teaching linguistic generalizations is debated, it is possible to achieve some success if the child is taught *only one sound association for each written symbol*. Less frequently occurring written forms of a phoneme should be taught as irregular words and learned through a visual process.

Spelling instruction can follow along the prescribed order of the linguistic reading program. This would ensure consistency across subject areas and would eliminate the confusion caused when a child is instructed in two conflicting reading and spelling series.

Formalized spelling instruction is begun in most commercial programs at the end of the first or the beginning of the second grade. However, it is possible to start earlier proceeding from the basic linguistic principles taught in primer level CVC (consonant-vowel-consonant) words. The following is a suggested sequence of a linguistic-spelling program which will guide the introduction of spelling words.

Suggested Linguistic-Spelling Program
General guidelines:

1. Teach 2–5 words per week.
2. Follow a weekly plan of instruction (such as the one suggested later in this chapter).
3. Integrate the week's spelling words in as many other classroom activities as possible (e.g., reading and writing).
4. Teach one related word group at a time. Not all words need to be taught in one lesson.
5. Review past words frequently.
6. Include one sight word in each lesson.

Lessons:
1. CVC (Consonant-vowel-consonant)
   a. Short *a* families (bat, hat, cat, sad, mad, had)
   b. Short *i* families (hit, bin, lid)
   c. Short *o* families (son, hot, mob)
   d. Short *u* families (bet, pen, fed, set)
   e. Short *e* families (bet, pen, fed, set)
2. CVCC (having short vowel sounds and ending in double letters)
   a. *ll* words (hell, sell, tell)
   b. *ss* words (kiss, moss, less)
3. CCVC (with short vowel sounds)
   a. Two-letter initial blends (*sh*-ship, *bl*-blend, *sw*-swim)
   b. Digraphs (*ch*-chat, *sh*-shot, *wh*-when)
4. CCCVC (three-letter blends with short vowel sounds) (*str*-string, *spr*-spring)
5. CVCV (long vowel sound, silent final e)
   a. Long *a* (make, cape, date)
   b. Long *i* (hike, bite, mile)
   c. Long *o* (joke, some, mode)

341

      d. Long *u* (cute, duke, tune)

      e. Long *e* (Pete)

  6. CCVCV (with long vowel sounds)

      a. Two-letter initial blends (*sp*-spade, -stick)

      b. Digraphs (*sh*-shame, *wh*-while)

  7. CCCVCV (three-letter blends with long vowel sounds) (*str*-stroke, *spr*-sprite)

  8. Alternate (soft) sounds of *c* and *g* (city, gear)

  9. *R* controlled vowels (*ar*-car, *er*-her, *ir*-sir, *ur*-fur)

10. Vowel digraphs (*ee*-teen, *ay*-say, *ai*-braid, *ea*-bead)

11. Silent letters (*knee, knot, honor, listen*)

12. Irregular words (the, said)

13. Root words

14. Prefixes and suffixes

15. Homonyms

*Adapted from: Mann, P., and Suiter, P. *Handbook in diagnostic teaching: A learning disabilities approach*. Boston: Allyn & Bacon, Inc., 1974, pp. 130–131.

For nonhandicapped learners many educators advocate an inductive approach in teaching linguistic generalizations. Using an inductive method, students are encouraged to discover spelling generalizations by analyzing several words which share a common linguistic property. Based on this analysis the students are asked to apply the generalization when spelling unfamiliar words.

A good example of an inductive teaching lesson is one which leads the children through the discovery procedure. Otto, McMenemy, and Smith (1973) specify the procedure for teaching the generalization that, "when the long *a* sound is the last sound in a word, the sound is usually represented by the letters *ay*."

1. Show the children a picture of a word containing the letters *ay* in final position (hay, tray, pray).
2. Have the children say the word the picture represents.
3. Write the word on the chalkboard.
4. Have the children supply their own speaking vocabulary words that have the same final sound (ray, delay, relay, sleigh, today, Chevrolet, holiday).
5. Ask the children to observe the spelling of words in which the final sound is long *a*.
6. Have the children verbalize the generalization they observe (when the long *a* sound comes last in a word, it is usually spelled *ay*).
7. Reinforce the generalization. (p. 258)

Although the inductive approach is a viable one for some children, it presents certain problems when working with many mildly handicapped youngsters. The cognitive abilities necessary for induction are of a higher order than those exhibited by some mildly handicapped children. Other students are unable to handle generalizations and rely heavily on visual imagery in order to spell. Finally, there are some children who may learn a generalization by rote but are unable to apply the principle in an unfamiliar situation. Instruction should be guided by the teacher's decision as to whether or not the child is capable of *learning* and *applying* linguistic generalizations.

A good rule of thumb for the majority of mildly handicapped children is to teach only those generalizations which provide the most utility. Beyond the basic grapheme-phoneme relationships the following rules are thought to be of value in spelling a large number of additional words.

1. The majority of nouns form their plural by adding *s*.
2. Nouns ending in *s, x, sh*, and *ch* are pluralized by adding *es*.
3. If a consonant precedes the final *y*, change *y* to *i* when adding a consonant except when the consonant begins with *i*.
4. Always follow a *q* with a *u*.
5. Drop an *e* at the end of a word when adding a suffix that begins with a vowel.
6. *I* before *e*, except after *c*, or when it sounds like *a* as in n*ei*ghbor and sl*ei*gh.
7. Form possessives by adding *'s*.

The mildly handicapped child who is capable of learning and applying spelling generalizations may need direct instruction in each rule. Repeated practice and exposure to words which consistently follow the generalization will assist the child's overlearning of the application.

Visual Approach

Mildly handicapped children, like their normal counterparts, differ widely in the way they learn to spell. Some may progress using the linguistic approach while many others need to concentrate on the development of a visual word image. The visual approach focuses on the appearance of the whole word, rather than on unique sound-symbol relationships. The goal of the visual technique is to create an impression of the word which the child can automatically reproduce in a writing task.

There are many instructional activities to help establish a visual image. A few examples are:

1. New spelling words can be posted around the room as a visual reminder. Such cues will be useful to the child until the word image has become firmly established.

343

2. The child may be asked to write the word using various mediums such as paints, large markers or string. The novelty of these experiences will maintain the child's attention while illustrating the whole word.

3. Emphasize the word image through identification of configuration drawings. The child may learn to spell the word by association with the configuration.

4. Matching tasks and fading configuration prompts can be used successfully (Figure 10.11) with some children. The key to configuration prompting is the highlighting of an outstanding feature.

It is difficult to say what element of a word will be a *hard* spot for any one child. Therefore, it is important to focus the child's attention on the *whole* word. Unless specific weaknesses are noticed (e.g., failure to follow a *q* with a *u*), or a certain element, such as a prefix (e.g., anti-), is being applied to old words, it is not generally advantageous to highlight word parts. The separation of elements hinders the development of a complete word image and does not lend itself to successful reproduction of the spelling pattern. An exception may occur when working with young children who have not yet developed the perceptual skills to focus on a whole word stimulus. In such cases, meaningful units of word sounds should be given specific attention (e.g., *n-ame*).

All irregularly spelled words (e.g., *knee, cough, said*) must be learned through visual memory. This is true in every case and for every child. Repetition is essential. The teacher should be cautioned to frequently check the child's spelling in order to prevent incorrect word patterns forming a strong visual image that may become a habit.

Efficient spellers write *most* words from memory and then rely upon visual feedback to check for the correct spelling. Mildly handicapped children whose word study habits afford them a strong visual image will improve their general spelling ability. The prescribed study method (Figure 10.12) is designed to stress the visual element and to prevent inappropriate spelling habits.

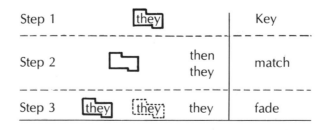

FIGURE 10.11   Matching Configurations

344

- Look at the whole word.
- Say the word.
- Close your eyes and say the word.
- Say the letters as you look at the word.
- Close your eyes and say the letters.
- Check.
- Write the word.
- Check.
- Repeat steps if an error is made.

FIGURE 10.12   *Prescribed Spelling Study Method*

Kinesthetic Approach

The movement of the muscles while forming the letter shapes provides important input for certain children when spelling a word. All of us remember teachers asking us to write the word in the air using an imaginary pen and encouraging exaggerated gross motor movements. These movements do offer additional sensory knowledge and may be important in the child's establishment of a memory pattern.

Such children relate to how the letter pattern feels and should be given activities which enhance motor association with words.

1.   Have the children practice writing words on the blackboard with a paint brush and water. Encourage large movements of the arm. The children should spell the word as they "write" it. Since the visual image disappears relatively fast, the major sensory awareness in this exercise is the kinesthetic input.
2.   Ask the children to "write" a word with the pointer finger on their writing hand across their other arm. Again, reinforce children for exaggerating letter strokes.
3.   Allow the children to practice writing words with finger paint or in sand (or salt) boxes. These techniques that provide larger surface areas on which children can practice movements will strengthen the kinesthetic feel of the letter.

A Functional Spelling Approach

Familiarity with a word influences a child's motivation, and therefore ultimately the ability to spell. Young children's speech centers around a limited number of high-frequency words which have relevance to them and

345

their environment. Learning to spell these commonly used words is a meaning-ful activity which enhances the child's written communication.

A functional approach to spelling is based on the premise that a child will learn to spell words that have a great deal of utility. In essence, the child realizes the importance of certain words for communication purposes and will want to learn to spell them. Spelling becomes an important tool for the child's written expression.

The foundation of a functional spelling approach can be based on either a predetermined list of frequently used words (Figure 10.13 presents an example of a frequency list), or a word list constructed from the child's own language experience. There will most likely be a great deal of overlap between these two methods, and, in fact, one may be used to supplement the other.

1. the	26. school	51. would	76. now
2. I	27. me	52. our	77. has
3. and	28. with	53. were	78. down
4. to	29. am	54. little	79. if
5. a	30. all	55. how	80. write
6. you	31. one	56. he	81. after
7. we	32. so	57. do	82. play
8. in	33. your	58. about	83. came
9. it	34. got	59. from	84. put
10. of	35. there	60. her	85. two
11. is	36. went	61. them	86. house
12. was	37. not	62. as	87. us
13. have	38. at	63. his	88. because
14. my	39. like	64. mother	89. over
15. are	40. out	65. see	90. saw
16. he	41. go	66. friend	91. their
17. for	42. but	67. come	92. well
18. on	43. this	68. can	93. here
19. they	44. dear	69. day	94. by
20. that	45. some	70. good	95. just
21. had	46. then	71. what	96. make
22. she	47. going	72. said	97. back
23. very	48. up	73. him	98. an
24. will	49. time	74. home	99. could
25. when	50. get	75. did	100. or

Source: Folger, S. The case for a basic written vocabulary. *The Elementary School Journal, 47,* 1, 1946. As found in DeHaven, E., *Teaching and learning in the language arts.* Boston: Little Brown and Company, 1979, p. 287.

FIGURE 10.13   *The 100 Words Most Frequently Used in the Written Work of Children in the United States*

In the language experience method, the child writes a "story," which may be only a phrase or a sentence, leaving a space or an attempted word spelling for any unknown word. The teacher then supplies the missing word and the child adds it to a personal spelling list. This strategy produces those words which the child perceives as most important.

A functional spelling approach establishes the curricula structure of the spelling program, but it does not specify the learning method. Words may be studied by a visual approach, linguistic analysis or a combination of these or any other method. The functionality of the program relates solely to word frequency and the implicitly meaningful spelling task. Since this technique relies on the child's own motivation to learn to spell a particular word, it is a positive approach for the mildly handicapped.

A Weekly Spelling Plan

Spelling instruction is often centered around a weekly plan which guides the child from acquisition to mastery of new words. Grouping children according to common spelling levels will simplify management of the weekly scheme and allow for activities involving peer interaction. With slight modifications the plan can provide for individual needs. Individualization will be based on the number and type of words selected for weekly study and the focus of the instructional activities. A weekly spelling plan can incorporate the elements of more than one approach and can offer the child the advantage of several study techniques.

A suggested weekly scheme would begin with a pretest and word analysis on Monday. Tuesday would be devoted to word study, while Wednesday and Thursday involve practice exercises. The weekly cycle is completed on Friday with a final test and word review.

An eclectic five-day spelling plan with specified daily activities could include the following:

Day 1: After a pretest is given the unknown words are added to the child's individual *words to learn* list. These words, along with those not mastered the week before, comprise the week's spelling words.

Working in small groups, new words are analyzed. The children are encouraged to find similarities with previously learned words, and when possible to apply a generalization. Word meanings are also emphasized. An appropriate activity would be to write each spelling word on an index card, with the word used correctly in a sentence on the reversed side.

Day 2: Working independently, the child follows the prescribed study method or the instructional program designed for him to learn to spell each word. This may mean using a whole word approach, a visual or a kinesthetic approach, or any combination that works well for the specific child. The goal is to increase the child's ability to produce the word at will.

Day 3: A variety of spelling games which incorporate word study and spelling practice can be used. Some suggested games are:
- Word puzzles can be made from a sheet of cardboard on which a single word has been written and cut into pieces. The child must complete the puzzle to spell the word.
- Hidden words can be buried in letter matrices. The child must find each spelling word spelt vertically, horizontally or diagonally in the matrix.
- The cloze technique is a useful practice exercise. The child must select the correct word spelling to complete the sentence.
- *Name That Word* is a game in which a child listens to a word being spelled on a tape. The child must write the word and pronounce the word before checking his answer.

Day 4: Working as partners children can provide classmates with practice, feedback, and immediate reinforcement.
- *Go Spell* is a card game played in the same way as *Go Fish* but the cards are marked with letters not numbers. The goal is to acquire the cards to spell as many of the week's words as you can.
- *Concentration* can be played similarly to the T.V. game but using cards with spelling words on them. Each player must turn over two cards at a time until they have a spelling match.
- Partners should give practice tests to prepare for the mastery exam at the end of the week. Partners check each other's spelling products and then help each other review any word spelled incorrectly.

Day 5: On the final day a mastery test is given to establish the child's spelling achievement. After checking the results, words are classified for further study. The words learned correctly are placed into a mastery bank (e.g., a *Pringles* can) and can be used for review activities. Any word incorrectly spelled should be placed on the words to be learned list and included in next week's pretest.

The amount of repetition necessary for many mildly handicapped children to learn mandates that review be built into the spelling program. A good practice is to develop a *review cycle* approximately every 4–6 weeks. The review cycle follows the five day plan but the pretest words are ones learned in the previous weeks.

Spelling Demons

Many words do not conform to linguistic patterns and as a result are troublesome to learn. Commonly referred to as "spelling demons," these words can present a particular problem for the mildly handicapped child. The most frequently misspelled words in the elementary grades are listed in Figure 10.14. The teacher should select the demon words which are appropriate to the child's spelling level and begin a program of intensive word study.

about	come	has	Mar.	said	think
address	coming	have	maybe	Santa Claus	thought
afternoon	couldn't	haven't	me	Saturday	through
again	cousin	having	Miss	saw	time
all right	daddy	he	morning	school	to
along	day	hear	mother	schoolhouse	today
already	Dec.	hello	Mr.	send	together
always	didn't	her	Mrs.	sent	tomorrow
am	dog	here	much	sincerely	tonight
an	don't	him	my	snow	too
and	down	his	name	snowman	toys
answer	Easter	home	nice	some	train
anything	every	hope	Nov.	something	truly
anyway	everybody	hospital	now	sometime	two
April	father	house	nowadays	sometimes	until
are	Feb.	how	o'clock	soon	vacation
arithmetic	fine	how's	Oct.	stationery	very
aunt	first	I	off	store	want
awhile	football	I'll	on	studying	was
baby	for	I'm	once	summer	we
balloon	fourth	in	one	Sunday	weather
basketball	Friday	isn't	our	suppose	well
because	friend	it	out	sure	went
been	friends	it's	outside	surely	were
before	from	I've	party	swimming	we're
birthday	fun	Jan.	people	teacher	when
bought	getting	just	play	teacher's	white
boy	goes	know	played	Thanksgiving	will
boys	going	lessons	plays	that's	with
brother	good	letter	please	the	won't
brought	good-by	like	pretty	their	would
can	got	likes	quit	them	write
cannot	grade	little	quite	then	writing
can't	guess	lots	receive	there	you
children	had	loving	received	there's	your
Christmas	Halloween	made	remember	they	you're
close	handkerchiefs	make	right	they're	yours

Source: Fitzgerald, James A. A Basic Life Spelling Vocabulary. Milwaukee: The Bruce Publishing Company, 1951 (pp. 144–50). Reprinted by permission of the Glencoe Press.

FIGURE 10.14   222 Spelling Demons for Second, Third, Fourth, Fifth, and Sixth Grades

Concentrated instruction and repetitive practice, such as advocated in the study method, will increase the visual image and help the child learn the spelling "demon." The use of mnemonic devices is another strategy that can assist some children in trying to remember the spelling of difficult words. The demands of learning mnemonics should not be placed on children who have trouble remembering them. However, even for these children they can be used as a means of motivating interest in learning word structures. Some examples of mnemonic devices are:

1. The princi*pal* is your *pal.*
2. A princi*ple* is a ru*le.*
3. Station*ary* means standing still.
4. A secret*ary* is station*ary* at her desk.
5. *All* (of us are) *ready.*
6. Station*ery* is used with a pen or pencil.
7. A spelling word is either *all wrong* or *all right.*
8. Only *full* has two *ll*'s, helpfu*l* and thankfu*l* have only one.
9. On Sat*ur*day we can have f*un.*

Remediating Spelling Problems

The importance of diagnostic information is its direct application to the spelling program. Hillerich (1977) advocates placing a child in a spelling level in which he knows 50–75 percent of the words. This establishes an instructional level from which the child can benefit without a great deal of frustration. Mastery of less than 50 percent of the words on a level indicates that the child does not know the words on the preceding list.

Often spelling errors follow a pattern that is repeated throughout the child's written work. As consistent spelling errors are diagnosed, the corrective procedure can be matched appropriately. The cause and correction chart in Figure 10.15 illustrates this direct relationship between the error and the remediation strategy. The child needs systematic instruction along with numerous opportunities to practice the corrective strategy.

Remedial Spelling Techniques

Spelling programs for the majority of learners are based on traditional group-centered strategies, such as those found in the basal spelling series. For many mildly handicapped children these programs may not provide the necessary individualization and modification to overcome their learning problems. The alternative is to use a remedial technique for spelling instruc-

Spelling Errors	Probable Cause	Remedial Procedure
"bad" for "bat" "cown" for "clown"	poor auditory discrimination	Give practice in hearing likenesses and differences in words that are similar. Have the student look at a word as it is pronounced to hear all the sounds and see the letters that represent them. Play rhyming games.
"enuff" for "enough" "clim" for "climb" "krak" for "crack"	poor visual imagery	Expose words that are not entirely phonetic for short periods of time and have the child reproduce them in writing from memory. Have child trace words with his finger and write them from memory.
"comeing" for "coming" "happyly" for "happily" "flys" for "flies" "payed" for "paid"	pupil has not learned rules for formation of derivatives	Stress visual imagery. Teach generalizations of forming tenses and adding suffixes.
"form" for "from" "abel" for "able" "aminal" for "animal" "mazagine" for "magazine"	poor attention to letter sequence in certain words	Have pupil pronounce words carefully. Stress sequence of sounds and letters.
"there" for "their" "peception" for "perception" "sasifactry" for "satisfactory"	carelessness	Discuss the importance of good spelling for social and vocational purposes. Encourage careful proof-reading of all writing.
"hires" for "horses" "bothry" for "brother" "meciline" for "medicine"	lack of phonics ability	Use a multisensory approach whereby the student sees the word, hears the word, says the word, spells the word orally, and copies the word.

Source: Otto, W., McMenemy, R., and Smith, R. Corrective and remedial teaching (2nd ed.). Boston: Houghton Mifflin Company, 1973.

FIGURE 10.15 Spelling Error—Cause and Correction Chart

tion. Kinesthetic activities are usually incorporated into the instructional activity to increase sensory input. The following are specific techniques which are commonly used for remediation purposes. Note the similarity between these strategies and those suggested in chapter 12 for the remediation of reading problems. Remember, however, the difference in desired outcomes between reading and spelling; reading is recognition of graphic symbols, while spelling is the production of letter patterns.

1. The Fernald (1943) approach is multisensory and follows several steps. The child is introduced to the word as the teacher writes and says it. Then the child repeatedly traces the word while saying it (tactile-kinesthetic-visual-vocal-auditory). The student continues to say the word as he writes it several times. Finally, the student writes the word from memory. If correct, the instruction precedes with a new word. If incorrect, the child is told to repeat each step beginning with tracing and saying the word.

2. Gillingham and Stillman (1970) suggest an alphabetic system in which sounds are built into words. The child learns sound-symbol associations first, followed by visual letter patterns and finally word patterns. As in the Fernald method, emphasis is placed on a visual-auditory-kinesthetic-tactile (VAKT) approach.

3. A visual sensory approach, which incorporates prompts (color cueing) for sight words and phonetic elements that must be memorized can be developed. Words which are highlighted are taught by tracing, saying them in a sentence, visualizing and writing.

4. The Phonovisual Method (Schoolfield & Timberlake, 1960) advocates a phonetic approach to training visual and auditory discrimination skills. Consonants and vowels are introduced by association with word pictures which key the visual image of the letter sound.

5. The Morphographic Spelling Program (Dixon, 1976) is designed for students in grades 4–12 who constantly misspell words even though they have mastered the basic sound-symbol relationships. It is a direct instructional approach consisting of 140 lessons, lasting 20 minutes apiece. The program is based on the belief that almost all English words can be analyzed and sets of rules developed which will lead to acceptable spelling. As with other direct instruction programs (e.g., Distar), Morphographic Spelling is a very structured program and includes two teacher presentation books, two student workbooks, placement test, progress charts, and student contracts. The three basic principles carried throughout the program are: introduction of morphographs (rules), application, and practice.

Before selecting a specific strategy the teacher should consult information gained from the modality preference test and other diagnostic measures. This prevents random selection of a remediation technique and will increase the likelihood of providing a successful match between learner capacity and program structure.

Teaching Dictionary Skills

No one can possibly remember the correct spelling (and meaning) of every word. The mildly handicapped child needs to realize this fact and to understand that dictionaries are a valuable resource in the task of correctly spelling unfamiliar words. The dictionary is a basic spelling tool and should be introduced to any child reading at or above a third-grade level.

Using a dictionary involves several skills which must be carefully taught to the mildly handicapped child at appropriate points in the language arts program. A hierarchy of these skills and suggested times to introduce them in the instructional sequence are provided in Figure 10.16. Alphabetizing is included in this list, although it is often considered a prerequisite to actual dictionary use.

Skill	Introduction in Instructional Sequence
1. Alphabetizing—sequencing of alphabet letters	1. Alphabetizing should be taught after completion of all letter name-symbol associations have been mastered.
2. Using guide words—recognizing words grouped by alphabetical similarities	2. Guide words are most effectively taught after alphabetizing has been mastered and when the child has a sufficient sight-vocabulary to learn word groupings.
3. Locating "mystery" words—being able to find words of uncertain spelling in a dictionary	3. This skill requires a foundation in grapheme-phoneme associations and can be introduced after all basic sounds have been learned.
4. Locating appropriate word meanings—being aware of and selecting multiple word meanings and appropriate word usage	4. The skill of selecting the appropriate meaning should be taught along with higher order comprehension skills.
5. Pronunciation marks—being able to interpret diacritical markings	5. The essential pronunciation marks can be taught after basic phonetic generalizations have been learned.

FIGURE 10.16   Dictionary Skill Sequence

353

P p

plan

This is a **plan** for a boat. It is a drawing that shows how the boat is to be built.

We **plan** to go.
We **expect** to go.

We will **plan** our trip before we go.
We will **think out** our trip before we go.

plane

An **airplane** is sometimes called a **plane**. The **planes** fly over our house on their way to the airport.

plant

A rose bush is a **plant**. Bushes, trees, grass, vegetables, flowers, and weeds are all called **plants**.

See John **plant** the seeds.
See John **put** the seeds **in the ground**.

Factories are sometimes called **plants**.

plastic

A **plastic** can be made into any shape, or into sheets or film. Many things that used to be made of wood, metal, or cloth are now often made of **plastic**.

Source: Wright, W. W. *The rainbow dictionary.* New York: The World Publishing Company, 1959.

FIGURE 10.17

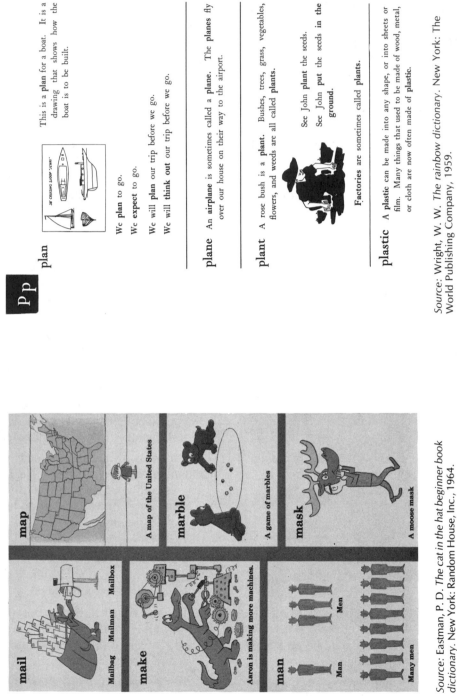

Source: Eastman, P. D. *The cat in the hat beginner book dictionary.* New York: Random House, Inc., 1964.

flicker—about 12 inches (30 centimeters) long

flourish (definition 4)

PETAL
SEPAL
STAMEN
PISTIL

flower (definition 1)
parts of a flower

float (definition 8)—The king of the parade rode by on a float.

224 flicker | flippant

flicked the dust from his shoes with a handkerchief.
3 make a sudden blow with: *The children flicked
wet towels at each other.* **1** noun, **2,3** verb.

flick er¹ (flik′ər), **1** shine or burn with a wavering,
unsteady light: *The firelight flickered on the walls.*
2 a wavering, unsteady light or flame: *the flicker of
an oil lamp.* **3** move lightly and quickly in and out,
or back and forth: *We heard the birds flicker among
the leaves.* **4** a quick, light movement: *the flicker of
an eyelash.* **1,3** verb, **2,4** noun.

flick er² (flik′ər), a large, common woodpecker of
North America, with yellow markings on the wings
and tail. See picture. *noun.*

flied (flīd). See fly² (definition 10). *The batter flied
to center field. verb.*

fli er (flī′ər), **1** person or thing that flies, such as a
bird or insect: *That eagle is a high flier.* **2** pilot of
an airplane; aviator. *noun.* Also spelled **flyer.**

flies¹ (flīz), more than one fly: *There are many flies
on the window. noun, plural.*

flies² (flīz). See fly². *A bird flies. He flies an
airplane. verb.*

flight¹ (flīt), **1** act or manner of flying: *the flight of
a bird through the air.* **2** distance a bird, bullet, or
airplane can fly. **3** group of things flying through
the air together: *a flight of pigeons.* **4** trip in an
aircraft. **5** airplane that makes a scheduled trip:
She took the three o'clock flight to Boston. **6** soaring
above or beyond the ordinary: *a flight of the
imagination.* **7** set of stairs from one landing or
one story of a building to the next. *noun.*

flight² (flīt), running away; escape: *The flight of the
prisoners was discovered. noun.*

flim sy (flim′zē), light and thin; slight; frail;
without strength; easily broken: *I accidentally tore
the flimsy paper. Their excuse was so flimsy that no
one believed it. adjective,* **flim si er, flim si est.**

flinch (flinch), **1** draw back from difficulty, danger,
or pain; shrink: *She flinched when she touched the
hot radiator.* **2** act of drawing back. **1** verb, **2** noun.

fling (fling), **1** throw; throw with force: *fling a
stone.* **2** a throw; **3** rush; dash: *In a rage the child
flung out of the room.* **4** move violently; plunge;
kick: *The excited horse flung about in its stall.* **5** time
of doing as one pleases: *He had his fling when he
was young.* **6** a lively Scottish dance. **1,3,4** verb,
flung, fling ing; 2,5,6 noun.

flint (flint), a very hard stone, which makes a
spark when struck against steel. *noun.*

flint lock (flint′lok′), **1** gunlock in which a piece
of flint striking against steel makes sparks that
explode the gunpowder. **2** old-fashioned gun with
such a gunlock. *noun.*

flip (flip), **1** toss or move by the snap of a finger
and thumb: *He flipped a coin on the counter.*
2 move with a jerk or toss: *flip the pages of a book.
The branch flipped back and scratched her face.*
3 snap; tap; sudden jerk: *The cat gave the kitten a
flip on the ear. The winner was picked by the flip of a
coin.* **1,2** verb, **flipped, flip ping; 3** noun.

flip pant (flip′ənt), too free in speech or action;
not properly serious or respectful: *His flippant
answer to my serious question annoyed me. adjective.*

Source: Thorndike, E. L., and Barnhart, C. L. *Scott, Foresman
beginning dictionary.* Dallas, Texas: Scott, Foresman
Publishing Company, 1976.

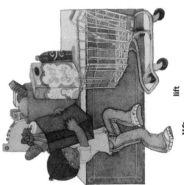

lift

lift

When you **lift** something it means that you
pick it up. It was hard for Mike to **lift** the
heavy bag. ○*See the picture.*

light

Light is something that comes from the sun in
the daytime. We can see things when we have
light. Lamps and candles are **lights.** The lamp
needs a new **light** bulb. Dad is going to **light**
a fire so we can cook the hot dogs.

lightning

Lightning is a quick line of light that you see
in the sky. There is **lightning** and thunder
when there is a storm.

like

like

1. Alice looks **like** her brother. An airplane in
the sky sometimes looks **like** a bird.
2. If you **like** something it means that it
makes you happy. Jack **likes** to eat ice cream.
○*See the picture.* June **liked** all the other
children in her class.

Source: The magic world of words: A very first dictionary. New
York: Macmillan Publishing Co., 1977.

355

In the early introduction of these skills the mildly handicapped child may be overwhelmed and confused by the format and composition of the dictionary. To alleviate this problem the teacher may wish to construct or use a commercially simplified "dictionary" consisting of a select number of the most frequently used words. An even more elementary step is to begin skill development with a picture-word dictionary in which the child can receive immediate feedback from the pictures. Samples of these instructional dictionary variations are located in Figure 10.17. Selection of the proper variation should be based on the child's level of skill development and chronological age. The pre-adolescent or older mildly handicapped student may consider the use of a picture dictionary as inappropriate. In such a case, instruction may begin on a few reproduced dictionary pages.

The dictionary can also be established as a self-checking procedure within the classroom. The dictionary may provide writing independence for the mildly handicapped child who is hesitant about the spelling and writing task. The child receives immediate performance feedback without relying on the teacher's presence. Although most spelling and language programs introduce dictionary skills, they often focus upon using the dictionary for pronunciation and meaning. This is quite different from using the dictionary for spelling and therefore, it may be up to the teacher to stress the importance of this dictionary function.

Every teacher has heard the refrain, "How can I look up a word if I don't know how to spell it?" It is possible to plan instructional activities which will solve this dilemma. To begin with, as soon as *some* phonics have been learned a teacher can present oral activities in which the children are asked, "What letter do you think *refrigerator* begins with?" This activity is followed with ones which incorporate alphabetizing and guide words in which the children must locate appropriate sections of the dictionary for a given word. The final activity stage is for children to learn to identify vowel sounds. Each of these tasks will help the children compile clues for locating the mystery word and guide them toward spelling independence.

SUMMARY

There is generally only one way to spell a word and the good speller is one who successfully arranges letter patterns in the appropriate manner. The most frequently spelled words in English are considered fairly consistent in their linguistic properties. However, for the mildly handicapped child the use of generalizations, which must be understood, learned and applied, may be problematic.

Efficiency in spelling relies heavily upon the rote reproduction of familiar words and the ability to produce unfamiliar words, either by generalizing linguistic principles or self-checking procedures. Spelling instruction is aimed at increasing the child's production of both familiar and unfamiliar words. The teacher must understand the components of the spelling process as denoted in the spelling skills chart (Figure 10.4) and be able to assess the child's facility in each skill.

Spelling skills may be both formally and informally assessed. Several sources of spelling assessment and specific strategies were offered in this chapter. It has been found that involving the child in immediate correction of pretests increases spelling efficiency. It is important that spelling be planned according to the child's ability and present communication needs.

Mildly handicapped children differ in the ways they best learn to spell. Approaches such as linguistic, visual and multisensory, should be examined for their appropriateness with each child. Direct instruction incorporated into a weekly plan of learning activities will provide the child with successful spelling habits. Several ideas for daily activities have been suggested which the teacher can expand upon according to the child's needs.

Remedial strategies for teaching spelling are similar to remedial reading techniques and include the Fernald method, the Gillingham-Stillman approach, and the Phonovisual system. Each of these strategies incorporates elements of kinesthetic and multisensory training.

There are many reasons why some children are poor spellers. These difficulties which are closely related to other areas of the language arts were summarized. It was proposed that an integrated language approach would be beneficial to the child's spelling ability as well as to other communication skills.

Finally, it was suggested that mildly handicapped children need systematic instruction in dictionary skills. Learning to use the dictionary will allow the child to locate unfamiliar word spellings and will increase independence in written expression.

POINTS FOR DISCUSSION

1. Using a basal spelling series, such as the *Merrill Linguistic Spellers,* develop an informal spelling inventory. Use the ISI to assess a child's spelling ability.

2. Using a study method, such as the one specified in this chapter, has proven useful in teaching spelling words. Discuss the rationale behind this type of study procedure and why it is effective for most mildly handicapped children.

3. Select twenty complex and generally unknown words from the unabridged dictionary. Working with a small group of your peers, use Westerman's Sensory Modality Preference Procedure to determine the instructional modality for each group member. Next, try the procedure with a mildly handicapped child.

4. The use of dictionaries is often limited when working with mildly handicapped children. A possible reason is the lack of structured programs and material to teach dictionary skills. The mildly handicapped child is uncertain as to how to use the dictionary for independent learning. Develop a series of activities to teach dictionary usage and alleviate this problem.

5. Collect samples of written expression created by a mildly handicapped child. Use the spelling error checklist to assess the child's spelling errors.

6. Review at least two different basal spelling programs. How are these materials alike, how are they different? What is the basic instructional approach and the primary method of study?

7. Carefully review the dictated spelling tests for Alex and Betty. What error pattern is evident for each child and what type of intervention program would you suggest?

    A.

Word List	Alex's Spelling	Problem
1. chair	1. shair	
2. slam	2. slam	
3. puppy	3. pupy	
4. smiling	4. smilin	
5. pencil	5. pensil	
6. ban	6. van	

    B.

Word List	Betty's Spelling	Problem
1. hat	1. het	
2. come	2. cum	
3. pin	3. pen	
4. hut	4. hat	
5. dot	5. dot	
6. man	6. men	

8. Review the list of spelling demons provided in this chapter and try to create some mnemonic devices which would aid in learning their spellings.

REFERENCES

Becker, W. C., Engelmann, S., and Thomas, D. R. *Teaching 2: Cognitive learning and instruction.* Chicago: SRA, 1975.

Beers, J. W., Beers, C. S., and Grant, K. The logic behind children's spelling. *The Elementary School Journal,* 1977, *77,* 238-242.

Beers, J. W., and Henderson, E. H. A study of developing orthographic concepts among first grade children. *Research in the Teaching of English,* 1977, *11,* 133-148.

Beery, K., Westerman, G. S., and Wilkinson, A. Sensory modality preference testing. In G. S. Westerman, *Spelling and writing*. Sioux Falls, South Dakota: Adapt Press, Inc., 1971.

Dixon, R. *Morphographic spelling*. Eugene, Oregon: E-B Press, 1976.

Eastman, P. D. *The cat in the hat beginner book dictionary*. New York: Random House, Inc., 1964.

Fernald, G. M. *Remedial techniques in basic school subjects*. New York: McGraw-Hill, 1943.

Fitzgerald, J. A. *A basic life spelling vocabulary*. Milwaukee: The Bruce Publishing Company, 1951.

Folger, S. The case for a basic written vocabulary. *The Elementary School Journal*, 1946, *47*, 1. Located in: DeHaven, E. *Teaching and learning in the language arts*. Boston: Little, Brown and Company, 1979, p. 287.

Fonerden, (Dr.) Mental embarrassments in orthography, as experienced by the relator, from his childhood to the twenty-fifth year of his age. *American Journal of Insanity*, 1850, *7*, 61–63.

Fries, C. C. *Linguistics and reading*. New York: Holt, Rinehart & Winston, 1963.

Gentry, J. R. Early spelling strategies. *The Elementary School Journal*, 1978, *79*, 2, 88–92.

Gillingham, A., and Stillman, B. *Remedial training for children with specific disability in reading, spelling, and penmanship*. Cambridge, Mass.: Educators Publishing Service, 1970.

Hanna, P., Hodges, R., and Hanna, J. *Spelling: Structure and strategies*. Boston: Houghton Mifflin Company, 1971.

Hillerich, R. L. Let's teach spelling—Not phonetic misspelling. *Language Arts*, 1977, *54*, 301–307.

Hodges, R. E., and Rudorf, H. E. Searching linguistics for cues for the teaching of spelling. *Research on handwriting and spelling*. Champaign, Ill.: National Council of Teachers of English, 1966.

Horn, E. *The curriculum for the gifted: Some principles and an illustration*. Twenty-third Yearbook, National Society for the Study of Education, Part I. Bloomington, Ill.: Public School Publishing Company, 1924.

Kauffman, J. M., Hallahan, D. P., Hass, K., Brame, T., and Boren, R. Imitating children's errors to improve their spelling performance. *Journal of Learning Disabilities*, 1978, *11*, 33–38.

Larsen, S. C., and Hammill, D. D. *Test of written spelling*. Austin, Texas: Academic Therapy, 1976.

Mann, P. H., and Suiter, P. *Handbook in diagnostic teaching: A learning disabilities approach* (abridged edition). Boston: Allyn & Bacon, Inc., 1974.

Moore, J. T., Jr. *Phonetic elements appearing in a three thousand word spelling vocabulary*. Unpublished doctoral dissertation, Stanford University, 1951.

Otto, W., McMenemy, R. A., and Smith, R. J. *Corrective and remedial teaching* (2nd ed.). Boston: Houghton Mifflin, 1973.

Partoll, S. F. Spelling demonology revisited. *Academic Therapy*, 1976, XI, 339–348.

Schoolfield, L., and Timberlake, J. *The phonovisual method*. Washington, D. C.: Phonovisual Products, 1960.

Smith, R. M. *Teacher diagnosis of educational difficulties*. Columbus, Ohio: Charles E. Merrill Publishing Co., 1969.

Smith, R. M. *Clinical teaching: Methods of instruction for the retarded.* New York: McGraw-Hill Book Company, 1974.

Stephens, T. M. *Teaching skills to children with learning and behavior disorders.* Columbus, Ohio: Charles E. Merrill Publishing Co., 1977.

Tarver, S. G., and Dawson, M. M. Modality preference and the teaching of reading: A review. *Journal of Learning Disabilities,* 1978, *11,* 17–29.

The magic world of words: A very first dictionary. New York: Macmillan Publishing Company, 1977.

Thorndike, E. L., and Barnhart, C. L. *Scott, Foresman beginning dictionary.* Dallas, Texas: Scott, Foresman Publishing Company, 1976.

Wallace, G., and Larsen, S. *Educational assessment of learning problems: Testing for teaching.* Boston: Allyn & Bacon, Inc., 1978.

Westerman, G. S. *Spelling and writing.* Sioux Falls, S.D.: Adapt Press, Inc., 1971.

Wright, W. W. *The rainbow dictionary.* New York: The World Publishing Company, 1959.

Zutell, J. Some psycholinguistic perspectives on children's spelling. *Language Arts,* 1978, *55,* 844–850.

11

Reading

When the mildly handicapped child is referred for academic support services, reading is the subject most frequently pinpointed as causing the learning problems. In almost every case a child's difficulty in reading has a cumulative effect and manifests problems throughout the language arts and other content areas. Poor reading is a stumbling block to further learning. Children who are deficient in this skill should be given the attention necessary to remove the educational barriers that are created when one is unable to work independently, use printed materials, or pursue personal reading interests.

In reading, as in all other areas, the mildly handicapped experience a broad range of disabilities. The continuum includes children who are experiencing reading problems due to improper instruction as well as those whose reading difficulties are a sign of more basic learning deficits. The teacher needs to understand reading theory, the sequence of reading skills, reading assessment, and the relevant features of the various reading approaches and remedial techniques in order to structure a reading program that can facilitate learning for the mildly handicapped child.

The reading problems presented by the mildly handicapped child are dealt with differentially throughout the school years. In fact, careful examination of the reading approach and program objectives established at each grade level would reveal an interaction between grade (age) level and program format. In the early elementary grades emphasis is placed on the development of reading skills aimed at making the child an independent reader. This focus strives toward mastery of both word analysis and comprehension.

As the mildly handicapped child experiences difficulties and proceeds into the intermediate grades, a greater amount of time is devoted to isolated skill development. By concentrating on deficient skills, it is hoped that the child will be able to acquire the fundamental competencies and develop reading independence. Emphasis on isolated skill acquisition often is associated with repetitive drills and reading practice. During this time, a parallel reduction in the child's motivation to read increases the learning problems. Whether this is due to the pre-adolescent's inability to recognize the relevance of the reading act, to the disinterest produced by practice drills, or to a combination of the two is uncertain. However, the interaction of these two factors has a profound influence on the resulting reading program.

At the secondary grade levels the importance of individual skill development is lessened somewhat and the reading program centers on the achievement of functional literacy. The high schooler becomes eager to achieve a certain proficiency in reading in order to successfully complete driver's training and to apply for and maintain employment. The anticipation of approaching adulthood and the urge toward self-sufficiency provide strong motivation for learning to read.

The intent of this chapter is not to advocate a specific reading method, nor is it to simply present critiques of some of the more prominent reading approaches. The field of reading is too comprehensive and each approach has been so intensely developed that they cannot be fully reviewed within this chapter. Therefore, we propose to examine elements of the reading program, highlighting positive directions for instruction of reading for mildly handicapped children.

Reading Program Objectives

Reading is a fundamental learning tool that is practically indispensible both in school and out. Day-to-day living would be increasingly difficult without the ability to read street signs, recipes, store ads, directions, entertainment guides, newspapers, and letters. The individual who learns to read is more likely to function as an independent, self-sustaining adult.

The objectives in a reading program for the mildly handicapped child are similar to those established for the normal child. The difference is one of priority, resulting from a practical need to emphasize the more basic skills for the mildly handicapped child with reading difficulties. Specifically, the objectives of the reading program are:

1. To develop a basic sight vocabulary directly related to the child's existing language skills.
2. To develop reading comprehension skills that allow the child to read for both information and pleasure.

3. To develop reading independence through word analysis skills.
4. To develop an interest in reading for information and entertainment (Cohen & Plaskon, 1978).

If in consideration of mildly handicapped children's learning disabilities, we lower our expectation for their achievement, we are doing them a true disservice and are in effect negating our teaching effort by undermining the importance of reading as a basic learning task. Reading requires a proficiency level of approximately 90 percent or better for the reader to attain meaning and to be comfortable in the task.

Literacy

The word literacy is often used to describe and classify individuals on reading ability with little understanding of the nature of the term or its application. Most efforts to define literacy have suffered in credibility due to their failure to detail observable skills, criterion levels, test materials, and situational differences. As a result, literacy has often been loosely used to refer to the ability to respond appropriately to daily reading tasks. Although this type of definition is acceptable for development of a reading goal, its usefulness is limited in explaining the reading process or prescribing reading methodology.

To be more specific, let us examine several levels of literacy and their appropriate application in daily life. Many people who consider themselves literate are only able to transpose print into spoken language at a very simple level and often with a great deal of difficulty. This minimal level of literacy is achieved at about the third- or fourth-grade level and is associated with practical competency in reading and comprehension. Recently the term *functional literacy* has been used to describe this level of attainment. Lichtman (1974) has listed daily life printed materials which the functional literate must learn to deal with (see Figure 11.1). Such materials contain limited, nontechnical vocabulary, and they are written in short, simple sentence constructions.

Special educators have begun to focus attention on a variation of functional literacy referred to as functional reading. As defined by Brown and Perlmutter (1971), functional reading is "discrete and observable motor responses to printed stimuli" (p. 75). This implies that the student learns to read the word and to indicate comprehension in an observable manner. Snell (1978) stresses the practical aspect of functional reading as a survival skill in our "word-dependent world" (p. 326), but indicates that there is no clearly determined range of difficulty which applies to this category.

A higher level of literacy is necessary for a person to read and understand articles in magazines, digests and general newspapers. The difficulty of the language structure and vocabulary complexity for these materials can be

1	2	3	4	5
Signs and Labels	Schedules and Tables	Maps	Categorized Listings and Indices	High-Interest, Factual Narrative
Road Signs	T.V. Guide	City/Street	Yellow Pages	Sports Events
Clothing Tags	Bus Schedule	Road	Book Indices	News Report
Medicine Labels	Train/Plane Schedule	Global Weather	Want Ad	Narcotics Article
Billboards	Work/ School Schedule		Dictionary	

6	7	8	9
Illustrated Advertisements	Technical Documents	Sets of Directions	Fill-in Blank Form
Department Store	Conditional Sales Contract	Recipe (Pizza)	Banking Forms
Yellow Pages	Insurance Policies	Use of Tools/ Machinery/ Equipment	Job Application
Food Store	Guarantees	Sewing with Pattern	Car Registration
Magazine	Apartment Lease		Credit Application
			Hospital Entry Form

Source: M. Lichtman. The development and validation of R/EAL, an instrument to assess functional literacy. *Journal of Reading Behavior*, 1974, 6, 172.

FIGURE 11.1   Daily Life Printed Materials

understood by the average child at the eighth-grade level or above. More complex social, political, and technical material such as those found in editorials, technical journals, and news magazines require a twelfth-grade or college-level mastery (Chall, 1975).

The relevance of these concepts (i.e., literacy through functional reading) for the mildly handicapped is the application of the individual's reading skills for functional and recreational purposes. The teacher and the student should be careful to keep sight of this utilitarian goal while concentrating on specific skill remediation. One way to maintain the proper perspective is to be aware of the child's environment, demands of peers, and future career orientation. Establishment of practical objectives ensures that the mildly handicapped child achieve at least functional literacy. This, however, is a minimal goal toward the child's attainment of adult self-sufficiency, and the teacher should work to bring the child as far beyond this level as possible.

The Reading Process

Understanding reading problems and remediation requires an awareness of the reading process. Many volumes written by reading authorities have been devoted to the formation of a reading definition and an appropriate reading theory. Although opinions differ, there has recently been a commonality in belief that "reading, thought and language are closely related" (Gillespie & Johnson, 1974, p. 33).

A definition of reading offered by Harris and Smith (1972) states: "Reading is the reader's interaction with a printed message across a range of thinking operations as guided by a purpose for reading" (p. 14). The reader's *interaction with a printed message* implies that the reader's background experiences play an important part in the interpretation of the material. The child's intellectual and perceptual skills also play a role in the process. This is illustrated in the definition by the phrase, *across a range of thinking operations*. The conclusion of the definition, *guided by a purpose for reading,* implies either a utilitarian or recreational goal.

Implicit in the Harris and Smith definition are the processes of *decoding* and *comprehension*. The ability to recognize a word through structural and word analysis is commonly referred to as decoding. The association of meaning to the perceived word is comprehension.

There are many explanations of the reading process. Common among them is the belief that reading is a complex behavior that involves the mastery of many different skills. Reading is often viewed in terms of stage development with each stage providing the foundations for the next one (Karlin, 1971; Kaluger & Kolson, 1978). Harris's (1970) stages of reading development are examples of this type of approach toward understanding the reading process:

Stage 1.   Reading readiness
Stage 2.   Initial reading acquisition
Stage 3.   Reading achievement
Stage 4.   Expansion of reading
Stage 5.   Refinement of reading

Another dominant point of view is represented by Dechant (1964) who sees reading as a perceptual process characterized as:

1.   A sensory process
2.   A perceptual process

365

3. A response process
4. A learned response
5. A developmental task
6. An interest
7. A learning process
8. Communication

Athough these processes help one to understand reading, they are not and cannot be used to explain the actual reading process. In this text we have selected one theory of reading to examine in detail. This theory was selected for its application to common reading problems experienced by many children.

The LaBerge and Samuels Model of Automatic Information Processing (LaBerge & Samuels, 1974) focuses on the role of attention in the reading process. According to these authors each of us is involved in two levels of attending: internal and external attention. During most of our daily activities within the classroom we are aware and deal with external attending behaviors. External behaviors are all those that are observable, such as eye contact, on-task behavior, and appropriate responding. Although external attending is a necessary condition for learning and for reading, it is not sufficient. The child must experience internal attending in order to both decode and comprehend the written passage.

Three characteristics of internal attention are noted as:

1. Alertness
2. Selective attention
3. Limited capacity

Alertness refers to the child's active attempt to become involved with information in the surrounding environment. The environment constantly bombards the child with stimulation, such as the noise in the classroom, the shuffling of paper, the teacher talking to another reading group, the noise of the pencil sharpener or the ticking of the clock, the visual elements of the bulletin board, the games in the corner, and so on. Because of the ability to selectively attend, the child is unaware of the majority of the stimulation and focuses only on certain components. Although many of us believe we can carry on two or more conversations at once, our limited capacity dictates that we only attend to one thing at a time.

Consider the children who watch TV while doing their homework. They appear to be attending to both, but actually they are switching their attention rapidly back and forth between the program and the math assignment. Attention is only given to one set of information at a time. Once we recognize these three elements of internal attention, we can apply them to the reading process and to the reading program within the classroom.

366

The theory of automatic processing goes on to assume that getting meaning from a printed word is a two-step process. The first step is decoding or translating printed symbols into spoken words. These words can be said aloud or subvocalized. The second step refers to comprehension, that is, getting meaning from the words we read. In comprehension, the relevent unit for reading is not the single word but the sentence. It is believed that single words can be comprehended automatically, however the interaction of a combination of words must be attended to. For instance, in the sentence, "The mother kissed her daughter," one must be aware of the agent-action-object phrase, which is, mother kissed daughter. In addition, one must understand the relationship between generations in order to fully comprehend the meaning of the sentence.

The LaBerge and Samuels model includes components of visual memory and phonological memory. In the visual memory hierarchy attention is given first to the features of the printed symbol (ol), then to the letter (d), followed by spelling patterns (da), and finally to words (dad). In the phonological memory hierarchy attention is given to sound features, then to phonemes, followed by syllables, and finally to words. Otto, Peters, and Peters (1977) indicate, however, that this process is reversible. They state that:

> In both the visual and phonological memory systems, it is possible, through the control of selective attention, to work from features up to words or from words down to features. When going from a whole word to features, a decomposition into parts takes place and teachers often call this process "analysis." For example, when the teacher asks the students to listen for the difference between /sat/ and /sad/, the process requires a top-down analysis from the whole into parts. On the other hand in reading, when a student sounds out the new word letter by letter and blends these sounds to form a word, it is a bottom-up process of synthesizing a word from its parts into a whole word. (pp. 27–28)

To comprehend the written passage, LaBerge and Samuels state that the reader relies on semantic memory which provides feedback as to word meaning. When material is familiar, the reader gains information that goes directly from visual memory to semantic memory. However, in the case of difficult material the reader tends to subvocalize the words and the information transfer process is from visual memory to phonological memory to semantic memory.

Let us review what we know so far about attention and reading. First, at any given point, the child can only attend to one thing. Next, reading is considered a two-step process involving decoding and comprehension. Then, the dilemma of the beginning reader is: if the child attends to decoding, can comprehension be achieved? The answer relates back to attention switching and our example of children who watch TV while completing their math homework. In a similar way beginning readers switch their attention back and forth from decoding to comprehension. Once children become proficient at the decoding task, they can turn their attention to comprehension. Basically this is what is done by fluent readers who decode the printed word at the automatic level and concentrate on comprehending the passage. When reading more technical material with unfamiliar words, advanced readers once again switch their attention back and forth between decoding and comprehension.

This theory can be used to describe certain common reading problems found among mildly handicapped children. Many children experiencing reading difficulties become *word callers,* meaning that they can recognize words but are unable to comprehend them. Accordingly a child experiencing this difficulty would be attending completely to decoding and unable to give any attention to comprehension. For such children the teacher should:

1. Provide material that is less difficult to decode but still provides the same basic content.
2. Encourage them to read a passage twice through focusing only on decoding.

Once the children feel fluent in the reading material, they can reread for comprehension and continue with the reading task.

Another common problem is when skilled readers complete a passage but are unable to remember what they have read. Again the concentration has been on decoding, which interferes with information passing from visual memory to semantic memory. The teacher should allow the child to read the passage once for decoding and then ask specific questions to focus the child's attention prior to rereading the material. In this way the child can attend to decoding and then to the specific meaning for the purpose of recalling significant passage elements.

When beginning to read, many mildly handicapped children hesitate when reading aloud. It is possible that the children are switching their attention to comprehension too soon and therefore are unable to attend to decoding the message. Again, the teacher should ask the child to read the passage through for decoding purposes only and not to attend to meaning. By turning the child's attention first to the decoding task and then to comprehension, the child is more apt to perform both tasks successfully without hesitation.

Reading Readiness

Reading readiness refers to the child's general state of maturity and involves factors relating to age, physical health, intelligence, perceptual abilities, social adjustment, and language skills. Since these factors vary among any group of children, the importance of readiness must be stressed. The mildly handicapped may enter school along with their chronological age-mates, but they may be less ready than their peers for the demands placed on the learner by reading instruction.

The reading program, if tailored to the mildly handicapped child's maturational and cognitive development, may need to have an extension of the readiness instructional component until the child is conditioned to the prerequisite reading skills.

> If the effects of reading are dependent upon the reader's condition at the time of reading, then the teaching of reading must include readying the student to interpret and respond to ideas we want him to experience. From this point of view a reading readiness program cannot be pressed into several workbooks, some experience charts, and a book of stories children love to hear. Rather, reading readiness must be concerned with the child's total development as a person in addition to selected instructional readiness activities. (Otto, McMenemy, & Smith, 1973, pp. 137–138)

During the readiness stage the instructional goal is to help the children develop a proper orientation to the reading task. Figure 11.2 provides readiness teaching activities and program objectives for the development of necessary prereading skills.

Readiness itself is not a general construct but rather a series of skills arranged in a quasihierarchial structure. For example, children are unlikely to develop reading comprehension if they have not achieved satisfactorily in listening comprehension skills. The dividing line between readiness skills and actual reading tasks is not always evident. The uncertainty arises, not in deciding which skills are necessary along the whole reading continuum, but in determining which skills are part of the reading act itself and not just preparatory for it. Examples of debatable readiness skills are rote memorization of the alphabet and letter identification. Some teachers and reading programs may classify these tasks as readiness while others include them within the reading program.

Current research is providing evidence that the commonly held belief in readiness skills as a strong predictor of later reading success may not be accurate (Larsen & Hammill, 1975; Newcomer & Magee, 1977). In fact, Newcomer and Magee (1977) found evidence that oral language deficits are as predictive, and in many cases better, than reading readiness skills. They suggest that oral language assessment be included in reading screening tests along with the basic reading readiness skills.

Reading is a complex process achieved through an integration of many skills, the foundations of which are developed during the readiness stage. In reading, as in all other language arts, the child's readiness is partly based on the evident desire to read. Prior to actual reading instruction a child

I. Skill: COMPREHENSION
   A. Listening Comprehension
      1. *Outcome:* The ability to understand and recall what one hears.
      2. *Teaching Tasks:*
         a. Read a simple story to the children showing pictures of each of the main characters and/or events. After the story is completed ask them to name each character or event and tell something that happened in the story.
         b. Using a flannel board, illustrate a story as you tell it. Have the children recreate the story in their own words using the flannel board pieces.
         c. Use either of the above techniques and ask the children to infer a relationship between the characters or a new ending for the story line. Children who can infer relationships and future events are functioning at a higher order comprehension skill.
         d. Orally present directions to the children to carry out a task: "Clap your hands two times" or "Color the circle blue."
   B. Visual Comprehension
      1. *Outcome:* The ability to understand and recall what one sees.
      2. *Teaching Tasks:*
         a. Show the children a drawing of an activity being performed by another child. Ask them to tell you what the child in the drawing is doing: "What does the picture say?"
         b. After looking at a nonsense picture, or a drawing of a common object, person, or animal with a missing part, ask the children to tell you: "What's wrong here?"
         c. Show the children a sequenced cartoon strip with the words cut out or covered over. Ask the children to provide appropriate dialogue. (Peanuts or Henry comics are excellent for this activity.)

II. Skill: DISCRIMINATION
   A. Auditory Discrimination
      1. *Outcome:* The ability to discriminate likenesses and differences among sounds.
      2. *Teaching Tasks:*
         a. After teaching the concept of rhyming words have the children name a color that rhymes with _____:
             head and bread _____ (red)
             fellow and bellow _____ (yellow)
             bean and teen _____ (green)
             fight and light _____ (white)
         or name an object word that rhymes with _____:
             hair and fair _____ (chair)
             up and pup _____ (cup)
             fish and wish _____ (dish)
             goat and moat _____ (coat)
         The same type of activity can be done with number words, animal words, and names of children in the class.

b. Present the children with objects or pictures and ask them to match names beginning with the same sound.

(bat)　　(bear)　　(house)　　(chair)

c. Provide the children with the key sound and ask them to clap their hands whenever they hear it. For example, if the sound is "t" they would clap once for table and twice for tattle.

B. Visual Discrimination
  1. *Outcome:* The ability to discriminate printed symbols from each other.
  2. *Teaching Tasks:*
    a. Ask the children to match similar shapes and patterns:

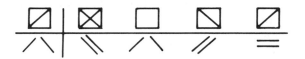

    b. Progress from shapes and patterns to letters and numerals:

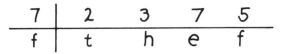

    c. Finally the children should be able to match identical words (letter patterns):

who	yes	who	where	now
can	cat	cast	can	come

III. Skill: MEMORY
  A. Auditory Memory
    1. *Outcome:* The ability to remember what one hears.
    2. *Teaching Tasks:*
      a. Using the direction activity suggested under the auditory comprehension skill increase the number of tasks the children must do. For example:
        Clap your hands.
        Clap your hands and stand up.
        Clap your hands, stand up, and go to the door.
        Clap you hands, stand up, go to the door, and turn around.
      b. After listening to a story involving a series of events, ask the children to tell or draw a picture of the proper story sequence.
  B. Visual Memory
    1. *Outcome:* The ability to remember what one sees.

   2. *Teaching Tasks:*
      a. Show the children a string of large beads of various colors. Start with only a few and ask the children to look at the beads (about five seconds) and then to make a string just like it. Increase the number of beads on the string, giving the children the chance to model each new addition.
      b. Show the children a picture of common objects. Remove the stimulus picture and have them name each of the objects (or animals) in the picture that they remember.

IV. Skill: ASSOCIATION
   A. Letter Name to Letter Symbol Association
      1. *Outcome:* The ability to identify letters by name.
      2. *Teaching Tasks:*
         a. Use as many modalities as possible when introducing each letter. For instance, have the children see "a," say "a," cut out "a," color over "a," make an "a" out of clay, and paint or write "a."
   B. Phoneme to Grapheme Association
      1. *Outcome:* The ability to associate a sound with its representative symbol.
      2. *Teaching Tasks:*
         a. Present each letter with a word and associated picture stimulus that begins with its representative sound. For example, sand-s, book-b, fish-f. The children should be able to identify each letter when given the appropriate key word.

V. Skill: ORIENTATION
   A. Visual Tracking
      1. *Outcome:* The ability to follow an object or a line of print across space.
      2. *Teaching Tasks:*
         a. Present a line of pictures of common objects for the child to name in order as the teacher points to them.

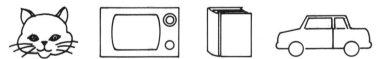

         b. Ask the children to complete a simple maze by moving a finger along the route.

Start ...... Finish

         c. Have the children trace different lines and shapes following from a marked starting point to a predetermined finish.
   B. Left to Right Orientation
      1. *Outcome:* The ability to read across a page from left to right.
      2. *Teaching Tasks:*
         a. Present materials with a green line drawn on one side and a red line on the other. Tell the children that we always begin reading

on the side of the green line and move across the page until we reach the red line. Have the children practice this by moving a finger across the page.

b. Have the children draw a series of lines across the page from left to right.

c. Have the children *read* colored dots from left to right across a page.

(Represented in colors: red, green, blue, blue, red.

FIGURE 11.2   Readiness Teaching Chart

may pretend to be able to read and carefully examine books and magazines. Some children use books as a grown-up status symbol and carry books around in imitation of older siblings. Another signal of eagerness to read is when the child points to letters and words and asks for their names. Teachers and parents should watch for these reading signs and encourage the child's curiosity about the printed word.

Reading Assessment

Reading diagnosis can occur at multiple points in the instructional sequence as is illustrated in Figure 11.3. The course of further instruction depends on the teacher's ability to interpret the diagnostic information and to adjust the reading program.

Diagnosis of reading abilities includes a variety of measures ranging from a review of personal files and classroom observation to formalized tests. The teacher needs to examine a combination of assessment techniques and to interpret the information in light of the child's previously noted learning style and difficulties. Figure 11.4 presents possible sources of information about the child's reading ability and the nature of the information that each source can provide. (See Figure 11.4 on pp. 376–378.)

Reading Batteries

Detailed information about a child's reading abilities is provided in individualized reading test batteries which include a variety of specific skill subtests. Analysis of subtest results allows the teacher to profile the child's strengths and weaknesses in reading skills. Most reading batteries can be

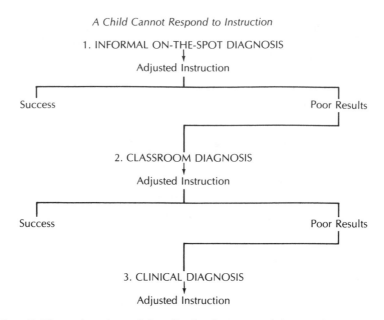

A Child Cannot Respond to Instruction

1. INFORMAL ON-THE-SPOT DIAGNOSIS

Adjusted Instruction

Success   Poor Results

2. CLASSROOM DIAGNOSIS

Adjusted Instruction

Success   Poor Results

3. CLINICAL DIAGNOSIS

Adjusted Instruction

Source: Wilson, R. *Diagnostic and remedial reading for classroom and clinic* (2nd. ed.). Columbus, Ohio: Charles E. Merrill Publishing Company, 1972, p. 28.

FIGURE 11.3   Sequence of Diagnosis

administered by the regular or special educator who has become familiar with the subtest procedures, scoring, and interpretation. However, because of the time required to administer reading batteries, they are usually given only to children experiencing moderate to severe reading difficulties. In cases where a teacher suspects a specific reading problem, it is advisable to give only select sections of a test and analyze them for diagostic-prescriptive purposes. Figure 11.5 presents information on five commonly used individual reading test batteries. (See Figure 11.5 on pp. 380–381.)

Informal Assessment

Within the daily classroom routine the teacher has a number of opportunities to observe and informally assess the child's reading performance. During reading groups, seatwork activities, group discussions, and individual instructional periods, the teacher may observe whether the child is interested in and able to complete the activities that involve reading. From these observations the teacher may also gain information related specifically to the child's word analysis and comprehension skills.

The use of a checklist allows the teacher to record the child's errors and to chart continuous progress. Figure 11.6 (p. 382) provides a checklist to help the teacher systematically observe the child and focus on specific problem areas. Wallace and Larsen (1978) note that interpretation of observational data "should be based upon current, multiple observations that have occurred over an extended period of time. In addition ... observations should be supplemented by data from formal or informal tests" (p. 318).

The most frequently used informal reading assessment format consists of the presentation of graded word lists and the oral reading of paragraphs followed by comprehension questions. Difficulty levels are controlled through vocabulary presentations which correspond to grade levels progressing from preprimer through the intermediate elementary grades.

Word recognition is examined by the graded word lists which provide an indication of the child's sight vocabulary, ability to *attack* unknown words, and the level at which reading instruction should begin. There are several published word lists, such as the Dolch (1950) Basic Word List, and Hillerich (1974) Word Lists, which are appropriate for informally screening the child's word recognition. In addition, word lists may be teacher developed and constructed by clearly printing or typing a list of 20–25 words randomly selected from the child's basic reading material. These may be chosen from the list of new words found at the end of most basal readers. Phonics skills that are representative of each level should be sampled. For instance, do prefixes, suffixes, and compound words sample the variety found in the text, and do the consonant blends and digraphs approximate those used throughout the text? A teacher-constructed word list has the advantage of relating directly to the instructional program and the reading levels found in the classroom materials.

Word lists are usually presented in two ways: a timed flash presentation and an untimed exposure for those words the child was unable to initially identify. The quick flash exposure tests the child's instant recognition or sight word vocabulary, while the untimed presentation allows the child to apply word attack skills to any unknown words. The child's performance is noted, and errors are properly indicated. After the word lists are administered, the teacher should look for specific error patterns.

During the second exposure the teacher of the mildly handicapped child may give prompts to assist word recognition. For instance, the teacher may provide an initial consonant sound, may suggest similar or rhyming words, or may help the child focus on a previously learned smaller word within the larger word. Prompts should be used only when the child seems unable to identify the word alone and each prompt should be carefully noted along with the child's errors. Prompts, like errors, can be analyzed for information regarding the child's skill level. The type of prompt that helps "unlock" the word mystery is a definite clue to the child's present level of functioning.

Errors are also noted during oral paragraph reading. While the child reads aloud, the teacher follows along and marks errors on a duplicate copy. Some of the most common word attack errors and the standard form of

Sources, Methods, and Instruments	Kinds of Information Obtained	What Was Learned about an Individual Student, Dick
1. School records	Scores on previous intelligence and achievement tests; school marks in all subjects; family size, economic and social background, language spoken, visual, auditory, and general health information; attendance; change of schools.	Dick is the oldest of seven children. His family is of low-middle socioeconomic status; white, Irish and German extraction. Poor English, but no foreign language is spoken. Kuhlmann-Anderson IQ 110; no recorded health problems; good attendance at the same school. Dick has done consistently poor work through the first year of high school.
2. Classroom observation of students engaged in oral reading, in group discussion, and other classroom activities	Success in completing a given assignment; oral and silent reading performance; indications of attitudes toward reading, school, and himself; interests; relations with other students; speaking vocabulary and sentence structure; uses made of reading; changes in attitudes, points of view, and behavior.	Dick seems to make no real effort to learn new and difficult words. He glides over them and does not stop to analyze or remember them. Even after the teacher has pointed out obvious errors in spelling, Dick makes the same errors again. On the same page he will spell a word both correctly and incorrectly. Other pupils choose him in games. Woodworking is his favorite subject.
3. Interest inventories and questionnaires	Reading interests and other interests.	Dick's main interest is sports. He checked several reading interests, but may just have thought this was the thing to do.
4. Reading autobiography and other introspective reports	Family reading habits, his own past and present reading interests, his analysis of his reading difficulties.	The family does little reading; Dick has read little in the past. At present he says he enjoys reading books on aviation.

Sources, Methods, and Instruments	Kinds of Information Obtained	What Was Learned about an Individual Student, Dick
5. Daily schedule	How he spends his time: in outdoor activities, TV, movies, chores, part-time work; alone, with friends, with family; kinds and amount of reading.	Most of Dick's free time was spent playing outdoors. After supper he usually watched TV. During the days recorded he did no voluntary reading.
6. *Dolch Basic Sight Word Test*	Sight recognition of basic words, words that he needs to study.	Dick failed to recognize at sight about one-fourth of the Dolch basic vocabulary.
7. Informal tests and group reading inventory	The free or creative-type response yields information about the pupil's approach to reading and inferences as to how his mind works when he reads. The short answer or multiple-choice questions give understanding of other aspects of comprehension.	Dick could not read independently books above the sixth-grade level. He picked out a few scattered ideas but saw no relation or sequence among them. He was able to identify most of the main ideas and supporting details in the multiple-choice questions. He made no application of the ideas to his own life.
8. Standardized reading tests	Different tests yield different kinds of information: speed of reading easy material, speed-comprehension ratio, special vocabulary in each subject, sentence and paragraph comprehension, ability to use index and reference material.	On the subtests as reported on the *Iowa Silent Reading Test,* Dick's vocabulary, sentence meaning, and directed reading seem to be very poor. He used the index well but slowly, had surprisingly high ability to get the main idea of a paragraph. His total reading score was at the 33rd percentile.
9. Listening comprehension tests	Relation between listening comprehension and silent reading comprehension on comparable material.	Dick comprehended much better when he listened than when he read.

continued

Sources, Methods, and Instruments	Kinds of Information Obtained	What Was Learned about an Individual Student, Dick
10. Diagnostic spelling test	Grade level of spelling ability, kinds of errors made.	Dick's spelling is about sixth-grade level; he is not word-conscious.
11. Classroom projective techniques, e.g., incomplete sentences, pictures	Attitudes toward self, family, and clues as to emotional conflicts, worries, etc.	Dick gave repeated indications of fear of failure and dislike of school.

Source: From R. Strang, *Diagnostic teaching of reading* (2nd ed.). New York: McGraw-Hill Book Company, 1969, pp. 19–21.

FIGURE 11.4   *Sources of Information on Reading Assessment*

marking them are presented in Figure 11.7. After oral and silent paragraph reading, the student is asked a series of questions. Comprehension questions should relate to factual recall, inference and vocabulary skills in order to assess the child's level of understanding. (See Figure 1.7 on p. 383.)

Informal Reading Inventory (IRI)

Among the most commonly used informal assessment procedures is the Informal Reading Inventory (IRI). The IRI may be either commercially produced (often associated with basal reading programs) or teacher constructed. In either case, the general format of the inventory is a combination of a graded word list and graded reading passages of approximately one hundred words, along with associated comprehension questions. The purpose of administering the IRI is to determine the child's independent functioning level, the point at which instruction is beneficial, and the level at which the child's frustration impedes learning. The IRI is also useful for determining specific strengths and weaknesses in reading skills and as a record of reading progress.

Construction of the IRI begins with a graded word list based on successive reading levels found in the classroom. The word list, developed and administered as suggested, provides information regarding:

1. The child's immediate sight vocabulary
2. Word analysis skills
3. An appropriate level for beginning the reading inventory

A good rule of thumb is to begin the reading inventory one level below that in which the child began experiencing difficulty on the untimed word list.

Passages for silent and oral reading are selected and typed in primary type along with comprehension questions on duplicate copies, one for the student and one for the teacher. Dittoed copies may be used for repeated testing. The teacher may decide to select passages from the back one-third of each basal level text (Mann & Suiter, 1974) or choose three passages; one from the beginning, one from the middle, and one from the end of each text. This latter procedure further delineates the child's functioning level and assists in a more accurate placement within the reading level.

Passage length is related to grade/age level as shown in Figure 11.8 (p. 383). The teacher should strive for a section containing a complete thought. The number of comprehension questions is also dependent on the child's general functioning level.

At the conclusion of the IRI, three separate reading levels can be established. Figure 11.9 (p. 384) gives the criteria designated for each level. The criteria for word recognition relates to the oral reading of passages and sight words, while comprehension refers to scores on questions based on oral and silent reading selections.

Independent Level
This is the level at which the child can read orally in a natural and easy manner, similar to a conversational tone. At the independent level there is no evidence of reading difficulty, such as finger pointing or hesitation. Reading for enjoyment is possible on material geared to this level. The 99 percent word recognition score means the child is making only one error in one hundred words with at least 80 percent comprehension.

Instructional Level
Functioning at the instructional level, a child can benefit from planned teaching. The child is generally relaxed during oral reading with little or no signs of difficulty and can recognize 95 percent of the words read. Comprehension at this level is accurate at 75 percent or more. Although still in the process of learning, the child can comfortably deal with the material. This is the optimum level for instructional activities.

Frustration Level
Material at this level causes a child to experience a great deal of difficulty, to show signs of tension when reading, or even to refuse to read.

Test	Publisher	Subtests	Grade/age level	Comments
Gates-McKillop Reading Diagnostic Tests	Teacher's College Press	Oral reading; word presentation; phrase presentation; word part analysis; phoneme-grapheme identification; and auditory blending. Supplementary tests: spelling, oral vocabulary, syllabrication, and auditory discrimination.	Grades 1–8	Two alternative forms of comparable difficulty allow for re-peated testing. Provides thorough examination of word-analysis skills; however, if given in its entirety it can be lengthy and laborious.
Durrell Analysis of Reading Difficulty	Harcourt, Brace, Jovanovich	Oral reading; silent reading; listening comprehension; word recognition; word analysis; letter identification; sounds; learning rate; spelling; and handwriting.	Ages 6–11	Provides a useful Checklist of Instructional Needs by which the teacher can note reading difficulties. Test manual presents helpful information for remediation and program planning.

Diagnostic Reading Scales	California Testing Service	Word recognition; reading and comprehension skills; phonics (eight supplementary tests).	Grades 1–8	Provides three word recognition lists and 22 passages of increasing difficulty as well as eight phonics supplementary tests. Results provide three reading levels per student: instructional, independent, and potential.
Woodcock Reading Mastery Tests	American Guidance Service, Inc.	Letter identification; word identification; word attack; word comprehension; passage comprehension.	Grades K–12	Separate norms are provided for boys and girls and groups. Two forms are provided for repeated testing and a *Mastery Scale* helps the teacher predict the child's success with reading tasks at different levels.
Gray Oral Reading Test	Bobbs-Merrill Co.	Oral reading rate and accuracy, comprehension.	Grades 1– College	Available in four alternate forms. Manual provides suggestions for detecting reading error patterns.

FIGURE 11.5   *Individualized Reading Batteries*

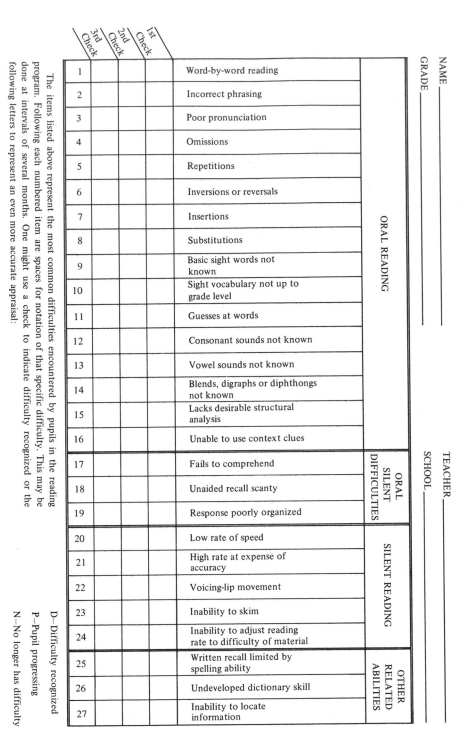

NAME

GRADE

TEACHER

SCHOOL

The items listed above represent the most common difficulties encountered by pupils in the reading program. Following each numbered item are spaces for notation of that specific difficulty. This may be done at intervals of several months. One might use a check to indicate difficulty recognized or the following letters to represent an even more accurate appraisal:

D—Difficulty recognized
P—Pupil progressing
N—No longer has difficulty

	3rd Check	2nd Check	1st Check		
1				Word-by-word reading	ORAL READING
2				Incorrect phrasing	
3				Poor pronunciation	
4				Omissions	
5				Repetitions	
6				Inversions or reversals	
7				Insertions	
8				Substitutions	
9				Basic sight words not known	
10				Sight vocabulary not up to grade level	
11				Guesses at words	
12				Consonant sounds not known	
13				Vowel sounds not known	
14				Blends, digraphs or diphthongs not known	
15				Lacks desirable structural analysis	
16				Unable to use context clues	
17				Fails to comprehend	ORAL SILENT DIFFICULTIES
18				Unaided recall scanty	
19				Response poorly organized	
20				Low rate of speed	SILENT READING
21				High rate at expense of accuracy	
22				Voicing-lip movement	
23				Inability to skim	
24				Inability to adjust reading rate to difficulty of material	
25				Written recall limited by spelling ability	OTHER RELATED ABILITIES
26				Undeveloped dictionary skill	
27				Inability to locate information	

Source: Ekwall, E. E. *Locating and correcting reading difficulties*. Columbus, Ohio: Charles E. Merrill Publishing Company, 1977, p. 5.

FIGURE 11.6 *Reading Diagnosis Checklist*

Type of Error	Notation	Example
Omission	Circle the omitted word(s).	My shoe (is) gone.
Substitution	Write the substitution over the correct word.	are Where is my shoe?
Reversal	Use an elongated line to indicate the two elements which were reversed.	Here is my shoe.
Repetition	Place a wavy line under the words which are repeated.	I like my shoes.
Insertion	Place a caret marking the place of the insertion and the word that was added.	too Do you like my shoes?
Mispronunciation	Write the mispronunciation over the intended word.	wed My shoes are red.
Unknown or aided words	Underline the assisted word(s).	My shoes have laces.
Self-correction	Place a check mark over the correct word.	My shoes are new.

FIGURE 11.7   Coding Reading Errors

The child misses more than one out of every ten words read and comprehension is reduced below 50 percent. No benefit is gleaned from material written on the child's frustration level.

Administration of an IRI will enable the teacher to appropriately match the child with suitable reading material. This procedure, although time

Grade Level	Approx. No. of Words	Approx. No. of Comprehension Questions
Primary	50	2 recall 2 vocabulary 1 inference
Intermediate	100	2 recall 2 inference 1 vocabulary
Secondary	150	2 recall 2 inference 1 vocabulary

FIGURE 11.8   IRI Passage Selection

Reading Level	Word Recognition (%)	Comprehension (%)
Independent	99	90
Instructional	95	75
Frustration	90 (or less)	50 (or less)

[a] Criteria selected from: Johnson, M. and Kress, R. *Informal reading inventories.* Newark, Del.: International Reading Association, 1965.

FIGURE 11.9   IRI Criteria[a]

consuming, reduces the chance that the child will experience failure and frustration. Periodic retesting is a good means of determining reading growth.

Reading Skills

Although there is no one accepted definition of reading, there is some consensus on the identifiable skills basic to the reading act. These are the skills which are generally included in the *scope and sequence* of the reading program. Specifically, scope refers to the breath of content included in the reading program, while sequence indicates the order of instruction. Different programs vary in the emphasis given to particular skills as well as in the order in which they are presented. The major classification of reading skills are word recognition, word analysis, and comprehension.

Word Recognition

The fluent reader is able to instantly identify the printed word. A sight vocabulary (word recognition) refers to those words the child can read at the automatic level, without the assistance of word analysis, context clues, or prompting.

Most basal readers include a list of sight words to be learned with each reading text. The goal is for the child to recognize each word in isolation or in context. To achieve this, the child must be given repeated exposures to each word. As the child learns to instantaneously recognize a word in a variety of situations, its meaning is better understood.

It is debatable whether it is best to teach sight words out of context or within a contextual framework. Samuels and his associates (Samuels, 1967; Samuels, Begy, & Chen, 1975–1976; Singer, Samuels, & Spiroff, 1973–1974) have hypothesized that words presented in context provide syntactic and grammatical cue distractions which prevent the child from focusing upon specific word features. Opposing this view is Goodman (1965; 1973), whose research shows that children are able to identify many words in context which are unknown in isolated lists. In an attempt to resolve the issue, Kirkman, Endo, and Crandall (1979) found that the presentation method had little effect upon four low intelligence, mildly handicapped children's rate of acquisition, generalization and retention.

A child's ability to recognize words on sight is based upon visual memory of the word image. The *look-say* approach to reading emphasizes the visual recognition of words for initial reading instruction. Selected, meaningful words are presented in repetitive sentence sequences (See Dick run. See Sally run.) and the child learns to identify the whole word through practice.

If a child has difficulty learning sight words, merely more practice may be needed. If the problem is not resolved, the teacher may want to develop a systematic instructional sequence designed to increase the visual image. This is especially significant for irregular words when it is important to stress sight recognition. The following instructional sequence will help increase sight vocabulary.

1. *Introduce the word(s) in context.* Write one or two simple sentences on the board, being sure that the child is already able to identify the majority of words and can derive meaning.
2. *Create a visual image* of the new word. Emphasize configuration by outlining the word image. Have the child close his eyes and "picture" the word.
3. *Write each word from memory.* This may take repeated practice and each successful attempt should be reinforced.
4. *Identify the word in isolation on flashcards and in context* in order to provide instant recognition.

Word Analysis

Word analysis enables the reader to decode the many words which he may encounter that are not included in the reader's sight vocabulary. Word analysis, sometimes referred to as "word attack skills," includes phonics, structural analysis, and context clues. For all practical purposes, as May and Eliot (1978) state, word analysis skills are any skill which assist in word recognition other than visual memory.

Phonics allows the reader to decode unknown words according to grapheme-phoneme associations. The breakdown of phonic elements includes; consonants, consonant blends, consonant digraphs, vowels, vowel dipthongs, and vowel digraphs. Each of these elements was presented in chapter 10 (Spelling Instruction) and is included in Figure 11.10 for the purpose of review.

- Consonants—all letters except vowels
- Consonant blends—two or three consecutive consonants representing related but separate phonemes
- Consonant digraphs—two consecutive consonants representing one phoneme
- Vowels—letters *a, e, i, o, u* (and semivowels k, y, and w).
- Vowel dipthongs—(blends) two vowels representing related but separate sounds
- Vowel digraphs—two vowels representing a single phoneme.

FIGURE 11.10   *Phonics Element Chart*

Phonics instruction has been the center of educational debate for almost thirty years. Phonics has been exclaimed by some as the panacea for all reading problems, and as the cause of all reading problems by others. At present, research has added little to resolve the controversy. Two studies (Carnine, 1977; and Jeffrey & Samuels, 1967) found a slight indication that phonics training is better than sight word training in transferring to new word lists. However, there was no attempt to verify this effect in sentence transfer where the children may have benefited from semantic and syntactic clues.

The majority of basal reading programs include some basic phonics training. It is generally believed that children who are able to apply phonics strategies can predict the letter sounds of unknown words. Such prediction, however, does not guarantee reading success. The child must be able to associate the predicted letter sounds with a familiar word which is appropriate to the sentence syntax.

Some mildly handicapped children have trouble learning many phonics rules. In fact, because of this, phonics should be taught without emphasis on rules. It is best to simplify the phonics program and to teach it slowly using the principles of repetition, practice, and generalization. A synthetic approach which teaches direct sound-symbol relationships will be most effective.

Phonics employs auditory skills to decode letter patterns. Instruction begins with training in auditory discrimination and auditory memory. Can the child distinguish common sounds, letter sounds, and sound combinations (sat-set)? Is the child able to repeat a series of sounds, a list of numbers, or a complete sentence? The answer to each of these questions is important to the establishment of grapheme-phoneme relationships and to sound blending.

The following steps outline a suggested phonics program which builds on the establishment of one sound per graphic symbol. Words with less frequently used letter sounds should be taught as sight vocabulary.

1. Teach the child to sound blend two-sound words, then three-sound words, etc. Kirk, Kliebhan, and Lerner (1978) suggest that

386

the child must be able to sound blend across a two-second interval, since this is the amount of time a beginning reader requires to recognize a graphic symbol and associate its relevant sound. The two-second interval allows the child to recall one sound while decoding the next.

2. Introduce consonant sounds—*b, d, f, c* (hard), *k*—only five sounds at first, followed by the vowel sound, ă (short *a*).

3. Teach words that supply meaning. Nonsense syllables are too abstract for many mildly handicapped children and should not be used.

4. Introduce additional consonants followed by other short vowel sounds. Leave the difficult short ě sound for last.

5. Present combinations of letter sounds, such as *ee* (feed), *ay* (pay), *oo* (food). By associating each letter pattern with only one sound, the child can learn the relationship more easily.

6. For each sound-symbol association establish a key word, such as *b* - ball; *s* – Sam; or *ai* – maid.

7. Teach additional combination sounds, such as *en, an, ing,* and *est.*

8. Selection of the phonics sequence should be based on the child's ability and the words presented in the child's reader. Do not expect the child to sound out a word without having been taught the sound. Teach the letter sounds of the words the child will soon encounter to help him retain the association.

9. Teach syllabication, suffixes, and prefixes. Each syllable contains only one vowel sound. Identifying the correct number of syllables helps the child apply phonics skills in decoding new words.

10. Teach infrequent sound-symbol associations and irregular words as sight words concentrating on their visual image.

Adapted from: Kirk, S., Kliebhan, J. M., and Lerner, J. *Teaching reading to slow and disabled learners.* Boston: Houghton-Mifflin Company, 1978.

Structural analysis refers to the identification of meaningful word units, such as prefixes, suffixes, and roots. These units which are meaning-oriented are known as morphemes. Relative to the total number of English words, there are a limited number of morphemes (Savage & Mooney, 1979). The child begins structural analysis when he begins to identify independent word parts. Some words, such as "fire," are intact morphemes. The compound word "fireman" contains two meaningful units and the reader must attend to both.

Structural analysis should be taught in the primary grades and should be closely associated with the child's own vocabulary. Structural analysis is the decoding of meaningful word units. After the child has learned some basic phonics generalizations structural analysis of the following elements should be integrated into the reading program.

1. *Compound words*—made up of two or more smaller and familiar words whose combined meaning make a new word.
2. *Suffixes*—meaningful word endings.
    a.   forming plurals
    b.   comparative forms
    c.   possessives
    d.   others
3. *Root words*—main element of a word
4. *Prefixes*—meaningful word beginnings
5. *Contractions*—shortening of a word by omitting specific sound-symbols.
6. *Syllabication*—pronunciation units within a word.

Context clues are sometimes considered separately from word analysis. When the child is unable to identify a word he may be able to figure it out based on an understanding of the words which surround it. For instance the word "fast" in the sentence, "This was a fast day," may not be meaningful unless one follows the context in which it was written. The *fast day* could refer to a religious celebration or a busy day that went by quickly. The complete context in which the word is used will provide the answer.

Context clues are helpful only when the child already has the decoding skills to identify the majority of words in the sentence and needs to determine the pronunciation of an unknown word. When using context clues the child is *predicting* the unknown word based on the syntax and semantics of the other words.

Mildly handicapped children who have problems in generalization will need direct instruction in order to use context analysis. The teacher can help the child determine the unknown word by:

1. Having the child preview the material silently to get the general meaning and to locate any unknown word.
2. Asking the child to supply words that would make sense in the sentence. For example in the sentence, "The boy _____ goodbye to his mother," *said, waved,* and *yelled,* are all possible answers.
3. Having the child identify the beginning sound of the unknown word. "The boy w_____ goodbye to his mother," limits the answer to the word, *waved.*

Context analysis skills can be trained by asking children to fill in missing words in a sentence or story. Practice in context clues should start with oral presentations with visual cue associations.

Sample Sentence: *(oral) "This is a picture of an _____."   (picture*
                                       stimulus of an elephant)

Possible Answer: *animal, elephant*

The next step is to provide the written sentence along with the oral presentation and the picture stimulus.

Sample Sentence: *(Written) "This is a picture of an e_____."*

Gradually introduce written sentences with a teacher presentation and no picture stimulus.

Sample Sentence: *"The teacher asked the girl a q_____."*

Finally have the child read the sentence without teacher assistance and locate and determine the unknown word.

One problem that mildly handicapped children may have in decoding is an inability to try alternative word attack strategies. Fluent readers do not hesitate to approach an unknown word in a different way, if they have not been able to decode it. The deficient reader, however, may not know how to alternate strategies and may give up in frustration.

Hansen and Eaton (1978) successfully used a series of corrective feedback statements to train five mildly handicapped boys in the use of alternative decoding strategies.

The corrective feedback hierarchy is provided in Figure 11.11. Each of the five strategies was given sequentially until the child either identified the word or the teacher had to supply it. Helping children use alternative decoding strategies in a systematic fashion appears to lead to identification of unknown words. This teaching sequence of corrective feedback can be adapted to assist any child who experiences decoding problems.

Comprehension

Comprehension—the ability to gain meaning from the printed word—typically includes the skills of: locating the main idea, recalling facts, determining causation, inferring future events, drawing conclusions, and evaluation. Smith (1969) simplified comprehension into four broad categories which extend from the lower functioning skills, such as recognition, to higher order skills involving problem solving. Smith's classification is as follows:

1. *Literal comprehension*—refers to the ability to gain facts and literal information. Although the majority of teacher questions are aimed

No.	Cue	Explanation	Rationale
1	Try another way	Cue the student that he has read a word incorrectly	The student should be allowed to first choose his own method of correction
2	Finish the sentence and guess the word	Cue the student to use the context for correction	Syntax and semantics are the basic methods of word recognition
3	Break the word into parts and pronounce each one	Cue the students to analyze the segments of the word	Morphological elements are the largest meaning bearing units of words
4	The teacher covers over parts of the word and asks the child to decode each part	Provide the student with an aided visual cue to decrease the amount of stimuli	Aided visual cues provide a transition between morpho-logical and phono-logical cues
5	What sound does _____ make	Provide the student with a phonic cue to indicate the location of his error within the word	Phonological elements are the smallest sound bear-ing units in words
6	The word is _____	Provide the student with the correct word	After the word has been analyzed unsuccessfully, it should be provided by an outside source

Source: Hansen, C. L., and Eaton, M. D., Reading. In N. G. Haring, T. C. Lovitt, M. D. Eaton, and C. L. Hansen (Eds.). *The fourth R: Research in the classroom.* Columbus, Ohio: Charles E. Merrill Publishing Company, 1978, p. 73.

FIGURE 11.11   Corrective Feedback Hierarchy and Linguistic Rationale for Correction Cues.

at this level of meaning, Van Etten (1978) points out that literal comprehension includes no "thinking" skills.

2. *Interpretation*—is the ability to gain meaning which is not precisely stated in the reading. Making inferences, comparisons and generalizations are skills developed through interpretive question-ing.

3. *Critical reading*—allows the reader to make personal evaluations about the text. The ability to judge the value of the writing in terms of quality accuracy and personal taste is important as one grows older.

4. *Creative reading*—as the higest level of comprehension, encompasses all of the skills of the first three levels. Creative reading refers to answering a question or solving a problem through reading and the application of original thought.

The Smith classification system is representative of many of the taxonomic models of comprehension employed by most basal reading programs and supplementary reading material. Implicit in the taxonomic model is the teacher's task of developing sequential lessons and questions which assist the child's comprehension. Throughout this model the reader is passive, reacting only when the stimulus question is presented.

A more current view of comprehension involves the reader in an active role. Comprehension occurs after decoding and integrates the child's background experiences, language ability, motivation, and cognitive skills with the meaning of the passage which was intended by the author.

Research on instruction in comprehension has shown that behavioral techniques are effective in developing this skill. Studies by Jenkins, Barksdale, and Clinton (1978) and Proe and Wade (1973) found that contingent reinforcement of comprehension was generalizable across time. These studies differed, however, in whether or not comprehension improvement was associated with oral reading improvement. Hansen and Eaton (1978) agree with Proe and Wade that for some children there is a direct correspondence between decoding and comprehension, whereas Jenkins, et al. found none to exist.

In describing a case study of a ten-year-old fluent reader with comprehension problems, Hansen and Eaton (1978) reported a teaching sequence that employed comprehension clusters ("what, who, where, when, locating the answer on the page, sequence, retell, main idea and inference," p. 70). Each component cluster was taught by the following sequence:

1. Picture cue
2. Picture cue and written question (teacher read)
3. Picture cue and written question (child read)
4. Written question (teacher read)
5. Written question (child read) (p. 70)

The child was slowly lead to the point of mastering comprehension of reading material.

391

Increasing Reading Rate

A basic principle for instruction is to achieve accuracy first and then increase rate. This is true in reading. Once words have been learned it is necessary to help many mildly handicapped children increase their reading speed in order for them to complete assignments on time and to keep up with other members of the class. Harris and Sipay (1971) suggest four strategies for increasing word perception.

1. Abundant practice of the most commonly used words.
2. Timed reading of selections, using reinforcement and continuous charting of progress.
3. Flashing of words and phrases with a gradual reduction in exposure time.
4. Controlled reading through presentations such as a language master.

The teacher who uses any one of these methods will need to plan for transfer of the accelerated rate in the practice sessions to other activities. Once the child has demonstrated word mastery and increased speed, a program of reinforcement can be established to help the child maintain success in various reading situations.

The Mildly Handicapped Child as a Reader

The majority of classroom reading programs are designed for group instruction with little regard to specific learning problems presented by individual children. Such programs are insufficient for the instructional needs of mildly handicapped children. The general learning characteristics often displayed by these children have direct implications for the teaching of reading and should be considered when selecting or modifying a reading approach.

Children who experience reading difficulties may exhibit any of the following learning traits which have implications for the selection of reading material. Remember, however, that *such characteristics are not associated with every mildly handicapped child and even within children they vary in intensity.*

1. Mildly handicapped children are most likely to learn new skills from concrete materials that have meaning to them and their environment. The child's own experiences should provide the structure for selecting sight words and reading stories.
2. Although mental age is an indicator of the child's learning ability, chronological age is an indicator of motivation and interest levels.

Selected reading materials should be of high interest to the child and have a controlled vocabulary to help reduce frustration and increase instruction and enjoyment.

3. Mildly handicapped children approach many learning situations with an expectancy to fail. Structured success in reading activities can be achieved by providing immediate reinforcement, breaking the learning task down into small, attainable units, sequencing learning and allowing opportunities for the child to experience reading for self-enjoyment.

4. Poor retention of previously learned reading skills and sight words can be alleviated by periodic review beyond criterion. Reading practice should be distributed throughout the school day giving the children frequent opportunities to exercise their skills.

5. Since mildly handicapped children often remember material best when it is presented in small segments, their word lists, stories, and skill exercises should be divided into manageable work units. This also allows the children to experience closure on each activity and achieve a feeling of success.

6. Many mildly handicapped children have difficulty transferring concepts, and as a result, skills may be learned in isolation. By providing a variety of reading experiences and relating reading skill exercises directly to reading tasks the teacher can help these children generalize a concept's application.

7. Distractibility and an inability to attend to relevant word stimuli are two additional problems that may affect the child's reading competence. Attention can be trained. The teacher should emphasize similarities and differences among words and provide reading experiences in a variety of learning modes.

8. Mildly handicapped children need continuous feedback during the initial skill learning stages. During reading they should be given immediate knowledge as to the correctness of the response. When the response is appropriate, positive reinforcement will strengthen the reading skill. If, however, the response is incorrect, repeat the trial and prompt them toward an accurate response. (Cohen & Plaskon, 1978)

Mildly handicapped children hear words spoken in relation to the people, objects, and activities around them and are initially eager to expand their world through reading. By understanding their learning characteristics and the associated instructional principles, the teacher can achieve optimal learning conditions. These conditions will:

1. Decrease the chance of error.
2. Maintain a high level of motivation.

3. Provide feedback for learner effort.
4. Increase attention to relevant stimuli.
5. Promote material retention and skill generalization.

An Analysis of Developmental Reading Approaches

Once the mildly handicapped child's learning characteristics are understood in regard to reading, the teacher can begin to appropriately adjust the reading program. Beyond an understanding of the child's needs, the teacher must be aware of the philosophy and general approach of the reading program used in the classroom. As with normal youngsters *there is no one reading method or program that works best for all mildly handicapped children.*

The reading process may be insensible to the mildly handicapped child simply because the structured approach does not meet his learning needs. Elements of the philosophical and/or instructional framework of the reading program may not be suited to the manner by which the child acquires and retains information. Without an appropriate match between instructional strategies and learning strategies a program is destined to encounter failure. Keeping in mind the specific learning characteristics of the student it is possible to analyze the advantages and disadvantages of specific reading approaches. The majority of developmental reading programs fall within the following classification: a basal approach, linguistics approach, programmed instruction approach, phonics approach, alphabetic approach, and language experience approach. Each of the six reading methods has had an impact on public school programs, some being more successful than others.

Developmental reading implies a normal pattern of reading growth. It is a term used to refer to the sequence of development followed by children with a normal expectancy for reading achievement. Developmental reading approaches incorporate the methods and materials which form the basis of the regular classroom reading program.

The analysis given in Figure 11.12 should provide insight into the reasons for developmental reading program effectiveness-ineffectiveness when considered in light of the mildly handicapped student population. A two-step analysis, such as the one provided, examining the learner's specific difficulties and needs and then delineating the structural advantages and disadvantages of the program in relation to these needs, may suggest avenues of remediation for the mildly handicapped child. (See pp. 396–400.)

Remedial Reading Methods

Although developmental reading approaches are commonly adapted for individual student needs, they have not received complete success with special populations of learners. Therefore other approaches have been designed with the problem reader specifically in mind. These *remedial reading strategies* include specialized teaching procedures and materials aimed at problem intervention. Many such remedial reading programs were originally created for teaching reading to retarded individuals. However, use of these techniques has not been limited to this population. The selection of one method over another should be based on:

1. The learning needs of the individual child.
2. The teacher's familiarity with and comfort in using the method and materials.
3. The availability of specified program materials.

Several of these remedial techniques will be discussed. The reader is encouraged to go beyond this review in learning about each method by:

1. Observing the method in use.
2. Perusing pertinent material.
3. Reading related research.
4. Actual practice in teaching the remedial technique.

The Gillingham Method

The Gillingham Method (Gillingham & Stillman, 1936, 1968) uses a multisensory approach to teach sound units or letters for reading, writing, and spelling. The method was designed for language-disordered children who, because of lack of cerebral dominance, experience confusion in learning to read.

The child *sees* the letter, *hears* the letter sounded, and *traces* and *writes* it in accordance with prescribed procedures.

The method emphasizes drill and repetition of three phonics-association levels: Association I involves learning the name and sound of the letter (V-A); Association II asks the child to name the letter associated with a certain sound (A-A); Assoication III includes writing the letter when hearing a certain sound (A-K). Later, letters are blended into consonant-vowel-consonant (CVC) words, such as *hat.* A highly specified manual accompanies the materials which include phonics drill cards, phonics words, syllable concept cards and stories.

Critics of the Gillingham Method (Frostig, 1966; Dechant, 1970) cite overly rigid and boring procedures and the lack of adaptation for children with auditory disabilities as major disadvantages. However, commercial variations of this approach (Slingerland, 1974; Traub & Bloom, 1970) as well as teacher made modifications have been used successfully.

Approach	Advantages for Mildly Handicapped Children	Disadvantages for Mildly Handicapped Children
Programmed Instruction The reading program is presented in small sequential segments known as frames. For each frame the child is asked to make a response and immediate feedback is given as the child checks his own work. This provides reinforcement before going on to the next step. The program may have a phonics or a linguistics orientation.	1. The child is encouraged to proceed at his own pace with reinforcement provided at each learning step. 2. Continuous recording of the child's errors provides a learning profile for instructional planning. 3. Learning is designed for the individual child rather than for a group. 4. Instruction is provided in short units made up of many small segments.	1. Some children are not self-directed learners and therefore have trouble initiating and pacing their learning. 2. Many children lose their initial high motivation and become distracted. 3. The repetitive material often becomes boring and loses the child's attention. 4. Short frames do not allow the child to experience the flow of written language. 5. It is difficult to program advanced comprehension skills within the short frame structure. 6. The instructional frames do not lend themselves to interesting stories. The child may not develop a desire for reading.

396

Alphabet Approach Nontraditional orthographic programs (e.g., Initial Teaching Alphabet—ITA) establish consistent grapheme-phoneme relationships. Several new symbols are created along with diacritical markings to enable this consistency.	1. Simplifies reading by making a direct sound-symbol association. 2. Provides successful experiences which reinforce and motivate the child to continue reading. 3. There are no exceptions to the rule. Therefore children may learn to read more rapidly than by other approaches.	1. The child must take the transition from the alphabet approach (e.g., ITA) to the traditional orthography. This is often very difficult for the child to do because of an inability to generalize. 2. The child sees the traditional alphabet outside of school and becomes confused. 3. The program does not induce transfer from reading instruction to other academic areas.
Phonics Approach Phonics is based on grapheme-phoneme associations. There is no one phonics program. Teaching is based either upon the synthetic method (teaches individual letter-sound blended into words) or the analytic method (teaches phonics principles from words the child already knows).	1. Emphasis on word recognition leads to independent reading. 2. Increases interest in reading as the child learns to figure out new words. 3. Helps the child to associate sounds and printed letters representing them.	1. Isolation of speech sounds is unnatural. The children often cannot blend the sounds to form complete words. 2. The child learns to read word-by-word and may become frustrated by emphasis upon sound blending. 3. The emphasis on word recognition is often at the expense of comprehension. 4. There are many exceptions to every rule. The child may become confused, unable to differentiate the rule from the exception.

continued

397

Approach	Advantages for Mildly Handicapped Children	Disadvantages for Mildy Handicapped Children
Basal Approach A comprehensive approach providing a series of reading materials extending from preprimer through the eighth grade. The series includes a teacher's manual to guide instruction on skills and suggested activities. Along with the reader, each child has a skills workbook that focuses upon skill development. The majority of reading programs in the United States use a basal approach.	1. A sequentially ordered, comprehensive approach from early readiness to advanced reading levels. 2. Skills are divided into small units for systematic teaching of word recognition and comprehension. 3. Establishes a basic vocabulary repeated throughout the sequence. 4. Provides diagnostic tools for pinpointing strengths and weaknesses. 5. Gives the individual teacher guidance in establishing the reading program focus. 6. Many basals emphasize a sight word learning method. 7. The teacher may easily expand or adjust the materials to meet the individual needs of mildly handicapped children.	1. Organizes the teaching of reading for groups of children rather than for individuals. 2. Limited vocabulary stresses reading in the basal series and also de-emphasizes reading in content areas. 3. The material is often too difficult for the children at the lower end of the learning continuum. Using books designed for younger students reduces motivation. 4. Workbooks for skill development result in isolated learning. The student is often unable to make the transfer from skill practice to the reading text or to other reading materials.
Linguistic Approach Using mostly regular words, the linguistic method teaches children to decode graphemes by seeing differences in letters in word families (cat, sat, fat) and to understand the difference in word meanings. The chil-	1. Stresses the transition from spoken to written talk by showing the child the relationship between phonemes and graphemes. 2. Arranges learning from familiar, phonemically regular words to ones	1. Most teachers are not skilled enough in linguistics to develop the necessary program for individual learners. 2. The vocabulary is too controlled and does not approximate the

(continued)	
dren are not directly taught letter sounds but learn them through minimal word differences. 3. The child learns to spell and read the word as a whole unit. 4. Creates an awareness of sentence structure so the child learns that words are arranged to form sentences. 5. Teaches reading by association with the child's natural language facility.	child's speaking skills so that the child has difficulty relating to it. 3. Creates word reading, losing the flow of the sentence. 4. Use of nonsense words for pattern practice is irrelevant and reduces comprehension training. 5. The emphasis on auditory memory skills will make this approach extremely difficult for children who have deficits in this area.
Language Experience Approach (LEA) The child's oral language is the basis for the reading program. The LEA integrates speaking, listening, writing and reading. The child learns to read the material he has created. The teacher must provide the necessary skill development at appropriate times during reading acquisition. 1. Employs the child's current oral language abilities as the focus of the reading program. 2. Combines speaking, listening and writing skills into the reading program. 3. Utilizes direct experiences so the child can relate to the written language form. 4. Adaptable to individual or small groups according to learner and teaching needs. 5. Flexible style involving narratives, descriptions, and/or recordings of event sequences. This allows an expansion of the child's reading style.	1. Requires a prolonged attention span which is difficult for many children. 2. May be too complex an activity as several language skills are involved. 3. May be limited to the child's speaking vocabulary and may not provide a structured enough approach to vocabulary development. 4. The LEA may not have enough consistency in vocabulary or control over syntax to teach and reinforce sequential skills for the child. 5. Relies heavily on the child's own experiences and ability to relate them as the basis of the reading program.

FIGURE 11.12 Developmental Reading Approaches

Adapted from: Cohen, S. and Plaskon, S. Selecting a reading approach for the mainstreamed child. *Language Arts*, 1978, 55, 966–970. Copyright © 1978 by the National Council of Teachers of English. Reprinted by permission.

The Fernald Method

This multisensory approach provides visual-auditory-tactile-kinesthetic stimulation in combination with a language experience approach to the teaching of reading. Designed by Grace Fernald and Helen B. Keller (Fernald, 1943) to teach reading to "word-blind" individuals of normal intelligence who could not learn to read through auditory and visual approaches. This method has been used successfully with retarded children (McCarthy & Oliver, 1965).

It is an extremely slow and laborious techinque structured around a four stage-learning process. The word is written for the child, the child traces the word, says the word and memorizes the word prior to it being added to a story and into a word bank. In stage 2 the tracing is discontinued and in stage 3 the child learns from the printed word without it being rewritten by the teacher. Finally, in stage 4, the child learns to generalize and to recognize new words from similarities with previously learned words.

Distar

The *Distar Reading Program* (Engelmann & Bruner, 1969) was developed for young disadvantaged children who express below-average communication skills. Emphasis is on the development of decoding skills. The program is based on *directive teaching,* a structured behavioral approach which specifies the teacher's words and actions as well as appropriate learner responses. Reinforcement and error corrections are also provided in the manual.

Distar levels I, II, and III provide the basis of the program which is suitable for children through the third grade. A follow-through program for advanced remedial skills is contained in the *SRA Corrective Reading Program,* for older students.

The fast pace and consistent programming provides effective remediation for many children. However, the program's rigidity and emphasis on auditory skills have been found to be weaknesses for some students and teachers.

Edmark Reading Program

The *Edmark Reading Program* (Edmark Associates, 1972) is a sight word approach to teaching severely limited readers. The learner needs only to be able to imitate verbalizations and to point to a response prior to beginning this program. Limited to only 150 vocabulary words the program serves as a good beginning approach to reading. The 227 lessons involve word recognition, direction books, picture-phrase matching, and story books. Having completed the Edmark Reading Program, the child should have enough foundation in reading to begin a more sophisticated approach. A teacher well versed in the reading sequence may wish to supplement the Edmark method with initial phonics training.

Rebus Reading Program

Rebus reading involves the decoding of pictures or symbols as printed words. *The Peabody Rebus Reading Program* (Woodcock & Clark, 1969) uses a series of 120 rebus words to teach initial reading through a programmed instruction technique. Words are gradually introduced using a fading strategy to replace the rebus with the printed symbol. A supplementary lessons kit provides activities for group instruction.

Hegge-Kirk-Kirk Remedial Reading Drills

This remedial reading method is designed specifically for young children who have not learned to read within the first few years of school. The *Hegge-Kirk-Kirk Remedial Reading Drills* are phonics oriented and are based on the learning principles of repetition, social reinforcement, consistency, and gradual change.

Over fifty drills are divided into four parts: the most frequently used sounds, combinations of frequent sounds, less frequently used sounds, and sound exceptions. Each drill can serve as an instructional lesson, or for initial reading, the materials can be used as a complete program.

Additional Remedial Suggestions

There are many possible causes of reading problems, as well as numerous choices for adaptations to the reading program. Many of the more severe difficulties can be appropriately dealt with by using a remediation method such as those described earlier in this chapter. Less intense problems may be alleviated through simple adjustments to the reading task. The following Problem Remediation Guide (Figure 11.13) offers suggestions for some frequently occurring reading difficulties which can easily be incorporated into the reading program.

Commercially produced materials are often helpful in locating and remediating reading problems. Three excellent examples of reading resources that each teacher would find useful are:

1. Carrillo, L. W. *Informal reading readiness experiences* (revised). New York: Noble & Noble Publishers, Inc., 1971.

401

Problem	Suggested Remediation
1. Child is unable to follow a line of print on a printed page.	a. Provide reading markers to highlight only one word, phrase, or line of print at one time.
	b. Cut the passage lines into strips allowing the child to read one strip at a time.
2. Child has trouble responding to comprehension questions after reading a passage.	a. Provide the child with a study guide consisting of focus questions prior to reading the passage.
	b. Tape-record the child's reading. Have the child listen to the tape while silently reading the passage. This may increase comprehension.
	c. Ask the child to read the passage twice through for decoding and then once for comprehension.
3. Child has difficulty learning new sight vocabulary.	a. Use a multisensory approach to learning the word(s). Attending and retention should increase along with stronger modality input.
	b. Have the child focus upon configuration cues. This increases attention to similarities and differences among words.
	they there that
4. Child has difficulty transferring words learned in isolation to context reading.	a. Highlight newly learned words in a passage with yellow marker. Gradually fade this stimulus cue.
5. Child is unable to generalize phonetic rules.	a. Use the following steps to assist transfer from rule learning to context reading.
	—Learn the rule in isolation.
	—Restate the rule when given several words the rule applies to.
	—Select words from a list of words that the rule applies to.
	—Select words from a passage that the rule applies to.
	b. Emphasize sight vocabulary development.

FIGURE 11.13 Reading Problem Remediation Guide

2. Ekwall, E. E. *Locating and correcting reading difficulties* (2nd ed.).
    Columbus, Ohio: Charles E. Merrill Publishing Co., 1977.
3. Russell, D. H., and Karp, E. E. *Reading aids through the grades* (2nd
    ed. by Mueser, A. M.). New York: Teachers College Press, 1975.

High-Interest, Low-Vocabulary Materials

Many problem readers, as they grow older, become discouraged when confronted with books geared to their interest level since such materials are often
beyond their reading ability. Because this problem is common, many materials are now being produced as high-interest, low-vocabulary books. These
books are written with an easy vocabulary while maintaining an interest level
appropriate for the more mature reader. The teacher needs to be certain that
the child has access to high-interest, low-vocabulary materials and that they
cover a variety of topics relevant to the child's age, sex, and interest.

The following list (Figure 11.14) provides information concerning
high-interest, low-vocabulary books.

Reading in the Content Areas

Throughout the school year the influence of reading is such that mildly
handicapped children may experience problems in all content areas if their
reading ability is below their grade level. When such a discrepancy exists, the
task in a content subject becomes twofold: to manage the subject reading
material and then to learn the properties of the subject. The responsibility
rests with the teacher to provide the child with the needed content knowledge and skills without being hindered by reading problems. Many techniques of individualized instruction are helpful, such as peer tutoring, audio
and visual media usage, small group activities and discussion, and project or
performance evaluation instead of written tests. Other means of coping with
the dilemma of reading in content areas are:

1. The application of a readability formula
2. The development of multilevel reading material
3. Directed reading activities (DRA)

Readability Formula

A readability formula estimates the reading level of a book or material
and is used most often with supplementary materials which are not clearly

403

Publisher	Title	Reading Grade Level	Interest Grade Level
Allyn & Bacon	*Breakthrough Series*	1–6	7–12
Benefic Press	*Animal Adventure Series*	PP–1	1–4
	Butternut Bill Series	PP–1	1–6
	Button Family Adventures	PP–3	1–3
	Cowboys of Many Races	PP–5	1–6
	Cowboy Sam Series	PP–3	1–6
	Dan Frontier Series	PP–4	1–7
	Mystery Adventure Series	2–6	4–9
	Moonbeam Series	PP–3	1–6
	Racine Wheels Series	2–4	4–9
	Sailor Jack Series	PP–3	1–6
	Space-Age Books	1–3	3–6
	Space Science Fiction	2–6	4–9
	Sports Mystery Stories	2–4	4–9
	What Is It Series	1–4	1–8
	World of Adventure	2–6	4–9
Book-Lab	*The Hip Reader*	PP–3	4–9
	Young Adult Sequential Reading Action Program	6	6–9
Bobbs-Merrill	*Childhood of Famous Americans*	4–5	4–9
Children's Press	*About Books*	1–4	2–8
	Fun to Read Classics	5–8	5–12
	The Frontiers of America Series	3	3–8
	I Want To Be Series	2–4	4–6
	Rally Series	4–5	7–10
	True Book Series	2–3	3–6
John Day Publishing	*Reading Fundamentals for Teenagers*	3–4	6–8
	Let's Visit Series	4–7	7–10
Doubleday	*Signal Books*	4	5–9
Field Educational Publications	*Americans All Series*	4	3–9
	Checkered Flag Series	2–4	6–12
	Deep Sea Adventures	2–5	3–11
	Jim Forest Readers	1–3	1–7
	The Morgan Bay Mysteries	2–4	4–11
	The Reading Motivated Series	4–5	4–10
Fearon Publishers	*Pacemaker Classics*	2	7–12
	Pacemaker True Adventures	2	5–12
	Pacemaker Story Books	2	7–12

Publisher	Title	Reading Grade Level	Interest Grade Level
Finney Co.	Finding Your Job	2–5	4–10
Follett	Interesting Reading Series	2–3	7–12
	Turner Career Guidance Series	5–6	8–10
	Turner-Livingston Communication Series	5–6	11–12
	Turner-Livingston Reading Series	4–6	7–9
	Vocational Reading Series	4–6	9–12
Frank Richards	The Getting Along Series	3–5	4–8
	Getting and Holding a Job	3–5	4–10
Garrard Publishing	American Folktales	3–4	2–6
	Basic Vocabulary Series	1–2	1–4
	Discovery Books	2–3	2–5
	Junior Science Books	4–5	6–9
	Folklore of the World Series	3–4	2–8
	First Reading Books	1–2	1–4
	Myths, Tales, and Legends	5	4–7
	Pleasure Reading Series	4–5	3–7
	Regional American Stories	4	3–6
	Sports	4	3–6
Globe Book	Stories for Teenagers	6	6–12
Grosset & Dunlap	We Were There Series	4–7	7–9
	How and Why Wonder Books	4–7	7–9
E. M. Hale	Getting to Know Books	4–5	4–9
	How and Why Series	4–5	4–9
	Story Of Series	3–4	3–9
Harper & Row	American Adventure Series	3–6	4–8
Harr Wagner	Jim Forest Readers	3–6	4–8
	Reading Motivated Series	2–6	3–8
	Deep Sea Adventure Series	4–8	5–10
	Wildlife Adventure Series	4–6	5–10
	Morgan Bay Mysteries	4–6	5–10
D. C. Heath	Teen-Age Tales	4–6	6–11
	Reading Caravan Series	3–6	5–10
Longmans, Roberts & Green	Tempo Books	7–8	9–11
Mafex Associates	Magpie Series	1–3	4–8
	Target Series	2–4	4–9
	Citizens All	1–3	4–8

continued

Publisher	Title	Reading Grade Level	Interest Grade Level
William Morrow	Morrow's High Interest/Easy Reading Books	1–8	4–10
Oxford University Press	Wildrush Books	3–4	5–9
Pyramid Books	Hi-Lo Reading Series	3–8	5–12
Random House	All About Books	4–6	4–11
	Gateway Books	2–3	3–8
	Landmark Books	5–7	5–11
	Step-up Books	2–3	3–9
	World Landmark Books	5–6	5–11
Readers Digest Services	Reading Skill Builders	1–4	2–5
	Adult Readers for Slow Learners	3–7	4–10
Scholastic Magazine and Book Services	Action Libraries	2–3	4–7
Steck-Vaughn	Reading Essential Series	1–8	4–10
	Read Better With Jim King Series	2–8	4–10
Watts Franklin	First Book Series	4–7	7–9
	Let's Find Out Series	2–4	5–6
Xerox Educational Publications	Know Your World	3–5	4–8

Source: Kirk, S., Kliebhan, J., and Lerner, J. Teaching reading to slow and disabled learners. Boston: Houghton Mifflin Company, 1978, pp. 248–250.

FIGURE 11.14   High-Interest, Low-Vocabulary Chart

marked according to level. Many of the early formulas involved time-consuming calculations and resulted in inaccurate estimates at certain levels (Bormuth, 1969). However, more recently developed formulas have overcome these difficulties and are beneficial in determining and adjusting reading levels for mildly handicapped students.

The Fry Readability Formula is a sample technique which is easy to use, quick to compute, and applicable throughout the range of grade levels. The following directions and graph will guide the teacher in using the Fry procedure (Figure 11.15).

A readability formula is correctly used to evaluate the application of reading material for a child of a certain reading ability. After computing readability, the teacher can decide whether it is appropriate to place the child

Average number of syllables per 100 words

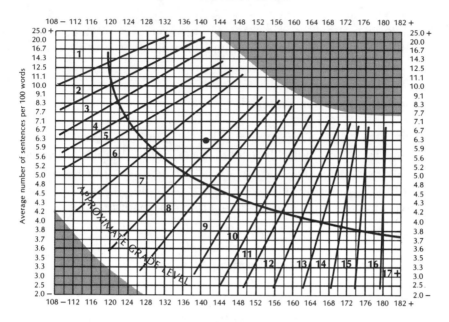

Source: E. Fry, Rutgers University Reading Center.

FIGURE 11.15   The Fry Readability Graph

Expanded Directions for Working Readability Graph

1. Randomly select three (3) sample passages and count out exactly 100 words each, beginning with the beginning of a sentence. Do count proper nouns, initializations, and numerals.
2. Count the number of sentences in the hundred words, estimating length of the fraction of the last sentence to the nearest one-tenth.
3. Count the total number of syllables in the 100-word passage. If you don't have a hand counter available, an easy way is to simply put a mark above every syllable over one in each word, then when you get to the end of the passage, count the number of marks and add 100. Small calculators can also be used as counters by pushing numeral 1, then push the + sign for each word or syllable when counting.
4. Enter graph with *average* sentence length and *average* number of syllables; plot dot where the two lines intersect. Area where dot is plotted will give you the approximate grade level.
5. If a great deal of variability is found in syllable count or sentence count, putting more samples into the average is desirable.
6. A word is defined as a group of symbols with a space on either side; thus, *Joe, IRA, 1945,* and *&* are each one word.
7. A syllable is defined as a phonetic syllable. Generally, there are as many syllables as vowel sounds. For example, *stopped* is one syllable and *wanted* is two syllables. When counting syllables for numerals and initializations, count one syllable for each symbol. For example, *1945* is four syllables, *IRA* is three syllables, and *&* is one syllable.

407

with the material or whether adjustments in reading level are necessary. Readability is the first step in the development of multilevel reading materials.

Multilevel Reading Material

Often textbooks, worksheets, task cards, and other content area reading material are at too difficult a level for a mildly handicapped child to handle. However, it is possible to adjust the reading level to that of the student without losing the relevant content. A material may be adapted to several levels in order to accommodate a range of reading abilities within the classroom.

Procedure for Adjusting Reading Material
1. Apply a readability formula to the original work and determine the reading level.
2. Decide on the level(s) of difficulty to which the material needs to be adjusted.
3. Rewrite the material, reducing sentence lengths and using more easily read synonyms for complex words. Use the readability formula to check the new level.
4. Type the new passage for easy reading. It is also preferable to mount or laminate the new material for repeated use.
5. Reproduce (cut and paste) illustrations, graphs, and charts from the original work and attach them to the new selection.
6. Develop comprehension questions equivalent to those associated with the original work.

For a textbook or any large material it is preferable to develop a series of short passages which contain the most essential information. The materials may be adjusted by parent volunteers, older students, or more advanced peers who can summarize the material they have read. Although this task may seem formidable, it is possible to achieve, and in some cases may be necessary if appropriate high-interest, low-vocabulary materials are not available.

Directed Reading Activity

The directed reading approach is used to facilitate comprehension by helping the student focus on and learn the most relevant parts of a content material. For a mildly handicapped child whose primary reading problems are associated with attention and/or comprehension this approach may be extremely helpful. According to Otto, Peters, and Peters (1977) a directed reading activity consists of the following strategic steps:

1. Technical vocabulary should be taught. After introducing the word and using it in a sentence, help the student understand its phonetic components and its associated meaning.
2. Formulate purposes for reading and state them as a series of questions. These will help the student focus on essential aspects of the content. Holding a class discussion while learning the technical vocabulary might allow the students to develop their own questions.
3. Guide the student during the beginning oral reading passages to help in applying vocabulary and the questioning procedure.
4. Allow the student to complete the material silently and to pursue questions and solutions independently.
5. Discuss the questions with the student to check for comprehension and to emphasize transfer and application of the material.

SUMMARY

Reading is a fundamental learning tool which is important for both academic and social independence. To appreciate reading requires an understanding of such terms as literacy, functional literacy, and functional reading. Mildly handicapped children experience a broad range of reading abilities, and program goals must be adjusted accordingly.

This chapter explored the reading process (theory and skill acquisition) and related structural components of prominent reading programs to the learning problems of mildly handicapped children. Following a diagnostic-prescriptive format attention was given to assessment of reading abilities and then to instructional and remedial strategies. Finally the importance of reading in the content areas was discussed and practical applications for adapting subject matter were given.

POINTS FOR DISCUSSION AND ACTIVITIES

1. Select a variety of supplementary readings (library books, social studies materials, arithmetic workbooks) from different grade levels. Apply Fry's readability formula and ascertain the reading level. Does it correspond with the intended grade level? Are the structural elements of the material (print size, illustrations, colors, subject matter) compatible with the reading level?

2. During the course of a day, record all phrases, words, etc., that you encounter and that you feel are essential for you to comprehend in order to function normally. Compare your list with others in the class. Make a composite list and discuss how life would change if you were unable to read and comprehend these words.

3. Give an Informal Reading Inventory to a child. Develop the inventory from a graded reading series or use a commercially produced one. Analyze the information and write a report for the child's classroom teacher.

4. Try to read a technical manual or a law brief. Afterwards, record whether you attended to decoding or comprehension of the material. Try to assess how you "attacked" unfamiliar words.

5. Next time you are at a party or in a large, talkative group, focus your attention on someone who seems to be attending to two or more conversations at once. What are they actually doing? Discuss with the person how much of each conversation he was able to attend to.

6. Examine three different reading approaches, carefully reviewing the materials, teacher's guides, and supplementary readings. Make a list of elements which you feel would be advantageous for teaching problem learners.

7. It is commonly believed that the most significant variable in the success of a reading program is the teacher and not the approach itself. What teacher variables do you think would influence reading success?

8. Field test the effectiveness of using a directed reading activity in a content area. To do this, select two passages of equal length and difficulty. Use the DRA approach with one and with the other, ask the student to first read and then answer questions. Are the results significant enough to support the use of DRA?

REFERENCES

Bormuth, J. The cloze readability procedure. *Elementary English*, 1968, *45*, 429–436.

Brown, L., and Perlmutter, L. Teaching functional reading to trainable level retarded students. *Education and Training of the Mentally Retarded*, 1971, 6, 74–84.

Carnine, D. Phonic versus look-say: Transfer to new words. *The Reading Teacher*, 1977, *30*, 636–640.

Chall, J. Report of the committee on reading, National Academy of Education. In J. Carroll and J. Chall (Eds.), *Toward a literate society*. New York: McGraw-Hill Book Company, 1975.

Cohen, S. B., and Plaskon, S. P. Selecting a reading approach for the mainstreamed child. *Language Arts*, 1978, *55*, 966–970.

Dechant, E. V. *Improving the teaching of reading*. Englewood Cliffs, N. J.: Prentice-Hall, Inc., 1964, 1970.

Dolch, E. W. *Teaching primary reading* (2nd ed.). Champaign, Ill.: Garrard Press, 1950.

Edmark Associates. *Edmark Reading Program, Teacher's Guide.* Seattle: Edmark Associates, 1972.

Ekwall, E. E. *Locating and correcting reading difficulties* (2nd ed.). Columbus, Ohio: Charles E. Merrill Publishing Company, 1977.

Engelmann, S., and Bruner, E. C. *Distar reading: An instructional system.* Chicago: Science Research Associates, 1969.

Fernald, G. *Remedial techniques in basic school subjects.* New York: McGraw-Hill Book Company, 1943.

Frostig, M. The needs of teachers for specialized information on reading. In W. M. Cruickshank (Ed.), *The teacher of brain-injured children.* Syracuse, N.Y.: Syracuse University Press, 1966.

Fry, E. B. *The Journal of Reading,* April 1968, *11,* 513–616.

Gillespie, P. H., and Johnson, L. *Teaching reading to the mildly retarded child.* Columbus, Ohio: Charles E. Merrill Publishing Company, 1974.

Gillingham, A., and Stillman, B. *Remedial work for reading, spelling, and penmanship.* New York: Hackett and Wilhelms, 1936.

Gillingham, A., and Stillman, B. *Remedial teaching for children with specific disability in reading, spelling, and penmanship.* Cambridge, Mass.: Educator's Publishing Service, 1968.

Goodman, K. S. A linguistic study of cues and miscues in reading. *Elementary English,* 1965, *42,* 639–643.

Goodman, K. S. (Ed.). *Miscue analysis: Application to reading instruction.* Urbana, Ill.: National Council of Teachers of English, 1973.

Hansen, C. L., and Eaton, M. D. Reading. In N. G. Haring, T. C. Lovitt, M. D. Eaton, and C. L. Hansen (Eds). *The fourth R: Research in the classroom.* Columbus, Ohio: Charles E. Merrill Publishing Company, 1978.

Harris, L. A. *How to increase reading ability* (5th ed.). New York: David McKay Company, 1970.

Harris, L. A., and Sipay, E. *Effective teaching of reading* (2nd ed.). New York: David McKay Company, 1971.

Harris, L. A., and Smith, C. B. *Reading instruction* (2nd ed.). New York: Holt, Rinehart and Winston, 1972.

Hillerich, R. L. Word lists—Getting it all together. *The Reading Teacher,* 1974, *27,* 353–360.

Jeffrey, W. E., and Samuels, S. J. The effect of method of reading training on initial learning and transfer. *Journal of Verbal Learning and Verbal Behavior,* 1967, *6,* 354–358.

Jenkins, J. R., Barksdale, A., and Clinton, L. Improving reading comprehension and oral reading: Generalization across behaviors, settings and time. *Journal of Learning Disabilities,* 1978, *11,* 607–617.

Kaluger, G., and Kolson, C. J. *Reading and learning disabilities* (2nd ed.) Columbus, Ohio: Charles E. Merrill Publishing Company, 1978.

Karlin, R. *Teaching elementary reading.* New York: Harcourt Brace Jovanovich, 1971.

Kirk, S., Kliebhan, J., and Lerner, J. *Teaching reading to slow and disabled learners.* Boston: Houghton Mifflin Co., 1978.

Kirkman, P. K., Endo, G. T., and Crandall, J. A. Contextual versus noncontextual word presentation techniques on acquisition, generalization, and retention with EMR children. *Education and Training of the Mentally Retarded*, 1979, *14*, 137-142.

LaBerge, D., and Samuels, S. J. Toward a theory of automatic information processing in reading. *Cognitive Psychology*, 1974, *6*, 293-323.

Larsen, S. C., and Hammill, D. D. The relationship of selected visual-perceptual abilities to school learning. *Journal of Special Education*, 1975, *9*, 281-291.

Lichtman, M. The development and validation of R/EAL, an instrument to assess functional literacy. *Journal of Reading Behavior*, 1974, *6*, 167-187.

Mann, P. H., and Suiter, P. *Handbook in diagnostic teaching: A learning disabilities approach*. Abridged ed. Boston: Allyn and Bacon, Inc., 1974.

May, F. B., and Eliot, S. B. *To help children read*. 2nd ed. Columbus, Ohio: Charles E. Merrill Publishing Company, 1978.

McCarthy, W., and Oliver, J. Some tactile-kinesthetic procedures for teaching reading to slow learning children. *Exceptional Children*, 1965, *31*, 419-421.

Newcomer, P. L., and Magee, P. Predictive indices of reading failure in learning disabled children. *Educational Research Quarterly*, 1977, *2*, 17-23.

Otto, W., McMenemy, R., and Smith, R. *Corrective and remedial teaching* (2nd ed.). Boston: Houghton Mifflin Co., 1973.

Otto, W., Peters, C., and Peters, N. *Reading problems: A multidisciplinary perspective*. Menlo Park, Calif.: Addison-Wesley Publishing Co., 1977.

Proe, S., and Wade, D. The effects of contingent praise upon the achievement of a junior high school student in oral reading accuracy in probes above functional grade level, 1973 (ERIC No. ED 104 042).

Samuels, S. J. Attentional processes in reading: The effect of pictures in the acquisition of reading responses. *Journal of Educational Psychology*, 1967, *58*, 337-342.

Samuels, S. J., Begy, G., and Chen, C. C. Comparison of word recognition speed and strategies of less skilled and more highly skilled readers. *Reading Research Quarterly*, 1975-1976, *11*, 72-86.

Savage, J., and Mooney, J. *Teaching reading to children with special needs*. Boston: Allyn and Bacon, Inc., 1979.

Singer, H., Samuels, S. J., and Spiroff, J. The effect of pictures and contextual conditions on learning responses to printed words. *Reading Research Quarterly*, 1973-1974, *9*, 555-567.

Slingerland, B. H. *A multi-sensory approach to language arts for specific language disability children*. Cambridge, Mass.: Educators Publishing Service, 1974.

Smith, N. B. The many faces of reading comprehension. *The Reading Teacher*, 1969, *22*, 249-259, 291.

Snell, M. E. Functional reading. In M. E. Snell (Ed.), *Systematic instruction of the moderately and severely handicapped*. Columbus, Ohio: Charles E. Merrill Publishing Company, 1978.

Strang, R. *Diagnostic teaching of reading* (2nd ed.). New York: McGraw-Hill, 1969.

Traub, N., and Bloom, F. *Recipe for reading*. Cambridge, Mass.: Educators Publishing Service, 1970.

Van Etten, G. A look at reading comprehension. *Journal of Learning Disabilities*, 1978, *11*, 30-39.

Wallace, G., and Larsen, S. C. *Educational assessment of learning problems: Testing for teaching.* Boston: Allyn & Bacon, 1978.

Wilson, R. *Diagnostic and remedial reading for classroom and clinic* (2nd ed.). Columbus, Ohio: Charles E. Merrill Publishing Company, 1972.

Woodcock, R. W., and Clark, C. R. *Peabody rebus reading program.* Circle Pines, Minn.: American Guidance Service, Inc., 1969.

12

Active Expression and Nonverbal Skill Development

How much of what we say is contained in the mannerisms that we utilize to get our messages across? At what point in the conversation do we recognize that gesture, facial expression, distance, and body movement are important to overall communication effectiveness? When do we realize we are unable to communicate with someone because of how that individual physically conducts him or herself? By the same token, how often are we very comfortable with someone else because of the very positive nonverbal messages that are sent? The nonverbal aspects of a communication encounter that complement the linguistic parameters are often elusive and difficult to isolate. When pointed out, however, most people realize that nonverbal actions do constitute a very important segment of communication activity.

A child's teacher should be concerned equally with one's ability to interpret and to utilize nonverbal cues and clues as with the skills of oral speaking, auding, composition, handwriting, spelling, and reading. The language arts program should focus attention on nonverbal skill development to much the same extent that activities, drills, and instruction are devoted to the other areas. At least *some* of the materials that are introduced into the

415

classroom should examine the role that nonverbal activity plays in message encoding and decoding.

All too often, the demands of the curriculum necessitate the removal or elimination of various parts of a topic or subject. Unfortunately the language arts curriculum is no exception. It seems that the emphasis on teaching the basics of reading and writing has overshadowed the development of general communication effectiveness—of which skill in the utilization of nonverbal elements is a key ingredient. How can the teacher incorporate into the language arts curriculum work in nonverbal skill development? What aspects of this seemingly difficult component of the communication act does one elect to include, to focus attention on, and to exercise in the classroom? Where does one begin with the mildly handicapped or the normal child in nonverbal communication skill awareness? What must be taken into account *before* an instructional program can begin?

Nonverbal Communication and Communication Models

In an earlier chapter considerable attention was given to various communication models to emphasize the role that the teacher can play in developing an awareness in children of the act of communication. In each model, stress was placed on the manner in which a particular message was transmitted from person A to person B via a particular channel. Naturally, it was understood that a number of factors affect the degree to which a message transmission succeeds or fails. In each two-way model, the interpretation of the message hinged to a large extent on the ability of *both* parties to respond to the numerous subtle features of the exchange and to judge the activity accordingly.

The discussion of the models of communication did focus, to some extent, on the role that nonverbal ingredients in a communication encounter played. The Byker and Anderson (1975) definition of communication as "the sharing of information" did imply that the information exchange process embodied the nonverbal elements. Byker and Anderson's notion of consubstantiality (see chapter 3) included the fact that the "on-going, co-active, developmental sharing of information" between Person A and Person B necessitated that a common ground be reached in terms of two individuals:

• Ability to reason
• Ability to organize tendencies and/or dispositions
• Sensitivity to language utilization along both verbal *and* nonverbal lines
• Attitudes and feelings towards each other

Only when some overlap exists in each of these areas can communication take place. The nonverbal elements in the model were certainly not singled out as being more or less important than reasoning ability, or attitudes, or dispositions towards a topic, but they were included as *essential* aspects of the communicative act. In fact, the very wording of the reference indicates that language sharing activity is not complete unless it is linked to nonverbal considerations.

Earlier models of the communication act, such as those advanced by Aristotle, Plato, and Socrates, were as strong in their orientation to the role that nonlanguage elements played in determining the successfulness of an encounter as those of more recent origin. Aristotle's view of communication activity as an act of persuasion is as much a study of the role nonverbal activity plays in shaping opinion as is the work of Faust (1970) who focused attention on body language alone.

In Aristotle's time the oration was the primary vehicle for the dissemination of information. A single speech could determine the fate of a fellow worker, the degree to which taxes would be levied, or the extensiveness of political policy. The way the orator constructed the presentation, both in terms of the language that was used *and* the mannerisms that were employed, would serve to rally an audience to offer support or would discourage the casting of votes. It was virtually essential that the political figures in ancient Greece be masters of oration and experts in the usages of gestures, facial expressions, and body language. Without such skills, it is doubtful that the system of government as it then existed would have achieved the level of greatness and importance in historians' eyes that it did.

In today's society, the role that persuasion plays in the shaping of policy is no less important. Certainly, public speaking is no longer the sole means by which messages and information are conveyed and attitudes are shaped, yet a major portion of personal day-to-day living involves what might be called "persuasive behaviors." So very often children, as well as adults, find themselves in situations that warrant careful explanation, support, justification, or compromise. Such communicative activity is no less significant than the major orations of Aristotle's time in terms of the impact on a single individual. It is not unlikely that one's ability to construct a message will result in a particular success, promotion, or profit that might have otherwise been unobtained. Surely, the individual's utilization of nonverbal elements can be said to account for a portion of the success of such encounters.

Nonverbal Communication in the Classroom

In the school environment the interactions that take place between the teacher and the student on a daily basis rely heavily on nonverbal cues and clues. The decision a child may make in the classroom to do or not to do a particular thing for a particular person depends to a large extent on how the child interprets the nonverbal messages accompanying a statement. The teacher must be sensitive to the numerous situations that may signal a child's inability to key into nonverbal elements. One might notice, for example, the following:

- Failure on the part of the child to change a particular behavior or to stop an activity, *even though* the tone of voice, the gestures, and the facial expressions indicate displeasure with what the child is doing.
- An inability to change topics of conversation when it is obvious that the listener is having trouble following the discussion and is showing signs of boredom or disinterest.
- Consistent attempts to respond to questions that are asked rhetorically and the nonverbal cues clearly indicated that no response is called for.
- The degree to which the child successfully interacts with peers in game-like activities or on the playground and the ease with which other children can "read" a child's feelings about a particular assignment, task, or topic.

Much of what occurs in the classroom revolves around a nonverbal signal system. At work in each educational setting is an informal set of rules that are evoked and adhered to by the informed group nonverbally. Such unspoken codes of behavior are reinforced continually by the actions and the activity of the class. The child who has difficulty keying in to this management technique and behavioral regulation procedure by being observant and sensitive to nonverbal clues and cues is bound to experience frustration and alienation. The classroom teacher must be aware of the manner in which each child "reads" and "understands" the role that nonverbal communication plays in daily living.

Nonverbal Communication and the Mildly Handicapped

Sanders (1976) has indicated that in any communication encounter, each participant must work to establish a common set of referents or values, share a similar symbol system, and possess a knowledge of the manner in which those symbols can be combined to express a pattern of ideas or thoughts. Both participants in a communication exchange, therefore, must be capable of making whatever adjustments and generalizations that the situation may call for in order to achieve a particular goal or objective, and thus communication success.

It has been noted previously that one of the characteristics of the mildly handicapped child is an inability to make generalizations and to transfer information from one situation to another. The mildly handicapped child does not effectively encode and decode linguistic information. Whether this is a result of poor attention, low intellectual abilities, a low tolerance for frustration, or the result of a physical disability (e.g., visual or hearing impairment) is certainly difficult to assess. What is quite apparent, however, is the fact that *there is more than a casual relationship between handicappism and difficulty in communication* (Lloyd, 1976, p. xi).

Since the communication act involves both the verbal and the non-verbal elements, it is essential that the participants in an exchange focus attention on both these aspects. If a major portion of the information contained in message conveyance is embedded in nonverbal clues and cues, the listener must be a competent interpreter of such signs. Much of this ability is thought to be taken for granted by most speakers and listeners. One almost assumes that a partner in a communication encounter is attending *totally* to his or her counterpart. Such, however, may not be the case. It is quite common for a communication exchange to break down simply because of drifting attention on the part of one individual. With the handicapped, problems in communication may be the result *primarily* of just such attentional deficits.

It has been noted that nonverbal features in a communication exchange consist primarily, but not exclusively, of gesture, facial expression, and body movements. Some treatments of the topic, as have been presented in chapter 3, include still other aspects of communication such as distance usage and paralinguistic phenomena such as intonation, pitch, stress, and juncture. Since, however, gesture, body movement, and facial expressions constitute the "purist" nonverbal ingredients in the communication models studies to date, it is important to examine just how the handicapped have been found to respond to such factors.

Thomas (1978), who has summarized a number of studies of handicapped individuals' facility at interpreting and attending to nonverbal cues in communcation settings, has come to the conclusion that "people differ in their ability to decode emotions from nonverbal behavior" (p. 37). This statement is based on the fact that research investigations have indicated that:

1. There is a low but positive correlation between intelligence and the ability to identify facial expressions (Kanner, 1931; Weisenberger, 1956).
2. While there were no significant differences between 96 college students, 61 mental retardates, and 50 mental patients in their ability to judge the emotional states of individuals shown in still photographs, the differences in ratings between the groups suggest that individuals may differ in their ability to evaluate emotional states based on nonverbal cues as pathological considerations are taken into account (Levy, Orr, & Rosenzweig, 1960).

3. Learning-disabled adolescents when compared to a control group matched for age and intelligence appear to consistently misinterpret emotional states (e.g., frustration, joy, fear, embarrassment, or anger) when nonverbal factors alone are the basis for decision making (Wiig & Harris, 1974; Bryan, 1974).

Many of the difficulties handicapped individuals experience in information sharing seem to be the result of a possible inability to respond appropriately to social cues in a communication encounter.

Developing Instructional Programs

It would not be difficult to elaborate even more extensively on the notion that nonverbal skills *are* a requirement for successful communication. While such information would document the necessity of dealing with this neglected skill in the language arts curriculum, especially with the mildly handicapped child, the question would remain: What can the teacher of the mildly handicapped child do to develop an ability in this social skill area?

We suggest that the teacher of the mildly handicapped child focus at least a part of the language arts curriculum on the development of nonverbal communication skills. It is clearly an open-ended mandate. There are numerous alternative activities available to the teacher. The specific approach that is taken is more a function of the "creativity" of the teacher and the degree of willingness to experiment with unusual and different approaches to curriculum.

In terms of actual instruction in this very essential, yet sometimes subtle area, we suggest a focus on the role that *active expression* can play in developing a child's ability in this aspect of communication. It was stated in chapter 8 that role-playing activities are proven strategies for instruction with mildly handicapped children. This focus on the development of a language arts curriculum that incorporates active expression as a vehicle for strengthening nonverbal skills is a highly recommended approach to take. We have found in working with both regular and special educators involved in the mainstreaming of mildly handicapped children that, even though teachers are willing to work with the handicapped child in the regular school curriculum and even though they possess the skills necessary to do so, many teachers often lack a strategy for implementing change. The area of language skill development is no exception. In fact, this particular curriculum component—that of nonverbal skill sensitivity training—is quite often completely avoided because a vehicle for presentation is lacking.

Active Expression—A Historical Perspective

In exploring various alternatives to the development of skills in the domain of nonverbal communication, active expression has consistently revealed itself to be an excellent blend of theory and practice. To better appreciate this particular approach to nonverbal skills development, consider the long history that active expression has had in education.

Active expression, in the form of creative dramatics, was first introduced into the curricula in the School of Speech at Northwestern University in 1924 by Winifred Ward (Karioth, 1970). It was basically through her insistence that drama, as a vehicle for communication skill development, was brought into the ranks of higher education.

Prior to that time, active expression was for the stage, for actors, and for paying audiences. With the unprecedented move by Ward in 1924, drama came into the educational setting. Historically, creative dramatics was at first purely aesthetic, focusing attention on the production of plays. Investigations of the impact such training was having on participants, however, led to the expansion of departments of dramatic arts and to the introduction of such activity at the secondary and elementary school levels. Quite assuredly, the emphasis originally was on "theatre" more so than on movement or communication skill development. Yet, underlying the play presentations was the unspoken rationale that such work was indeed beneficial to children and adults in terms of communication effectiveness.

Active Expression in Fostering Social, Emotional, and Academic Performance

The concept of active expression incorporates itself exceptionally well into the language arts curriculum because of its correspondence to the developmental stages of young children. Cohen (1971) has stated that children's overall movement activity is directly related to their particular developmental stage. According to Cohen, the teacher can see competency, experimentation, testing, and the development of attitudes toward the self as well as the joy the child experiences from simple physical activity and the sharpening of physical ability. Based on direct observations, it is apparent that young children express themselves almost totally through body movements. The child's entire posture, gesturing, level of activity, pace, and positioning provides the alert teacher with clues as to the quality and meaning of the message that the child is conveying. If such a reservoir of information is contained in such nonverbal activity, it is a skill that should be developed and utilized in the curriculum. Active expression does just that.

In terms of academic development, Merow (1970) has stated that creative dramatics provides children with still another vehicle for self-expression, self-exploration, and information processing and presenting. Active expression lays the groundwork for academic advancement for many children because of the degree to which it fosters the growth of a positive self-concept. Generally speaking, the more aware of their own particular abilities in a given area children become, the more positive the learning experience is. Most teachers agree that once a "problem" child has been introduced to an activity in which success can be achieved, a marked improvement in behavior, attitude, and performance is noted as well. Howard (1967) noted that almost *all* children experience success in active expression activities. Children generally are not afraid to express their emotions in role-playing, pantomime, drama, or movement activities. This built-in "success quotient" is still another reason why active expression as an aid to the development of nonverbal skill development should be incorporated into the school curriculum. Undoubtedly, the activity will serve to benefit both the normal and the mildly handicapped child.

From the point of view of socialization, active expression is equally as powerful. Drama, because of its close association with life-like situations that can be couched in fanciful or real experiences provides a vast supply of situations from which both the child and the teacher can draw. Few children find it difficult to express themselves dramatically. In many cases, the children willingly volunteer to "act out" a situation for a variety of reasons, be it class or teacher recognition or simply a way to recount something involving the child. Howard (1967) has noted that even the most shy, self-conscious child is drawn out by creative dramatics and movement in the classroom. Once the child, and in particular the mildly handicapped youngster, is involved, the door is opened to multiple experiences on which to capitalize.

Drama, when properly introduced to the class and implemented, socializes the child by involvement in peer activity. Randall (1967) stressed that communal drama, which places no pressure on a particular individual, results in a temporary loss of self-consciousness, and therefore can serve to draw out even the most isolated and shy individual. Randall further notes that creative dramatics does help children adjust to difficult life situations and improves overall awareness of them, thereby causing successful socialization and adjustment. Dramatic activity stressed, with its emphasis on the nonverbal elements, is undoubtedly a great equalizer of children. Everyone seems to experience the same fears, frustrations, and anxiety associated with dramatic play, yet all profit to the same extent from the experience.

Active expression plays a role in personality development as well as in academic, social, and emotional growth. When the term "personality" is taken to mean the way in which the child views and responds to the surrounding world—objects and persons alike—drama seems, according to

Crosby (1956), to be able to provide a genuine opportunity for expressing those views and perceptions. Crosby noted that with each dramatic play opportunity, the child experiments with preconceived notions of the world about him or her, enlarges upon them, and integrates such interpretations into the overall world view. As a result, these types of activities give the teacher insights into the child's character and emotional state. It is as though the teacher is able to discover through dramatic presentations that which is in no other way communicable. The nonverbal elements, the message conveyance, and the overall posturing that the child takes in such situations is a real key to personality.

Active Expression and Language Development

Just what is the relationship between active expression and language development? To what extent does the teacher effectively foster the development of nonverbal skills by making use of role-playing, movement, and/or pantomime? Up until now, we have stressed the advantages that apparently exist socially, emotionally, and academically from the inclusion of active expression in the language arts curriculum. What specifically does such activity do in terms of communication effectiveness?

Moffett (1968), writing in his *Student Centered Language Arts Curriculum: A Handbook for Teachers,* reinforces the notion that there is a distinct relationship between movement, creative dramatics, and language development. Moffett writes:

> Though movement to sound or pantomime does not seem at first glance related directly to the development of speech, it does in fact lay an important base for it. Nonverbal expression can provide the best pathway to speech development. (1968, p. 41)

It is upon these particular statements that our program for nonverbal skill development focusing on creative dramatics is founded. Children apparently prefer movement and nonverbal means of communication over speech, particularly at an early age (Moffett, 1968, p. 41). Speech only becomes, after a period of time, a specialized way of communication. Young children do not seem to single out speech or print from movement and gesture. The separation occurs at a later point in the child's development when the child runs up against the limitations of movement as a means of expression. The forced awareness that movement cannot express his or her fullest thought causes the child to look to other means for communication—thereby learning the utility of speech. Certainly the movement, gesture, and other nonverbal aspects of

423

earlier means of communication are not simply thrown aside, but are instead used to supplement and to enhance the communication encounter. In Moffett's own words, "speech suddenly begins to accompany other action and justifies itself only when it can do what other actions cannot" (1968, p. 35). The speech act thus emerges from the nonverbal forms.

Active Expression in the Language Arts Curriculum

The following pages are devoted to procedures by which the teacher can incorporate active expression directly into the language arts curriculum as a vehicle for teaching awareness of nonverbal communication cues and clues. Basically, the teacher is teaching awareness of the body, how it works, and how it moves, to reinforce that the mannerisms that we employ supplement the messages that we send verbally. In practice, the teacher is "helping the child discover for himself what arms, legs, hand, and feet can do" (Mosser, 1970, p. 60). By taking just such a posture, the teacher of both the normal and the mildly handicapped child is providing *direct* training in the development of nonverbal communication abilities.

The suggested program for active expression in the classroom for the normal and the mildly handicapped child is outlined below. The teacher should remember that what follows *is a model of an instructional program with suggested activities and techniques*. This is a recommended technique for introducing nonverbal skill training into the classroom. There may well be additional variations on the procedures that are outlined here. In fact, each teacher *will have to* alter the manner in which instruction in nonverbal skills is provided for a particular population. What is recommended, however, is that the instructional program incorporate creative dramatics and movement. The following is a teaching sequence.

Suggestions for Developing an Awareness of Nonverbal Aspects of Communication through Active Expression

Introducing Active Expression to the Class

When the teacher decides to initiate the program, emphasis should be placed on the fact that *all* the children in the class can respond spontaneously and freely. *Any* response is acceptable. There are no right or wrong movements.

Role of the Teacher

There is no need for expertise in the introduction of movement and creative dramatics. From the teacher the children need:

- Supportive encouragement
- A solvable problem
- Anything *but* demonstration!

The Situation

It is recommended that in staging the activity, whether it is a single approach or a weekly or even daily occurrence, the teacher should:

- Allow the children to stand anywhere.
- Make sure that the children do not get in each other's way.
- During nonlocomotor activities make sure each child stays in his or her own space. (To ensure boundaries, draw a chalk circle around the children, or have them stretch their arms and swing around in a circle.)
- Make sure that the children thoroughly understand the problem that is presented.
- Decide in advance on a signal for starting and stopping each movement (e.g., whistle or clap).

The Skills and Activities

Once the setting has been arranged and the ground rules established, the instructional activities can be introduced. Here, the focus is on basic movements, relationships, and problem solving. Examples of each are as follows:

I. Basic Movements
  1. *Locomotor*—movements that propel the body through space
      a. Move about the room or in your own space as many ways that you can.
      b. Skip around the room. Walk. Run. Hop.
      c. Walk to make your name on the floor.
  2. *Nonlocomotor*—movements that a body can do in a fixed space
      a. How can you make yourself tall while sitting down?
      b. Try reaching for one leg as far as you can in any direction.
      c. Hold your shoulders still, reach with your head.

II. Relationships
  1. *With People*
     a. Choose a partner. Face him; move all around him.
     b. Do the same in groups of four to six. Have a leader walk around without touching anyone in the group.
  2. *With Objects*
     a. Can you bounce a ball? Do it.
     b. Can you tap it with your foot? Do it.
     c. Can you tap the ball to make a square on the ground? A circle?
III. Problem Solving
  1. *Hand and Arm*
     a. Pick up a very hot cup of coffee with a saucer.
  2. *Trunk and Arm*
     a. Move a very heavy object.
  3. *Foot and Leg*
     a. Cross a creek stepping only on the stones. Don't get wet!

Developing the Skill

Once the class has been exposed to movement and the way in which it can be incorporated into pantomime and dramatic activity, emphasis can be placed on the development of the skill in terms of knowledge of space utilization and quality of movement.

I. Quality of Movement
  1. *Time—speed of movement*
     a. Walk around the room to the beat of a drum.
        Vary the drum beat. Vary the method of movement.
     b. Walk in quick little steps. Walk in slow, deliberate steps.
  2. *Force—strength of movement*
     a. Can you walk lightly? What kind of animal could you be?
     b. Walk with more force. How is this different from the way you walked before?
     c. Walk with heavy steps.
     d. Push a box that is empty.
     e. Push a box that is full.
II. Space
  1. *Personal space—where you move*
     a. Swing one part of your body. Two. Three. Your whole body. How many parts can you move?

   b. Move one part in quick, sudden movements and another
      more slowly.
   c. Kneel down and move. Lie down and move.
2. *General spaces*—very large areas
   a. Walk and cover as much space as possible
   b. Walk diagonally only.
   c. Walk backwards, sideways.
   d. Move as close to the floor as possible.
   e. Be as tall as possible.
3. *Body shapes*—patterns
   a. Make a line. Was it straight or crooked?
   b. Be small.
4. *Flow*—smooth or broken movements
   a. Walk smoothly.
   b. Use a broken motion. What are some broken motions?

Any of these activities may be done individually or in pairs by matching or by having children contrast movements.

Applying the Skill to Other Activities

Once the children in the class have had ample opportunity to practice, experiment, and explore various alternative nonverbal ways to express themselves through movement, these activities can serve as a means for still other creative dramatic activities. Some of these might be:

- The use of short introductory pantomimes that other children try to guess through observation
- Short plays, improvised or created, that are based on the children's ideas
- Improvisation with assigned parts, a partially scripted play, or the acting out of missing sections
- Discussion or investigations into the uses of drama, movement in advertising
- Exploring still alternative modes of nonverbal expression through body movement—perhaps now incorporating gesture and facial expression to a greater extent.

Source: Adapted from Mosser, G. Movement education: The why and how. *Grade Teacher*, December 1970.

Single Activities to Focus Attention on Nonverbal Communication

Having explored the numerous activities and techniques that can be utilized to teach nonverbal skills through active expression, the teacher can introduce single-session activities that reinforce many of the same awarenesses that a lengthier program in creative dramatics accomplishes. In some situations, it may be more appropriate to use a single event to teach a particular concept or awareness than to develop an entire unit of study.

The following tasks have been brought together from a number of sources, the most notable of which is Hennings' (1974) text titled *Smiles, Nods, and Pauses.* These instructional situations have been grouped according to the nonverbal elements of gesture, facial expression, body language, and activities that focus attention on a combination of these elements in determining the meaning of a particular message or event (see Figure 12.1). The activities that follow should serve as idea starters themselves.

Focus on Gestures

1. Interpreting Impressions (Hennings, 1974, p. 189)
    a. *Objective:* To understand how certain gestures can create an impression.
    b. *Procedure:* Ask volunteers to create the impression of being:
        • Bored
        • Not interested in what the speaker is saying
        • Engrossed in a project, not wanting to be disturbed
        • Relaxed and enjoying a social gathering
        • Confident
        • Shy and afraid
        Then divide children up in groups and have them list the kinds of gestures, motions, poses, or facial expressions that they interpret as showing interest, boredom, relaxation, confidence, shyness, and others.
    c. Discussion: What conclusions can we draw? How can gestures create an impression?
2. Both Hands Tied
    a. Objective: To experience the difficulty of communicating without the use of gestures.
    b. Procedure: Have each child in the class experience the frustration of trying to explain how to perform a particular task, or to give directions without being able to use his or her hands. In this case, one might have the child place both hands in a pillowcase or cloth sack, thus limiting hand movement. If a paper bag is used, a considerable amount of noise will be

428

Focus	Activity Number & Title	Source
Gestures	1. Interpreting Impressions	Hennings, 1974
	2. Both Hands Tied	Cohen & Plaskon, 1979
	3. Speech Without Gestures	Foerster, 1974
Facial Expressions	4. Poem to Paint	King, Katzman, & James, 1976
	5. You Must Have Been a Beautiful Baby	Wiemann & Wiemann, 1975
	6. Who Would You Like to Play With?	Wiemann & Wiemann, 1975
	7. Faces	Hennings, 1974
	8. Read the Picture	Hennings, 1974
	9. Write the Script	Hennings, 1974
	10. How Do You Feel Today?	Hennings, 1974
	11. Read the Message	Hennings, 1974
	12. How Do We Know?	Hennings, 1974
Body Language	13. Watch the Teacher Speak	Hennings, 1964
	14. Watch the Students Speak	Hennings, 1974
	15. We're on T.V.	Hennings, 1974
	16. Ways of Saying It Without Words	Hennings, 1974
	17. Physical Posture	Galvin, Book, & Buys, 1972
Combined Effects of Gesture, Facial Expression & Body Language	18. TV Star	Hennings, 1974
	19. Silent Movies	Hennings, 1974
	20. They're on TV	Hennings, 1974
	21. TV Commercials	Hennings, 1974

FIGURE 12.1   A List of Activities Related to Nonverbal Skill Development and Active Expression

produced every time an unconscious effort is made on the part of the child to use a gesture.

   c. Discussion: How did it feel to have your hands in the sack when you were talking? What kinds of things weren't you able to do? What would have been easier to say if you could have used your hands?

3. Speech Without Gestures (Foerster, 1974, p. 442)

   a. Objective: To find out the effect of verbal language without nonverbal behavior.

   b. Procedure: Go behind a screen or sheet and give an emotional speech or tell a story. Then do it in front of the students.

   c. Discussion: How did the gestures and facial expressions affect the speech? Were they necessary or needed?

Focus on Facial Expressions

4. Poem to Paint (King, Katzman, & James, 1976, p. 90)
   a. Objective: To relate emotions or feelings with facial expressions.
   b. Procedure: Read the poem below to the children and then have them paint faces with different emotions or model them in clay.

"Faces"

I painted a face that was angry
I painted the mouth in a frown

I painted a face that was puzzled
I painted the head upside down

I painted a face that was curious
I painted the eyes large and bright

I painted a face that was sad
I painted it all dark as night

I painted a face that was proud
I painted the chin straight and high

I painted a face that was happy
I painted a gleam in the eye

   c. Discussion: When you are angry, sad, or happy, what does your face look like? Can you think of other feelings that our face expresses?
5. You Must Have Been a Beautiful Baby (Wiemann & Wiemann, 1975, p. 27)
   a. Objective: To recognize that facial expressions can influence one's decisions.
   b. Procedure: Have children bring in baby pictures and write captions for their own and other children's pictures.
   c. Variations: Use current school photos and have each student write a caption for his own picture. Then as a game, have student match the written description with the pictures.
   d. Discussion: How accurate are the captions? What clues prompted you to write the captions? Were some facial expressions easier to write captions for? Were some pictures able to be interpreted in different ways? Did certain facial cues help you match particular pictures with the descriptions?
6. Who Would You Like to Play With? (Wiemann & Wiemann, 1975, p. 17)
   a. Objective: To recognize that facial expressions can influence one's decisions.

    b. Procedure: Cut out children's faces from newspapers and magazines. Line them up on the board and give students a questionnaire: "Who would you pick:

        • To have as a boyfriend?
        • To have as a girlfriend?
        • To play with at recess?
        • To be president of the class?
        • To go to the principal with you?
        • To introduce to your parents?
        • To be lost in the woods with?
        • To help you with your homework?
        • To be the one who always tells the truth?
        • To be the one who stole the candy from the store?
        • To be the one who was involved in a fight?

    c. Discussion: What influenced your decisions? Which decisions were hard to make? How did the faces and eyes influence your decision?

7. Faces (Hennings, 1974, p. 181)

    a. Objective: To realize that messages can be sent through facial expressions.

    b. Procedure: Read the book *Faces* by Barbara Brenner.

    c. Discussion: What are the different ways people can show they are happy? How can we have an expression that covers up how we really feel? Can a smile show different feelings?

8. Read the Picture (Hennings, 1974, p. 177)

    a. Objective: To look at expressive faces in books and see how they show different emotions.

    b. Procedure: Look at various books with pictures expressing emotion or feelings, such as Maurice Sendak's *Where the Wild Things Are,* Dr. Seuss's *Horton Hatches the Egg,* Evaline Ness's *Sam, Bangs and Moonshine,* Mercer Mayer's *A Boy, A Dog, and A Frog,* and *A Boy, A Frog, and A Friend,* and John Hamberger's *A Sleepless Day* and *The Lazy Dog.* Also, wordless books are good for interpreting mood and action.

    c. Discussion: What is happening? How do you know how the characters are feeling? What do their faces express?

9. Write the Script (Hennings, 1974, p. 179)

    a. Objective: To interpret facial expressions and actions from a filmstrip.

    b. Procedure: Have children look at wordless filmstrips and write a story for it. Educational Enrichment Materials puts out silent filmstrips of wordless books like Martha Alexander's *Out! Out! Out!* and *Bobo's Dream,* and Mercer Mayer's *Frog, Where Are You?* Or use sound filmstrips without sound, put out by Scholastic Magazines, Inc.; Teaching Resources, Inc.; Weston Woods; or Miller-Brody Productions. Have the children write a plot and then listen to the soundtrack to see who came the closest to the actual story.

    c. Discussion: How do the characters feel? How do we know? Do they look happy, angry, or fearful?

10. How Do You Feel Today? (Hennings, 1974, p. 181)

    a. Objective: To be able to link facial expressions with emotions.

    b. Procedure: Put a mirror along with this chart over a sink or counter:

```
┌─────────────────────────────────────────────┐
│ HOW DO YOU FEEL TODAY?                        │
│        LOOK AND SEE                           │
│   HAPPY?                   LONELY?            │
│   SAD?                     NERVOUS?          │
│   TIRED?                   MAD?               │
│   CURIOUS?                 ANGRY?             │
└─────────────────────────────────────────────┘
```

    c. Discussion: What does your face look like when you are sad, happy, angry? How do we know you are mad?

11. Read the Message (Hennings, 1974, pp. 181–182)

    a. Objective: To be able to interpret emotions from facial expressions.

    b. Procedure: Divide the class into two teams. One member leaves the room, while another member draws a slip with an emotion written on it (boredom, exhaustion, lonely, fear, hopelessness, irritation). The team member comes back and tries to guess the emotion only from the teammate's facial expressions. No physical activity is allowed, and the time limit is two minutes. One point is scored for each correct answer.

    c. Discussion: Which emotions were easier to get across than others? Why? Why are some people better at it? Was it easier using the face or the body to convey emotion?

12. How Do We Know? (Hennings, 1974, pp. 182–183)

    a. Objective: To discover when someone is expressing an emotion through facial expressions.

    b. Procedure: Have a discussion on emotions and feelings. Have children describe the way they look when they have certain feelings and then have them act it out if they want.

    c. Variations: Let the children draw, fingerpaint, or make puppets to depict happy, sad, or mean people. Or, have them do creative writing on "How they look and feel when they are sad, scared, or mean?'' and ''What makes them feel that way?''

d. Discussion: What do we mean when we say ''You look happy today''? How can we tell when someone is happy, mean, lonesome, tired, or sad? How would you look if you felt sad or happy? What word(s) describe this face?

Focus on Body Language

13. Watch the Teacher Speak (Hennings, 1974, pp. 196–197)
    a. Objective: To become more aware of the motions that the classroom.
    b. Procedure: Make a large chart entitled ''The Teacher Speaks,'' and put it on a bulletin board. Have the children keep notes throughout the day on meanings they associate with each motion and the conditions when a motion takes on a certain meaning. Then, at the end of the day, add the observations to the chart.

THE TEACHER SPEAKS		
MOTIONS	MEANINGS	CONDITIONS
Points		
Walks toward student		
Nods head		
Claps hands		
Scratches head		

    c. Discussion: How is body language used? What conclusions can we draw? (For example, a certain gesture, such as pointing, has different meanings depending on the situation.)
14. Watch the Students Speak (Hennings, 1974, p. 197)
    a. Objective: To become more aware of the motions that the students themselves use in the classroom to communicate.
    b. Procedure: Have children work in groups and fill out the same chart as the one above but with the title ''The Students Speak.'' Have them take notes throughout the day and then compile them as a group at the end of the day. To help the students begin, give them an example of a student motion, such as raising their hands.
    c. Discussion: How do you use body language? What conclusions can you draw?
15. We're on TV (Hennings, 1974, p. 198)
    a. Objective: To identify and understand the meaning of the nonverbal language in the classroom.

433

b. Procedure: Focus the video-tape on the entire class, and then replay the tape, so the class can identify the meanings from their facial expressions and gestures. Have them fill out the chart shown above.

c. Discussion: What can we tell from your actions? Do they convey any meanings?

16. Ways of Saying It Without Words (Hennings, 1974, p. 199)

a. Objective: To discover the various conditions in which actions can have different meanings.

b. Procedure: At the beginning of the week, put the sign: "25 Ways to Say 'That's Good!'" on the bulletin board. Have the children in their spare time write suggestions on strips of paper and tack them up. Other signs could be devised: "25 Ways to Say 'I like you' Without Opening My Mouth" or "25 Ways to Say 'Yes' ('No') Wordlessly" or "25 Ways to Say 'I don't like that' Without Words."

c. Discussion: At the end of the week, discuss the different answers. Under what conditions do the actions mean "That's good"? Under what conditions would the actions have a different meaning?

17. Physical Posture (Galvin, Book, & Buys, 1972, p. 19)

a. Objective: To discover how bodies express feelings.

b. Procedure: Show children pictures of physical stances: sitting, standing, kneeling, running, reaching, and others.

c. Discussion: How does this person feel? How does he use his body to express feelings?

Focus on the Combined Effects of Gesture, Facial Expression, and Body Language

18. TV Star (Hennings, 1974, p. 188)

a. Objective: To interpret facial expressions, stance, and other nonverbal clues of people on television.

b. Procedure: Divide the children up in small groups and have them pick a TV star to watch for several weeks and fill in an interpretation guide. Then have each group write a nonverbal description of the person, including mannerisms, stance, use of eyes, facial expressions, dress, appearance, and speed of activity. Remind them not to include the name of the performer or the program. Put the descriptions on a bulletin board labeled "Guess the Star." Have them write down their guesses and put them into an envelope underneath the description. Later, open

434

the envelopes and examine the answers. Finally have each team name its star.

```
┌─────────────────────────────────────────────────┐
│         INTERPRETATION   GUIDE                    │
├───────────────────────────────────────────────── │
│ Name of observer _____ │
│ Occasion of observation _____ │
│ Gestures used _____ │
│ Facial expressions _____ │
│ Stance or posture _____ │
│ Overall body motions _____ │
│ Dress _____  │
│ Mannerisms _____ │
│ Other _____ │
└─────────────────────────────────────────────────┘
```

    c.   Discussion: What nonverbal clues were most important in determining the TV star?

19. Silent Movies (Hennings, 1974, p. 179)

    a.   Objective: To interpret a movie without the soundtrack.

    b.   Procedure: Turn off the soundtrack and talk with the children about what is going on from the action and background clues. Then, look at the film with the sound.

    c.   Discussion: What nonverbal clues were most important in basing our interpretation?

    d.   Variations: First, divide the children up in groups. Have them watch the soundless movie and write down the plot. Then, watch the movie with sound to see what group came closest to the correct interpretation.

20. They're on TV (Hennings, 1974, p. 198)

    a.   Objective: To study and understand other people's nonverbal communication outside the classroom.

    b.   Procedure: Video-tape various school activities (lunch, gym, or assemblies), meetings, or a street scene. Have children identify the different nonverbal behaviors.

    c.   Discussion: What do their actions mean? Does the situation influence the meaning of their nonverbal language?

21. TV Commericals (Hennings, 1974, p. 200)

    a.   Objective: To begin to interpret the nonverbal message of TV commercials.

    b.   Procedure: First, have the students list or draw the ways a certain commercial character says something. Then, have them each do one commercial and write down on a notecard the various nonverbal devices the producer uses to get the message across—gestures, face expressions, action, and props. Put the notecards on the bulletin board with the title "What's the TV Message?"

    c.   Discussion: What nonverbal devices does the commercial use to persuade viewers to go out and buy the product whether they need it or not? What messages are the commercial characters sending through their gestures, distance, timing, touch, and stance?

    The development of nonverbal skills on the part of the handicapped child does not differ dramatically from the techniques that are recommended for use in the regular school program. It should be understood that in the case of nonverbal skill development, the teacher should be focusing attention on the *providing* of opportunities to experience, to use, and to interpret the meaning conveyed by nonverbal activity. Little is known specifically about the percentage of information that is transmitted by facial expression versus body movement, for example, or to what extent gesture embodies the bulk of emphasis over tonal patterns. It seems that much still remains to be learned about the role nonverbal elements play in the act of communication. No specific classification systems, no real analysis procedures, and no methodology exists to date with respect to the study of nonverbal communication. What *is* known is that nonverbal message units *are* essential to the communicative act. Without an awareness of these factors, successful communication is doubtful. Too many day-to-day interactions require subtle shifts of focus, changes in tone, and careful selection of words, descriptors, topics, and phrasing all because of the nonverbal signs that are transmitted from one individual to another.

    All of the activities that have been included in this chapter are meant to serve as models, ideas, or starting points for the teacher. Whether the concern is for a particular mainstreamed mildly handicapped child or for the normal youngsters who will have to interact with this child makes no real difference. The concerns here *are* basically the same. Certainly, there are differences in abilities and in perceptions, yet *all* children have been shown to profit from creative drama, movement, pantomime, role-playing, and training in nonverbal communication effectiveness. What one is essentially talking about is a matter of degrees in programming, in presentation, in reinforcement, and in instruction.

SUMMARY

    This chapter has dealt with the development of skills in interpreting nonverbal clues and cues in communication encounters. The communication models that were introduced in chapter 3 were reviewed in terms of the degree to which nonverbal elements influence the effectiveness of message transfer. In each setting, numerous nonlinguistic factors impact on the exchange of information. Handicapped populations have been found to deviate from normal populations in the ability to judge emotional states based on nonverbal signs alone. Such information indicates that some training in nonverbal skills is required if mainstreamed children are to interact well with their peers. In developing instructional programs for children, emphasis was placed on the role that active expression can play in training a child to respond to nonverbal aspects of communications. Historically, active expression has been shown to impact the ability of children and adults to develop social, emotional, academic, and personality traits that are characteristic of successful communicators. In education, only recently has attention been given to the incorporation of nonverbal skill development in the language arts curriculum. A technique by which a teacher can incorporate active expression into the classroom and over twenty different activities focusing attention on the use of gesture, facial expression, and body movement were presented. These starting points were presented as models, ideas, and stepping-stones to a program suitable for use with a given population, class, or individual child.

It is our belief that nonverbal skill awareness is as important to the process of learning to communicate effectively as is oral language, listening skill development, composition, spelling, and handwriting. In fact, unless we take time to deal with the subtleties of our language that are embodied in nonverbal communication concerns, we are doing nothing more than taking a child through the motions of language learning. The skill of interpreting gesture can make a child sensitive to a speaker. An awareness of inconsistencies in facial expressions and comments can make a sixth grader a perceptive evaluator of the comments of peers. And, the handicapped fourth grader's skill at understanding the use of distancing contributes significantly to the child's ability to accept and to be accepted socially in school. The teacher has the responsibility of building into the curriculum training and exposure to the role that nonverbal skills play in communication. Such activity should become the commonplace rather than the rare occurrence in today's school environment.

POINTS FOR DISCUSSION

1. It was pointed out that language arts curricula very seldom incorporate nonverbal communication skills into their scope and sequence. Obtain from your curriculum laboratory or a local school a copy of the language arts curriculum guide. Examine the guide to see if nonverbal communication skills are incorporated into it. If they are, list them for discussion in your next class period. If none is available, indicate where they might be incorporated and what type they might be.

2. In this chapter, we pointed out several behaviors that might signal a child's inability to key into nonverbal clues and cues. Reread those examples and try to

generate at least five more indicators that a child is experiencing difficulty with nonverbal aspects of communication.

3. The literature on the mildly handicapped and nonverbal skill development seems to indicate that handicapped individuals have difficulty interpreting social cues in conversation. If you have worked with a handicapped child or adult in the recent past, share your experiences with the class. In your presentation, try to focus on the communication encounters you had. Were they unusually difficult? Easy? Were you aware of the ability of the handicapped individual to make use of nonverbal signs to convey a message? Were you aware of their inability to do so? Do you feel that your communication encounter with this person was successful? Unsuccessful?

4. In this chapter, an emphasis was placed on active expression as a means by which children could be taught to respond to the nonverbal elements in a communication exchange. Discuss with a small group whether or not you see the advantages academically, socially, emotionally, and linguistically that have been cited here. If you disagree with the discussion contained in this chapter, indicate why.

5. As a technique for teaching nonverbal skills to both the mildly handicapped and the normal child in the regular classroom, an instructional sequence in active expression was presented. If possible, implement either the complete sequence or segments of it with a group of children. Evaluate the activity. If you are not able to work with a class in a local school, try the instructional sequence in your own class with your colleagues.

6. Take the instructional sequence that is contained in this chapter for active expression and develop a similar one of your own. Follow the same format Mosser has suggested, but develop your own activities for the basic movements, relationships, and problem-solving.

7. Once children have learned something about the way they move and express themselves nonverbally, the activity can be extended to other areas. Work in groups of two and generate at least eight possible extensions of the activity. Be sure your list does not duplicate those activities contained in this chapter.

8. Single-session activities have been cited as being effective in heightening children's awareness of how they make use of facial expressions, gestures, and body movement. Take the ideas that are contained in this chapter and develop a unit plan for nonverbal communication that make use of these single-session activities. You may need to develop still others to develop a complete unit, or you may need to modify some to work within your particular environment. Either way, be sure that what you develop is useful to you and a plan that can be used with children.

REFERENCES

Bryan, T. An observational analysis of classroom behaviors of children with learning disabilities. *Journal of Learning Disabilities*, 1974, 7, 26–34.

Byker, D., and Anderson, L. *Communication as identification.* New York: Harper & Row, 1975.

Cohen, D. Learning to observe—observing to learn. *Address to NAEYC-AAHPER Conference,* February, 1971.

Crosby, M. Dramatics as a developmental process. *Elementary English,* 1956, *33*(2), 13–18.

Faust, J. *Body language.* New York: Simon and Schuster, 1970.

Foerster, L. Teach children to read body language. *Elementary English,* 1974, *51,* 440–442.

Galvin, K., Book, C., and Buys, W. *Speech communication: An interpersonal approach for teachers.* Skokie, Ill.: National Textbook, 1972.

Hennings, D. *Smiles, nods, and pauses: Activities to enrich children's communication skills.* New York: Citation Press, 1974.

Howard, S. The movement education approach to teaching in English schools. *JOHPER,* 1967, *38*(1).

Kanner, L. Judging emotions from facial expressions. *Psychological Monographs,* 1931, *41* (3, Whole No. 186).

Karioth, J. Creative dramatics as aid in developing creative thinking abilities. *Speech Teacher,* 1970, *19*(4).

King, J., Katzman, C., and James, D. *Imagine that! Illustrated poems and creative learning experiences.* Pacific Palisades, Calif.: Goodyear, 1976.

Levy, L., Orr, T., and Rosenzweig, S. Judgments of emotion from facial expressions by college students, mental retardates, and mental hospital patients. *Journal of Personality,* 1960, *28,* 342–349.

Lloyd, L. *Communication assessment and intervention strategies.* Baltimore, Md.: University Park Press, 1976.

Merow, E. Every child on stage. *Instructor,* 1970, 79(10).

Moffett, J. *A student-centered language arts curriculum grades K-6: A handbook for teachers.* Boston: Houghton Mifflin, Co., 1968.

Mosser, G. Movement education—The why and how. *Grade Teacher,* December 1970.

Randall, G. Origins and uses of creative drama. *Opinion,* 1967, 11(3).

Sanders, D. A model for communication. In L. Lloyd. (Ed.), *Communication assessment and intervention strategies.* Baltimore, Md.: University Park Press, 1976.

Thomas, C. *An investigation of the sensitivity to non-verbal communication of learning disabled and normal children.* Unpublished doctoral dissertation proposal, University of Virginia, 1978.

Weisenberger, C. Accuracy in judging emotional expressions as related to college entrance. *Journal of Psychology,* 1956, *44,* 233–239.

Wiemann, M., and Wiemann, J. *Non-verbal communication in the elementary classroom.* Urbana, Ill.: ERIC Clearinghouse on Reading and Communication Skills, Falls Church, Va.: Speech Communication Association, November 1975.

Wiig, E., and Harris, S. Perception and interpretation of non-verbally expressed emotions by adolescents with learning disabilities. *Perceptual and Motor Skills,* 1974, *38,* 239–245.

13

Variant
English Speakers

The variant or nonstandard English speaker has been the subject of a great many papers, books, and research reports in education. The focus of concern has been on the implications for teaching language-related subjects (speaking, writing, and reading) to children whose language in some way is manifestly different from that of the general school population and what is thought to be the accepted standard speech form of education.

Within the American culture a wide variety of English language forms can be found. There is no one standard English dialect. English language patterns vary in a continuum across regions, ethnic backgrounds, and socioeconomic levels and the versatility of the language provides a great deal of variation. A wide range of language behavior is acceptable within standard English. This diversity reflects the pluralism of the general society.

Labov (1967), a noted sociolinguist, has estimated that persons using nonstandard speech patterns in 20 to 30 percent of their conversation are generally thought of as variant speakers. The major implication is that people are often stereotyped by the language they use and that this occurs even within the existing wide range of acceptable speech patterns. A person's language plays an important role in his interaction with other members of the immediate environment and his ultimate acceptance by society. Language usage is a key factor in establishing identification with one's own community.

Later, as the individual seeks social mobility and acceptance by a new segment of society, language becomes a vital tool. The interrelatedness of language and society has been incorporated within the growing field of sociolinguistics. Teachers of variant English speaking children should be aware of how environment and culture influence children's language patterns and language-related academic tasks.

In this chapter, the term *variant English* is used interchangeably with the terms *nonstandard English* and *dialect*. Emphasis is placed on the reality of language variation. There is no intent to denote a substandardization of any English language used by a specific population, or to segregate a group by dialectical differences. Stated more precisely by Bryen, Hartman, and Tait (1978):

> First, dialect variation is not a racial issue and it is not isolated to Blacks in America. We reject the term nonstandard because "standardness" is a situational phenomenon—standard English in one situation would not be considered the standard in another. Second, we have rejected the term nonstandard because of the frequent (and erroneous) myths and negative attitudes that become associated with a dialect so termed. The term *Variant English,* on the other hand, reflects the realities of language. Language *does* vary and may result in varieties or dialects of any language system. (p. v)

English language variations can be seen in three fundamental speech components: pronunciation, vocabulary, and grammar. The way a person pronounces a word, the choice of expressions, and the structural aspects singularly or in combination denote differences in language. Illustrations of each of these language differential components are:

Pronunciation: De boy rode on de train.
          (The boy rode on the train.)
Expression: Mash the button.
          (Press the button down.)
Structure: She be happy.
          (She is always happy.)

Differences in English speech patterns result from: geographic location, profession, social class, race, and age. Each variable influences the person's pronunciation, word choice, and sentence construction. Although the two primary influences on children who speak an English dialect are geography and social class membership, ethnicity is often cited because of the composition of the American society and the influences of economics and regionality.

Language Disorder versus Language Difference

The language exhibited by the mildly handicapped child is of great interest to the classroom teacher and should be considered during instructional planning. Language plays an essential role in the learning process, and a breakdown or variation in language production may impede the child's acquisition of new skills. However, the extent of the interference and the means of instruction varies according to whether the child demonstrates a language *disorder* or a language *difference*.

The term *language disorder* refers to a broad classification of communication difficulties including delayed speech, vocabulary disorders, syntactical abnormalities, and poor comprehension. The child who has a language disorder may not be able to remember words (dysnomia) and may substitute "whatchamecallit" for unknown names and objects. Another child may have the appropriate vocabulary but may not be able to organize words into a comprehensible sequence. As a result the simple sentence, "This is my book," may be spoken as, "My this book is." Disorders such as these, reflected in the process of producing language, are known as expressive disorders or expressive aphasia.

Receptive language disorders (receptive aphasia) are manifested as poor comprehension. Some children may have difficulty understanding small units of a word ("ed" as in "walked"), while others will be unable to comprehend whole word meanings or more complex units such as sentences. For instance, in "The boy ran after the girl" it may be difficult for certain children to comprehend who was doing the chasing.

Speech disorders are also of concern to the classroom teacher in that they can interfere with the flow of communication and make learning more difficult. A speech disorder refers to problems of voice, articulation, and fluency, and can be differentiated from the larger category of language disorders. A child who stutters, or consistently mispronounces the initial "r" sound, or speaks in an extremely high-pitched voice has a speech disorder.

Language differences may also affect the child's learning ability, however the "problem" is based upon sociolinguistic variation rather than clinical pathology. Children who come from homes and communities where the primary language is a variant form of English are considered language different. In most cases, language different children are not language deficient. Their language development and language usage are appropriate for their environment and there is no implication of existing language deficits or inferior language abilities.

The differential between the child's language system and standard English may result in learning problems. Language different children have been shown to experience difficulty in learning language related skills and especially in reading skill development (Shuy, 1972). Teachers working with variant English speaking children on language arts skills need to display a positive and accepting attitude toward the children and their culture and to understand the affect the children's language difference has on the learning process.

Although language differences and language disorders are not necessarily associated, a child may be both language different and language disordered. Such a child is a variant English speaker who demonstrates a particular language problem. Among the mildly handicapped student population many children may actually be representative of these two language classifications.

Identification of Mildly Handicapped Variant Speakers

To begin to understand the instructional needs of the mildly handicapped, variant English speaker it is necessary to establish guidelines for identifying such children. Identification starts with the determination of a handicapping condition, such as those specified in chapter 1, and then is extended to include any child whose language is recognizably different from the standard English speaker in pronunciation, vocabulary, or grammar. A variant English speaker is one whose language differences are not solely the result of pathological difficulties.

Mildly handicapped children from several major ethnic and socioeconomic groups may be expected to use a variation of English in their communication process. In fact, it has long been noted that special classes and services are heavily populated with minority group children (Dunn, 1968; Mercer, 1973) who are variant English speakers. These may include:

1. Black children in both northern urban centers and rural southern regions.
2. Chicano Americans (of Mexican, Puerto Rican, and Spanish descent).
3. Chinese children.
4. Poor, rural white children (e.g., Appalachian children).

Appendix B contains inventories showing elements of variant language forms for each of these major groups. In surveying the inventories the teacher should keep in mind that not all children use all the features that are listed, and the frequency of any feature is unique to the individual and his personal environment. The importance of becoming linguistically familiar with the language differences of the child you are teaching cannot be underestimated. A teacher who is linguistically naïve may not be able to differentiate among a student's learning problems, true language problems, and variant speech usage.

To more fully understand the language differences employed by the variant speaker, a base of comparision is necessary, that is, a standard language. It would be helpful to refer back to chapters 2 and 8 on language acquisition and oral skill development and to review elements of standard language and language related problems for the mildly handicapped learner. It is a difficult and complex task to differentiate the learning problems of the average variant speaker and the mildly handicapped child whose language happens also to be nonstandard.

The mildly handicapped, variant English speaking child is a major concern for many teachers. The problems presented are unique and the instructional program must be adjusted to best serve the child. It is not sufficient to attend to the child's learning problem regardless of variant language framework, nor is it appropriate to assume that language orientation is solely responsible for the child's learning failures. The teacher must develop instructional plans for the learning deficits with consideration and attention given to the language variation. Unfortunately, almost nothing has been done in this area and many of the pedagogic problems remain unsolved.

Variant Speakers—Linguistically Different not Deficient

In the language arts classroom, concern is given primarily to the development of communication skills. The variant English speaker must be recognized as a child who possesses an intact language system. Variant English speakers should not be classified as intellectually inferior, immature in language acquisition, genetically deviant, or naturally representative of lower-class homes. Persons subscribing to any of these "myths" commonly assigned to nonstandard English speakers, succumb to a *deficit model* of language development. Accordingly, it is believed that such children lack facility with standard English due to a cognitive limitation which makes them unable to reason and make use of abstract thinking.

The deficit model was illustrated by Bereiter and Engelmann's (1966) conclusions that variant speakers are unable to use causal logic because of the lack of an if-then structure and the use of double negation and unspecified plural forms. The misconception is not in the language usage of the variant speaker, but in the assumption that such usage implies a cognitive limitation.

An example of an erroneous assumption would be:

Child: I didn't do nothing.
Interpretation: I did do something.

Those believing in the cognitive deficit theory would not recognize the negative element of the statement, but would postulate that the double negatives cancel each other out resulting in a positive statement (i.e., *I did something*). However, familiarity with the rules of variant English would disprove this assumption and verify the child's use of the negative form.

A second and more acceptable theory of variant English is a *difference model* of development (Baratz & Shuy, 1969; Cohen & Cooper, 1972). In this approach, the variant English speaker's language is seen as systematic and as structured as that of standard English. Persons using variant English have the ability to communicate, reason, and think. There is no implication of cognitive dysfunction or inferiority. From a linguistic point of view the differences between standard and variant English are evident but not significant to the point that one is more effective than the other.

> In general, the deep structures of sentences and the underlying representations of lexical items are the same in the two dialects. And so are most of the rules that operate on them: transformation of deep structures and phonological rules on underlying representation. (Dale, 1976, p. 274)

Examined from this context the difference theory is a more viable one. The child's own language is a rich instructional resource as the child already understands and speaks English.

Instruction of the mildly handicapped variant speaking child should be considered within the framework of language difference. Teaching should logically proceed from the individual child's language system with the objective of helping the child develop more effective communication. Although many of the examples in this chapter pertain to Black dialect, the information can often be applied to the teaching of children with other variant languages.

The Instructional Program for the Variant Speaker

Mildly handicapped variant speakers need to develop communication skills which will help them integrate into the mainstream of society. The compounding of their handicapping condition and language difficulties presents even greater urgency to establish and achieve communication skills. There is no intent to imply that mildly handicapped children will most likely be variant English speakers or vice versa that variant speakers are mildly handicapped. The overlap that often occurs between these two groups is a reality, and the responsible teacher must deal with both variables as they impinge upon the child's language skill development. The primary objective is the same for all mildly handicapped children, that is, to remove barriers to effective communication. Labov (1966) has determined eight priority areas for communication instruction of nonstandard speakers. In order of greatest significance they are the abilities to:

1. Understand spoken English in order to learn from the teacher
2. Read and comprehend printed material
3. Communicate to others in spoken English
4. Express themselves in writing
5. Use standard English for written communication
6. Spell correctly
7. Use standard English in oral communication
8. Use appropriate pronunciation in order to avoid stigmatization

Note the sequence of Labov's objectives—from basic communication to the use of standardized English forms. The hierarchy is aimed at helping the child pass through stages which ultimately lead to standard language usage at an automatic level of functioning. At this point the child can attend to what is said rather than how it is said.

Several important principles for language development and language arts curriculum are suitable for instruction of the mildly handicapped variant English speaking child. Although listed as separate points, they should be considered in total with the understanding that language is an integrated function.

1. There is no "perfect" or standard English speech form. English is flexible and has a range of acceptable speech patterns.
2. English instruction must be based on description and use of English as it exists today and not upon strict Latin of the past. The language of the child's environment and the standard of the community are of primary importance.
3. When the English language of the child's community varies from the standard, the child should be taught to recognize the difference and the parallel forms of the standard and variant languages.
4. Mildly handicapped children should not be taught formal grammar but instead should be directed toward understanding an *intuitive* grammatical structure; how to use language, not why we use it.
5. Children should be given *daily, repeated,* and *realistic* opportunities to use the language system and to express themselves freely.
6. Talking in spontaneous dialogues and structure drills are most beneficial when balanced in the instructional plan.
7. *Do not expect* children to repeat the language rule or to explain appropriate usage. *Do expect* them to make the transition to a standard form once they have had ample opportunity to learn it and are old enough to be motivated and ready to switch.

447

8. Children need a great deal of time to achieve bidialectalism and this will probably not fully occur until secondary school age. However, the foundations for attaining successful bidialectalism should be built at an early age and should be part of the instructional plan throughout the school years.

The pertinent issue in language instruction is the development of realistic expectations in communication skills for the mildly handicapped speaker.

> ... a nonstandard speech performance does not signal the absence of language competence, but simply indicates that the speaker has learned his language in an environment that uses this language system for communication purposes. (Ruddell, 1974, p. 264)

Style Shifting

All speakers shift style from formal language through a continuum of informality to an occasional level of slang or jargon. This acceptable style shift depends on the speaker's audience and the purpose of the communication. When speaking to a group of college students in a lecture hall, the professor is most likely to present a formal, highly structured language pattern. The same instructor coincidentally meeting a student on the street would be less apt to speak as formally and would be even more informal during a casual conversation in the home of a friend who happens also to be a student in the lecture class.

Style shifting is a natural aspect of language competence and should be expected and encouraged in the variant speaker who is learning to adjust to appropriate uses of standard English. The child must learn to differentiate situations that require a more formalized oral or written communication from those that allow an informal approach.

The important element of style shifting, the discrimination among situations requiring a decisive selection of speech form, is illustrated in Figure 13.1.

Case I represents situations in which only standard English is appropriate and any other language form would be counterproductive. For instance, a job interview or a business letter requires standard language usage. Case II, however, signifies the opposite end of the continuum when the variant language is the practical and acceptable form. Speaking to a close friend or writing an informal note to a parent would exemplify Case II situations. In both Cases I and II, language structure should be automatic. Finally, the importance of the child's ability to move along the language continuum and determine the appropriateness of either standard or nonstandard lan-

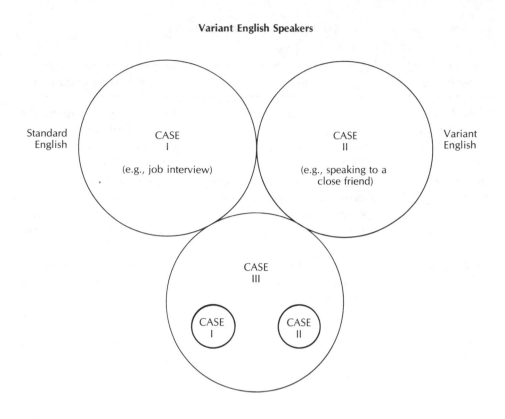

Standard
English

CASE
I

(e.g., job interview)

CASE
II

(e.g., speaking to a
close friend)

Variant
English

CASE
III

CASE
I

CASE
II

Decision Point

FIGURE 13.1   Style Shifting Selection

guage for a given situation is illustrated in Case III. Examples of Case III would
be meeting new people or a social engagement with a business associate.

If a teacher has problems understanding a child's written or oral
communication, then language arts instruction should naturally start at these
points. Any language deviation that interferes with the progression of communicative skill development should be immediately addressed.

The majority of nonstandard speech forms will present little or no
problem to the listener or reader. In addition most differences will not deter
the child's own comprehension. However, in some cases the child's variant
language ultimately affects comprehension, as for example in the absent use
of past tense markers, possessives, and future tense markers. Figure 13.2
contains examples of nonstandard English sentence forms and explanations
of the possible comprehension errors that may result.

The examples in Figure 13.2 clearly show that the teacher must pay
close attention to the child's semantic intentions. Another area of miscom-
munication may result from phonological differences, such as *toe* for *toll;*
pin for *pen;* and pronouncing *marry, merry,* and *Mary* similarly. When
working with mildly handicapped children it may be necessary to have the
children expand upon their statements in order to clarify their intention for

Sentence	Error Form	Comprehension Problem
When I passed by, I read the posters. (Labov, 1967)	Without the past tense marker, *ed,* it becomes: *When I pass by, I read the posters.*	Use of the past tense marker in the word pass*ed,* influences the pronunciation of the word *read.*
This is John's street.	Without the possessive form form of the proper noun the sentence changes to: *This is John street.*	Absence of the possessive marker in *John's* could change the sentence meaning to imply that the name of the street is John.
You'll like this movie.	The removal of the future tense marker you'*ll* leaves the sentence as: *You like this movie.*	Without the future tense marker the sentence can be interpreted as either an interrogative sentence or a declarative present tense sentence depending on inflection.

FIGURE 13.2   *Examples of Comprehension Errors*

the listener (teacher) or to restate what they "heard" the teacher say. In this way, comprehension can be checked and misunderstanding can be avoided.

Motivating Language Development

The child's feelings of self-worth, cultural identity, and attitudes are of primary consideration. It is unfortunate that teachers and others within society often discriminate on the basis of language variation. Many negative connotations, such as "poor," "wrong," and "bad," are applied to variant English forms. The effect of such bias on the teaching process for the mildly handicapped nonstandard speaker can be very detrimental. The problem learner's feelings of insecurity in the learning situation are serious enough to warrant attention without the additional problems of prejudice. A teacher with a negative attitude will be unsuccessful in motivating and instructing these children.

Motivation becomes the all-important factor. Many nonhandicapped variant speakers will desire to learn standard English forms at adolescence when the student becomes naturally aware of the need for effective communication within the adult community. Both Johnson (1969) and Burling (1973) state that standard oral language will not be successfully adopted by

450

the variant speaker until that individual has the desire to learn it. For the mildly handicapped child a lack of motivation will be even more of a problem and will possibly set the child even further apart. However, it must be understood that persistence in nonstandard oral language does not exclude the child's motivation or ability to comprehend speech or to learn to read.

The teacher's job has a dual function. The first is to motivate, that is, to help the child recognize the importance of learning appropriate usage of standard speech. The second is to plan and implement a program of speech development aimed at standard language acquisition.

Instructional Alternatives

The question of which instructional approach is appropriate for teaching the mildly handicapped variant English speaker is very difficult. Although often debated there are at present three possible approaches for teaching nonstandard speakers:

1. Eradication of the nonstandard language form
2. Complete acceptance of the variant language form
3. Bidialectalism

A closer examination of each of these choices for the mildly handicapped child may prove helpful.

Eradication

The child comes to school speaking and comprehending the language of the family environment. This language is purposeful and well established. Beyond the early school years, the peer group continues to exert the most substantial influence on the child's language and in the majority of cases the peer group represents the variant language. At the end of each school day the child returns to this same environment where use of the variant language form is functional for all members of the community. There will always be situations in which the variant language form is appropriate and its eradication would be a disservice.

The mildly handicapped child may be even more likely to need the social acceptance of peers, and to do so, a firm commitment to the nonstandard language form may need to be made. It would be unwise to underestimate the child's need for social acceptance and to try to remove this tangible bond. In fact, it may even be considered impossible to eradicate evidence of the variant language.

451

Acceptance of the Variant Language

The ultimate goal of the educational process is for the mildly handicapped child to assimilate as much as possible into the general society. Complete maintenance of the variant language limits the child's eventual social and economic rewards. The child's language system should be accepted along with the child, however, stylistic variation must be introduced and the child made aware of social needs and alternative speech patterns.

Bidialectalism

This third alternative is most commonly preferred as it allows the child to fluctuate effectively to meet the language demands of specific occasions. Bidialectalism is not easily established and may be an added frustration to the mildly handicapped child who is already experiencing language problems. The effective teacher will help the child learn the major elements of standard English to gradually shift the language pattern.

Not everyone agrees with the approach of bidialectalism. Some parents and professionals feel that it is an unnecessary language requirement which places too many needless demands on the child. They believe that the teaching of bidialectalism suggests that the language and culture of the variant speaking child are wrong and that the child must learn the right way to communicate. This bias can be avoided by teaching bidialectalism in a manner that suggests that both standard and variant English are useful and correct given the appropriate situation.

Oral Language Instruction

At the early stages of oral language instruction it is important for children to first feel comfortable as speakers. They must be able to stand in front of a group to present information or exchange intimacies in a conversation without feeling overly anxious, stammering, or becoming confused. *The child's natural language in its variant form should be the springboard for oral expression.* Lessons for developing more acceptable language patterns should be structured around practical and meaningful situations.

Variant English seldom causes oral communication problems in the classroom. Bryen, Hartman, and Tait (1978) stress that the majority of classroom oral communication problems are attitudinal in nature.

> Many teachers constantly correct the language and speech of their youngsters until these youngsters view communication as yielding, at

best, corrective measures and, at worst, punitive ones. As a result, these youngsters may feel that the safest course is to use minimal language in the classroom. (pp. 231–232)

Oral language transition occurs with appreciation of language variation and that language may acceptably shift depending on the specific social situation. Therefore, it is important that the child be given both structured and spontaneous speech situations in order to learn how and when to transfer from informal variant speech to formal standard speech. Correcting random errors in oral language is an unsystematic and almost useless task. On the other hand, to start at the very beginning of language development and build a new language system fails to make use of the child's enormous amount of language achievement (Burling, 1973). The dilemma can be resolved by systematic instruction of the oral language using:

1. Appropriate modeling
2. A comparative program of parallel language sequencing
3. Activities for planned practice of standard speech forms

Mildly handicapped children need a great deal more practice in order to reorient their speech pattern. Emphasis should be placed on grammatical structuring rather than pronunciation differences. People in general will tolerate mispronunciation to a greater extent than other language variations. Oral language should be carefully modeled for the child but there should be no attempt to correct the child's speech by having him repeat the proper form. For instance:

Teacher: "What is Clyde doing?"
Child: "He running."
Teacher: "Yes, he is running awfully fast."

or:

Teacher: "Alice likes you. She is willing to share her ball with you."
Child: "She a friend."
Teacher: "Yes, she is a good friend."

In each case the teacher presented the correct model, without penalizing the student in any way.

When language is the primary objective of the activity, corrective feedback and immediate reinforcement are essential.

Teacher: "Look at this picture of trees and water. What do we call the water?"
Child: "Scream."

453

Teacher: "Yes, but we say, *stream.* Can you say *stream?"*
Child: "Stream."
Teacher: "Very good, stream."

It is important and probably more effective to call as little attention as possible to standard speech when language is spontaneous. The child is more likely to imitate teachers, peers, and others that he admires and whose respect he seeks. Content should elicit the most attention followed by standard usage. In this way, emotional stress is avoided, communication is developed, and self-confidence can be established. Each of these three elements is particularly sensitive for the mildly handicapped learner.

Oral language skills can be developed using a variety of activities such as the following:

1. *Name the action.* A child selects a picture card that represents an activity or movement. The child must describe the action using standard English. The student who successfully states the activity also using standard English selects the next card.
2. *Sell it.* The teacher selects two children to role play a salesperson and a customer. The teacher tells the salesperson what to sell or gives the salesperson something to sell. The task is to convince the customer that he really needs and wants this "object."
3. *Sentence completion.* Each student in the room begins a sentence stopping in the middle for the next person to pick up and complete. Sample sentences might be:
   Yesterday I . . .
   He was a very . . .
   I went to the store and . . .
4. *Motivation.* Brainstorm all the situations that require the speaker to use standard English. Keep a class list and review it often. Use the situations on the list to motivate the child to want to learn standard speech.
5. *Role play.* Develop a series of situations which require *either* standard (formal) speech or nonstandard (informal) speech. The child must decide which is the appropriate speech form and act out the situation in that manner. Sample situations are:
   • Trying to convince the baseball team coach to let you pitch the big game.
   • Asking the store manager for an after-school job.
   • Telling a friend about a movie you watched on TV last night.
   • Explaining your art project to a panel of judges.
6. *Say it another way.* The teacher or an appointed child begins by saying a sentence in either standard or nonstandard speech form.

The next child must repeat the sentence translating it into the opposite speech form. For example:

Standard: People are not ready for winter yet.
(Peop'es ain't ready fouh winner, ya know.)
Standard: I have lived here.
(I have live here.)
Nonstandard: He be workin'.
(He is always working.)

The purpose of activities such as these is to provide the variant speaking child with practice in:

1. Using standard English
2. Making decisions about using an appropriate speech form
3. The paralleling and acceptance of standard and variant language patterns

The complexity of the task will need to be adjusted to match the skills of the mildly handicapped learner.

Written Language Instruction

There has been very little research or literature related to the process of teaching writing skills to the variant speaker. What there is closely ties writing to speaking and reading skill development. Burling (1973) presents an explicit comparison of the writing styles and corresponding instructional techniques of standard speakers (Style I) and nonstandard speakers (Style II). Figure 13.3 illustrates five techniques presently used to teach, what Burling refers to as the acceptable, "literary style" (Style III). The chart commentaries are based on Burling's explanations of each technique as it applies to the nonstandard speaker.

A major conclusion of Burling's discussion is that Style I and Style II speakers are often differentially treated for instructional purposes. Style II speakers commonly exhibit difficulties which are increased by the negative attitudes of teachers. An implication for the mildly handicapped variant speaker is that instructional methods may be similar to those used with other mildly handicapped children with two exceptions. First, the teacher's expectation and attitude must convey a positive approach to the child concerning his colloquial expressions and his culture. Second, the necessary time frame for writing achievement must be extended to allow for the gradual acquisition of the new language form.

Technique	To Style I (Standard) Speakers	To Style II (Nonstandard) Speakers	Commentary
1. Teach new spoken forms to young children, feeling that these are pre-requisites to learning to read.	Never	Sometimes	An attempt is made to switch the Style II speakers to a more standard oral form before writing is begun. It is a false assumption in such cases to believe that the standard spoken and written forms are the same.
2. Correct the written work of small children vigorously when it reflects their colloquial style.	Rarely	Often	Style II writers are often more criticized for mechanical and colloquial expressions than are Style I speakers. The reality is that the expressive power of the written content is often secondary to the standardization of writing conventions and expressions.
3. Expect literary style to be un-consciously absorbed from reading.	Yes	Yes	Teachers can do little to directly assist a child in absorbing a language form through the reading process. However, we do know that Style II speakers tend to read more poorly and therefore read less often. The result is a slower ab-sorption process.
4. Rephrase diffi-cult passages into "different words" (into a a colloquial style) when that	Yes	No	When a Style II speak-er has difficulty com-prehending, teachers seldom will rephrase the expression into variant English form.

Technique	To Style II (Nonstandard) Speakers	To Style I (Standard) Speakers	Commentary
helps a child to understand.			The teacher's attitude against the variant form along with a lack of understanding of the linguistic nature prevent the rephrasing into the Style II colloquial expression. Although teachers may restate the phrase in a second standard form it is not always helpful to the Style II speaker.
5. Leave until high school, or even college, deliberate instruction in overcoming colloquialisms in written style.	Usually	No	Written compositions of most Style I speakers are not evaluated for expression other than to assist the child in clarity and writing mechanics. Style II speakers are often edited for colloquialisms at a much earlier age and with a much more concerted effort.

Adapted from: Burling, R. *English in black and white.* New York: Holt, Rinehart and Winston, Inc., 1973, pp. 151–155.

FIGURE 13.3 Techniques for Teaching Written Expression

The techniques described by Burling refer to the written language style. The underlying conflict is between determining "good" writing from mechanically "correct" writing. This is a point which Corbin (1966) clearly makes by differentiating between logically and clearly stated expression and writing which contains no errors in spelling, vocabulary, and punctuation. Bryen et al. (1978) expound upon this point with direct implication for the variant speaker.

> ... the assumption can be made that the speakers of variant dialects are faced with no greater handicaps in learning to write a "good" composition than are speakers of standard dialects. What might be expected,

457

however, is a greater incidence of a mechanically "incorrect" composition because of the divergence between syntactical and phonological structures of variant dialects and those structures which have come to be accepted as "correct". (p. 214)

The mildly handicapped variant speaker's writing difficulties are compounded by stylistic bias and mechanical errors. Following Burling's analysis, the reader should be aware of differences in approaching the teaching of writing to variant and standard speakers. It becomes necessary to systematically examine the effects of variant language on specific mechanical writing practices, such as spelling and word usage. Other writing conventions remain relatively unaffected by the language difference and therefore will not be covered in this section. Refer to chapter 9, Written Expression, for a review of instruction in writing conventions. The information provided here expands on the methods already discussed.

Spelling

The presentation on spelling instruction in chapter 10 established the lack of a perfect phoneme-grapheme correspondence of the English spelling system. Yet, there is enough consistency that the child who can use a sound-symbol relationship will be at an advantage in learning to spell. For the nonstandard speaking child many phonological features will not be accurately represented in standard written form. Figure 13.4 examines several phonological elements which may cause difficulty for variant speakers in learning how to spell. (See p. 460.)

The teacher must be alert to the variability of the children in the class in order to differentiate between a child whose spelling difficulties are the direct result of nonstandard speech rather than of a more serious nature. For some mildly handicapped children this may be a very difficult task indeed.

The child who spells *sing* as *sin* has probably not pronounced the final phoneme g, and has left it off the written word. Each phoneme that was pronounced was spelled. Therefore, it would be appropriate to say that this child has a pronunciation problem and not a spelling problem. However, the child who spells *house* as *dleus* has a spelling difficulty, the inability to associate appropriate graphic symbols for letter sounds.

A major difficulty arises when the teacher utilizes a different pronunciation than the student. The teacher needs to be sensitive to the child's own pronunciation. This involves careful listening, fine tuning to variations among children, and conscious probing. A series of questions and pointers for identification of different pronunciations are listed below. Three techniques can be used to have a child identify speech sounds.

458

Technique	Procedure
Picture Stimulus	Show the child a set of pictures or words and ask him to identify them. For example, numeral three and a tree; or single pictures such as a *school* (does he leave off the final *l?*).
Questioning	Ask the child to answer specific questions to establish variability. • What number comes after three? (*four* or *foe*) • People who have no money are _____? (*poor* or *pour*) • When you have a cut it is called a _____? (*sore* or *saw*) • The person at the back of the line is _____? (*las* or *last*)
Repetition	Have the child repeat a series of sentences after you or tell you a story using certain key words. (Attend to the possible spelling, not the grammatical errors.) Teacher: I had a cold last week. Child: (I have a *coal las* week.) Teacher: The answers on the test were all right. Child: (The answers on the *tes* was *arat*.)

Spelling for a variant speaking child whose pronunciation does not correspond with the grapheme-phoneme regularities of standard English is a much more difficult task. This is mainly due to the large number of speech sounds which do not exist within the variant language form and the increased number of homophones generally found in such speech. These techniques will help the teacher establish what words the child says as homophones as well as what sounds (and in what position) the child leaves out of his speech. In many cases, the child will not even be able to differentiate the phoneme differences when heard. For instance, a child who says *walk* instead of *walked* may not even be able to recognize, let alone repeat, the final sound.

Spelling instruction largely becomes a visual memory task. The child must learn to portray the graphic symbols of sounds not said (*dumb* for *dum*) or which are said alike but spelled differently (*peel* and *pail*). In many cases the child will need to be given additional instruction in learning to differentiate words based on meaning. *Words which are being taught visually must be taught in context.* Only in this way will the child learn to associate the visual representation with the appropriate word meaning.

Bryen et al. (1978) asked two fourth-grade variant speakers to spell a series of dictated sentences (Figure 13.5). Ignoring grammatical errors, analyze the sentences by circling spelling errors which are caused by variant language differences and underlining errors which most likely cannot be explained by variant speech differences.

Phonological Feature	Standard English	Variant English
r-lessness	skirts	skits
	teenagers	teenages
	sore	saw
l-lessness	always	aways
	help	hep
	school	schoo
a/an article	an apple	a apple
n/ng	everything	everythin
	going	goin
consonant cluster simplification	understand	understan
	test	tes
	closest	closes
e-i merger	pen	pin

Source: Bryen, D. N., Hartman, C., and Tait, P. E. *Variant English*. Columbus, Ohio: Charles E. Merrill Publishing Co., 1978, p. 216.

FIGURE 13.4   Dialect Influences on Spelling

Student 2 has a serious spelling problem which will need remediation including intensive work on sound-symbol associations. For Student 1, the teacher needs to draw attention to standard spellings and provide practice drills for rote memorization.

Usage

Other major writing problems of the variant language speaker are the selection of words and the construction of expressions. Although, many of the variant language forms found in spoken language are not found in written compositions (e.g., "ain't," often said, is seldom written) many other variant phrases are present. Ross (1976) believes that certain expressions do not appear because they are so deeply opposed in the school environment. Children may recognize the relative formality of writing as opposed to the informality of speaking.

Many of the differences of the variant speaker are consistent grammatical changes. Dialect based grammatical differences which interfere with language are found in Figure 13.6.

Instruction for errors such as those listed in Figure 13.6 can be centered upon teaching bidialectalism, that is, parallel forms of standard and

Dictated Sentences

1. He walked along the street.
2. I asked him if he was hungry.
3. She runs two miles every day.
4. I will never do anything bad.
5. John wants an apple to eat.
6. His shirts are always good looking
7. on him.

Student 1

1. He walk along the street.
2. I ask him was he hungry.
3. She run 2 miles a day.
4. I will never do everthin bad.
5. John want a apple to eat.
6. His sirt aways good looking
7. on hem.

Student 2

1. He walk a long the street.
2. i ask him ef he was hungered.
3. She run to minse areay bay.
4. I will never bo ineaything bad.
5. Jochon wasn an epple to eat.
6. his shits aways good looking on him.

Answers

Student 1

1. (walk)
2. (ask)
3. (everthin)
4. (a)
5. sirt (aways)
6. (hem)

Student 2

1. (walk) a long
2. (ask) ef hungered
3. to minse areay bay
4. bo ineaything
5. Jochon wasn epple
6. (shits) aways

Source: Bryen, D. N., Hartman, C., and Tait, P. E. *Variant English.* Columbus, Ohio: Charles E. Merrill Publishing Co., 1978, pp. 217–218.

FIGURE 13.5 *Dictated Spelling Samples*

Feature	Written Responses
Zero copula	She a nice person.
Subject-verb agreement	She have a pleasant smile.
Absence of plural marker	The feeling of other people ...
Absence of past tense marker	They offer me ... individual help me.
Absence of possessive marker	This is Joan coat.
"If" construction	I ask him was he hungry.
Pronominal predicate markers	The man who had the fight, he ...

Source: Bryen, D. N., Hartman, C., and Tait, P. E. *Variant English*. Columbus, Ohio: Charles
E. Merrill Publishing Co., 1978, p. 219.

FIGURE 13.6   *Dialect-Based Grammatical Interference in Writing*

nonstandard English. The teacher should present the child with the alternative way of saying (writing) a phrase or sentence. Gladney (1972) presented the two forms as *school talk* and *everyday talk*. The bidialectal language program, devised for the Chicago schools, incorporated spoken and written language as well as reading. The children were introduced to *school talk* (standard language) as an alternative way of getting their message across. Children were taught to translate (again both in speaking and writing) from one form to the other.

Some simple sentences are included in Figure 13.7. See if you can correctly translate them into the alternate language form.

For the variant English speaker writing can be a very frustrating activity if it is consistently "red penciled" and considered "wrong." The teacher should establish the purpose of the writing exercise and make corrections accordingly. The mildly handicapped variant speaker may be even more

School Talk	Everyday Talk
• I have a mama.	
	• I got a sister.
• When I am running, my teacher says, stop that.	
	• When I be talking my teacher she say, stop that.
• Yesterday, I passed the police station.	

Adapted from: Gladney, M. R. A teaching strategy. In Hodges, R. E., and Rudorf, E. H. *Language and learning to read*. Boston: Houghton-Mifflin Co., 1972, pp. 73-83.

FIGURE 13.7

reluctant to produce a written product because of past failures. Encouragement and motivation are essential. Allow the child to write freely, reinforcing the meaning of the expression while teaching appropriate usage separately. At a later time, "good" writing and "correct" writing can be merged.

Problems in Reading Achievement

Causes of reading failure among variant English speakers have drawn a great deal of attention among professional educators, linguists, and sociologists. The controversy that centers on the influences of language variance on reading achievement has not been fully resolved, and the research thus far has resulted in conflicting points of view.

Emphasis on *language interference* in reading ability has centered on several significant factors. Some writers contend that the often present mismatch between the teacher's dialect and the child's dialect causes conflict when the teacher tries to get the child to pronounce each word as the teacher would say it. The teacher's reaction to variant language translations as reading errors handicaps the child in learning to read (Rigg, 1978; Cunningham, 1976–1977). Whether or not the child differentiates the pronunciation between *oil* and *all* or *since* and *cents* in the same manner as the teacher is of little importance. The child who reads: *I had eight since in my pocket,* understands that he is referring to money and not time. The child does not need to be corrected because of phonological differences. The child whose language varies from the teacher's is as accurate in pronunciation as the teacher may be. The purpose of reading is meaning, not simply the sounding of letters and words. Grapheme-phoneme associations are simply a means to comprehending the printed word.

Dialect differences often result in *miscues,* differences between the printed words and the reader's oral presentation. Goodman (1965) first presented the idea of a direct relationship between the difference in the reader's dialect and the language of the printed material, and that this conflict will affect reading success. Miscues, which occur because authors and readers have dialect differences, can appear in pronunciation, syntax, and semantics. The important element of the miscue is that comprehension remains intact regardless of the variation between the reader's language and the author's writing. Phonological mismatches between the child's language and the standard printed form are not to be considered reading errors any more than are teacher-student dialect mismatches. In most cases teachers can, and do, ignore mispronunciations if they are consistent with the student's reading level and nonstigmatizing common speech. For instance, "I had ice cream *an* cake *las* night," will generally be acceptable. However, "*Dat* boy *et* my food," will present a more noticeable stigma and will tend to be cor-

463

rected by most teachers as a reading error. In both instances the reader understood the author's intent and derived accurate meaning from the reading, yet, one is considered more of a variation than the next.

Syntactic and semantic miscues are more often attended to by teachers who are naïve in linguistic training and reading instruction. The child may read, *He jump up high,* for *He jumped up high,* or *Dana mother cook a good dinner* for *Dana's mother cooked a good dinner.* These changes do not influence the deep structural meaning of the sentences. The teacher needs to be aware that the child who is translating from the author's dialect into variant English is going through a complex process of recognizing the graphic symbol and then rearranging verbal output to fit natural expression. The child has presented the writing in a manner which is simply more comfortable.

Miscues occurring in oral reading do not affect comprehension. The question of comprehension during silent reading has also been researched, unfortunately with equivocable results. Comparisons of results of children's reading comprehension on material printed in standard English and nonstandard English were reported to show no significance by Simons and Johnson (1974) and Liu (1975-1976). Both of these studies, however, had methodological problems which must be considered when interpreting the results. Harber (1977), on the other hand, found a significantly higher achievement in standard orthography when reading standard English material than nonstandard English.

It is interesting to compare these findings with those on listening comprehension tasks which show no significant differences according to standard or variant language form (Harber, 1977; Levy & Cook, 1973). The implications are that variant language speakers may be receptively bidialectal at a fairly early age due to mass media, school instruction, and community interaction. Listening comprehension skills for standard English, contrary to reading comprehension skills, may be spontaneously acquired for the variant language speaker.

Suggested Methods of Reducing Reading Problems

Several alternatives have been suggested for ameliorating the reading problems which often result from the inconsistencies between spoken and written language. The most commonly referred to alternatives are:

1. Teaching standard English prior to beginning reading instruction
2. Developing and using materials printed in nonstandard language forms
3. Teaching children to read materials with certain neutralized features
4. Using standard materials but allowing children to read a nonstandard form

Each of these alternatives has been fully reviewed with relevant research by Shuy (1972), Somervill (1975), and Bryen et al. (1978). The reader would be well advised to pursue one of these sources. The discussion that follows is limited to direct implications of each alternative for teaching reading to the variant English speaker.

Teaching Standard English Prior to Beginning Reading Instruction

The development of standard language must begin at a very early age in order not to delay reading instruction. Many prescribed studies, such as those conducted by Bereiter and Engelmann (1966), although highly structured and somewhat successful, failed to carry over into the primary school years. In addition, this alternative is associated with a cognitive deficit approach and provides little benefit.

Developing and Using Materials Printed in Variant English

It has been suggested that dialect-based reading materials be used for *initial* reading instruction. Gradually a transition to standard materials would be programmed. "The rationale behind this approach is that the task of beginning reading involves decoding the written word as being representative of already meaningful spoken language" (Bryen et al., 1978, p. 197).

Somervill (1975) among others has suggested that there would be no need to use anything other than traditional orthography (standard spelling), since all children learn to read words that are not phonetically consistent. At present there is no evidence to either support or dispute this contention and the disagreement has resulted in a weakening of advocacy for the approach.

Some success has been achieved with the method of developing and using materials printed in nonstandard English, primarily because of the confidence it provides the early reader by eliminating a mismatch between the reader and the printed material. However, disadvantages do exist. Teachers must be very well versed in linguistic variance, since not all children in a class may have the same dialect. Also, the teacher will need to be able to create additional reading materials when necessary.

Teach Children to Read Using Materials with Neutralized Features

This is a less extreme approach than developing and using materials printed in nonstandard English. It is also primarily an initial teaching approach which emphasizes the similarities between the standard and nonstandard language forms. The major disadvantage is that the many differences among dialects render it almost impossible to decide which features should or should not be neutralized.

Use Standard Materials but Allow Children to Read in a Variant English Form

Dialect reading of existing materials is the most practical solution in that it requires no additional or alternative materials. The early discussion of miscues is applicable to this alternative. The teacher instructs the child in grapheme-phoneme correspondence and allows the child to transpose the instruction into dialect. The child is able to make use of natural language while learning to gain meaning from the printed page.

Somervill (1975) does caution, however, that certain children who may have no trouble in pronunciation differences may be confused by having to make ". . . a mental translation of grammatical features while attempting to read" (p. 254). In fact, it may be that only fluent readers can make dialect translations during oral readings. A teacher, therefore, should not be too concerned about a child who is able to make dialect switches . . . this may be an encouraging feature.

A great deal more research needs to be done before any one approach can be endorsed. The relationship between reading ability and language variation is still uncertain. The major point for instructional emphasis, however, should be to achieve comprehension both in oral and silent reading. The approaches discussed relate directly to oral reading only. The specific purpose of oral reading is diagnosis. Before diagnosing a true reading problem of a variant English speaker, the teacher must understand the language variation used by the child and be able to differentiate between actual reading problems and language miscues.

Specific Reading Methods

Two major methodological approaches other than adaptations of basal texts, such as those discussed in the previous section, which have been used with variant speakers are the language experience approach and the direct instruction model.

Since the language experience approach was discussed in chapter 11, Reading Instruction, and chapter 10, Written Expression, the remainder of this section will focus on the *direct instruction model*. Described by Becker, Engelmann, and Thomas (1975) the approach is designed for low-functioning and/or language variant children whose oral language is below the level necessary for basic basal reading instruction. The program incorporates behavioral principles and basic instructional techniques. First written for Head Start programs, the materials have been extended to include Follow Through classrooms in the primary years.

Commercially the program is being produced as the Distar Reading Program (SRA) and has proven successful with many high-risk reading children. The important elements of the Direct Instruction model can easily be incorporated into any classroom. The major principles, with appropriate suggestions for implementation, are as follows:

1. *Work in small groups,* and arrange the seating so that all children can face the teacher and be within touching distance. This enables

the teacher to maintain attention and to offer physical prompts and reinforcements when appropriate.

2. *Provide sequenced, daily lessons.* Task analyzing the material to sequence small learning steps is extremely important if the child is to grasp the information and acquire the language and reading skills.

3. *Teaching begins with attention* which can be gained by either a verbal signal ("class") or physical signal (clap hands). Never begin an instructional sequence without first gaining attention, being sure that all children are ready to learn.

4. *Use prompts* to alert the child to the learning task. Both visual and verbal prompts are essential to the reading activity. The child should always be given the prompt during the initial learning stages. ("Look at this word. It says cat. What does this word say?") Later, prompts may be reduced ("Look at this word. What does it say?"), as the child learns the reading task.

5. *A presentation-question-and-answer format* is the appropriate structure. This provides the child with information to ensure that he is aware of the material and then verify his understanding (present, prompt, question).

6. *Pacing is essential.* By moving along the presentation at a relatively fast and steady pace children are motivated to stay with the learning activity. If a child can not respond within 3–5 seconds, additional prompting is necessary.

7. *Questions should initially be answered in unison* by all group members. This allows any child who does not know the material at first to imitate the example set by peers. Individual responses may follow group answers so that each child's understanding can be checked.

8. *Correction or reinforcement should always follow a response.* This provides immediate feedback for each participating child.

9. *Scripted lessons* are important in order to ensure proper sequencing and pacing. Have all materials and teacher cue cards available prior to the lesson beginning. Know what you, as the teacher, will say and what you expect in response. Stay with your lesson script in order to keep the lesson moving at the right pace and covering the material you had planned.

10. *Monitor achievement.* Continuous progress assessment is extremely important if lessons are to be tailored to group and individual needs.

The use of the Direct Instruction Model will prove successful if the teacher follows the steps outlined. Small group reading instruction should last approximately 20–30 minutes. The aim is to provide each child with a structured teaching situation which will provide sequenced reading skills.

Although one may have little choice in selecting reading materials for the classroom, the teacher can make a real difference in the nature of the reading instruction. A positive attitude toward working with the mildly handicapped variant English speaking child is the key factor. The teacher must understand and accept the child's culture and language and must be willing to incorporate basic linguistic principles into sound instructional sequences.

SUMMARY

A great deal of attention is now being given to the language arts program for the variant speaking child. In this chapter we presented a definition of the variant English speaker and then expanded the definition to include mildly handicapped children when it is appropriate. Standard language is seen as a continuum of language forms with a range of acceptability. A child who is a variant speaker may have difficulty learning academics prepared in standard language form and may not be able to pass into the mainstream of society. The *deficit model* and the *difference model* of variant language development were described, emphasizing the difference model as a more appropriate approach.

Three major areas of language arts performance for variant speakers were reviewed: oral language, written language, and reading. Research related to instruction and actual teaching techniques were provided. The teacher of the variant language speaker must be able to motivate the child toward learning and using standard speech in situations that call for it. A teacher who is linguistically naïve may not be able to differentiate elements of the child's variant speech patterns from true language difficulties. It is of primary importance that the teacher accepts the child's language and culture while helping the child to expand his language performance to include standard English.

POINTS FOR DISCUSSION

1. There is a continuum of dialects within American society. Make an inventory of unusual expressions, pronunciations, and words which are peculiar to either certain sections of the country or to certain subgroups of the populations. Are all of the people who use these elements on your list variant English speakers?

2. Review each of the reading approaches for teaching reading to variant speakers. Select two approaches for comparison. Develop or locate materials for each approach and try to teach a variant language speaking child to read using each procedure. What are the results? Which approach are you most comfortable with?

3. Make a tape recording of a variant speaker reading. After transcribing the tape, decide which errors are consistent with the child's dialect and which are serious reading mistakes.

4. The word miscue was defined in this chapter as: pronounced differences between the printed word and the reader's presentation. Agree or disagree with the statement that dialect miscues do not affect reading for comprehension and should therefore not be corrected by the teacher.

5. Collect samples of spelling errors made by variant speaking children. Referring to the appendix on variant language forms, decide which errors are the result of linguistic differences (i.e., pronunciation problems) and which ones are the result of spelling difficulties.

6. Review the major elements of the direct instruction model. Do you think this procedure would be effective for teaching almost any academic skill to problem learners? Why or why not? What do you see as the major advantages of this program?

7. Style shifting is a phenomenon observed in all speakers. Try to attend to your own shifts during a one day or one week period. Keep a record of when and in what way you changed your manner of presentation.

8. In a small group session discuss each of the following points and agree or disagree.
    a. A standard speaking teacher will not be able to fully accept a variant speaker's language pattern.
    b. Bidialectalism is a fully feasible goal of the educational process for variant English speaking children.
    c. A person's primary language form can never be completely eradicated.
    d. When the variant speaking child writes a composition, it is not possible to separate "good" writing from mechanically "correct" writing due to the numerous dialectal expressions.

REFERENCES

Baratz, J. C., and Shuy, R. W. (Eds.). *Teaching black children to read.* Washington Center for Applied Linguistics, 1969.

Becker, W. C., Engelmann, S., and Thomas, D. R. *Teaching 2: Cognitive learning and instruction.* Chicago: SRA, 1975.

Bereiter, C., and Engelmann, S. *Teaching disadvantaged children in the preschool.* Englewood Cliffs, N. J.: Prentice-Hall, Inc., 1966.

Bryen, D. N., Hartman, C., and Tait, P. E. *Variant English.* Columbus, Ohio: Charles E. Merrill Publishing Co., 1978.

Burling, R. *English in black and white.* New York: Holt, Rinehart and Winston, Inc., 1973.

Cohen, S. A., and Cooper, T. Seven fallacies: Reading, retardation, and the urban disadvantaged beginning reader. *Reading Teachers,* 1972, 26, 38–45.

Corbin, R. *The teaching of writing in our schools.* New York: Macmillan, 1966.

Cunningham, P. M. Teacher's correction responses to black-dialect miscues which are non-meaning-changing. *Reading Research Quarterly,* 1976-1977, *4,* 637–653.

Dale, P. S. *Language development: Structure and function* (2nd ed.). New York: Holt, Rinehart and Winston, 1976.

Dunn, L. Special education for the mildly retarded: Is much of it justifiable? *Exceptional Children,* 1968, *35,* 5–22.

Gladney, M. R. A teaching strategy. In R. E. Hodges and E. H. Rudorf, *Language and learning to read.* Boston: Houghton Mifflin Co., 1972, pp. 73–83.

Goodman, K. Dialect barriers to reading comprehension. *Elementary English,* 1965, *42,* 853–860.

Harber, J. R. Influence of presentation dialect and orthography form on reading performance of black inner-city children. *Educational Research Quarterly,* 1977, *2*(2), 9–16.

Johnson, K. R. When should standard English be taught to speakers of non-standard Negro dialect? *Language Learning,* 1969, *20,* 19–30.

Labov, W. *The social stratification of English in New York City.* Washington, D.C.: Center for Applied Linguistics, 1966.

Labov, W. Some sources of reading problems for Negro speakers of nonstandard English. In A. Frazier (Ed.), *New directions in elementary English.* Champaign, Ill.: National Council of Teachers of English, 1967.

Levy, B. B., and Cook, H. Dialect proficiency and auditory comprehension in standard and black nonstandard English. *Journal of Speech and Hearing Research,* 1973, *16,* 642–649.

Liu, S. S. F. An investigation of oral reading miscues made by non-standard dialect speaking black children. *Reading Research Quarterly,* 1975-1976, *11,* 193–197.

Mercer, J. R. *Labeling the mentally retarded.* Berkeley: University of California Press, 1973.

Rigg, P. Dialect and/in/for reading. *Language Arts,* 1978, *55,* 285–290.

Ross, S. B. On syntax of written black English. *TESOL Quarterly, 1976, 10,* 115–122.

Ruddell, R. B. *Reading-language instruction: Innovative practices.* Englewood Cliffs, N.J.: Prentice-Hall, Inc., 1974.

Shuy, R. W. Speech differences and teaching strategies: How different is enough? In R. E. Hodges and E. H. Rudorf (Eds.), *Language and learning to read.* Boston: Houghton Mifflin, 1972, pp. 55–72.

Simons, H. D., and Johnson, K. R. Black English syntax and reading interference. *Research in the Teaching of English,* 1974, *8,* 339–358.

Somervill, M. A. Dialect and reading: A review of alternative solutions. *Review of Educational Research,* 1975, *45,* 247–262.

14

Instructional Programming and the Language Arts

Teaching the language arts to the mildly handicapped child requires a keen sense of organization. The teacher of the mildly handicapped child needs to be alert to the various points throughout the school day at which specific language skills can best be taught. Reading may be a far more enjoyable activity for both the teacher and the child when done in conjunction with a story that the child might be completing for the class or school newspaper. Composition skills may be more readily attended to when they are discussed in the context of an entrance hall bulletin board that the children are preparing, rather than when they are taught in a lesson format from the classroom textbook series. Regardless of the situation, the language arts teacher should realize that the mastery of speaking, listening, reading, and writing depends to a great extent on the number of opportunities that a child has to practice these skills and that such activity *is not limited to a single period each day*. The successful teacher of the language arts is one who:

1. Can capitalize on the interrelatedness of the language arts.
2. Is capable of integrating instruction in each of the language arts in the entire curriculum.

3. Can utilize the entire school day as a vehicle for teaching the language arts.

The Interrelatedness of the Language Arts

Throughout this text each of the language arts may appear to have been dealt with in an isolated manner. The conventions of print limit the alternatives for presenting the essential information. The organization of the individual language arts chapters should not be construed as advocating isolation in language arts instruction. In the actual teaching of the language arts, there is a considerable amount of overlap between speaking, listening, reading, and writing. These skills cannot and should not be taught in isolation.

The perceptive language arts teacher realizes that in teaching aural language skills, for example, one is in fact dealing to a large extent with spoken language as well. Being a "good" listener is in part a requirement of being a "good" speaker. The child who excels in conversational settings is often the one who attends carefully to what is being said by a peer. When teaching aural language skills, it is not unlikely to find that discussion, dialogue, and conversation—the very same activities utilized in the teaching of oral language—play an important role.

This interrelatedness of the language arts extends to composition, handwriting, reading, and spelling as well. Throughout this text, numerous examples demonstrated how instruction in one of the language arts can affect ability in another. In many instances, the relationships are clear (e.g. handwriting to spelling), however, it is quite likely to find that instruction in one area will in some manner influence the acquisition of another more subtly related language skill. Reading instruction that focuses on word-attack skills might impact a child's overall composition abilities, even though a more logical assumption would be that instruction in word-attack skills will result in improved performance in spelling. Such events occur because of the unique nature of the language arts, of the entirely individual way in which language skills are developed, and the unsuspecting and unpredictable ways in which skills are internalized by individuals. Language skills are mutually dependent on each other in ways often unaccounted for, and the interrelatedness of the language arts is clearly one of the defining characteristics of the composite skills.

In designing instructional programs for the mildly handicapped, the interrelatedness of the language arts is an important point to remember. The instructional program developed for a child who has been experiencing difficulty in expressive and/or receptive language must be multifaceted. Work in two or more areas of the language arts might be necessary to achieve both the long- and short-terms goals established for a child.

The interrelatedness of the language arts can be exemplified in the construction of an Individualized Educational Program (IEP). In many cases, the mildly handicapped child who is being mainstreamed requires an instructional program that focuses on all the components of the language arts curriculum. In the example provided in this chapter, Benjamin is shown to have an IEP that stresses skill development in reading, listening, spelling, and writing. These aspects of the language arts curriculum are clearly compatible and the interrelatedness that exists between them enables the teacher to plan a multifaceted program for the child.

In planning and programming language arts for the mildly handicapped, every effort should be made to capitalize on this characteristic interrelatedness. In fact, by doing so, the teacher should find that instruction in the language arts in general becomes a much more enjoyable and profitable experience for both the student and the teacher.

Integrating the Language Arts into the Entire Curriculum

Besides relating well to each other, components of the language arts supplement various aspects of the general elementary school curriculum. Science, social studies, and mathematics as well as the fine arts programs that involve music, art and/or drama, are school day activities that can be approached from a language arts point of view. It is possible to develop a program that revolves entirely around the language arts. Such an approach to instruction can be referred to as *theme teaching*.

Theme teaching can be accomplished in a traditional self-contained classroom or implemented in a more open, space program. The physical environment itself has little bearing on this particular technique for intergrating the language arts into the entire school curriculum. As a result, many teachers find this strategy appropriate for their individual settings and for working with the mildly handicapped.

To develop an instructional program that revolves around a single theme, the teacher must:

1. Identify a single topic, subject, area, or issue around which an entire instructional program can be built. A topic of current interest to the general public (therefore to the children) provides a fertile field for planning an entire curriculum. Examples include themes selected from television specials, investigative newspaper reports, best sellers, local development projects, sports events, and issues of social significance.
2. Present the selected topic to the class for consideration. It is sometimes desirable to present several different options. In the course of discussion, additional areas of interest may be mentioned that had

not been previously considered. Do not discount such spontaneous suggestions. In fact, some of the most successful theme-related instructional programs have been generated unexpectedly by the children themselves!

3. Having reached a consensus, the teacher should determine the extensiveness of related resources with which the theme can be developed. It does little good to isolate a topic related to Asian studies, for example, if the school library has few books on that subject. A successful theme teaching program requires supplemental materials such as study prints, photographic essays, tapes, slides, books, and similar teaching tools. The sea is an example of a theme that is readily supplemented by most school libraries and thus can be quite well developed.

4. Develop a web of interest with the children that specifies the various subject areas related to the topic selected. This is certainly a form of curriculum planning, but each content area must be explored to determine just how science, social studies, and mathematics can be developed by this theme and the various language arts. The web building process is especially valuable in teaching mildly handicapped children due to the extent to which the child can become involved in discussion and dialogue with peers and with the teacher. It permits the mildly handicapped child to identify areas of interest that perhaps overlap with other children's. The mildly handicapped child becomes involved at a very early stage in the development of this theme. A web of study using the sea as a theme is presented in Figure 14.1.

5. Present the completed web of study to the class for the express purpose of implementing the program. To begin instruction it is advisable to permit the children in the class to select areas of study. For example, a small group might wish to begin exploring the myths, folktales, or science fiction stories that use the sea as their focus. Another group might opt for a more structured investigation into the impact the exploration and development of the sea as a resource has had on society. It is recommended that small groups be formed and that the mildly handicapped child be included where appropriate. The teacher will be required to guide the development of their areas of interest. It is not inappropriate, however, to have a single child wish to investigate a topic independently. Such work should be permitted.

6. As the groups are formed, the teacher should provide a focus for the work by helping each group select one of the language arts to serve as a vehicle for the investigation and reporting process. It is here that the theme teaching process effectively utilizes the language arts as an integrating mechanism. The reading that is done on the im-

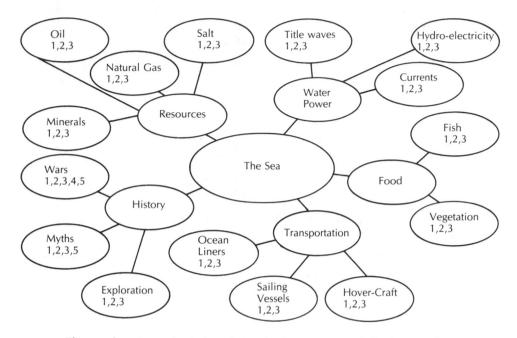

The numbers in each circle refer to the language arts skills that can be brought into play as each topic is developed: 1 = Reading; 2 = Oral Reporting; 3 = Writing & Composition; 4 = Aural Language; 5 = Dramatic Play

FIGURE 14.1   A Web of Interest Centering around a Sea Theme

pact of the sea on society is in fact a social studies lesson. Those children who explore the production of oil on off-shore drilling rigs and the resultant impact in the marketplace can complete a whole range of computational problems. Children who elect to write to their representative or to a petroleum company executive regarding recent oil spills and their impact on the environment are combining science and composition skills in a most appropriate manner.

7. Finally, the teacher should decide at what point the theme will conclude and the means of evaluation. A reasonable amount of time to spend on a particular theme certainly depends on the children involved, the availability of resources, the depth to which the topic is explored, and whether or not there is current public interest in the topic. In many cases, an eight- to ten-week period of time has been found to be a comfortable time frame for focusing on any one topic. Teachers who have utilized a theme teaching approach have developed simple assessment instruments to determine just what science concepts, social implications, and mathematical skills have been attained during the period the theme was explored. These assessment devices are generally teacher-made and related specifi-

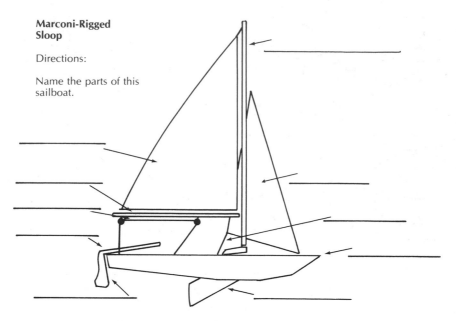

Marconi-Rigged Sloop

Directions:

Name the parts of this sailboat.

FIGURE 14.2   Sample Assessment Technique

cally to aspects of the theme to which the children have been exposed. Because of the unique nature of the theme approach to teaching, commercially prepared materials are not always available. It is up to each teacher to construct "tests" that relate directly to the theme. Figures 14.2, 14.3, and 14.4 are examples of assess-

A Modern Luxury Liner

Directions: Name the parts of this luxury liner.

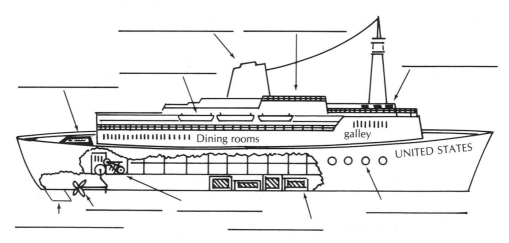

FIGURE 14.3   An Example of a Simple Assessment Instrument

476

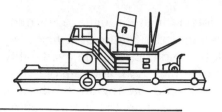

Kinds of Ships

Directions:
Name each of these
ocean-going vessels.

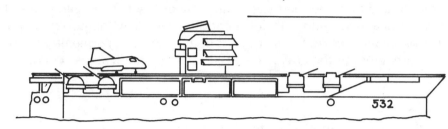

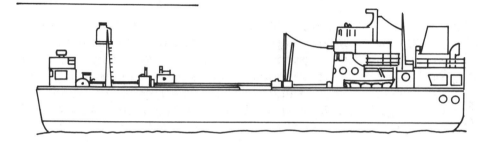

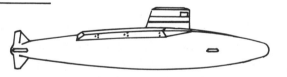

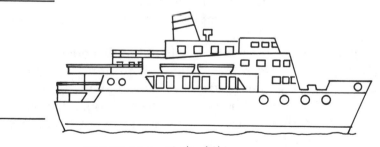

FIGURE 14.4   Kinds of Ships

ment devices developed by a classroom teacher that tests the children's knowledge of various sailing vessels. The sea theme that was made use of in this classroom resulted in the children's exploring various ocean going ships. These are typical of the assessment procedures that can effectively measure knowledge obtained during a theme study program.

The theme teaching approach to integrating the language arts into the entire school curriculum is extremely open-ended. Because of its flexibility, it is well suited to the teaching of the mildly handicapped. The availability of multiple options in focus of study, depth of exploration, and rate of learning, enables the teacher to individualize the instructional program for the mildly handicapped child without unnecessarily disrupting the activity of other children. In addition, the theme approach encourages the integration of the mildly handicapped child into instructional groups. A theme approach to instruction capitalizes on the fact that the language arts permeate the entire school curriculum to the advantage of the mildly handicapped child.

Using the Entire School Day for Language Arts Instruction

In the process of developing a theme approach to instruction, it is not un- likely to find that the entire school day revolves around the theme selected. What were once periods for mathematics, science, or social studies, become times for different group activities related to developing interests in the topic under consideration. Isolated units of instruction give way to discussions, reports, readings, and writings that relate to the theme at hand. The school day, from start to finish, legitimately can be occupied with related language arts.

One factor that often discourages teachers from attempting a theme approach to instruction is that of scheduling. It seems as if the entire school day is simply too short or too crowded with instructional and noninstruc- tional activities. It is impossible to conceive cf a day not bound by a fixed schedule. Many teachers feel that unless time and lessons are legislated, little if anything at all will be accomplished. Nothing could be farther from the truth!

In working with children, scheduling becomes a central factor in determining just what can be accomplished during a given time period. It would be naïve to ignore the fact that some system for classroom manage- ment must be developed to achieve task completion. By providing a structure within which children can work, the entire school day can be effectively utilized to teach the language arts.

To help manage the school day, the teacher should develop a system for keeping track of children. A sign-in/sign-out board made of laminated name tags, cup-hooks, or pegboard (or particle board) can be an extremely useful addition to the classroom. With modification, the board can be used by the children throughout the entire day. For examples, if a section of the board is marked off for the library, resource room, or even the restrooms, children could learn to move their name tag from one section to the other if they plan to leave the room.

A procedure for scheduling activities needs to be developed that is simple to use and easy to understand. If the teacher elects to utilize the entire school day for theme teaching, it will be necessary to control what is done, when, and by whom. Experience has shown that unless a schedule board is developed, children loose track of time, forget assignments, and fail to organize themselves to accomplish specific tasks. It is the teacher's responsibility to assist children in the management of their time. A simple technique for organizing children's daily schedules that was developed and utilized by one of the authors consists of a three-panel free-standing screen made out of pegboard, a pine frame, and coathangers. This scheduling board contained 180 numbered cards, 30 for each of six time periods, that the children learned to use to "program" their own activities each day. The scheduling board operates as follows:

1. After signing in each morning, the children go to the scheduling board to plan their school day.
2. Looking at the board, the children see in the first row:

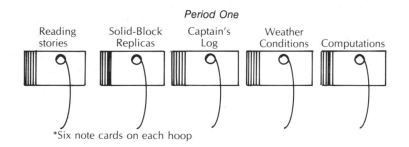

*Six note cards on each hoop

The first row represents the first time frame for the school day and the five different activities in which the child can be engaged. The children simply decide what they want to accomplish first. Assume that this class has selected the sea theme and that there are five different activities:

a. Reading select stories
b. Working on a solid-block replica of an ocean-going vessel
c. Making an entry in a personal "captain's log" regarding the days events
d. Listening to a recording of the weather conditions from the weather stations set up in the science section of the room
e. Completing a set of computations (prepared by the teacher) regarding a ship's course, contents, fuel consumption, and ballast.

Since, in this case, a child wants to work on the solid-block construction during the first period of the day, the child simply slips down a card on wire number two, titled "Solid-Block." The other

479

children can see that one person had already elected to work in the art area on this particular activity.

3. Now the child looks at the board's second row which represents the second period of the day and looks identical to the first row. Thus, the child sees:

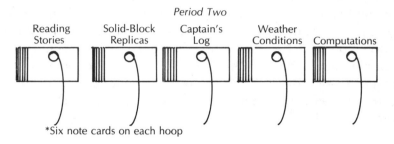

*Six note cards on each hoop

The child repeats the process realizing that now there are only four alternatives from which to choose. The child decides that, after working on the solid-block, he would like to read for a while, so he flips down a single card on the first wire hoop.

4. The child continues through this process until he has selected an activity for each of the instructional periods in the school day. Since at noon all the children have lunch, the fourth period is designated as a lunch period, but the child can select in advance which table he would like to sit at in the cafeteria. Thus, a card on hoop number one indicates that he will be sitting at Table 1.

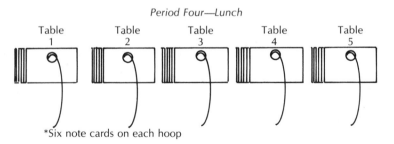

*Six note cards on each hoop

This system for time allocation has different advantages. Among them are:

1. Children are allowed to organize their own school day.
2. Child can elect to work on projects and assignments in the order that appeals to him the most.
3. The children in the class are effectively grouped without interference by the teacher. At any one point during the school day, no more than five children at a time are working on any one activity. Once all the cards are flipped down on a wire hoop, that activity for that period is closed.

4. Children can construct their own groups. For example, two children can agree before going to the scheduling board that they will work together on their computations after lunch. So, when they go to the scheduling board, they both flip down a card on the computation hoop for period five and thus occupy two spaces in the math center.

5. This scheduling system is flexible to the extent that the choices presented can fluctuate as the theme is developed and assignments or topics are completed. It is not a fixed system and can be adapted to accommodate events such as an assembly or a visiting teacher.

6. The teacher can organize the day for the mildly handicapped child in the classroom without upsetting the daily routine for that child. For example, the teacher may want to work with a child who needs additional help in completing the computations assigned for this sea unit. The teacher merely decides which period to work with the child and flips down a single card to occupy a space. The teacher can do this prior to the children's arrival in the morning. Just explain, when the class assembles, that one spot in the mathematics activity section is already occupied for the first period. It might be advisable to mark on the mildly handicapped child's schedule sheet that during a particular period the child is to meet with the teacher to work on the math problems. Since this system is so flexible, if more than one child requires special attention, the teacher can simply occupy more than one space during any single time period as the situation calls for.

7. This system lets the teacher easily group children together in order to engage a mildly handicapped child in a peer tutoring situation. All that is required is identifying the child in the class who will provide the peer instruction. This child is simply asked to schedule daily activities along with the mildly handicapped child so that the two children could work together throughout the day or during a specified period.

While this particular system may seem to be without teacher direction, note that the teacher does need to be quite involved, on a daily basis, in perhaps the following activities:

• Planning the next sequence of activities to occupy the time frames.
• Observing to assess the extent to which the activities currently in progress are being developed by the children.
• Assisting on a regular basis throughout the day the children as they complete the various projects related to a particular theme.
• Developing individual or small group assessment tools and techniques.
• Providing resources as the situations may require.
• Locating materials that are required to complete assignments.

- Correcting and evaluating those activities that are completed and turned in for display, for presentation to the class, or to be brought home.
- Assisting the mildly handicapped child in those areas requiring particular skill development or attention.
- Organizing subsequent themes, units, or lessons that have been identified as natural "spinoffs" from the topic under consideration.

The teacher who implements this management system will find that a greater proportion of the school day *is* spent in instructional activities. In many cases, the teacher finds that he has even more time to spend dealing with problems on a one-to-one basis as the majority of the class is productively occupied in activities of their own choosing. The teacher of the mildly handicapped child will find that such an arrangement permits the development of academic skills and the type of instructional integration that is so often difficult to achieve.

To help children remember the choices that they made, the teacher should develop a weekly schedule sheet, such as the one shown in Figure 14.3. As the child selects an activity, she marks on the sheet in the appropriate space the number or the name of the activity that she is going to engage in during that period. The teacher should develop a system for storing the individual weekly schedule forms for easy reference by the teacher and the child. A successful technique for storing and displaying schedule sheets is to nail a single clothespin for each child to a piece of plywood. (See Figure 14.6.) After the schedule form has been completed, hang it on the clothespin. Thus, at any point during the day, the teacher and the child can refer to the schedule sheet as a reminder of the order in which activities were to be completed.

The clothespin system can also serve to store "work completed" throughout the day. If there are particular assignments that require the com-

	Period 1	Period 2	Period 3	Period 4	Period 5
Monday					
Tuesday					
Wednesday					
Thursday					
Friday					

FIGURE 14.5   Sample Weekly Schedule Firm

482

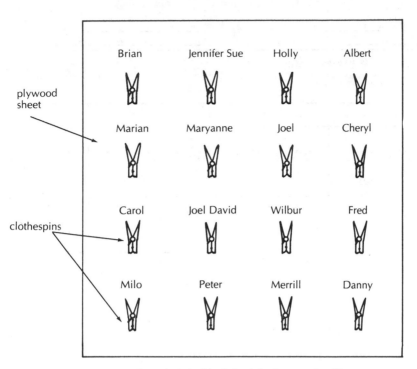

FIGURE 14.6   Sample Weekly Schedule Storage Facility

pletion of work sheets, the child can clip her paper to the board when it is finished. At the end of the day, the teacher removes the papers the children placed on the board and corrects them that evening. By the same token, it is quite easy to pass papers back to the children by putting them on the board as they are corrected and recorded.

This scheduling system complements the theme teaching approach. It is flexible and adapts to a variety of situations. It is not bound by routine and permits individual choices. It is unique to the extent that it enables the teacher to successfully integrate instruction in the language arts into the entire school day. The activities listed on the scheduling board can be specific language arts (e.g., reading, writing, oral reporting, dramatic play or presentations, and composition). And, the system can take into account those varied events that so often turn an otherwise normal school day into one unexpected event after another. The entire school day can be utilized by the language arts teacher if a management system such as the one described here is developed. It can and has been done successfully by many teachers.

Developing an Individualized Educational Program

It was pointed out earlier in this chapter that the development of the Individualized Education Plan (IEP) for the mildly handicapped child experiencing

TEACHING LANGUAGE ARTS SKILLS

Student: Benjamin

Grade Level: 5

Teacher: Mrs. Macher

Special Services: Resource Room–daily 1½ hrs.

Present Level of Functioning:
PIAT – Math –3.8
    Reading Recognition – 3.3
    Reading Comprehension – 3.3
    Spelling – 3.7

General Information – 2.2
Total – 3.2

TOWL – 3.6
Woodcock Reading Inventory
Word Attack – 2.5
Word comp. – 2.3
Passage comp. – 3.8

Annual Goals	Short–Term Objectives	Evaluation	Suggested Teaching Strategies
Reading: •Benjamin will demonstrate the ability to read for instruction in level 9 of the Young American Basic Reader.	•Benjamin will be able to identify basic sight vocabulary of level 9 of Young Americans.	Word cards will be read with 90% accuracy (timed).	•Use flash cards. •Create a visual image by having child write words in sand box. •Color code new vocabulary as they are introduced. •Create a "Word Bank"
	•Benjamin will be able to identify the 220 Basic Dolch Sight Words.	Word cards will be read with 95% accuracy (timed).	
	•Benjamin will be able to name the short vowel sounds in the CVC and CVCC patterns when dictated or written.	•On written work sheets Benjamin will identify the short vowel sound with 90% accuracy. •In dictation Benjamin will identify the short vowel sound with 90% accuracy.	•Make a list of word families. •Match words and picture cards representing these sounds. •While listening to a list of of words being read, Benjamin will clap his hands whenever he hears a certain sound. •Sort word cards according to vowel sound found in the word. •Play vowel Bingo.
	•Benjamin will be able to identify the long vowel sound in CVVC and CVCC patterns when dictated or written.	•On written work sheets or in dictation, Benjamin will identify the long vowel sound with 90% accuracy.	•Make a chart of words representing each vowel sound. •Mark flash cards according to long or short vowel sound (-) (-). •Color code words that have the same vowel sound.
	•Benjamin will recognize r-controlled vowels (er, ir, ur, ar).	Benjamin will identify the two letters (er, ir, ur, ar) in each dictated word.	•Listen to a tape of words having the same r–controlled vowel until Benjamin becomes familiar with that sound. •Play tic–tac–toe using r–controlled vowel words as the stimulus.
	•Benjamin will be able to identify frequent letter patterns, such as ee, ea, ay, ant, ing, en, in.	Given a list of words using the selected letter patterns, Benjamin will correctly identify the words with 90% accuracy.	•Develop a list of words using each pattern. •Color code the significant feature. •Practice hearing, reading, hearing the word on the Language Master.
	•Benjamin will be able to read for comprehension.	•Benjamin will find and express the main idea in 5 short paragraphs. •Benjamin will be able to retell a story he read with the proper sequence of events included. •Benjamin will answer comprehension questions with 85% accuracy on a story he has read in the Young American Series.	•Circle the main idea on worksheets. •"News telecaster" Benjamin will report to the class on something he read in the paper (2 times a week). •Outline main events in a story. •Use a tape recorder to have Benjamin retell stories he has read. •After reading each story have Benjamin answer 5 comprehension questions.

Spelling: •Benjamin will be able to correctly spell a group of representative words selected from his basal spelling and reading books.	•Benjamin will be able to spell CVC and CVCC words (short vowel) when they are dictated to him.	•Given 20 words, Benjamin will spell them from dictation with 90% accuracy. •Given 10 misspelled words, Benjamin will correct the spelling with 90% accuracy.	•Use Dr. Spello activities. •Apply the spelling study method to each word. •Play Scrabble. •Complete crossword puzzles. •Practice writing spelling words using various mediums (paint, string). •Play Name that Word.
	•Benjamin will be able to spell CVCe and CVVC words (long vowel) when they are dictated.	•Given 10 CVCe and 10 CVVC (long vowel) words, Benjamin will spell them with 90% accuracy from dictation. •Given 10 misspelled words, Benjamin will correct the spelling with 90% accuracy.	
	•Benjamin will be able to spell words from a selected list of sight vocabulary in level 9 of the Young American series.	On a Cloze test of 20 words, Benjamin will complete the spellings with 95% accuracy.	
	•Benjamin will be able to spell words selected from a list of spelling demons.	On a Cloze test of 20 words, Benjamin will complete the spellings with 95% accuracy.	
Listening: •Benjamin will increase his listening skills.	•Benjamin will be able to discriminate dissimilar auditory stimuli. •Benjamin will be able to discriminate between two similar auditory stimuli.	After listening to a given sound, Benjamin will be able to select that sound from a series of sounds.	•Using tape recordings and headphones practice discriminating between sounds. •Using a series of different bells, match the correct bell to a given tone.
	•Benjamin will be able to comprehend what he hears and to demonstrate his understanding.	•Benjamin will be able to retell a story he has heard including all relevant events in proper sequence. •Benjamin will follow oral directions. •Benjamin will be able to answer comprehension questions on a story which was read to him with 90% accuracy.	•Play Telephone and pass a message along. •Listen to tape recordings and follow the directions they give (e.g., draw a picture from directions). •Retell a story. •Report on a radio show. •Write the main idea of a story which was told aloud. •Identify common sounds.
Written Expression: •Benjamin will be able to write a paragraph expressing a main idea.	•Benjamin will be able to write a complete sentence when given a stimulus.	•When asked 5 simple questions, Benjamin will write the answers in complete sentences (90%).	•Make a sentence by matching two phrases. •Respond verbally to questions using sentences. •Circle all sentences in a list of sentences and nonsentences. •Match sentences with picture stimuli. •Write a series of statements about an object, event or picture.
	•Benjamin will be able to sequence a list of related sentences.	•Given 5-8 sentences, Benjamin will put them in a proper sequence to express an idea or story.	•Arrange picture cards in sequence to tell a story. •Retell a story changing the sequence to have a new ending. •Start with 2 sentences, arrange in proper sequence, then 3, 4, 5, etc.
	•Benjamin will be able to write a paragraph about a given stimulus.	•Benjamin will write a story when given a title.	•Write letters to friends. •Write a story about your favorite _____ (TV show, ice cream flavor, pet, street, etc.). •Write a short story about "The Most Exciting Thing That's Ever Happened."

485

language difficulties should capitalize on the interrelatedness of the language arts. In the sample IEP that is shown, annual goals and short-term objectives for a child functioning well below grade level are constructed along with evaluation and suggested instructional activities. In this particular instance, the annual goals for Benjamin are expressed in specific terms of reading, spelling, listening, and writing. Because of the overlapping nature of these skills and the manner in which they mutually reinforce each other, the activities are not discrete and can be used to supplement each other. As the language arts teaching theme is developed, the teacher can integrate many of the suggested teaching activities that correspond with the IEP objectives.

SUMMARY

This chapter has demonstrated the manner in which the language arts teacher can effectively integrate the language arts into the entire school day and into the general school curriculum. The teacher of the mildly handicapped child needs to be alert to the many opportunities that present themselves on a daily basis for instruction in the language arts. Because the language arts are so interrelated and because speaking, listening, reading, and writing are so compatible to each of the content areas; a theme teaching technique can be successfully utilized.

While the concept of an integrated approach to instruction is a valid one, without a management system for scheduling activities and events, the implementation of the theme teaching approach will fall short of the teacher's expectations. For this reason the language arts teacher must develop a system for scheduling that organizes children into groups, permits choices, and is flexible in design. The scheduling board was presented as an example of a procedure that has been successfully utilized.

Each language arts teacher of the mildly handicapped will find it necessary to develop an Individual Education Plan. In this chapter, a model for an IEP that incorporates the interrelated aspect of instruction for the language arts was presented. When dealing with a mildly handicapped child, the establishment of annual goals in the language arts often requires attention to more than one of the components skills of the curriculum. This is, in fact, exactly what should happen, since the language arts can not effectively be dealt with in independent units. The hypothetical situations presented in this chapter reflect the interrelatedness of the language arts and the fact that speaking, listening, reading, and writing can be integrated into the school day and into the curriculum.

Descriptions of the Commonly Referred to Language Assessment Instruments

Assessment of Children's Language Comprehension by R. Foster, J. Giddan, and J. Stark. Palo Alto, California: Consulting Psychologists, 1969, 1973.

Foster, Giddan, and Stark (1969) developed an instrument capable of measuring the number of units or words a child can remember. They felt that most of the currently available tests "do not provide a measure of the child's ability to comprehend syntactic units where the number of elements in a unit is a determining factor" (Foster et al., 1969, p. 2). Therefore, Foster et al. designed a test that examines the auditory comprehension ability of most children. The ACLC attempts to describe the level at which the child is able to process various lexical items. The normal child, according to the manual, has little difficulty learning various syntactic relationships. A child who is language delayed and suffers from a particular disorder may require intensive training to develop an ability to better retain words.

The ACLC contains fifty items—all selected because of the ease with which they could be illustrated, the fact that they are commonly occurring, and that they contain no more than two syllables.

The ACLC is designed to test the child's ability to respond to an increasingly more complex statement. It begins at what is termed the one critical level, where the child is required to identify only common nouns, and proceeds through two, three, and four critical element statements. An example of a two critical element statement would be: "Horse standing." "Chair and horn." "Dirty box." Three critical elements would be: "Ball under the table." "Happy lady sleeping." And, four critical elements: "Happy little girl jumping." "Cat standing under the net."

The ACLC measures the child's ability to understand the language that is presented without having to make any particular productions. With the presentation of each stimulus item, an appropriate plate of pictures representing the statement and containing distractor items is available for the child to respond to. The ACLC closely models the PPVT and the NSST in this respect. On hearing the stimulus, the child indicates which of the pictures is correct. The response that is made helps the examiner determine which critical element the child is responding or attending to. For example, in the two critical element level ("Horse standing"), the child will respond probably to just the first critical element, "Horse," and ignore the second critical element "standing." The score sheet that is provided assists the examiner in determining which critical elements the child responds to correctly and those which are responded to incorrectly.

Once administered, the test can be interpreted to help define a starting point in training for a particular child. The test assesses three major areas: Part A—core vocabulary development; Parts B, C, and D—comprehension of an increasing number of lexical items (2, 3, or 4 critical elements); Parts B, C, and D—consistency of pattern of words missed within a sequence—(is the first, second, third, or fourth critical element missed with consistency?). By examining the child's performance in each of these areas, a program for language training can be developed. The results obtained on the ACLC provide the speech therapist with information regarding the child's current developmental stage.

Carrow Elicited Language Inventory (CELI) by E. Carrow. Boston: Teaching Resources Corporation, 1974.

The Carrow Elicited Language Inventory (CELI) is another diagnostic tool. It attempts to provide a systematic procedure to measure a child's syntactic maturity. The Carrow test varies considerably from the DSS and the NSST in both its construction and administration. The DSS technique is built on the child's spontaneous speech. The NSST uses prepared sentences and picture plates. The CELI consists of 52 stimuli that are sentences and one phrase. The test is designed so that the administration does not require extensive knowledge of linguistics and can be given by any trained examiner with a background in psycholinguistics and perhaps language disorders.

The CELI is based on the assumption that data-collecting procedures and language testing cannot rely on spontaneous speech samples alone. Carrow (1974) states that:

> Sentence imitation has been found to be a fruitful source of information relative to the development of language comprehension and expression in children (Menyuk, 1964, 1969; McNeill, 1970; Lenneburg, 1976). Ervin (1964) indicated that the grammar of a child's spontaneous speech and the grammar of his imitations of the adult utterance are not different. The child tends to omit from the surface structure those linguistic elements that cannot be related to deep structures; i.e., children will reproduce a sentence using the rules they know; they filter it through their own productive system (McNeill, 1970). (Manual, p. 2)

Carrow, in designing her elicited language inventory, apparently felt quite comfortable in the development of an instrument based on imitation. By selecting stimulus sentences that were appropriately constructed and extended beyond the child's abilities in terms of pure recall, a considerable amount of insight into the child's awarenesses and uses of various grammatical constructions could be obtained. Table A.1 summarizes the grammatical forms that are included in the CELI.

The administration of the CELI follows the procedures used in many instruments. The child should be tested individually in a quiet room, and the stimulus sentences presented in a live voice and recorded on high-fidelity audio tape equipment. There are practice exercises and instructions available for the experimenter. The following is an example of the testing procedure:

> We are going to play a game and this is how we play it. I am going to say some words; when I stop, I want you to say the same thing I said. Some of the things I say will be very easy and some will be hard. Just do your best. Let's try some words to see if you understand. I'll hold this mike up to your mouth like this when you talk. (Demonstrate.)
>
> *Examiner:* I like candy.
> *Response:* I like candy.
> *Examiner:* Mother went to the store.
> *Response:* Mother went to the store.
>
> Very good. Remember! 1) Listen carefully. 2) Don't start talking until I finish. 3) Say the same thing I did. 4) Speak up and talk in a loud, clear voice. (Carrow, 1974, p. 11, Training Guide)

These instructions can be modified depending on the age and ability level of the child. It is recommended, however, that all stimulus sentences be

Table A.1   Summary of CELI Grammatical Forms

Form	Number
PRONOUNS	41
Indefinite (it, no one, everyone, both, what, whatever)	9
Personal	
1st & 2nd person (I, me, my, mine, you)	12
3rd person (he, she, her, hers)	10
Plural (we, they, their)	7
Demonstrative (those, that)	2
Reflexive (himself)	1
PREPOSITIONS (to, by, in, between, under, on, with)	14
Contexts: modifying copula *is*	4
modifying auxiliary *is* + *ing*	2
modifying auxiliary *is* + *ed*	2
modifying main verbs	6
CONJUNCTIONS (and, because, if, or, before, than, that)	7
ARTICLES (the, a)	41
Contexts: occurring initially	16
occurring medially	25
ADVERBS (fast, where, outside, how, down, up, now)	9
WH- QUESTIONS (where, why, whose)	5
NEGATIVE (not, n't)	13
Contexts: with copula	2
with auxiliary	8
with modal	3
NOUNS	
Singular	50
Plural	9
ADJECTIVES AND PREDICATE ADJECTIVES	7
VERBS	103
Main Verbs (uninflected, *s, ed*)	46
Contexts: singly	14
with auxiliary + (neg)	17
with modal + (neg)	5
with infinitive	5
with auxiliary + neg + infinitive	2
with modal + auxiliary + neg	1
with modal + auxiliary + infinitive	1
with gerund	1
Copula ('s, is, are, been)	14
Contexts: singly	11
with neg	2
with modal + auxiliary	1

Table A.1 *continued*

Form	Number
Auxiliary (am, is, are, has, have, has been, have been, do, does, did)	26
Contexts: with verb (ing, ed) + (neg)	20
with neg + verb + infinitive	2
with modal + neg + verb	2
with modal + verb + infinitive	1
with modal + copula	1
Modal (can, could, will, would, may)	8
Contexts: with verb + (neg)	5
with auxiliary + copula	1
with neg + auxiliary + verb	1
with auxiliary + verb + infinitive	1
INFINITIVES	8
GERUND	1

Source: Carrow, E. *Carrow elicited language inventory,* 1974. Reprinted by permission of E. Carrow and Teaching Resources Corporation, Hingham, Mass.

spoken with the stress and intonation of conversational speech. Care should be taken to avoid exaggeration of words, and articulation should be clear and precise. If the child does not imitate the sentence the first time it is given, it is recommended that the clinician test the next three items then return to the unimitated sentence to see if the child will repeat it on the second trial. Only two trials may be given.

With respect to scoring procedures, the CELI is rather unusual. The scoring analysis forms that are provided require the clinician to transcribe the child's responses. It is recommended that the clinician use phonemic notation for all transcriptions. Once the transcription has been completed, it will be possible to score the child's performance.

The test scoring procedure is based on an error analysis. There are five categories of error types:

1. Substitutions
2. Omissions
3. Additions
4. Transpositions
5. Reversals

The clinician is required to note each type of error on the scoring analysis form. After the entire test has been scored, a tally should be made of the number and type of errors made in each grammatical category. Because the scoring procedure is somewhat complex, a training guide is provided. Before administering and scoring the test, the clinician should take the time to practice with the training tape. If the clinician has become familiar with the error categories and the transcription process, the test becomes relatively easy to administer and to score.

In the case of the CELI, both percentile ranks and standard scores are provided. The test was normed on a group of 475 children. Percentile ranks and stanine scale scores corresponding to total raw scores obtained are provided for children ages three through twelve. It is possible, then, to determine a child's relative performance on the CELI in relation to other children.

With respect to interpretation of the results obtained, Carrow points out that:

> The CELI is most stable for total error scores for all age groups and for subcategory scores for three- and four-year-old children. With the exception of the verb subscore in the type subcategories, the performance of the 5-, 6-, and 7-year-old children in the subcategories was relatively homogeneous within each age group. Consequently, the percentile scores must be interpreted with caution. The most stable categories for the total group are articles, pronouns, verbs, and negatives. (Manual, p. 20)

Memory, attitude, and familiarity with the experimenter will influence the test results. The score obtained on the CELI cannot be used as a definitive measure of the child's level of syntactic maturity. Yet, it does provide the best possible estimate. It is recommended that other test scores be used in conjunction with the CELI in order to obtain an adequate diagnosis of the child's disability.

Developmental Sentence Scoring by L. Lee and S. Canter. Evanston, Illinois: Northwestern University Press, 1971, 1974.

Lee and Canter's (1971) *Developmental Sentence Scoring* (revised, 1974) procedure is another technique that can be used to determine the child's level of syntactic maturity. The Developmental Sentence Scoring (DSS) is a formalized language assessment procedure. There is both normative data and a standardized technique by which values are assigned to particular constructions. DSS can be time consuming and tedious to complete. It does, however, provide specific information with respect to the level of syntactic development of a particular child.

According to Lee and Canter (1971, p. 317), an adequate corpus of sentences for the DSS analysis can be obtained from a sample of fifty complete, different, consecutive, intelligible, nonecholalic sentences elicited from a child in conversation with an adult using stimulus materials, pictures, and toys in which the child is interested. Given this criteria, the speech clinician can analyze a child's language sample and can arrive at a DSS score.

The DSS technique rests on an analysis of:

1. Indefinite pronouns and/or noun modifiers
2. Personal pronouns
3. Main verbs
4. Secondary verbs
5. Negatives
6. Conjunctions
7. Interrogative reversals
8. *Wh-* questions

Within each of these categories, items have been grouped in terms of their developmental sequence. A weighted scale had been used to assign numerical value to the items subject to analysis. Table A.2 contains the eight analysis categories and the corresponding scored items contained in each.

Once the sample has been obtained and transcribed, it is necessary to identify those items occurring in each of the eight analysis categories. A score sheet similar to the one shown in Table A.3 is necessary. The sentences provided here for examples are those developed by Lee and Canter to illustrate the DSS scoring technique.

Though a tedious and rather difficult process to pace oneself through, the Developmental Sentence Scoring procedure provides information that is by far superior to that which can be obtained from an informal assessment technique or the currently available screening devices. The DSS technique also provides the classroom teachers, special educator, or speech therapist with information regarding the child's development of specific grammatic forms. An instructional program can be devised based on the information obtained from the DSS analysis. While there are problems associated with the assessment procedure, it is a most useful tool.

The Illinois Test of Psycholinguistic Abilities by S. A. Kirk, J. J. McCarthy, and W. D. Kirk. Urbana, Illinois: University of Illinois Press, 1968.

Another instrument that the teacher might encounter, depending on the results obtained from various screening devices, is that of the Illinois Test of Psycholinguistic Ability (ITPA). The ITPA developed by Kirk, McCarthy, and Kirk (1968) is perhaps the most comprehensive language assessment measure currently available. The ITPA has been used extensively in both school and clinical settings in order to pinpoint particular difficulties experienced by children with deviant or delayed language habits. The ITPA is a diagnostic instrument. It is not designed to categorize disabilities or to classify children. Its objective, according to the manual, "is to delineate specific abilities and disabilities in children in order that remediation might be undertaken where needed" (Kirk et al., 1968, p. 5). The ITPA, therefore, provides a model not only for diagnosis but also for instruction.

Table A.2 Developmental Sentence Scoring Scale

	INDEFINITE PRONOUNS OR NOUN MODIFIERS	PERSONAL PRONOUNS	MAIN VERBS	SECONDARY VERBS
1	is, this, that	1st and 2nd person: I, me, my, mine, you, your(s)	A. Uninflected verb: I see you. B. copula, is or 's: It's red. C. is + verb + ing: He is coming.	
2		3rd person: he, him, his she, her, hers	A. -s and -ed: plays, played B. Irregular past: ate, saw C. Copula: am, are, was, were D. Auxiliary am, are, was, were	Five early-developing infinitival complements: I wanna see (want to see) I'm gonna see (going to see) I gotta see (got to see) Lemme [to] see (let me [to] see) Let's [to] play (let [us to] play)
3	A. no, some, more, all, lot(s), one(s), two (etc.) other(s), another B. something, somebody, someone	A. Plurals: we, us, our(s) they, them, their B. these, those		Non-complementing infinitives: I stopped to play I'm afraid to look. It's hard to do that.
4	nothing, nobody, none, no one		A. can, will, may + verb: may go B. Obligatory do + verb: don't go C. Emphatic do + verb: I do see.	Participle, present or past: I see a boy running. I found the toy broken.

#			
5	Reflexives: myself, yourself, himself, herself, itself, themselves		A. Early infinitival complements with differing subjects in kernels: I want you *to come.* Let him [*to*] *see.* B. Later infinitival complements: I had *to go.* I told him *to go.* I tried *to go.* He ought *to go.* C. Obligatory deletions: Make it [*to*] *go.* I'd better [*to*] *go.* D. Infinitive with wh-word: I know what *to get.* I know how *to do it.*
6	A. Wh-pronouns: who, which, whose, whom, what, that, how many, how much I know *who* came. That's *what* I said. B. Wh-word + infinitive: I know *what to do.* I know *who(m)* to take.	A. could, would, should, might + verb: *might come, could be* B. Obligatory does, did + verb C. Emphatic does, did + verb		
	A. any, anything, anybody, anyone B. every, everything, everybody, everyone	(his) own, one, oneself, whichever, whoever, whatever Take *whatever* you like.	A. Passive with *get*, any tense Passive with *be*, any tense B. must, shall + verb: *must come*	Passive infinitival complement: With *get:* I have *to get dressed.*

continued

	INDEFINITE PRONOUNS OR NOUN MODIFIERS	PERSONAL PRONOUNS	MAIN VERBS	SECONDARY VERBS
7	C. both, few, many, each, several, most, least, much, next, first, last, second (etc.)		C. have + verb + en: I've eaten D. have got: I've got it.	I don't want to get hurt. With be: I want to be pulled. It's going to be locked.
8			A. have been + verb + ing had been + verb + ing B. modal + have + verb + en may have eaten C. modal + be + verb + ing could be playing D. Other auxiliary combinations: should have been sleeping	Gerund: Swinging is fun. I like fishing. He started laughing.

NEGATIVES	CONJUNCTIONS	INTERROGATIVE REVERSALS	WH- QUESTIONS
it, this, that + copula or auxiliary is, 's, + not: It's not mine. This is not a dog. That is not moving.		Reversal of copula: Isn't it red? Were they there?	A. who, what, what + noun: Who am I? What is he eating? What book are you reading?

	and	B. where, how many, how much, what . . . do, what . . . for *Where did it go?* *How much do you want?* *What is he doing?* *What is a hammer for?*
can't, don't	Reversal of auxiliary be: *Is he coming? Isn't he coming?* *Was he going? Wasn't he going?*	
	A. but B. so, and so, so that C. or, if	when, how, how + adjective *When shall I come?* *How do you do it?* *How big is it?*
isn't, won't	because	A. Obligatory do, does, did: *Do they run? Does it bite?* *Didn't it hurt?* B. Reversal of modal: *Can you play? Won't it hurt?* *Shall I sit down?* C. Tag question: It's fun, *isn't it?* It isn't fun, *is it?*

continued

NEGATIVES	CONJUNCTIONS	INTERROGATIVE REVERSALS	WH-QUESTIONS

All other negatives:
A. Uncontracted negatives:
    I can *not* go.
    He has *not* gone.
B. Pronoun-auxiliary or pronoun-copula contraction:
    I'm *not* coming.
    He's *not* here.
C. Auxiliary-negative or copula-negative contraction:
    He was*n't* going.
    He has*n't* been seen.
    It could*n't* be mine.
    They are*n't* big.
			why, what if, how come
			how about + gerund
			Why are you crying?
			What if I won't do it?
			How come he is crying?
			How about coming with me?

A. where, when, how while, whether (or not), till, until, unless, since, before, after, for, as, as + adjective + as, as if, like, that, than I know *where* you are. Don't come *till* I call. B. Obligatory deletions: I run faster *than* you [run]. I'm *as* big *as* a man [is big]. It looks *like* a dog [looks]. C. Elliptical deletions (score 0) That's *why* [I took it]. I know *how* [I can do it]. D. Wh-words + infinitive: I know *how* to do it. I know *where* to go.	A. Reversal of auxiliary have: *Has he* seen you? B. Reversal with two or three auxiliaries: *Has he been* eating? *Couldn't he have* waited? *Could he have been* crying? *Wouldn't he have been* going?	whose, which, which + noun *Whose* car is that? *Which* book do you want?

Source: Lee, L. *Developmental sentence analysis.* Evanston, Ill.: Northwestern University Press, 1974, pp. 134–135. Reprinted with the permission of the publisher and the author.

Table A.3 DSS Score Sheet

Name:
Recording date:
Birth date:
CA:
DSS: 13.63

Hypothetical Corpus of Thirty Sentences Illustrating Developmental Sentence Scoring

	Indef. Pro.	Pers. Pro.	Main Verb	Sec. Verb	Neg.	Conj.	Inter. Rev.	Wh-Q	Sent. Point	Total
1. Boy eat.			—						0	0
2. Boy eat cookie.			—						0	0
3. The boy is eating a cookie.			1						1	2
4. The boys are eating cookies.			2						1	3
5. They ate them.		3,3	2						1	9
6. They didn't eat them.		3,3	6		7				1	20
7. Didn't they eat them?		3,3	6		7		6		1	26
8. Why didn't they eat them?		3,3	6		7		6	7	1	33
9. Why didn't they?		3	inc.		7		6	7	1	24
10. All the cookies were eaten.	3		7						1	11
11. I want to eat some cookies.	3	1	1	2					1	8
12. I want him to eat some cookies.	3	1,2	1	5					1	13
13. I tried to find some cookies.	3	1	2	5					1	12
14. Could you find them?		1,3	6				6		1	17

500

Sentence									S.P.	Total
15. You couldn't find them, could you?		1,3	6		7		6		1	24
16. Nobody knows where to find them.	4	3	2	5		8			1	23
17. Who knows where she keeps them?		2,3	2,2			8		2	1	20
18. I looked but I couldn't find them.		1,1,3	2,6		7	5			1	26
19. I like eating cookies.		1	1	8					1	11
20. Nobody told me that I shouldn't eat them.	4	1,1,3	2,6		7	8			1	33
21. I only ate a few.	7	1	2						1	11
22. Somebody else must have eaten all the rest.	3,3		8						1	15
23. Let's eat some more.	3,3		1	2					1	10
24. Mommy said, "Don't eat those cookies."		3	2,4		4				1	14
25. That isn't what she said.	1	6,2	1,2		5				1	18
26. Him can't have some.	3				4				1	8
27. What you eating?		1					—	2	0	3
28. Her don't gots any.	7	1			—				0	7
29. Mommy find out.		—	—						0	0
30. You want to get spanked?		1		7			—		0	8
									TOTAL	409

409/30 = 13.63 DSS

Source: Lee, L. *Developmental sentence analysis.* Evanston, Ill.: Northwestern University Press, 1974, p. 164. Reprinted with the permission of the publisher and the author.

At first glance, the ITPA appears to be a formidable instrument. The twelve subtests that comprise this particular instrument are as follows:

1. Auditory reception
2. Visual reception
3. Visual sequential memory
4. Auditory association
5. Auditory sequential memory
6. Visual association
7. Visual closure
8. Verbal expression
9. Grammatic closure
10. Manual expression
11. Auditory closure
12. Sound blending

As can be seen from this list of test areas, the ITPA attempts to determine the child's ability in each area thought to be instrumental in the determination of language ability. These twelve subtests were not arrived at at random. The fact that the ITPA tests ability in each one of these areas stems from the overall definition of language constructed by the authors. Figure A.1 is a representation of the three-dimensional model of the ITPA. Examining the figure it is possible to understand the reasons for the inclusion of these twelve subtests. It is believed by Kirk et al., that language and language activity involves at one level auditory stimuli, verbal stimuli, vocal responses, and pure motor responses. At another level, it involves both automatic and representational activity, and at a third level it consists of receptive, organizing, and expressive processes. This three-dimensional model of the ITPA results in the view that the subtest includes all tests the various skills required in order to produce either a vocal or motor response. Figure A.1 shows the flow from stimuli to response and the intermediary steps and processes according to Kirk et al., necessary to produce appropriate and acceptable responses. This model, then, is useful in understanding the construction of the ITPA as well as providing an alternative view of the language process.

The ITPA is truly a complicated instrument. Each of the subtests are to be presented in a specified sequence. In some cases, basals and ceilings are determined to provide reference points for the beginning and ending of testing. The examiner is provided with a record form for scoring items as well as space for noting responses. When the testing procedure is concluded, a profile can be plotted that visualizes the performance of the child on each of the subtests. Figure A.2 is an example of an ITPA ability profile.

The ITPA must be interpreted with caution. As with most comprehensive instruments, there is tendency to attribute specific behaviors to a child depending on the results obtained from the administration of this single

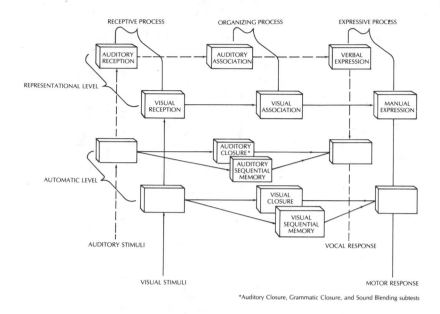

RECEPTIVE PROCESS   ORGANIZING PROCESS   EXPRESSIVE PROCESS

*Auditory Closure, Grammatic Closure, and Sound Blending subtests

Source: The Illinois test of psycholinguistic abilities by S. Kirk, J. McCarthy, and W. Kirk, © 1968. Reprinted with permission of University of Illinois Press.

FIGURE A.1   The Language Process

instrument. Since it is such a comprehensive test and because such discrete categories exist, one might be inclined to attribute a child's difficulty to an inability to function in a particular area in which a low score appears, when this may not be the case at all. There may be a number of factors influencing the child's performance. Only when the results of the ITPA are used in conjunction with information obtained from other instruments can statements regarding the child's ability or disability be made. One would also expect to find, in cases of language delay or language deviation, that scores would represent a pattern of behavior rather than indicate isolated areas of disability. It is, therefore, the overall pattern that can be arrived at from the profile that is of significance. It is stated by the authors that:

> Test scores from any test, including the ITPA are not infallible. Tests cannot replace expert diagnosticians. They are tools used by diagnosticians as aids to diagnosis. Therefore, the interpretation of discrepancies ... should take into consideration other relevant information. Additional information regarding the child's behavior is obtained from other tests as well as from reports from teachers and parents. (Kirk et al., 1968, p. 96)

Certainly the ITPA is the most comprehensive instrument currently available to assess language ability. It heightens one's sensitivity to the various levels of language activity, and it examines many of the behaviors gener-

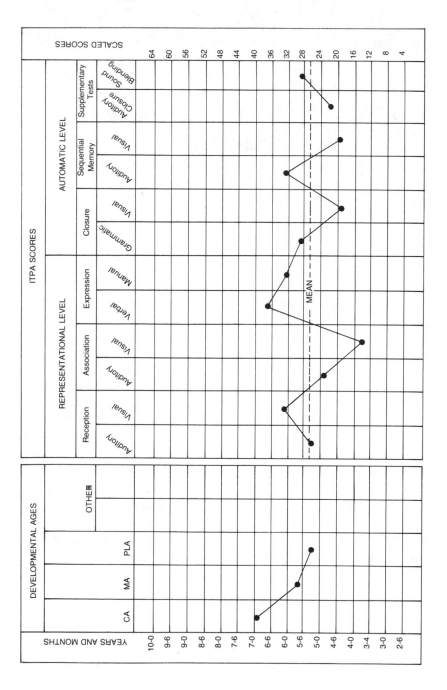

Source: The Illinois test of psycholinguistic abilities by S. Kirk, J. McCarthy, and W. Kirk, © 1968. Reprinted with permission of University of Illinois Press.

FIGURE A.2   *ITPA Ability Profile*

ally associated with language functioning. The test is certainly one that can be used effectively and can provide information that will be extremely useful to the classroom teacher, special educator, and speech therapist who is designing a language training program for a particular child.

Peabody Picture Vocabulary Test (PPVT) by L. Dunn. Circle Pines, Minnesota: American Guidance Service, 1959, 1965.

The Peabody Picture Vocabulary Test (PPVT) is not in a strict sense a language assessment instrument. It was devised as a measure of intelligence rather than that of receptive language ability. Given the construction of the instrument, however, it is in essence a measure of receptive language ability.

The PPVT concerns itself primarily with nouns. Neither sentences nor phrases are presented for the child to consider. The child's previous experience is a large factor in determining relative performance on this test. In recent years, the PPVT has received considerable criticism because of its apparent cultural bias. The use of the instrument, however, has not been subject to severe curtailment. The PPVT is still a widely used assessment measure.

The PPVT consists of 150 plates, each containing four pictures. A stimulus word is provided and the child is requested to identify the correct picture. Figure A.3 is an example of a plate associated with the stimulus word "chair." As can be seen in this example, the child's attention is directed to the distracting items of a "fish," a "man," and a "banana." In this situation the child must discriminate among those items and correctly identify the picture that corresponds to the word "chair." The test proceeds in this fashion until the child has made six errors in eight consecutive responses.

While the administration of the PPVT is relatively simple, there are several important rules provided in the manual. It is recommended, for example, that the test be given in a quiet room and that distractions be kept to a minimum. The manual encourages the tester to motivate the child to do his best and to lavish praise on the child. The administration of this instrument requires no adherence to a specific time limit and usually takes fifteen minutes. The child is tested only over a particular range of items that have been determined as being appropriate. The starting point, basal, and ceiling will vary from child to child.

With the PPVT the total raw score is the number of correct responses. Since this test requires that a basal and a ceiling be established, it is assumed that all the items below the basal would be responded to correctly and that all the items above the ceiling would produce errors. To obtain the raw score, one needs to simply subtract the number of errors that occur from the number of the last item mentioned or the ceiling item.

Point to "chair."

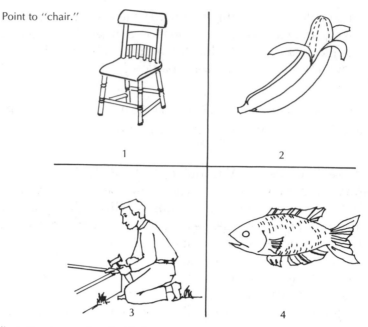

Source: This illustration is reproduced with the special permission of the author of the PPVT, Lloyd M. Dunn.

FIGURE A.3   Sample Plate of the PPVT

Once the raw score has been determined, it must be converted to one of three types of derived scores:

1. Age equivalent or mental age
2. A standard score equivalent or intelligent quotient
3. A percentile equivalent

The PPVT provides raw score conversion tables.

Once the scores have been obtained, the experimenter has the responsibility to appropriately interpret the age equivalent or standard scores. In this case, as in all testing procedures, certain variables may need to be taken into account. The score that is obtained cannot be assumed to be the final word on the child's language ability. There may be errors in pronunciation on the part of the experimenter or dialectical differences that have not been controlled for. There may be cultural differences influencing the child's reactions to the various words and pictures, and there may be a lack of exposure on the part of the child to the various concepts and items that comprise this particular assessment instrument. As in all testing situations, the PPVT is one component of the child's overall assessment. The findings that are obtained on this instrument need to be confirmed and viewed in relation to other instruments the child may have been required to take.

Northwestern Syntax Screening Test (NSST) by L. Lee. Evanston, Illinois: Northwestern University Press, 1971.

The Northwestern Syntax Screening Test is also an instrument that is made use of on a widespread basis by speech clinicians. This instrument is intended for use as a screening device with children ages three to eight. It is, according to the manual, "in no sense to be considered a measurement of a child's general language skill or even as an in-depth study of syntax" (p. 1, 1971). The NSST consists of a series of twenty plates for both the expressive and receptive language categories. In each situation, the child is presented with a pen-and-ink drawing and is asked to respond by either pointing to a picture or by stating a sentence which has been given that appropriately describes a picture. The NSST has both receptive and expressive norm tables. It is possible to isolate the comparative performance of a child on the NSST by comparing the score obtained on either the receptive or expressive categories to those listed in the norm tables.

In the administration of the NSST, the speech clinician is instructed to make a statement similar to the following:

> *Receptive Item:* I'm going to tell you about these pictures. When I'm done, you show me the right picture. Look at all the pictures. Don't point until I tell you. (Show page 1.) *The cat is behind the chair. The cat is under the chair.* * Show me *the cat is under the chair.* * (Child points.) Now show me *the cat is behind the chair.* (Child points.)

This particular procedure is utilized through all ten receptive language pairs.

For the expressive items, the administrator will give instructions such as the following:

> *Expressive Item:* I will tell you about these pictures. When I am done, you copy me. Say just what I say. Don't talk until I tell you, though. Ready? Listen. (Show page 1.) *The baby is sleeping.* * *The baby is not sleeping.* Now what is this picture? (Examiner points to asterisk picture and child replies.) Now what's this one? (Examiner points to unasterisked picture and the child replies.)

This procedure is also used in the ten expressive language sentence pairs. Figures A.4 and A.5 are examples of the plates that comprise the NSST.

A score of one is given for each correct response. A child could obtain a score of 0, or 2 on each of the twenty pairs of sentences. With respect to failure, the manual states that on the receptive portion a failure is a wrong picture identification in response to the spoken sentence. For the expressive portion of the instrument, however, failure may be:

1. Any change of the examiner's spoken sentence which affects the test item is considered a failure even though the child's response is grammatically and semantically correct.

Ex.:   The baby is not sleeping.
Child: The baby is awake.
(Score incorrect. The test item, negative placement, is omitted even though the child's sentence is grammatically and semantically correct.)

2.   Any response which contains a grammatical error, even though it is not the test item is considered a failure on the ground that the test item, though correct, may have introduced enough complexity to cause other structures to be dropped.
Ex.:   The girl sees the dogs.
Child: Girls sees the dogs.
(Score incorrect. The omission of an article produces an ungrammatical sentence. It is possible that the child might have included the article if the sentence had not contained the further complication of the verb tense marker, -s.)

3.   The experimenter is reminded, however, that any change of the examiner's spoken sentence which does not change the test item and which still produces a grammatically and semantically correct sentence is acceptable and scores 1.
Ex.:   The baby is not sleeping.
Child: He is not sleeping.

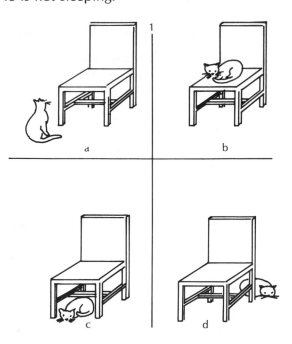

Source: The Northwestern syntax screening test (NSST) by L. Lee, © 1971. Reprinted with permission of University of Illinois Press.

FIGURE A.4   NSST Plate—Receptive Portion

508

FIGURE A.5   NSST Plate—Expressive Portion

(Score correct. The child's introduction of a pronoun does not affect the test items, *not,* and the sentence is grammatically and semantically correct.) (Lee, 1971, pp. 304)

It is recommended that incorrect replies to the expressive items be noted by crossing out words or word endings or otherwise changing the printed sentence on the record form to read exactly as the child replies. This process is recommended because it enables the examiner to look back over errors and to determine specific areas that could serve as the basis for instruction.

With respect to the interpretation of the scores obtained on the NSST, the manual states that: "In all cases, the clinician should use other language measures, investigate the child's social and emotional adjustment, and consider his intellectual level and classroom performance before deciding to enroll him for language teaching" (Lee, 1971, p. 7).

Certainly the interpretation of the scores extend beyond simply a comparison of the child's score to the percentile tables. The manual is quite detailed in its guidelines regarding the interpretation of the scores obtained on this instrument.

The NSST is a screening device. As stated originally, it is not intended as an in-depth study of syntax nor is it meant to be a measure of children's general language ability. It does provide, however, a means of identifying those children between the ages of three and eight years of age who are sufficiently deviant in syntax development to warrant further study.

Verbal Language Development Scale by M. Mecham. Circle Pines, Minnesota: American Guidance Service, 1958, 1971.

One of the most widely used formalized texts, in the sense that it is commercially available through the American Guidance Service, is that of the *Mecham Verbal Language Development Scale*. This particular instrument examines children's language ability in the area of listening, speaking, reading, and writing. It is to some extent a language inventory. Here, the speech therapist would simply mark each item the child passes with a plus (+) and give one point of credit. If a failure to perform a particular language skill could be determined, a minus (−) would be indicated on the score sheet and no credit would be assigned. In those cases where it was obvious that the language skill was emerging, a plus/minus (+/−) combination would be assigned and one half a point credit would be given. This instrument provides a language-age equivalent table. The score obtained can be compared to that of other children. Figure A.6 contains the items for one month through fifteen years that comprises the Verbal Language Development Scale.

KEY TO LETTER SYMBOLS:
L = Listening
S = Speaking
R = Reading
W = Writing

0–1 Year Level

S_____ 1. "Crows," laughs or smiles
S_____ 2. Produces consonant sounds reflexively
S_____ 3. Talks; imitates sounds
L_____ 4. Responds to name and "no-no"
L_____ 5. Comprehends "bye-bye" and "pat-a-cake"
S_____ 6. Echoes words (dada or mama)
L_____ 7. Follows simple instructions

1–2 Year Level

S_____ 8. Expressive vocabulary of at least two words
W_____ 9. Marks with pencil or crayon
L_____10. Recognizes names of familiar objects
L_____11. Recognizes hair, mouth, ears, and hands when they are named
S_____12. Expressive vocabulary of at least 25 words
S_____13. Uses names of familiar objects
L_____14. Identifies common pictures when they are named
S_____15. Talks in short sentences
S_____16. Can name common pictures

2–3 Year Level

S_____17. Verbalizes toilet needs
S_____18. Asks for "another"
S_____19. Uses plurals
S_____20. Vocabulary of 50 words or more in conversational speech
S_____21. Uses *I, me, you,* etc. in his speech
S_____22. Expresses vocally a desire to take turns
R_____23. Identifies action in familiar action pictures
S_____24. Names one color
S_____25. Names almost all common pictures

3–4 Year Level

S_____26. Says full name
S_____27. Relates experiences
S_____28. Says at least one nursery rhyme
S_____29. Recites poem or sings song from memory
S_____30. Names all colors

4–5 Year Level

R_____31. Reads by way of pictures
W_____32. Draws with pencil or crayon
W_____33. Prints simple words

5–6 Year Level

S_____34. Relates fanciful tales
S_____35. Names penny, nickel, dime
S_____36. Recites numbers to thirties
S_____37. Asks meaning of words

6–7 Year Level

S_____38. Uses telephone to communicate
S_____39. Can tell a familiar story
R_____40. Reads on pre-primer level
W_____41. Writes numbers from one (1) to fifty (50)

7–9 Year Level

S_____42. Names quarter, half-dollar, dollar, etc.
W_____43. Writes with pencil
R_____44. Reads on own initiative
W_____45. Writes occasional short letters

9–15 Year Level

S_____46. Can retell short story that he has read on his own
W_____47. Answers ads; purchases by mail
R_____48. Enjoys books, newspapers, magazines
W_____49. Writes by letter
S_____50. Follows current events and discusses them with others

Source: Mecham, M. *Verbal language development scale.* Circle Pines, Minn.: American Guidance Service, Inc., 1958, 1971.

FIGURE A.6   *Verbal Language Development Scale*

Appendix B

Inventories of Variant Language Forms

Black Variant Speakers

Homophones for the Variant Black Speaker.

Position	Standard Form	Nonstandard Form	To the Standard English Speaker ____sounds like____	
Initial	/str/	/skr/	stream	scream
			strap	scrap
Initial	/šr/	/sr/	shrimp	srimp
Initial	/đ/	/d/	this	dis
			that	dat
Initial	/θr/	/tr/	three	tree
			thrust	trust
Final	/θ/	/f/	Ruth	roof
Final	/đ/	/v/	bathe	bave
Final	/nt/	/n/	meant	men
			bent	Ben
Final	/ŋ/	/n/	sing	sin
Final	/sks/	/səs/	masks	masses
Before nasals	/i/	/e/	pin	pen
			since	cents
Before /r or l/	/ih/	/eh/	beer	bear
			peel	pail
Before /r/	/uh/	/oh/	poor	pour
Before /l/	/oy/	/ɔh/	boil	ball
			oil	ail
Any	/ay/	/ah/	find	fond
			time	Tom
Any	/aw/	/ah/	found	fond

Position	Standard Form	Nonstandard Form	To the Standard English Speaker _____sounds like_____	
Final, or before consonants	/l/	absent	tool	too
			toil	toe
			fault	fought
			help	hep
Final or Medial	/r/	absent	four	foe
			guard	God
			Carol	Cal
			carried	cade
Final	/d/	absent	road	row
Final	/g/	absent	log	law
Final	/k/	absent	back	baa
Final	/t/	absent	boot	boo
Final	/dnt/	/tn/	didn't	dit'n
			shouldn't	shut'n
Final	/skt/	/ks/	asked	axed
Final	/sts/	/s/	fists	fis

Phonological variations that affect the grammatical system.

Position	Standard Form		Nonstandard Form		To the Standard English Speaker sounds like		Grammatical Consequence
Final	/ft/		/f/		laughed	laugh	Past tense
				also	tuft	tough	not signaled
Final	/md/		/m/		simed	sim	Past tense
							not signaled
Final	/nd/		/n/		fined	fine	Past tense
				also	wind	wine	not signaled
Final	/st/		/s/		passed	pass	Past tense
				also	past	pass	not signaled
Final	/zd/		/z/		buzzed	buzz	Past tense
					raised	raise	not signaled
Final	/l/		absent		you'll	you	Future tense
					they'll	they	not signaled
					he'll	he	
					she'll	she	
Final	/dz/		/d/		loads	load	Agreement
							not signaled
Final	/lz/		/l/		holes	hole	Agreement
		also	/z/		holes	hose	not signaled
Final	/mz/		/m/		comes	come	Agreement
		also	/z/		comes	cuz	not signaled
Final	/nz/		/n/		runs	run	Agreement
		also	/z/		runs	ruz	not signaled
Final	/ts/		/t/		hits	hit	Agreement
		also	/s/		hits	his	not signaled
Final	/ks/		/k/		knocks	knock	Agreement
		also	/s/				not signaled

Morphological and syntactical variations.

DESCRIPTION	EXAMPLE
A. Use of verb forms	
1. Copula omitted, as in	He tired. You playing here. He running away.
2. Standard use of copula for greater emphasis, as in	He *is* tired. You *are* playing.
3. Use of *be* in place of other verb forms (may indicate extended time), as in	They always *be* messing around. Most of the time he *be* in the house.
4. Standard use of *be* verb forms in tag question sentence or response, as in	He ain't tired, *is* he? Yes he *is*.
5. Subject-predicate agreement a. Use of substitute *be* verb forms, as in	I *is* going. There *was* two boys. You *is* too much.
b. Third person singular in present tense, absence or alternate use of -s form, as in	My mother *look* at television a lot. He *know* it. or We *likes* to ride our bikes. They *runs* down the street. or Somebody get *hurts*.
6. Past tense forms a. Absence of regular verb ending -ed	He *pick* me. He *turn* around.
b. Use of *ain't* to signal past tense with verbs not changed in past tense, as in	He *ain't* see me yesterday. I *ain't* see it.
c. Use of *ain't* in place of *doesn't, don't, hasn't,* etc., and at the front of questions and declaratives with strong effect, as in	*Ain't* he finish? *Ain't* nobody see it; *ain't* nobody hear it.
7. Absence of future tense marker *will* or contraction *'ll*, as in	She be comin' home. He hit you tomorrow.
8. Alternate use of irregular verbs, as in	They *rided* their bicycles. I would've *took* him.

continued

DESCRIPTION	EXAMPLE
B. Use of noun forms	
1. Plural overgeneralization, as in	mens, peoples, teeths, mices
2. Absence of plural form cued by preceding word, as in	two dog, several cat
3. Absence of possessive markers with nouns, as in	That's *Roy* girl. *Calvin* old *man* car.
4. Omission of indefinite article with nouns which have plural forms (count nouns), and addition of it to nouns without plural forms (mass nouns), as in	Give me chair. Give me a cash.
C. Use of pronoun forms	
1. Substitution of *they* for *their* and *you* for *your,* as in	*They* eyes are brown. You brought it on *you* own self.
2. Substitution of *them* for *those* and use of *here* with *this,* as in	I have one of *them* hoops. This *here* book.
3. Substitution of *which* for *who* and in some cases the connector *and,* as in	Bill, *which* is six, is my brother. They were good, *which* we all was good.
D. Adjectives and adverbs	
1. Use of *more* with adjectives in comparative form using *-er.* or use of equative construction without a change in adjective, as in	He is *more* taller than you. That girl is *more pretty* than the other one.
2. Omission of *-ly* ending common to adverbs, as in	She treated him cruel.
3. Alternate placement of adverbs such as *mostly,* as in	That's what *mostly* we call 'em. This is a crazy world we *absolutely* livin' in.
4. Substitution of *it* for *there,* as in	*It* was one on the table this mornin'.
E. Sentence patterns	
1. Inversion of question forms, as in	He fixes that?
2. Omission of *do* forms in questions, as in	How he fix that? How it taste?
3. Redundant pattern elements	
a. Use of *at* in "where" questions, as in	Where you *at?* Where he work *at?*

DESCRIPTION	EXAMPLE
b. Double negatives—use of a negative with each indefinite pronoun or adverb, as in	Nobody don't know. I ain't never had no trouble wit' none of them.
c. Doubling of forms, as in	My brother he going. I didn't play with only but Wayne and Tyrone.

Variant English Speakers of Spanish Background:

English Form	Spanish Equivalent	For the Spanish-English pronunciation of: ____ the child may say ____ or To the English speaker ____ sounds like____	
/I/	/iy/	bit	beet
		pit	peat
/æ/	/e/ or /a/	bat	bet
		hat	hot

Variant English Speakers of Chinese Background:

English Form	Chinese Equivalent	For the Chinese-English pronunciation of ____ the child may say ____ or	To the English speaker ____ sounds like ____
/ly/	/i/	beat	bit
/ey/	/e/ or /æ/	bait	bet or bat
	/e/	came	come
/uw/	/u/	Luke	look
/b/	/p/ (final, unreleased)	rib	rip
/g/	/k/ (final, unreleased)	rig	rik
/d/	/t/ (final, unreleased)	rid	rit
/z/	/s/ (initial)	zoo	sue
/v/	/f/ (final)	have	half
	/w/ (initial)	vest	wast
/zh/	/s/	leisure	leaser
/θ/	/t/	thank	tank
	/s/	thank	sank
/đ/	/d/	that	dat
/š/	/s/	she	see
/č/	/č/ (final)	church	churchi
/ǰ/	/ǰ/ (final)	judge	judgi
/n/	/l/	need	lead
		good night	good light
/r/	/l/	rice	lice
		read	lead
		radio	ladio
/w/	/v/	will	vill

Variations in the grammatical system.

DESCRIPTION	EXAMPLE	
	English	Chinese
A. Use of verb forms		
1. Subject-predicate agreement	He lives in San Francisco.	He live in San Francisco.
2. Tense	I am working. You are talking. I had just finished watering the lawn.	I right at work. You right at talk. I just water finish lawn.
3. Use of *be*	He is sick.	He sick.
4. *Be* substitution	I was here yesterday.	I at here yesterday.
5. Negative	I cannot go.	I no can go.
B. Use of noun form		
1. Plural form	Many houses are beautiful.	Many house beautiful.
2. Omission of article with noun	George is the president.	George president.
C. Use of pronoun forms: no shift in person	You have known him a long time.	You know he long time.
D. Preposition omitted	I live in San Francisco.	I live San Francisco.
E. Connector omitted (conjunction)	You and I are alike.	You I alike.
F. Question form: word order	Are you going home? Will you come to my house for dinner?	You go home? You tonight come I of home dinner?

Source: Ruddell, R. B. *Reading language instruction: Innovative practices.* Englewood Cliffs, New Jersey: Prentice-Hall, Inc., 1974, pp. 268–271, 273–277.

Author Index

Subject Index